Race and Ethnicity in the United States

Race and Ethnicity in the United States

Issues and Debates

Edited by
Stephen Steinberg

BLACKWELL
Publishers

First published 2000
Reprinted 2000, 2002

Blackwell Publishers Inc.
350 Main Street
Malden, Massachusetts 02148
USA

Blackwell Publishers Ltd
108 Cowley Road
Oxford OX4 1JF
UK

Library of Congress Cataloging-in-Publication Data

Race and ethnicity in the United States: issues and debates/
edited by Stephen Steinberg.
   p.   cm.
Includes bibliographical references and index.
ISBN 0–631–20830–5 (alk. paper). — ISBN 0–631–20831–3 (pbk. : alk. paper)
1. United States—Race relations. 2. United States—Ethnic relations. I. Steinberg, Stephen.
E184.A1R247 2000
305.8'00973—dc21   99–16129
                                                     CIP

British Library Cataloguing in Publication Data

A CIP catalogue record for this book is available from the British Library.

Typeset in 10.5 on 12pt Sabon
by Newgen Imaging Systems (P) Ltd, Chennai, India
Printed in Great Britain by MPG Books Ltd, Bodmin, Cornwall

This book is printed on acid-free paper.

Contents

Contributors

Stephen Steinberg is a professor of sociology and urban studies at Queens College and the Graduate Center of the City University of New York. His books include *The Ethnic Myth: Race, Ethnicity, and Class in America* (Beacon Press, 1989) and *Turning Back: The Retreat from Racial Justice in American Thought and Policy* (Beacon Press, 1995).

Richard D. Alba is a professor of sociology at the State University of New York at Albany. His most recent book is *Ethnic Identity: The Transformation of White America* (Yale University Press, 1990).

Peter Beinart is a Senior Editor and frequent contributor to *The New Republic*.

Larry Bennett is a professor of political science at De Paul University. His most recent book is *Neighborhood Politics: Chicago and Sheffield* (Garland, 1997).

John Charles Boger is a professor of law at the University of North Carolina at Chapel Hill. He is co-editor (with Judith Welch Wegner) of *Race, Poverty, and American Cities* (University of North Carolina Press, 1996).

Vernon M. Briggs, Jr. is a professor of labor economics at Cornell University. His most recent book is *Mass Immigration and the National Interest* (M. E. Sharpe, 1996).

Sharon M. Collins is a professor of sociology at the University of Illinois, Chicago. Her most recent book is *Black Corporate Executives: The Making and Breaking of a Black Middle Class* (Temple University Press, 1997).

Nancy A. Denton is a professor of sociology at the State University of New York at Albany. She is co-author (with Douglas S. Massey) of *American Apartheid: Segregation and the Making of the Underclass* (Harvard University Press, 1993).

Troy Duster is a professor of sociology at New York University and the University of California at Berkeley. His most recent book is *Backdoor to Eugenics* (Routledge, 1990).

Ronald Dworkin is a professor of jurisprudence at Oxford University and New York University. His most recent book is *Life's Dominion and Freedom's Law: The Moral Reading of the Constitution* (Harvard University Press, 1997).

Todd Gitlin is a professor of journalism and sociology at New York University. His most recent book is *The Twilight of Common Dreams: Why America Is Wracked by Culture Wars* (Metropolitan Books, 1995).

Lani Guinier is a professor of law at the University of Pennsylvania. Her most recent book is *Lift Every Voice: Turning a Civil Rights Setback Into a Vision of Social Justice* (Simon & Schuster, 1998).

Amy Gutmann is a professor of politics at Princeton University. She is author (with K. Anthony Appiah) of *Color Conscious: The Political Morality of Race* (Princeton University Press, 1996).

David Hollinger is a professor of history at the University of California at Berkeley. His most recent book is *Postethnic America: Beyond Multiculturalism* (Basic Books, 1995).

Richard D. Kahlenberg is a fellow at the Center for National Policy. His most recent book is *The Remedy: Class, Race, and Affirmative Action* (Basic Books, 1996).

Robin D. G. Kelley is a professor of history and Africana Studies at New York University. His most recent book is *Yo' Momma's Disfunktional! And Other Essays on the Culture Wars in Black America* (Beacon Press, 1997).

Donaldo Macedo is a professor of English and director of the Bilingual/ESL Graduate Studies Program at the University of Massachusetts at Boston. His most recent book is *Literacies of Power: What Americans Are Not Allowed to Know* (Westview Press, 1994).

Douglas S. Massey is a professor of sociology at the University of Pennsylvania. He is co-author (with Nancy Denton) of *American Apartheid: Segregation and the Making of the Underclass* (Harvard University Press, 1993).

Thomas Muller is a professor of sociology at the University of California at Los Angeles. His most recent book is *Immigrants and the American City* (New York University Press, 1993).

Gary B. Nash is a professor of history at the University of California at Los Angeles, and director of the National Center for History in the Schools. His most recent book is *History On Trial: Culture Wars and the Teaching of the Past* (Knopf, 1997).

Geoffrey Nunberg is a professor of linguistics at Stanford University. His most recent book is the collection *The Future of the Book* (University of California Press, 1996).

Gary Orfield is a professor of education at Harvard University, and author of *Dismantling Desegregation: The Quiet Reversal of Brown v. Board of Education* (The New Press, 1996).

Joel Perlmann is Senior Scholar at the Jerome Levy Economics Institute of Bard College. His most recent book is *Ethnic Differences: Schooling and Social Structure Among the Irish, Italians, Jews, and Blacks in an American City, 1880–1935* (Cambridge University Press, 1988).

Diane Ravitch is a professor of history and education at Teachers College, Columbia University. Her books include *The Troubled Crusade: American Education, 1945–1980* (Basic Books, 1983).

Adolph Reed, Jr. is a professor of political science on the graduate faculty of the New School for Social Research. His most recent book is *W. E. B. Du Bois and American Political Thought* (Oxford University Press, 1997).

Peter Schrag is editorial page editor of the *Sacramento Bee*. His most recent book is *Paradise Lost: California's Experience, America's Future* (The New Press, 1998).

Carol M. Swain is a professor of politics and public affairs at the Woodrow Wilson School, Princeton University. Her most recent book is *Black Faces, Black Interests: The Representation of African Americans in Congress* (Harvard University Press, 1993).

Roger Waldinger is a professor of sociology at the University of California at Los Angeles. His most recent book is *Still the Promised City? African-Americans and New Immigrants in Postindustrial New York* (Harvard University Press, 1996).

Michael Walzer is a professor at the Center for Advanced Study at Princeton. His most recent book is *On Toleration* (Yale University Press, 1997).

Doris Y. Wilkinson is a professor of sociology at the University of Kentucky. She is co-editor of *Race, Class, and Gender: Common Bonds, Different Voices* (Sage Publications, 1996).

Acknowledgments

I would like to thank Susan Rabinowitz, the acquisitions editor at Blackwell, for her enthusiasm and support, and Jenny Tyler for her impeccable editing. Thanks also to my students at Queens College, who provided indispensable feedback as the volume evolved.

The author and publishers gratefully acknowledge the following for permission to reproduce copyright material:

Alba, Richard D., "Assimilation's Quiet Tide" reprinted with permission of the author from *The Public Interest*, no. 119 (Spring 1995), pp. 3–18. © 1995 by National Affairs, Inc.

Beinart, Peter, "Degree of Separation at Yale" reprinted by permission of *The New Republic*, November 3, 1997 © 1997, The New Republic, Inc.

Bennett, Larry and Reed, Adolph, Jr., "The Complexities of a Public Housing Community," excerpted from Adolph Reed, Jr. (ed.), *Without Justice For All* (Westview Press, 1999), pp. 195–202 and 207–8. Copyright © 1999 by Westview Press, a member of Perseus Books, L.L.C. Reprinted by permission of Westview Press.

Boger, John Charles, "The Kerner Commission Report in Retrospect" from John Charles Boger and Judith Welch Wegner (eds.), *Race, Poverty and American Cities*. Copyright © 1996 by the University of North Carolina Press. Used by permission of the publisher.

Briggs, Vernon M., Jr., "Immigration Policy and the U.S. Economy: An Institutional Perspective," *Journal of Economic Issues*, Vol. 30 (June 1996).

Collins, Sharon M., "Bursting the Bubble: The Failure of Black Progress" from *Black Corporate Executives: The Making and Breaking of a Black Middle Class*. © 1997 by Temple University Press. All Rights Reserved.

Duster, Troy, "Understanding Self-Segregation on the Campus," *Chronicle of Higher Education*, September 25, 1991.

Dworkin, Ronald, "Is Affirmative Action Doomed?" *The New York Review of Books*, November 5, 1998, reprinted with permission from The New York Review of Books. Copyright © 1998 NYREV, Inc.

Gitlin, Todd, "The Rise of 'Identity Politics,'" *Dissent* 40 (Spring 1993).

Guinier, Lani, "Democracy's Conversation." Reprinted with permission from January 23, 1995 issue of *The Nation* magazine.

Guinier, Lani, "Groups, Representation, and Race Conscious Districting" from *The Tyranny of the Majority* (The Free Press, 1994).

Gutmann, Amy, "Should Public Policy Be Class Conscious Rather than Color Conscious?" from K. Anthony Appiah and Amy Gutmann, *Color Conscious*

(Copyright © 1996 by Princeton University Press. Reprinted by permission of Princeton University Press).

Hollinger, David, "The Ethno-Racial Pentagon" from David A. Hollinger, *Postethnic America* (Basic Books, 1995).

Kahlenberg, Richard D., "The Case for Class-Based Affirmative Action," *New Labor Forum* (Spring 1998).

Kelley, Robin D. G., "Identity Politics and Class Struggle," *New Politics* (Winter 1997).

Macedo, Donaldo, "English-Only: The Tongue-Tying of America" reprinted from *Journal of Education*, Boston University School of Education (1991), Vol. 173, no. 2, with permission from the Trustees of Boston University (copyright holder) and the author.

Massey, Douglas S. and Denton, Nancy A., "The Future of the Ghetto" reprinted by permission of the publisher from *American Apartheid*, Harvard University Press, Mass., copyright © 1993 by the President and Fellows of Harvard College.

Muller, Thomas, "The Immigrant Contribution to the Revitalization of Cities" from *Immigrants and the American City* (New York: New York University Press, 1993).

Nash, Gary B., "The Great Multicultural Debate," *Contention*, 1992.

Nunberg, Geoffrey, "Lingo Jingo: English-Only and the New Nativism" reprinted with permission from *The American Prospect*, 33 (July–August 1997). Copyright © 1997 The American Prospect, P.O. Box 383080, Cambridge, MA 02138. All rights reserved.

Orfield, Gary, "Turning Back to Segregation" from Gary Orfield and Susan E. Eaton, *Dismantling Desegregation* (New York: The New Press, 1996).

Perlmann, Joel and Waldinger, Roger, "Are the Children of Today's Immigrants Making It?" reprinted with permission of the authors from *The Public Interest*, no. 132 (Summer 1998), pp. 73–96. © 1998 by National Affairs, Inc.

Ravitch, Diane, "Multiculturalism: E Pluribus Plures" reprinted from *The American Scholar*, Vol. 59, no. 3 (Summer 1990). Copyright © 1990 by the author.

Reed, Adolph, Jr., "Yackety-Yak About Race," *The Progressive*, December 1997.

Schrag, Peter, "When Preferences Disappear" reprinted with permission from *The American Prospect*, 30 (Jan.–Feb. 1997). Copyright © 1997 The American Prospect, P.O. Box 383080, Cambridge, MA 02138. All rights reserved.

Steinberg, Stephen, "The Liberal Retreat from Race" adapted from chapter 5 of *Turning Back* (Boston: Beacon Press, 1995), and excerpted here from a revised version published in Wahneema Lubiano (ed.), *The House That Race Built* (New York: Pantheon Books, 1997), pp. 13–47.

Steinberg, Stephen, "Occupational Apartheid and the Origins of Affirmative Action" adapted from chapters 8 and 9 of *Turning Back* (Boston: Beacon Press, 1995), and excerpted here from Adolph Reed, Jr. (ed.), *Without Justice For All* (Boulder: Westview Press, 1999), pp. 215–33.

Swain, Carol, M., "The Future of Black Representation" reprinted with permission from *The American Prospect*, 23 (Fall 1995). Copyright © 1995 The American Prospect, P.O. Box 383080, Cambridge, MA 02138. All rights reserved.

Walzer, Michael, "What Does It Mean To Be an 'American'?" *Social Research*, Vol. 57, no. 3 (Fall 1990), New York.

Wilkinson, Doris Y., "Integration Dilemmas in a Racist Culture," *Society*, March/April 1996, pp. 27–31. Reprinted by permission of Transaction Publishers. Copyright © 1996 by Transaction Publishers; all rights reserved.

The publishers apologize for any errors or omissions in the above list and would be grateful to be notified of any corrections that should be incorporated in the next edition or reprint of this book.

Note to the Reader

I was a freshman at Brown University in 1959, a year that the nation was in the throes of the civil rights revolution. I had enrolled in a course on "Race Relations," and decided to write my term paper on "Desegregation in the South." In a conference with my professor, I asked him if I should end the paper with some reflections on what could be done to resolve the problem. "Sure," he responded, "but label it 'sermon.'"

My professor's flip comment reflected a prevailing belief about the relationship between academic sociology and the world of "politics." The general view, famously enunciated by Max Weber in his essay on "Science as a Vocation," was that social science must scrupulously maintain a posture of value neutrality, and avoid becoming entangled in the seamy business of politics. As a private citizen I might be outraged at the blatant violation of the civil rights of African Americans. However, as a sociologist I was obligated to avoid taking sides. Yes, I could methodically trace the origins of the caste system, and yes, I could expound on its deleterious consequences (providing my language was circumspect). But as a social scientist, with the emphasis on the latter half of this term, I must avoid taking an advocacy position. To propose solutions would amount to preaching, which would violate the Olympian self-concept of social scientists as above the fray – neutral observers of the conflict that fractured the mortal world below.

Ironically, it was the civil rights conflict that forced social scientists to surrender their guise as impartial observers. How was it possible to remain "neutral" when fire hoses and police dogs were turned on peaceful demonstrators demanding nothing more than elementary civil rights? Did "objectivity" require that the social scientist remain on the sidelines as the forces of racism and anti-racism were locked in bloody struggle? Didn't sociologists, in their professional capacity, have a role to play in the resolution of a conflict that was tearing the society apart? As Howard Zinn put it in the title of his autobiography, "You Can't Be Neutral on a Moving Train." Many social scientists still reject Zinn's brand of intellectual advocacy. However, rare is the professor who would instruct a fledgling student to affix the word "sermon" to the concluding section of a paper that ventures into the realm of social policy.

In recent decades social policy has emerged as a legitimate extension of most academic disciplines. Indeed, the theme of the 1998 Meeting of the American Sociological Association was "Inequality and Social Policy." The preamble to the program began as follows:

> The past quarter century has witnessed rising inequality in the distribution of income and wealth and declining job stability for many groups of workers. Sociologists have been at the forefront of research on the causes of these trends, the role of social policy in intensifying or alleviating them, and the unintended

consequences of policy outcomes. Sociology's presence in policy analysis, once a subject of contention, is now an established fact.

No longer is it deemed enough to identify inequality as a problem, and to measure it with scientific precision. As the preamble went on to say, it is also the mission of sociology "to help the lay public, policymakers, and public officials recognize the relevance of sociological research for public policy."[1]

Not only is social policy accepted as an extension of traditional social science, but it has emerged as a field unto itself. Schools of public policy, including doctoral programs, dot the academic landscape. Moreover, with the help of subsidies from government and foundations, a host of institutes and think tanks have cropped up that define their mission in terms of public policy. Nor do they maintain even a pretense of value neutrality. Some, such as the Heritage Foundation and the American Enterprise Institute, are avowedly conservative. Others, such as the Institute for Policy Studies and the Economic Policy Institute, are unabashedly progressive. Still others have a reputation as being "centrist" – the Brookings Institution, for example. Never before have the lines of separation between social science, political advocacy, and social policy been so blurred.

This volume evolved from a course that I developed at Queens College on "Race, Ethnicity, and Public Policy." I quickly discovered that there is a dearth of books on this subject, and that much of the material published in scholarly books and journals was too narrowly focused on minute detail and failed to address broad policy issues. I found myself foraging for reading that provided sweeping and critical analyses of policy issues. As a teacher, I also sought readings that would engage the interests of students, tap their life experiences and concerns, and stimulate thought and discussion.

Increasingly, my foraging led to publications that make a concerted effort to break out of the straitjacket of scientific discourse, and to reach a larger audience of sophisticated readers. Most of the selections in this volume were culled from books and journals that exemplify engaged scholarship, and that combine intellectual rigor with effective writing. It is a pleasure to compile these readings in a single volume, and to bring them to a wider audience of students. Note that all thirty selections were published since 1990, twenty-two of them since 1995.

Originally I planned to adopt the point-counterpoint format that is a familiar feature of other anthologies, pairing selections that represent polar positions on key issues. Upon reflection, I rejected this format. I came to think that presenting polar positions often amounts to little more than shouting across the ideological divide. It is the intellectual equivalent of a ping-pong match, or perhaps more aptly, a fencing contest. It becomes a spectacle of jousting and parrying, rather than dialogue and intellectual engagement.

I had a second reason for rejecting the point-counterpoint format. I did not want to give venue to positions that I consider retrograde, idiotic, antidemocratic, or immoral. Granted it would inject "controversy" to have a selection from *The Bell Curve*, in which Richard Herrnstein and Charles Murray reinstate old canards about the intellectual inferiority of blacks and other groups.

Or Dinesh D'Souza's *The End of Racism*, which contends that the problems that afflict black America have little or nothing to do with white racism, but are a byproduct of black cultural pathology. Or Peter Brimelow's *Alien Nation*, which frets about how American culture is imperiled by the alien hordes. But instead of furthering discussion, polar positions have the opposite result: they are so far apart that they thwart a genuine give-and-take, and they tend to deflect discussion in directions that are rarely productive.

Yet this is not an attempt to skirt controversy. On the contrary, this volume is sizzling with controversy. For each of the fifteen issues under examination, I have included two readings. In some instances the readings build upon one another, but in most instances they provide sharply divergent viewpoints. However, these articles are generally predicated on similar values and assumptions so that, even in their disagreement, there is a basis for productive intellectual exchange. Instead of being presented with two stark alternatives and being forced essentially to choose one, as readers you may well see merit in both positions, even when they reach antithetical conclusions.

This brings to mind a small tale. A man and woman go to a rabbi to discuss their marital problems. The man presents his litany of grievances, to which the rabbi responds, "You are right." The wife then presents her side with equal fervor, to which the rabbi again responds, "You are right." "But rabbi," the couple exclaim, "how can we both be right?" With undisguised irony the rabbi responds: "You are right."

At the risk of stretching the analogy too far, let us suppose that our mythical rabbi were presented with two positions on, say, immigration policy. One vilifies immigrants for polluting the national culture and imperiling the national future. The other contends that immigrants contribute population, labor, and resources, and therefore have positive value. It is doubtful that even our omniscient rabbi would find merit in both positions. Nor would there be much basis for reconciling differences or finding a sensible middle ground.

My point is that many policy issues do not lend themselves to a binary judgment of right and wrong. Often principles and objectives – each legitimate and worthy – are in conflict. We are thus presented with a choice between equally problematic alternatives, or we must assess whether or not the benefits of a policy outweigh the costs. This is the rationale for pairing readings that offer divergent viewpoints. As readers, you will be challenged to confront the complexities and moral ambiguities surrounding these contested policy issues. Above all, my purpose has been to provide you with the raw materials for thought and discussion.

Note

1 Preliminary Program, "Inequality and Social Policy: A Challenge for Sociology" (Washington, D.C.: American Sociological Association, 1988), p. 1.

Part I

Anti-Racist Public Policy in the Post–Civil Rights Era

Introduction to Part I:
Two Steps Forward and
One Step Backward

Throughout American history the anti-racist struggle has conformed to the pattern of two steps forward and one step backward. As Gunnar Myrdal wrote in his classic study, *An American Dilemma*:

> The Revolutionary War started a development which ultimately ended slavery in all Northern states, made new import of slaves illegal and nearly accomplished abolition even in the South – though there the tide soon turned in a reaction toward fortification of the plantation system and of Negro slavery. The Civil War gave the Negro Emancipation and Reconstruction in the South – though it was soon followed by Restoration of white supremacy. The First World War provided the Negro his first real opportunity as a worker in Northern industry, started the Great Migration out of the South, and began the "New Negro" movement – though the end of the War saw numerous race riots and the beginning of a serious decline in employment opportunities.[1]

Thus, in each instance the expansion of freedom and opportunity was followed by a period of backlash in which previous gains were lost, though as Myrdal noted, "not as much ground was lost as had been won."[2]

Published in 1944, *An American Dilemma* failed to anticipate even the possibility of a grassroots protest movement that would tear down the walls of Southern segregation. Yet Myrdal raises the paramount issue concerning the post–civil rights era: will the current backlash wipe out the gains that were wrung out of white society through the civil rights movement? Are we, as a nation, repeating history by taking that metaphoric step backward?

To address this question, we need conceptual clarity about the nature and limits of the civil rights revolution. This was primarily a struggle for liberty, not equality. That is to say, the civil rights movement sought to dismantle the system of official segregation that had been erected in the aftermath of slavery, and to secure full rights of citizenship for African Americans. This was accomplished with the passage of the 1964 Civil Rights Act, which banned discrimination in schools, employment, and public accommodations, and the 1965 Voting Rights Act, which secured the right to vote for African Americans.

The abiding faith of the movement and its leaders was that once the walls of segregation came tumbling down, blacks would be free to assume their rightful place in American society. Even before the landmark civil rights legislation was passed, however, it became clear that legislation alone would not address the deep-seated inequalities that were the legacy of two centuries of slavery and another century of Jim Crow. As Martin Luther King, Jr. put it: "What good is to be allowed to eat in a restaurant if you can't afford a hamburger?"[3] Thus, the achievement of the legislative goals of the civil rights movement led to a growing realization among movement leaders that abolishing legal racism alone would not produce racial equality, and that new strategies would be necessary to deal with the cumulative disadvantages inherited from the past.[4]

This was also acknowledged by President Lyndon Johnson in a commencement address at Howard University in June 1965, the very month that the Voting Rights Act received Congressional approval. As he told the graduating class:

> [F]reedom is not enough. You do not wipe away the scars of centuries by saying: Now you are free to go where you want, do as you desire, choose the leaders you please. You do not take a person who, for years, has been hobbled by chains and liberate him, bring him to the starting line and then say, "You are free to compete with all the others," and still justly believe that you have been completely fair. We seek not just freedom but opportunity – not just equality as a right and a theory but equality as a fact and as a result.[5]

Johnson's oratory was followed by the outbreak of racial violence in the Watts section of Los Angeles only two months later. In the ensuing years there were hundreds of other "riots" that threw the entire society into crisis. This crisis forced political elites to confront the issue of equality as well as liberty.

The most immediate result was the War on Poverty. Though conceived as a war on "poverty," the political impetus derived from the black protest movement, and the bulk of programs were targeted for minority communities. In a sense the War on Poverty fulfilled William Julius Wilson's vision of "a hidden agenda" that camouflaged programs for minorities under the rubric of universal programs that ostensibly helped "everyone."[6] According to Wilson, programs specifically targeted for minorities are not politically viable since they lack the necessary support from the white majority.

However, race-neutral public policies also have inherent limitations. Though blacks are disproportionately poor, they constitute only a minority of the poor, and given their racial isolation, race-neutral programs are apt to reach them last and least. Such programs, therefore, amount to a liberal version of filter-down economics. By their very nature, race-neutral programs are not equipped to deal with the unique problems that beset minority communities. For example, they provide no remedy or relief for discriminatory barriers that blacks encounter in jobs, schools, and other opportunity structures. Wilson has been widely quoted for his statement that affirmative action did nothing to help the poorest segments of the black community.[7] However, the same thing can be said in reverse about the War on Poverty: it did nothing to break down *racial* barriers that denied blacks access to jobs, housing, and schools.

During the 1960s and 1970s pressures mounted for public policies to counter institutionalized racism. By far the most important such policy initiative was affirmative action. The key assumption, encapsulated in the name itself, was that banning discrimination did not go far enough to compensate for past wrongs and to overcome persistent racial barriers. Rather, it was imperative for employers to actively seek out protected groups in the recruitment, hiring, and promotion of workers. Eventually it became apparent that even good-faith efforts on the part of employers were inadequate, and affirmative action programs were backed up with specific goals and timetables in order to assure the desired results.

A second race-targeted policy was school desegregation. The logic was embedded in the 1954 Supreme Court decision in *Brown v. Board of Education*. Having declared school segregation unconstitutional, the Court then ordered schools to implement desegregation plans. Initially policy was aimed at de jure segregation in the South, but later desegregation plans were directed at de facto segregation in the North as well.

A third race-targeted policy involved the creation of black-majority districts for the purpose of Congressional elections. The logic paralleled the popular wisdom that being allowed to eat in a restaurant was of little value if you couldn't afford the price of a hamburger. In this case the logic ran as follows: what good is it to be able to vote if blacks never get a chance to elect blacks to Congress? This was the reasoning that led to a policy whereby, under specified circumstances, state legislatures were obligated to draw up electoral districts that put minorities in a majority.

All three of these policies have been engulfed in controversy. All three have been eviscerated by recent Supreme Court decisions. The question thus presents itself: having so grudgingly made concessions granting "liberty," is the nation currently reneging on its commitment to "equality"?

The readings in Part I of this volume focus on the contentious debates concerning anti-racist public policy. We begin with two general readings that are intended to provide historical perspective on the current period of racial backlash. John Charles Boger uses the 1968 Kerner Commission report as a baseline for assessing where we stand on race three decades later. My article traces a parallel development in social science discourse: the retreat from "race" (read: racism) during the post–civil rights era, as scholars and policymakers reverted to victim-blaming explanations for persistent racial inequalities.

Next, we examine Lani Guinier's hopeful proposal for a national conversation on race, followed by Adolph Reed's trenchant critique ("Yakety-Yak About Race") of President Clinton's race initiative. Guinier sees a need "to discuss race openly and without partisan rancor," but Reed derides the preoccupation with "racial healing," insisting that "we need a clear commitment by the federal government to preserve, buttress, and extend civil rights."

We then examine a number of specific policy issues:

The racial division of labor   My article on "occupational apartheid" provides historical perspective on the racial division of labor that eventually gave rise to affirmative action policy. In "Bursting the Bubble," Sharon Collins argues that insofar as the black middle class is the product of affirmative action policy, it does not signify a deracialization of labor markets. Collins found that most black corporate executives in her study were placed in marginal positions, typically serving "minority" functions, and cut off from the corporate mainstream.

The race versus class debate   Richard Kahlenberg responds to the popular backlash against affirmative action by proposing to base affirmative action on class rather than on race. In contrast, Amy Gutmann develops a logical and historical defense for basing affirmative action on race as well as class.

The future of affirmative action   In "When Preferences Disappear," Peter Schrag sees a silver lining in the rollback of affirmative action. He suggests that admission officers and employers will be forced to devise fairer standards that will increase access, not only for blacks but for other underrepresented groups as well. A far less sanguine view is offered by Ronald Dworkin in "Is Affirmative Action Doomed?" Dworkin makes a case for the constitutionality of affirmative action, and worries that if the Supreme Court strikes down affirmative action, this will reverse decades of minority progress in employment and college admissions.

Should the ghetto Be "dismantled"?   In "The Future of the Ghetto," Douglas Massey and Nancy Denton contend that racial segregation exacerbates the effects of poverty, and propose "a bold new initiative to eradicate the ghetto and eliminate segregation from American life." In "The Complexities of a Public Housing Community," however, Larry Bennett and Adolph Reed Jr. caution against the tendency to portray low-income, inner-city neighborhoods as riddled with pathology and social disorganization, leading to proposals to "dismantle the ghetto" and disperse its residents. In their case study of the Cabrini-Green public housing development in Chicago, they show that residents benefit from an array of social networks and neighborhood organizations, and those who are being dispersed in the name of "urban renewal" will be worse off than before.

School desegregation   In "Turning Back to Segregation," Gary Orfield reviews recent Court decisions that have effectively nullified the historic 1954 decision in *Brown v. Board of Education*, and will result in the resegregation of public education. A wholly different tack is taken by Doris Wilkinson in her article, "Integration Dilemmas in a Racist Culture." Against the background of the failures of school integration, Wilkinson considers the emotional and social costs to black children, and asks whether school integration can work in a nation still steeped in racism.

Racial districting   In "Groups, Representation, and Race Conscious Districting," Lani Guinier argues the case for racial districting in order to ensure that black interests will be represented by blacks in Congress. However, this practice has recently been struck down by the Supreme Court. This may have paradoxical consequences, according to Carol Swain in "The Future of Black Representation." Swain believes that blacks and whites will be more apt to form interracial coalitions that will result in the election of liberal Democrats. In her view African Americans "need more representation of their liberal views of policy than they need people who look like them."

As the annotations make clear, all these issues have generated heated and often acrimonious debate. Note, however, that the lines of debate do not correspond neatly to lines of race or political ideology. Blacks disagree among themselves over the legitimacy and practicality of the policies under examination. So do liberals and conservatives. There is a stream of liberal/left thought that subsumes race to class, and seeks to address racial inequalities with policies that are race-neutral. Others on the left argue the centrality of race, and the necessity, as a moral and political imperative, of pursuing anti-racist public policy. On the other hand, conservatives at times have supported such policies as affirmative action and racial districting, and today champion the same charter schools that are advocated by some black leaders. Other conservatives invoke the principle of the civil rights movement and insist on strict adherence to color blindness in public affairs.

Insofar as positions on the issues and policies examined in this volume defy easy classification as "black" or "white" or as "liberal" or "conservative," this presents a challenge for you as readers. You will have to sort out for yourselves whether a particular policy is defensible, and at what price. And you will be challenged to step back from the debates over particular issues and confront the ultimate question: are we as a nation repeating history by taking one step backward?

Notes

1 Gunnar Myrdal, *An American Dilemma*, original edition 1944 (New York: McGraw-Hill, 1994), p. 997.
2 Ibid., p. 997.
3 Martin Luther King, Jr., "Showdown for non-violence," *Look*, April 16, 1968, p. 28.
4 Lee Rainwater and William L. Yancey, *The Moynihan Report and the Politics of Controversy* (Cambridge, Mass.: MIT Press, 1967), p. 11.
5 Quoted in Rainwater and Yancey, *The Moynihan Report*, p. 126.
6 William Julius Wilson, *The Truly Disadvantaged* (Chicago: University of Chicago Press, 1987), ch. 7.
7 "Programs of preferential treatment applied merely according to racial or ethnic group membership tend to benefit the relatively advantaged segments of the designated groups. The truly deprived members may not be helped by such programs." Ibid., p. 115.

1

The Eclipse of Anti-Racist Public Policy

The Kerner Commission Report in Retrospect

John Charles Boger

Nearly three decades have passed since the Kerner Commission issued its final report in March 1968, a searing indictment of America's urban and racial policies. Even if the nation had somehow managed in the intervening decades to resolve its urban and racial challenges, this extraordinary document would invite historical reflection. Yet the problems outlined by the Kerner Commission continue to defy solution by the nation's policymakers, and reflections on the Kerner Commission Report have keen contemporary significance. As the 1992 Los Angeles rebellion emphasized, millions of the urban poor still find themselves without full-time employment, adequate education, affordable health care, decent housing, or social welfare programs that meet their basic needs. Moreover, the black–white racial divisions that dominated the Kerner Commission's vision of urban life in 1968 remain sharp, although they have been complicated by the emergence of other ethnic groups – Cubans, Puerto Ricans, Mexican Americans, Latinos from Central and South America, Japanese, Chinese, Vietnamese, Cambodians, Thais, Koreans, and others – whose legitimate claims for participation in American urban life make political, social, and economic relationships more challenging.

Meanwhile, America's cities in 1995 continue to face serious, burgeoning social ills, many of which are closely intertwined with race and ethnicity: a decline in manufacturing and other blue-collar jobs, inadequate public schools, an explosion of gang- and drug-related violence and crime among the young, the AIDS epidemic and other looming public health challenges, an increasingly

Excerpted from *Race, Poverty and American Cities*, ed. John Charles Boger and Judith Welch Wegner (Chapel Hill: University of North Carolina Press, 1996), pp. 3–76. Copyright © 1996 by the University of North Carolina Press. Used by permission of the publisher.

impoverished citizenry, an inadequate tax base, and private disinvestment in urban projects. Many urban mayors today find themselves with less money than in 1968 and fewer clear ideas about what can be done.

To be sure, the urban scene has changed significantly since 1968, and in some respects, as we document below, conditions have improved. *Yet the principal theme of this essay is that the fundamental social and economic diagnoses of the Kerner Commission remain pertinent nearly three decades later, while its policy prescriptions remain largely ignored.*

In this essay I undertake two preliminary tasks: first, to review the Kerner Commission's principal findings and recommendations; second, to provide readers with a statistical snapshot of the altered circumstances that face African Americans and America's cities in 1995.

*   *   *

The Urban Crisis of the Mid-1960s and the Kerner Commission Report

During the mid-1960s the nation witnessed five consecutive summers of racial unrest in its cities. These riots followed a decade of mounting white violence, targeted especially against African Americans who had challenged the South's system of legalized segregation. During the decade between 1954 and 1964 scores of southern black churches had been fire-bombed, and dozens of blacks had been killed in the civil rights struggle. In July 1967, following the especially deadly and destructive riots by African Americans that spring and early summer, President Lyndon B. Johnson issued Executive Order No. 11,365, creating the National Advisory Commission on Civil Disorders. The president charged the commission to investigate "the origins of the recent major civil disorders in our cities, includ[ing] the basic causes and factors leading to such disorders," and to propose "methods and techniques for averting or controlling such disorders," including "the appropriate role of the local, state and Federal authorities." Nine months later, in March 1968, the commission, chaired by then-governor Otto Kerner of Illinois, delivered a comprehensive report to the American nation. The report began with a memorable warning:

> Our nation is moving toward two societies, one black, one white – separate and unequal. ... Reaction to last summer's disorders has quickened the movement and deepened the division. Discrimination and segregation have long permeated much of American life; they now threaten the future of every American.
>
> This deepening racial division is not inevitable. The movement apart can be reversed. Choice is still possible. Our principal task is to define that choice and to press for a national resolution.
>
> To pursue our present course will involve the continuing polarization of the American community and, ultimately, the destruction of basic democratic values.[1]

At first glance this warning of a deepening racial division seemed to point to a racial pattern as old as American history. From colonial times, America's white majority had insisted on and legally enforced the separate and unequal status of blacks. The Constitution itself implicitly recognized chattel slavery, ensuring the growth of a nation "half slave and half free." Even in the non-slaveholding areas outside the South prior to 1861, most free blacks endured intense social segregation and legally enforced discrimination. The Civil War ended chattel slavery as an institution but brought no real end to the legal subordination of blacks. Instead, less than a decade after adoption of the Fourteenth and Fifteenth Amendments – garlanded with promises of equal protection under the laws, full citizenship, and political enfranchisement – national political and judicial leaders abandoned their short-lived experiment in racial equality, acquiesced in renewed racial discrimination, and collaborated to block further participation in the democratic process by millions of African American voters. The white majority, in effect, repudiated the legal promises crafted during Reconstruction and chose instead to shape twentieth-century American life and law in the image of Jim Crow.

Yet the Kerner Commission Report, in retelling this history, made clear that its alarm in 1968 proceeded not merely from the perpetuation of these old racial divisions but from a dangerous new form of separation that was unfolding in the mid-1960s, one that would "threaten the future of every American." Some critics objected that the commission had failed to appreciate new and positive trends in America's racial relations. After centuries of oppression, African Americans appeared poised to achieve the equal rights denied them for 350 years. Decades of patient planning and struggle by National Association for the Advancement of Colored People (NAACP) lawyers had culminated in 1954 in the remarkable success of *Brown v. Board of Education*, a decision in which the Supreme Court had formally renounced Jim Crow. The Warren Court subsequently presided over a remarkable campaign to restore the Fourteenth and Fifteenth Amendments as guarantors of equal rights for black citizens.

Moreover, a decade of direct political activity organized by the Southern Christian Leadership Conference, the Congress of Racial Equality, the NAACP, and the Student Nonviolent Coordinating Committee had prompted Congress in 1964 and 1965 to enact the two most sweeping civil rights statutes ever written into American law: the Civil Rights Act of 1964 and the Voting Rights Act of 1965. Together these acts were designed to end racial discrimination in public education, employment, voting, and governmental programs. Surely, these observers reasoned, the promising developments from 1954 to 1965 spelled the end of America's history of racial division. Surely the nation was moving forward, not backward.

Yet the Kerner Commission's verdict was strongly to the contrary. Neither *Brown v. Board of Education* nor the Civil Rights Act of 1964 nor the victories of Dr. King nor any of the hard-won accomplishments of the second civil rights revolution would suffice to heal America's racial wounds. Instead, the commission implied, the riots were clear proof that antidiscrimination laws alone could never fully redress the residual injuries of slavery and segregation. Ironically, after a decade of remarkable achievements in court and Congress, America faced a racial divide more profound than any in its segregated past.

The Kerner Commission's vision of the future

The commission's stern analysis began with a description of two related social movements, each set in motion during the early 1900s, that had gathered force steadily after World War II. The first was the migration of African Americans from the rural South to the urban North; the second was the almost simultaneous departure of urban whites from northern cities to suburban enclaves. According to the report the resulting residential separation was virtually absolute:

- Almost all Negro population growth (98 percent from 1950 to 1966) is occurring within metropolitan areas, primarily within central cities.
- The vast majority of white population growth (78 percent from 1960 to 1966) is occurring in suburban portions of metropolitan areas. Since 1960, white central-city population has declined by 1.3 million.
- As a result, central cities are becoming more heavily Negro while the suburban fringes around them remain almost entirely white.[2]

These demographic shifts, the commission observed, were not the product of private choice or other race-neutral explanations. "What white Americans have never fully understood – but what the Negro can never forget – is that white society is deeply implicated in the ghetto. White institutions created it, white institutions maintain it, and white society condones it."[3]

In a series of point-by-point forecasts, the commission urged that these developments, if unchecked, would undercut the positive effects of the Civil Rights Act and the judicial decrees of the Warren Court. First, the commission reasoned, the accelerating residential segregation would frustrate black efforts to secure equal employment, since "most new employment opportunities... are being created in suburbs and outlying areas – and this trend is likely to continue indefinitely."[4] The exclusion of blacks from this emerging suburban workforce would be catastrophic; black unemployment (and underemployment) would become "the single most important source of poverty among Negroes"[5] and a principal source of family and social disorganization as well: "Wives of these men are forced to work, and usually produce more money. If men stay at home without working, their inadequacies constantly confront them and tensions arise between them and their wives and children. Under these pressures, it is not surprising that many of these men flee their responsibilities as husbands and fathers, leaving home, and drifting from city to city, or adopting the style of 'street corner men.'"[6]

The adverse effects of the developing urban/suburban "mismatch" between jobs and minority workers, the commission forewarned, would extend beyond individual family circles. Central cities, increasingly inhabited by low-paid or unemployed African Americans and other ethnic minorities, would experience – indeed, already were experiencing – the interrelated social effects of concentrated poverty: high rates of crime, inadequate health care, inadequate sanitation, and exploitative retail services ....

The commission foresaw unhappy social consequences for urban housing and municipal governance flowing from the increased racial isolation. While inadequate housing was not a problem faced solely by urban blacks, the commission nonetheless contended that, because of their higher relative rates of poverty and the pervasive discrimination they faced in the broader urban housing market, African Americans would experience the adverse effects of poor housing disproportionately. "Discrimination prevents access to many nonslum areas, particularly the suburbs, and has a detrimental effect on ghetto housing itself. By restricting the area open to a growing population, housing discrimination makes it profitable for landlords to break up ghetto apartments for denser occupancy, hastening housing deterioration. By creating a 'back pressure' in the racial ghettos, discrimination keeps prices and rents of older, more deteriorated housing in the ghetto higher than they would be in a truly free and open market."[7]

Having cataloged the adverse effects on individual citizens, the Kerner Commission next examined the cumulative effect of urban racial isolation on the financial health of the nation's cities:

> As a result of the population shifts of the post-war period, concentrating the more affluent parts of the urban population in residential suburbs while leaving the less affluent in the central cities, the increasing burden of municipal taxes frequently falls upon that part of the urban population least able to pay them. Increasing concentrations of urban growth have called forth greater expenditures for every kind of public service: education, health, police protection, fire protection, parks, sewage disposal, sanitation, water supply, etc. These expenditures have strikingly outpaced tax revenues.[8]

The commission found little consolation in the likelihood that African Americans soon would gain political power in urban centers. Black mayors and city councils, the commission reasoned, would lack both the will and the capacity to increase taxes on already overburdened city taxpayers. Nor would additional sources of municipal revenues likely become available. Private industry was unlikely to make investments in the racial ghetto; the commission observed that "the withdrawal of private capital is already far advanced in most all-Negro areas of our large cities," and that even if "private investment continued, it alone would not suffice."[9] Only the federal government could command sufficient financial resources to step into the financial breach. Yet by the time African Americans came to power in urban centers, the commission predicted, "it is probable that Congress will be more heavily influenced by representatives of the suburban and outlying city electorate. These areas will comprise 41 percent of our total population by 1985, compared with 33 percent in 1960. Central cities will decline from 31 percent to 27 percent. Without decisive action toward integration, this influential suburban electorate would be over 95 percent white and much more affluent than the central city population."

The commission specifically addressed the crucial role played by the national media in shaping the nation's racial and urban understanding. It faulted the media less for their riot coverage than for their broader failure "to report adequately on the causes and consequences of civil disorders."

The Kerner Commission's prescriptions for national action

The Kerner Commission insisted that these accelerating trends toward racial isolation required an immediate, comprehensive, national response. Only three basic strategies were possible. The nation could adopt a so-called Present Policies Choice that maintained the current allocation of resources to urban areas and the poor. Alternatively it could pursue an Enrichment Choice that would offset the effects of continued Negro segregation with programs designed to improve the quality of life in disadvantaged central-city neighborhoods, a choice that "would require marked increases in federal spending for education, housing, employment, job training, and social services."[10] Finally, the nation could exercise an Integration Choice, "aimed at reversing the march toward two societies, separate and unequal."[11] This choice would provide strong incentives for African Americans to leave central-city residences, enlarging their choices in housing, employment, and education. It would also require large-scale public investments, on an interim basis, in the quality of central-city life for those residents who chose to remain behind.

Having sketched out the alternatives, the commission urged the nation to make the Integration Choice. ... In casting its institutional weight behind the Integration Choice, the commission insisted that this choice was (1) responsive to the expected job growth in the suburbs, (2) compelled by evidence that "socio-class integration is the most effective way of improving the education of ghetto children," (3) best adapted to create an adequate housing supply for poor and moderate income citizens, and (4) most faithful to American political and social ideals.

Many of the commission's specific policy recommendations to implement this strategy, however, actually focused on programs directed toward inner-city improvements. The commission proposed, for example, to improve employment prospects by (1) consolidating urban employment efforts, (2) increasing manpower and job training efforts in urban areas, (3) taking aggressive action against those employment practices with a racially discriminatory intent or effect, (4) providing tax credits to spur investment in rural as well as urban poverty areas, and (5) beginning "immediate action to create 2,000,000 new jobs over the next three years – one million in the public sector and one million in the private sector."[12] None of these employment proposals directly confronted the problem of residential segregation.

In the area of public education, while the commission supported general efforts to "reduce de facto segregation in our schools," especially the "racial discrimination in Northern as well as Southern schools,"[13] it stopped short of calling for mandatory, interdistrict school desegregation. Instead, most of its recommendations targeted inner-city schools and children for compensatory or supplemental aid.

Only in the area of housing did the commission prescribe solutions tailored to address the urban/suburban racial segregation central to its analysis of the underlying problem. The commission's suburban housing strategy was twofold. First, it called for "a comprehensive and enforceable federal open housing law to cover the sale or rental of all housing, including single family homes."[14] To implement the law, the commission urged "voluntary community action" to disseminate information about suburban housing opportunities to urban minorities and to provide education in suburban communities about "the desirability of open housing."[15] Second, the commission urged an expansion of federal housing programs that would target more low- and moderate-income units in suburban areas, to be implemented through a revitalized federal housing program that would add 6 million units to the federal low-income housing inventory within five years.

The national response to the Kerner Commission Report

The Kerner Commission warned America that it must choose among three mutually exclusive policy alternatives. Yet within a month after the commission issued its report, President Lyndon Johnson renounced a second presidential term, and later in 1968 Republican candidate Richard Nixon narrowly defeated the Democratic presidential candidate, Vice-President Hubert Humphrey. During the succeeding eight years, the urban and poverty programs crafted by Lyndon Johnson's administration – the War on Poverty and the Model Cities Program – gradually lost executive and legislative momentum. Gary Orfield has characterized the national political response as a near-total rejection of the basic Kerner prescriptions:

> With the election of Nixon and Reagan, whose administrations have set the basic social-policy agenda for the last twenty years, the country rejected the fundamental conclusions and recommendations of the Kerner Report. The issue of civil rights disappeared from national politics, and the idea that there was something fundamentally wrong with existing racial conditions, something that required strong governmental action, was rejected. ... Presidential politics polarized on racial grounds with four of the five elections since the Kerner Report won by the candidate who received virtually no black votes.[16]

It would be inaccurate, however, to suggest that the nation took no steps at all to address the social ills of segregation and isolated urban poverty. Prior to the 1968 presidential election, Congress passed two major pieces of housing legislation, both of which were prompted in part by the riots and the themes of the Kerner Commission Report. One was the Fair Housing Act of 1968, which had been hastily appended by Congress, after the assassination of Dr. Martin Luther King Jr. on April 4, 1968, to pending civil rights legislation that had been designed to protect citizens from violence or intimidation while exercising their civil rights. Under the Fair Housing Act, it became "the policy of the United States to provide within constitutional limitations, for fair housing throughout the United States."[17] The act expressly prohibited racial or religious discrimination by governmental or most multifamily private market actors in the sale or rental of dwellings, or in their advertisement, financing, or commercial brokerage.

The Fair Housing Act also required the Department of Housing and Urban Development (HUD) and other federal agencies to "administer their programs and activities relating to housing and urban development ... affirmatively to further the purposes" of fair housing. Yet the act provided very few federal tools to compel private compliance. Instead, it placed principal responsibility on the shoulders of aggrieved private litigants, who were authorized to file administrative complaints of housing discrimination with HUD and to initiate federal lawsuits if HUD failed to obtain "voluntary compliance" within thirty days. Apart from their conciliation responsibilities, however, federal authorities were given meaningful enforcement powers only if "the Attorney General ha[d] reasonable cause to believe that any person ... is engaged in a pattern or practice of resistance," and if "such denial raise[d] an issue of general public importance."[18]

Congress enacted a second piece of responsive federal legislation, the Housing and Urban Development Act of 1968, in the wake of the urban riots. This legislation created programs to spur low-income housing construction, including (1) new interest subsidies for low- and moderate-income homeownership, (2) a new program to subsidize interest rates for developers who would agree to build and lease dwelling units for low-income persons, (3) additional funding to increase public housing production by 375,000 units over the 1968–70 period, and (4) numerous urban renewal modifications.

Three years later HUD promulgated regulations that were designed to channel low-income housing subsidies toward suburban jurisdictions, and in 1974 Congress passed additional housing legislation that appeared on its face even more far reaching and directly responsive to the concerns of the Kerner Commission. The Housing and Community Development Act of 1974 (HCDA) declared that it was aimed at "the elimination of slums and blight ... and the deterioration of property and neighborhood and community facilities of importance to the welfare of the community, principally persons of low and moderate income."[19] The legislation promised to promote "the reduction of the isolation of income groups within communities and geographical areas and the promotion of an increase in the diversity and vitality of neighborhoods through the spatial deconcentration of housing opportunities for persons of lower income and the revitalization of deteriorating or deteriorated neighborhoods to attract persons of higher income."[20]

Yet the HCDA proved, in practice, to be unfaithful to the lofty assurances of its preamble, operating most often to undermine the real needs of the poor. The 1974 act abandoned narrowly tailored categorical grants in favor of broad, community development block grants that allowed local authorities to pursue locally developed priorities, subordinating the needs of the poor, who were usually politically powerless, to the desires of local political leaders. Although the HCDA formally required each community to develop a Housing Assistance Plan that would address likely future housing needs, HUD was granted no substantive power to reject a local plan or to withhold block grant funds ....

Thus, much like the Model Cities legislation that preceded it, the HCDA's Kerner-Commission-inspired goals of racial and economic deconcentration were thwarted by powerful political opposition. Indeed, the HCDA's insistence on "spatial deconcentration" of low-income housing soon led to ironic consequences. As John Calmore noted at the time,

> In the name of expanding housing opportunities, the government has actually restricted [the development of] housing for poor inner-city residents and has

adversely affected the social and political integrity of their communities...
Moreover, the occurrence of spatial deconcentration is too often merely a recon-
centration of people in a different space. Finally, in light of extensive urban reinvestment, many so-called impacted areas are really transitional areas; absent
more low-income housing in these areas, many poor will suffer displacement,
being replaced by the return of the middle-class to the inner city.[21]

*   *   *

The Urban Crisis of the Early 1990s:
The Kerner Commission Revisited

*   *   *

Residential patterns: segregation by race and class

The commission contended in 1968 that changing urban residential patterns
(most critically the growing concentration of blacks in the central cities and
the departure of whites to the suburbs) would, if unchecked, contribute to
the deterioration of every major aspect of urban life. In the decades since the
report was issued, many of the underlying demographic trends forecast by the
Kerner Commission have continued, although some have abated. The black
migration from the rural South largely has ceased, and there is evidence that
some African Americans are returning to the South from northern cities.
Overall, however, the United States in 1995 has become a significantly more
urbanized society than it was in 1968 and many of the nation's larger urban
centers, especially in the northeastern and north-central states, have retained
the urban characteristics sketched out in the Kerner Report: an older, central-
city area surrounded by expanding, more affluent suburbs. As predicted, the
populations of America's central cities have become disproportionately black,
Hispanic, and Asian, while suburban communities have remained disproportionately white.

The 1989 report of the National Research Council's Committee on the Status
of Black Americans (the Jaynes Committee) summarized the data as follows:

> Urban residential segregation of blacks is far greater than that of any other large
> racial or ethnic group, and there is extensive documentation of the purposeful
> development and maintenance of involuntary residential exclusion and segrega-
> tion. ... Black suburbanization rates remain low, and objective indicators of
> socioeconomic status that predict suburbanization for Hispanics and Asian-
> Americans do not do so for blacks. The social changes of the 1960s and 1970s
> that affected black status had only slight effects on the residential segregation
> of blacks in large cities. Blacks are not free to live where they wish, whatever
> their economic status. Thus, black-white residential separation continues to be a
> fundamental cleavage in American society.[22]

Within cities, some researchers report that poor residents have become
increasingly concentrated in certain black and Hispanic neighborhoods since
1960. ... Paul A. Jargowsky and Mary Jo Bane have studied the extent to which

"ghetto poverty" (defined to include all census tracts in which over 40 percent of the residents are poor) increased in the nation's standard metropolitan statistical areas (SMSAs) between 1970 and 1980.[23] ... Jargowsky and Bane note that while the absolute number of poor persons living in ghettos in metropolitan areas increased by 29.5 percent from 1970 to 1980, the increases were not spread uniformly among SMSAs. Instead, two-thirds of the increases came in only five eastern and north-central cities – New York, Chicago, Philadelphia, Newark, and Detroit – while southern and western cities, except Atlanta and Baltimore, saw decreases in their ghetto populations.

Alarming increases, however, came between 1970 and 1990. While only 2.69 million persons were reported living in census tracts with poverty rates above 40 percent in 1970, the numbers increased to 3.83 million in 1980 and rose to 5.49 million in 1990. That high-poverty-concentration population in 1990 was 57 percent African American, 23.8 percent Latino, and 15.5 percent non-Latino white.[24] Viewed differently, by 1990 some 21 percent of the black poor and 16 percent of the Hispanic poor (but only 2 percent of non-Hispanic white poor) had come to live in the high-poverty, inner-city neighborhoods portrayed in the Kerner Commission Report.[25] John Kasarda has recently documented precisely how "the number and percent of poor blacks concentrated in poverty tracts, extreme poverty tracts, distressed tracts, and severely distressed tracts increased" during the 1980s.[26]

Moving contrary to these trends, a significant percentage of middle-class blacks left central cities for suburban areas.[27] For example, while only 2 percent of Cleveland's African American population lived in the suburbs in 1960, by 1990 one-third did.[28] By 1992 a majority of all blacks in the Washington, D.C., metropolitan area lived not in the District of Columbia but in its suburbs.[29] Indeed, as of 1989 over 27 percent of all black households lived in the suburbs, and 43 percent owned their own homes.[30]

Yet even these moves by African Americans to suburban locations most often have led them not to "white" or racially integrated communities but, instead, to older, near-city suburbs whose residents were predominantly black or that quickly underwent racial transition to majority-black status after racial integration began.[31] Thus, suburban blacks in 1993 typically find themselves, as in yesterday's cities, residentially segregated from the white majority.[32]

Employment and income patterns: persistent racial disparities

Economically the years since 1968 have witnessed one decade of relative stagnation (the 1970s after 1973), seven years of vigorous economic expansion (1982–9), and three intervals marred by serious recessions (1974–5, 1980–2, and 1990–2). During this quarter-century, employment prospects and average personal incomes have improved for many African Americans who have entered the black middle class.[33] Yet overall higher rates of poverty have continued to plague African American communities, unemployment rates among blacks have remained nearly twice as high as those among whites, and significant wage differentials have persisted.

Poverty rates   In 1968 12.8 percent of Americans had incomes that placed them below the official poverty line. That percentage varied substantially by race; only 10.0 percent of whites but 33.5 percent of blacks were classified as officially poor.[34] The Census Bureau also reported that the poverty rate was substantially greater in central cities than in nonmetropolitan areas or the nation's suburbs.[35]

Progress toward the reduction of poverty between 1968 and 1995 has been slight. Poverty rates declined substantially between 1964 and 1973 but stagnated during the 1970s and rose again during the recessions of the early 1980s, failing to decline significantly even during the high-growth years of the middle 1980s. With the onset of the recession of 1990, poverty rates began climbing again; in 1992 the rate was 14.5 percent, higher than at any time since 1966 (except 1983, when the rate briefly hit 15.2 percent). Danziger and Weinberg have summarized recent data on poverty rates as follows:

> Poverty in America in the early 1990s remains high. It is high relative to what it was in the early 1970s; it is high relative to what analysts expected, given the economic recovery of the 1980s…; it is high relative to what [it] is in other countries that have similar standards of living. … In addition, the poverty rates for some demographic groups – minorities, elderly widows, children living in mother-only families – are about as high today as was the poverty rate for all Americans in 1949! This lack of progress against poverty over the past two decades – the fact that poverty in 1992 is higher than it was in 1973 – represents an American anomaly. For the first time in recent history, a generation of children has a higher poverty rate than the preceding generation, and a generation of adults has experienced only a modest increase in its standard of living.[36]

These overall statistics, furthermore, mask decidedly different experiences for some demographic subgroups. In 1993 only 9.9 percent of non-Hispanic white persons but 33.1 percent of blacks and 30.6 percent of Hispanics were below the official poverty line[37] [poverty rates in 1997 were 6.3 percent for non-Hispanic whites, 23.6 percent for blacks, and 24.7 percent for Hispanics[38]]. Thanks largely to the expansion of Social Security and Supplemental Security Income benefits during the past two decades, the poverty rate among the elderly, both blacks and whites, has fallen dramatically. Poverty among the young, however, has remained very high: 46.1 percent of all black children under the age of eighteen lived in poverty in 1993, as did 13.6 percent of non-Hispanic white children and 40.9 percent of Hispanic children. Moreover, among single-parent families headed by women – a growing percentage of all families during the past twenty-five years – poverty rates remain very high: 38.5 percent in 1992.[39]

Recent observers have suggested that current poverty rates are a product of several convergent factors: the stagnation in overall wage growth during the past fifteen years, a growing income disparity between higher-wage and lower-wage jobs, a substantial decrease in real dollar terms in federal and state financial assistance to low-income families, and changes in demographic composition in American families. One thing is clear: cities have been asked to bear the greatest burden of the new poverty. In central-city areas, poverty rates rose sharply, from 9.8 percent in 1970 to 15.4 percent in 1987, while suburban rates rose only slightly, from 5.3 percent to 6.5 percent during the same period. Nonmetropolitan poverty actually declined from 14.8 percent to 13.8 percent.

Viewed from another angle, central cities, which had housed only 27 percent of the nation's poor in 1959, by 1985 had become home to 43 percent of the poverty population. This growing concentration of urban poverty was especially high for African Americans; the proportion of poor blacks living in central cities climbed from 38 percent in 1959 to 61 percent in 1985.[40]

Employment rates   Professors Moss and Tilly have recently summarized the contemporary evidence on black male employment:

> Black men's fortunes in the United States labor market have taken a decided turn for the worse. Joblessness among black men has climbed through the 1960s, 1970s, and 1980s. Until the mid-1970s, growing joblessness was offset to some extent by the narrowing of racial wage differentials among men. But since the mid-1970s, the black/white wage gap has begun to widen anew....
>
> Black men's employment/population ratios have been falling since the 1950s, and have dropped relative to those of white men since the mid-1960s. During the 1960s and early 1970s, the relative fall was driven primarily by black men's more rapid decrease in labor force participation; since then a widening gap in unemployment rates has accounted for most of black men's relative decline.[41]

Christopher Jencks also confirms that black male unemployment rates have remained more than twice as high as white rates throughout this period.... Some have suggested that many central-city black males cannot find employment because they either have failed to develop sufficient skills to be marketable or have adopted cultural characteristics that render them unemployable. Joleen Kirschenman and Kathryn M. Neckerman report the outcome of surveys of Chicago-area employers, who quite candidly confess such assumptions: "Employers view inner-city workers, especially black men, as unstable, uncooperative, dishonest, and uneducated. Race is an important factor in hiring decisions. But it is not race alone: rather it is race in a complex interaction with employers' perceptions of class and space, or inner-city residence."[42] Other researchers report, however, that most inner-city residents are willing to work,[43] and in tight job markets, low-income, central-city blacks can and do find work, experiencing measurable gains in income.[44] If most African Americans in central cities are willing to work, what explains their very high rates of unemployment? Recent studies employing the "audit methodology" – sending "testers" of similar qualifications but different racial backgrounds to apply for the same job openings – have revealed substantial racial discrimination against blacks who seek entry positions in the Chicago and Washington, D.C., areas, especially for higher-level jobs.[45] Such discrimination is consistent with that reported by Kirschenman and Neckerman and with the long history of black exclusion from jobs in urban America.[46]

Income levels   As noted, African American workers have not only continued to face higher unemployment rates, but those with steady employment have continued to receive salaries that are, on average, notably below those paid to white employees. The most recent data on average weekly earnings among full-time wage and salary workers, reflecting the gains from the economic expansion of the 1980s (although unadjusted for educational attainment and job qualifications) confirm the picture of significant wage differentials by race – and by sex as well.

The Kerner Commission suggested in 1968 that wage disparities between white and black workers could be explained in large part by the limited range of jobs open to most urban African Americans: "The concentration of male Negro employment at the lowest end of the occupational scale is greatly depressing the incomes of United States Negroes in general. In fact, this is the single most important source of poverty among Negroes. It is even more important than unemployment."[47]

Since black educational attainment, measured by years of school completed, has largely overtaken that of whites, the racial wage gap should have closed if earlier wage differentials reflected no more than educational differences. Instead, the wage differential between black and white workers continued to widen throughout the 1980s.

Some respected scholars view the overall evidence on wages more positively. In summarizing black economic gains achieved during the forty years since Gunner Myrdal first issued his famous report in 1940, Smith and Welch wrote in 1986,

> The changes over the last forty years were dramatic. Fully 20 percent of work-ing black men in 1980 were still part of the poor black under-class, a reminder than many blacks remained left out and left behind. But placed in historical per-spective, such figures still represent enormous progress toward eradicating black poverty. Political rhetoric on the race issue must eventually balance two com-pelling truths. America has made considerable strides in reducing black poverty; but by the standards of a just society, black poverty remains at unacceptably high levels.
>
> However, the real story of the last forty years has been the emergence of the black middle class, whose income gains have been real and substantial. The growth in the size of the black middle class was so spectacular that as a group it outnumbers the black poor. Finally, for the first time in American history, a siz-able number of black men are economically better off than white middle-class America. During the last twenty years alone, the odds of a black man penetrat-ing the ranks of the economic elite increased tenfold.[48]

Yet Smith and Welch also acknowledged that, following 1979, black-to-white earnings ratios began to decline once again, and that this decline has contin-ued throughout the 1980s.

*   *   *

Educational changes: narrowed gaps in attainment and achievement

...[T]he black/white gap in academic achievement has narrowed significantly since 1968, as "both levels of schooling and rates of return to schooling [among black schoolchildren] have converged toward those of whites in recent years."[49] During the years 1969 through 1984, for example, the average performance of black children on national achievement tests improved more, at all grade levels, than did achievement among white children. Representative national data on reading performance illustrate the point.

The Jaynes Committee drew three conclusions from these and other relevant data:

> First, school achievement scores of blacks have increased at a faster rate than those of whites. Second, despite gains by blacks, substantial gaps in school achievement remain. Third, among the youngest age group and birth cohort, there is evidence of a possible decline in black performance relative to that of whites....
> ...The math and verbal SAT performance of blacks has also improved in absolute terms and relative to whites in the past several years.... Overall, the SAT results are consistent with other data. There is a fairly clear record of improving achievement test performance by blacks.[50]

During this period of rising black student achievement and school attendance, a large percentage of black children entered desegregated public schools, especially in the southern states. According to Gary Orfield, southern schools had become more racially integrated than schools in any other region by 1986.[51]

One principal question in 1993 was whether the significant gains in academic achievement among black schoolchildren resulted from – or merely coincided with – the increase in desegregated schooling during those years. Many researchers concluded that desegregation substantially improves the educational achievement and the "life chances" of African American children. Others, predictably, have disagreed.

A reliable answer is made less certain by several factors. As Robert Cram and Rita Mahard have stressed, much depends on how desegregation is implemented and on the factors that accompany it:

> Desegregation sometimes results in better curricula or facilities; it often results in blacks having better trained or more cognitively skilled teachers; it is frequently accompanied by a major effort to upgrade the quality of education; and it almost always results in socioeconomic desegregation. When desegregation is accompanied by all of these factors, it should not be surprising that there are immediate achievement gains half to two-thirds of the time. This suggests that desegregation is sufficient but not necessary to obtain these gains, since there are other ways to achieve curriculum reform or better teaching if the political will is present.[52]

In many officially desegregated schools, extensive racial isolation still exists at the classroom level. Moreover, since other compensatory educational programs have been implemented in both segregated and desegregated settings since 1968 – including preschool programs such as Head Start and compensatory educational services for poor children funded through the Title I/ Chapter 1 Program of the Elementary and Secondary Act of 1965 – difficult questions are posed about the relative educational impact of desegregation and these other compensatory programs.

Whatever its educational value, school desegregation – a chief focus of black educational reform in 1968 – became, by 1993, little more than a theoretical issue for many urban school districts. Supreme Court decisions in the 1970s severely limited the authority of federal courts to order school desegregation across school district lines. Given the high degrees of governmental fragmentation and the severe residential segregation that characterize many northern and western metropolitan areas, the crucial educational issue for central cities in these areas has become how to educate a public school population that is disproportionately poor and overwhelmingly nonwhite. Although numerous experiments with a variety of new educational approaches are under way in 1995, no firm consensus has emerged on how best to address the needs of urban minority schoolchildren. Indeed, there is some mounting evidence that high concentrations of low-income children in a student body, of whatever racial composition, reduces the educational achievement of all children in the school, whether from low-income or middle-income families. Such evidence, if substantiated, would suggest that no educational solution that fails to reduce the concentration of poor children in inner-city schools can be effective in providing meaningful educational opportunities.

Health care for urban African Americans: largely separate and still unequal

The Kerner Commission reported in 1968 that "the residents of the racial ghetto are significantly less healthy than most other Americans. They suffer from higher mortality rates, higher incidence of major diseases, and lower availability and utilization of medical services."[53] Even outside "racial ghetto" neighborhoods, the health of African Americans in 1968 was, on average, far poorer than that of whites, whether measured by infant mortality rates, life expectancy rates, or effective access to medical services.

Nearly three decades later, despite generally improving health care for all Americans, racial disparities in health care persist on a wide scale.[54] While infant mortality has dropped sharply in absolute terms, black infants remain over twice as likely as whites to die within the first year of life. Likewise, although both black and white life expectancies have improved significantly during this period, average black life expectancy is still years shorter than that of whites.[55]

* * *

Housing in 1992: scarce, expensive, and segregated

Chief among housing issues addressed by the Kerner Commission in 1968 was that of housing quality, primarily the prevalence of "substandard housing and general urban blight" in black residential areas. The commission found that large percentages of urban nonwhites lived in "housing units classified as deteriorating, dilapidated, or lacking full plumbing in 1960." The report noted greater overcrowding among nonwhite units, and it offered evidence that a higher proportion of nonwhites paid at least 35 percent of their incomes for housing in many cities.

Remedying these deficiencies, the commission proposed, would require a sharp increase in housing production for low-income citizens, with a target of 6 million new units in the 1968–73 period and a significant increase in antidiscrimination activities in order to assure urban minorities more housing options outside the central cities.

The ensuing decades have seen a broad deterioration in the housing plight of many low-income residents, especially minority residents. Several trends are positive: overall housing quality arguably has improved, and the percentage of poor renters receiving some form of housing assistance has grown substantially. William Apgar reports,

> According to the 1987 American Housing Survey, 4.3 million households resided in public housing or rental housing otherwise subsidized by federal, state or local governments. While growth in the number of subsidized households has slowed since the mid-1980s, the 1987 figure is up nearly 95 percent from the 2.2 million posted in 1974.
>
> Much of the increase in housing assistance in the last 15 years has gone to aid households at the lowest end of the income distribution. Among the very poor (incomes less than 50 percent of the poverty threshold), 919,000 (or 34 percent) received housing assistance in 1987, compared with only 225,000 (or 17 percent) in 1974. Among poor renters with incomes between 50 percent and 100 percent of the poverty threshold, the increase was more modest, rising from 681,000 (or 23 percent) in 1974 to 1,370,000 (or 33 percent) in 1987.[56]

Figures compiled for HUD tell a similar story. In 1989, 13,808,000 of America's 33,767,000 renter households (41 percent) were income-eligible for federally assisted housing. Among those 13.8 million eligible for federal assistance, only 4,070,000 renters (or 29 percent) received some form of federal housing assistance from HUD; 9,738,000 households, or over 70 percent, did not. In addition to rental assistance, federal assistance was provided for approximately 1 million low-income homeowners, bringing the total number of low-income renters and homeowners assisted to 5.4 million in fiscal 1988.

According to Apgar, over 3.2 million households below the poverty line in 1990 received neither federal housing assistance nor income assistance.[57] To compound the low-income housing problem, a shortage has developed in many low-income housing markets. The Center on Budget and Policy Priorities has put the shortage into stark numerical terms:

- In 1970, the number of low rent units was 9.7 million – approximately 2.4 million greater than the number of renter households with incomes of $10,000 a year or less.

- Between 1970 and 1978, there was a slight decline in the number of low cost units and a modest increase in the number of low income renter households. Despite these changes, *there were still 370,000 more low-cost units than low income households in 1978.*
- By 1985, however, there were 3.7 million fewer low rent units than there were low income renter households – 11.6 million renter households, but just 7.9 million low-rent units.[58]

* * *

As low-income housing units have become more scarce, incomes among low-income and minority persons have stagnated or declined, and public welfare payments have lost approximately 40 percent of their 1977 value in real-dollar terms. Thus, by the late-1980s low-income families, poorer in real-dollar terms than similar families had been in 1968, found themselves scrambling for shelter in markets characterized by a sharply diminished housing supply and sharply increased housing costs.

Among the consequences have been the emergence of a homeless population numbering in the hundreds of thousands in major cities,[59] unlike anything experienced in the United States since the depths of the Great Depression. Homelessness, however, is only the most visible sign of the new housing crisis; the growth in the number of poor families, especially African Americans and Hispanics, who pay unsustainable fractions of their incomes for rent has been far more pervasive. Overcrowding has also increased in many cities, as families struggle to avoid the streets, and "shelter children," the denizens of huge, warehouselike facilities or dead-end welfare hotels, are now a common feature of many cities.

The impact of these housing trends has been especially severe among the black and Hispanic urban poor. As one study noted, "In [1985], ... half of all poor Hispanic and black households spent more than 57 percent of their income for housing.... Some 37 percent of poor black households – or 1.1 million households – paid at least 70 percent of their income for housing costs."[60] Moreover, while the absolute number of households receiving federal housing assistance grew between 1979 and 1987, as of 1987 more than 70 percent of all renters below the poverty line received no federal housing assistance at all, either through access to public housing or through federal housing subsidies. During the Reagan years, furthermore, federal appropriations for low-income housing suffered the greatest cuts endured by any major federal program – a decline of over 80 percent.

Beyond the problems of housing availability and affordability that have plagued urban African Americans, continued racial discrimination has remained a serious impediment even for urban African Americans who could afford to pay higher housing costs....

[A]nalyses in the 1980s and early 1990s continue to show very high levels of residential segregation. The available evidence indicates that a substantial percentage of this segregation is not the product of private choice or income disparities between whites and blacks but, rather, of illegal discrimination against

African American buyers or renters, not only by sellers and landlords, but also by mortgage lenders and insurers.

Welfare in 1995: still a morass

The Kerner Commission undertook a broad examination of public welfare issues in 1968, explaining that "the burden of welfare – and the burden of the increases [in welfare recipient case rolls] – will fall principally on our central cities," and that "our present system of public assistance contributes materially to the tensions and social disorganization that have led to civil disorders. The failures of the system alienate the taxpayers who support it, the social workers who administer it, and the poor who depend on it."[61]

The commission identified several critical deficiencies in the welfare system of 1968: first, it excluded many who needed benefits; second, it provided "assistance well below the minimum necessary for a decent level of existence"; and third, it incorporated "restrictions that encourage continued dependency on welfare and undermine self-respect." ...

To address these deficiencies the commission proposed a variety of responses, including (1) a commitment by the federal government to assume greater financial responsibility for AFDC, in order to provide "more adequate levels of assistance on the basis of uniform national standards"; (2) the extension of welfare payments to a far broader range of potential recipients – at a minimum, two-parent families with children; and (3) the development of job training, day care centers, and other programs to enhance the self-reliance of welfare recipients.

The subsequent history of welfare policy is complex, since the nation has not adopted the Kerner Commission's recommendation to nationalize AFDC payments, and thus wide variations in state benefit levels and a welter of overlapping programs remain the rule. Nonetheless, some overall trends are discernible. Between the mid-1960s and early 1970s there was a substantial increase in the nation's AFDC population; one commentator, noting an expansion from 3.1 million recipients in 1960 to 10.8 million by 1974, described the increase as an "explosion."[62] By the mid-1980s this trend had prompted some to contend that AFDC was contributing to the perpetuation of a new welfare class, especially among the minority poor, who were being seriously deterred from entering the labor market by the receipt of welfare assistance.[63]

Nonetheless, the number of persons receiving AFDC payments remained virtually constant after 1975; indeed, the number actually declined slightly between 1975 through 1989, before rising again during the recession of 1990–2. Furthermore, the expansion in AFDC caseloads was not accompanied by a similar increase in benefits:

Since 1960, spending on cash assistance programs has gone through several distinct phases. ... Between 1960 and 1973 federal, state, and local spending on AFDC rose more than 400 percent, as average benefit and participation in the program soared. Real spending surged again in 1975 and 1976 in response to the severe 1974–75 recession. But in the 1970s eligibility conditions were tightened and nominal benefit levels failed to keep pace with inflation; in the eight years after 1976 real outlays declined 15 percent. ... At the end of the 1980s, participation in the program – and its cost – once again began to rise. Pushed up by the effects of the 1990–91 recession, AFDC caseloads and spending levels reached record highs in the early 1990s. Still, spending was only modestly higher than in the mid-1970s, when 2 million fewer people were collecting benefits.[64]

Thus while total AFDC payments, measured in absolute dollar terms, have increased substantially, the per capita increases have been far less significant. When adjusted for inflation, the maximum AFDC benefit for a family of three with no other income actually declined 42 percent between 1970 and 1991, and the average AFDC family of three currently receives an income no more than 42 percent of the poverty line.

Of course, since the mid-1960s a number of important noncash programs have been created or expanded to help low-income recipients, including the Food Stamp program, the Women, Infants, and Children Supplemental Nutrition Program (WIC), the National School Lunch Program, and the Medicaid program discussed earlier. There is debate over the net impact of these newer programs on the poor and on whether the traditional calculations of the poverty line, which exclude noncash benefits, provide an accurate indicator of the actual plight of poor persons who receive such benefits.

The most significant recent federal response to the "welfare problem" has been the Family Support Act of 1988. This legislation was designed to encourage more AFDC recipients to obtain education or job training and eventually to become economically self-sufficient by entering the job market. The actual impact of the act, however, has been far less revolutionary. The Job Opportunities and Basic Skills (JOBS) program that was central to the welfare-to-work approach of the Family Support Act is expected to move fewer than 1.3 percent of all AFDC families off public assistance and into full-time work by the end of 1995, embarrassingly short of the 20 percent goal originally envisioned by its sponsors.

The Family Support Act has since been branded as inadequate by both Democrats and Republicans. The Clinton administration announced a new legislative reform proposal, The Work and Responsibility Act of 1994, on June 21, 1994; the legislation was formally introduced into Congress a week later. Clinton's approach demands greater personal responsibility by AFDC recipients and requires that most AFDC parents find a private market job or accept a governmentally subsidized job after twenty-four months of AFDC payments. Although substantially more strict than the Family Support Act, the Democratic proposal is far less draconian than its Republican counterpart, the Personal Responsibility Act, which was offered during the early days of the 104th Congress in 1995 [and subsequently signed into law]. The Personal Responsibility Act would (1) end AFDC as an entitlement of all income-eligible families; (2) turn federal AFDC and related programs into a federal block grant given to each state, the amount to be frozen at fiscal year 1994 spending levels, with minor upward adjustments for population increases; (3) allow states almost unfettered control over reshaping or abandoning traditional public welfare programs; and (4) forbid even those states that would prefer to do so to grant federal AFDC payments to unmarried teenaged mothers under the age of eighteen, to their children, to children born while their mother is receiving cash benefits from the state, or to legal, resident aliens.

While the legislative future of these alternative welfare proposals is uncertain at present, the public mood seems perceptibly to have shifted against the more generous approaches of the early 1970s. Indeed, under the Family Support Act of 1988, numerous states had obtained formal waivers from federal requirements to experiment with new ways of designing and delivering public benefits. Most of these experimental state programs in the early 1990s were characterized by stricter requirements.

Some critics of these developments have contended that public emphasis on "welfare" and anger over AFDC payments are misplaced, since most poor and minority families are *not* on AFDC but instead are struggling in minimumwage or part-time jobs that simply do not pay enough to lift them from poverty.[65] President Clinton's legislative success in enlarging the Earned Income Tax Credit program during 1993 plainly proceeds on the recognition of these realities, since it was designed affirmatively to reward low-income householders already in the labor market by providing them with substantial tax credits that, with food stamps, would lift a family of four with a full-time, minimum-wage worker to the poverty line.[66] As public policy appears poised to tilt against public welfare benefits, one conclusion is clear: none of the three major recommendations of the Kerner Commission has yet been adopted. Millions of poor Americans remain ineligible for public assistance. There are no minimum national standards for AFDC recipients, and no state provides benefits that lift recipients above the poverty line. Most states withdraw Medicaid coverage and AFDC payments to AFDC recipients who enter the workforce, perpetuating the financial disincentives to self-reliance that the Kerner Commission identified in 1968.

Black political power: major political gains, formidable practical challenges

In no area has black progress during the past three decades been more dramatic than in the attainment of political power in the nation's cities. Aided in the South by passage of the Voting Rights Act of 1965 and in the North and West by the changing demographic composition of the urban electorate forecast by the Kerner Commission, African Americans have captured mayors' offices, school superintendents' offices, and other local power bases in dozens of major cities, including New York, Los Angeles, Chicago, Detroit, Philadelphia, Washington, Newark, Baltimore, Atlanta, Birmingham, New Orleans, and Denver.

This greater political control has frequently led to significant tangible gains for black constituents, including an end to formal discrimination by city agencies, substantial minority hiring in city departments and agencies, city construction and purchasing contracts with minority business enterprises, and meaningful appointments to city administrative boards and agencies.

African American municipal leaders have thus been able to achieve benefits "much in the same way earlier ethnic groups, such as the Irish, took advantage of the benefits of office."[67] In some cities, employment opportunities have improved dramatically; by 1987, for example, 43 percent of all employees of the city of Cleveland were black, as were 47 percent of all employees of the greater Cleveland Regional Transit Authority, 73 percent of all employees of the Cuyahoga County Housing Authority, and 52 percent of the more than 10,000 people employed by the Cleveland Board of Education. Such numbers were inconceivable twenty years earlier when, according to Norman Krumholz, "none of these agencies even had an affirmative action plan."[68]

Yet black political power, by and large, has done significantly less to bring major economic or social gains to the minority poor in these cities. Professors Gary Orfield and Carole Ashkinaze recently have offered a comprehensive look at Atlanta, Georgia, where two decades of exuberant metropolitan job growth and black political leadership might have been expected to lead to dramatic improvement for Atlanta's minority poor. Instead, Orfield and Ashkinaze report, the continued geographic segregation of Atlanta – a black central city surrounded by white suburbs and by separate and unequal black suburbs – has led instead to the development and expansion of a "dual market," in which most of the good jobs, the good schools, and the better neighborhoods continue to be reserved for suburban whites, with Atlanta's inner-city, predominantly black population left farther and farther behind. Other political scientists who had studied Atlanta tell a similar story. Clarence Stone has concluded, "Benefit from the city's 'supply-side' development strategy has accrued to the black middle class, but there is not much evidence the lower class has gained. Atlanta is second only to Newark, New Jersey, among American cities in its poverty rate."[69]

Orfield and Ashkinaze attribute these failures in part to inaction by Atlanta's black political leadership, describing "a kind of celebratory politics, where black middle-class leaders took the evidence of their own success as proof of progress and many low-income blacks accepted that [success] as proof of the possibilities within the system."[70] Yet Clarence Stone observes that, very often, "democratic politics mirrors resource inequalities." While Atlanta's black middle class has been able to contribute substantial resources to Atlanta's governing coalition, lower-income groups have lacked both the organized voting strength and the economic resources necessary to prompt government to act meaningfully on their behalf.

Moreover, even if city officials in Atlanta and elsewhere possessed the political determination to do so, they would lack power to overcome the root problems that afflict the urban poor:

> Local government is not nearly so powerful as state government, federal government, or the private sector in affecting broad social, economic, and educational problems. Local government controls limited resources and struggles every year to maintain existing staff and services. Cutting city budgets means cutting into the black middle class since city government tends to hire much larger proportions

of blacks than other large employers. Much of the discretionary money that used to fund new programs came from federal grants that fell sharply in the 1980s. Some critical programs, such as job training, were turned over to state government. Many of the programs cannot be solved, at any rate, within the boundaries of a single local government.…

The institutions and policies that most directly affect the mobility of young blacks are almost all outside the control of city leaders. City governments have no control of the suburbs, where most of the jobs are being created and almost all of the new housing is developed. The best opportunities for pre-college education are suburban. Educational funding, welfare policy, higher education, job training, and many other critical issues are decided largely at the state and federal levels, where suburban power is growing and city influence is shrinking as population disperses.[71]

Conclusion

There is some evidence that the conditions in which a substantial percentage of blacks live and work have improved in the last thirty years. Nonetheless, structural changes in the national and urban economies have, in the eyes of many observers, contributed to the apparent emergence, during the past three decades, of an "underclass" concentrated in America's cities – a very poor, disproportionately African American population living in drug-plagued, inner-city areas bereft of adequate job opportunities and hampered by inadequate public services. The most striking facts about this poverty are its intense concentration within the nation's major cities and its overwhelmingly racial cast. Douglas Massey and Mitchell Eggers have developed the term "hypersegregation"[72] to underline the multidimensional urban trap in which these urban poor find themselves. Massey and Denton have recently explained: "In a racially segregrated city, any increase in black poverty is confined to a small number of black neighborhoods; and the greater the segregation, the smaller the number of neighborhoods absorbing the shock and the more severe the resulting concentration of poverty. If neighborhoods are also segregated by class, not only is the additional poverty restricted to black neighborhoods, it is confined primarily to *poor* black neighborhoods."[73] Massey and Denton's work illustrates how race- and class-isolation extend their collective misery beyond individual households. During virtually any economic downturn such concentration quickly multiplies individual economic misfortune, producing a communitywide economic and social depression.

Michael Katz adds that the injury to these inner-city neighborhoods is not merely economic: "Many institutions have deserted inner cities; the ones that remain are failing; along with city government, their legitimacy has collapsed. … Institutional withdrawal and collapse not only rob inner cities of the services they need, they knock out the props that sustain a viable public life and the possibility of community. They destroy the basis of civil society."[74]

Are Massey, Denton, and others correct in forecasting that economic policies designed to overcome African American poverty, if pursued alone, are doomed to failure unless they simultaneously overcome America's all-but-universal patterns of residential segregation, especially in its large, metropolitan areas? This perennial question, at the heart of the Kerner Commission's 1968 report, was reopened in the late 1980s through the influential writings of William Julius Wilson and others.[75] It is surely the ultimate question that must be addressed.

Notes

1 *Report of the National Advisory Commission on Civil Disorders* (New York: Bantam Books, 1968) (hereafter cited as *Kerner Report*), p. 1.
2 *Kerner Report*, pp. 12–13.
3 Ibid., p. 2.
4 Ibid., p. 392.
5 Ibid., p. 255.
6 Ibid., p. 260.
7 Ibid.
8 Ibid., p. 393.
9 Ibid., p. 399.
10 Ibid.
11 Ibid., p. 396.
12 Ibid., pp. 24, 413–24.
13 Ibid., pp. 25–6.
14 Ibid., p. 28.
15 Ibid., p. 481.
16 Gary Orfield, "Separate Societies: Have the Kerner Warnings Come True?," in Fred R. Harris and Roger W. Wilkins, *Quiet Riots: Race and Poverty in the United States* (New York: Pantheon Books, 1988), p. 101. For other accounts of policy currents during this period, see Henry J. Aaron, *Politics and the Professors: The Great Society in Perspective* (Washington, D.C.: Brookings Institution, 1978); Sar A. Levitan, *The Great Society's Poor Law: A New Approach to Poverty* (Baltimore: Johns Hopkins University Press, 1969); Daniel P. Moynihan, *Maximum Feasible Misunderstanding: Community Action in the War against Poverty* (New York: Free Press, 1969); Charles Murray, *Losing Ground: American Social Policy, 1950–1980* (New York: Basic Books, 1984); Frances Piven and Richard Cloward, *Regulating the Poor* (New York: Pantheon, 1971), pp. 248–348; Alexander Polikoff, *Housing the Poor: The Case for Heroism* (Cambridge, Mass.: Ballinger, 1978).
17 42 U.S. Congress §3601 (1988).
18 42 U.S. Congress §3613.
19 42 U.S. Congress §5301 (c)(1) (1988 and Supp. II 1990).
20 42 U.S. Congress §5301 (c)(6).
21 John O. Calmore, "Fair Housing vs. Fair Housing: The Problems with Providing Increased Housing Opportunities through Spatial Deconcentration," *Clearinghouse Review* 14 (1980), pp. 7, 8.
22 Gerald David Jaynes and Robin M. Williams Jr., eds., *A Common Destiny: Blacks and American Society* (Washington, D.C.: National Academy Press, 1989), pp. 49–50.
23 Paul A. Jargowsky and Mary Jo Bane, "Ghetto Poverty in the United States, 1970–1980," in *The Urban Underclass*, ed. Christopher Jencks and Paul E. Peterson (Washington, D.C.: Brookings Institution, 1991).

24 John D. Kasarda, "Inner-City Concentrated Poverty and Neighborhood Distress: 1970 to 1990," *Housing Policy Debate* 4 (1993), p. 263.

25 Jargowsky and Bane, "Ghetto Poverty in the United States," p. 252.

26 Kasarda, "Inner-City Concentrated Poverty," p. 283. He added that "there was not only a greater growth in the number of black poor in the cities during the 1980s than the 1970s, but also a growth in the percentage of blacks who were poor during the 1980s, in contrast to the 1970s" (ibid., p. 266).

27 See Larry Long and Diana DeAre, "The Suburbanization of Blacks," *American Demographics* 3 (1981), p. 16.

28 Norman Krumholz, "The Kerner Commission Twenty Years Later," in *The Metropolis in Black and White,* ed. George C. Galster and Edward W. Hill (New Brunswick, N.J.: Rutgers Center for Urban Policy Research, 1992), p. 156. Nonetheless, an overwhelming percentage of all black suburbanites in Cleveland live in just one community, East Cleveland, which suggests that locational choices for blacks who have managed to move out of Cleveland's ghetto continue to be restricted. From 1960 to 1970 East Cleveland's population went from 2 to 51 percent black (ibid.).

29 Joel Garreau, "Candidates Take Note: It's a Mall World after All," *Washington Post,* weekly edn., August 10–16, 1992.

30 According to the Census Bureau, 57.9 percent of all African Americans lived in central cities in 1992, while 27.5 percent lived in suburbs and 14.5 percent lived outside metropolitan areas (U.S. Department of Commerce, Bureau of the Census, *Money Income of Households, Families, and Persons in the United States: 1992,* series P-60, no. 184 [Washington, D.C.: U.S. Government Printing Office, 1993], p. 3). About 39 percent of all Hispanic households lived in suburbs in 1989 (ibid., p. 4).

31 See generally Phillip L. Clay, "The Process of Black Suburbanization," *Urban Affairs Quarterly* 14 (1979), p. 405; John R. Logan and Linda Brewster Stearns, "Suburban Racial Segregation as a Nonecological Process," *Social Forces* 60 (1981), p. 61; Douglas S. Massey and Nancy A. Denton, "Suburbanization and Segregation in U.S. Metropolitan Areas," *American Journal of Sociology* 94 (1988), p. 592.

32 In the early 1980s, Lake reported that

> the suburbanization of blacks is being accompanied by the increasing territorial differentiation of suburbia along racial lines – and not by integration. Comparison of the experiences of black and white suburban homebuyers at the end of the 1970s provides strong evidence of a suburban housing market explicitly and implicitly organized along racial lines. ... The mechanisms in place to enforce and reproduce a structural pattern based on race mean that at the individual level, suburbanization for blacks connotes constrained residential choice, a restricted and less efficient housing search process, and limited opportunities for housing equity and wealth accumulation. (Robert W. Lake, *The New Suburbanites: Race and Housing in the Suburbs* [New Brunswick, N.J.: Rutgers Center for Urban Policy Research, 1981], p. 239).

33 In 1991, for example, 20.9 percent of all black households in the suburbs earned incomes of $50,000 or more, while 4.8 percent of all suburban blacks earned incomes in excess of $70,000 (U.S. Department of Commerce, Bureau of the Census, *Money Income of Households, Families, and Persons in the United States: 1991,* series P-60, no. 180 [Washington, D.C.: U.S. Government Printing Office, 1991], pp. 9–10).

34 U.S. Department of Commerce, Bureau of the Census, *Poverty in the United States, 1959 to 1968,* series P-60, no. 68 (Washington, D.C.: U.S. Government Printing Office, 1969), pp. 2–3.

35   In 1970 15.4 percent of the nation's central-city households had incomes below
      the poverty line, compared with 5.3 percent of the suburban households (Paul E.
      Peterson, "The Urban Underclass and the Poverty Paradox," in Jencks and
      Peterson, *Urban Underclass*, pp. 3, 7, tab. 1).

36   Danziger and Weinberg, "Historical Record," p. 18.

37   Center on Budget and Policy Priorities, *Despite Economic Recovery, Poverty
      and Income Trends Are Disappointing in 1993* (Washington, D.C.: Center
      on Budget and Policy Priorities, 1994), p. 5, tab. 1; see also Danziger and Weinberg,
      "Historical Record," p. 37, tab. 2.4 (reporting similar percentages for 1990).

38   U.S. Department of Commerce, "Poverty in the U.S., 1997," *Current Population
      Reports* (Washington, D.C.: U.S. Government Printing Office, 1997).

39   U.S. Department of Commerce, Bureau of the Census, *Poverty in the United
      States: 1992*, series P-60, no. 185 (Washington, D.C.: U.S. Government Printing
      Office, 1993), p. 14.

40   John D. Kasarda, "The Severely Distressed in Economically Transforming
      Cities," in *Drugs, Crime, and Social Isolation: Barriers to Urban Opportunity*,
      ed. Adele V. Harrell and George E. Peterson (Washington, D.C.: Urban Institute
      Press, 1992), p. 46.

41   Philip Moss and Chris Tilly, *Why Black Men Are Doing Worse in the Labor
      Market: A Review of Supply-Side and Demand-Side Explanations* (New York:
      Social Science Research Council, 1991), pp. 3–4.

42   Joleen Kirschenman and Kathryn M. Neckerman, "'We'd Love to Hire Them,
      But ...': The Meaning of Race for Employers," in Jencks and Peterson, *Urban
      Underclass*, pp. 203, 204.

43   In one recent study of the attachment of inner-city residents of Chicago to the
      labor market, researchers found that "willingness to work was the norm in
      Chicago's inner city" and that "at most, 6 percent of adults in Chicago's inner-
      city neighborhoods would meet our criteria for being shiftless" by being idle,
      able-bodied, and unwilling to work (Marta Tienda and Haya Stier, "Joblessness
      and Shiftlessness: Labor Force Activity in Chicago's Inner City," in Jencks and
      Peterson, *Urban Underclass*, pp. 135, 151–4).

44   Richard B. Freeman, "Employment and Earnings of Disadvantaged Young Men
      in a Labor Shortage Economy," in Jencks and Peterson, *Urban Underclass*,
      pp. 103, 119–20 (finding that labor market shortages significantly improve both the
      employment prospects and the wages of disadvantaged young men, "particularly
      blacks"); Paul Osterman, "Gains from Growth?: The Impact of Full Employment
      on Poverty in Boston," in Jencks and Peterson, *Urban Underclass*, pp. 122, 131
      (noting that while evidence exists of a "significant minority" with no attachment
      to the labor force, in general, lower-income "blacks have benefited a good deal
      from full employment in Boston [and]...given opportunity, they evidently
      responded in 'acceptable' ways").

45   See generally Michael Fix and Raymond J. Struyk, eds., *Clear and Convincing
      Evidence: Measurement of Discrimination in America* (Washington, D.C.: Urban
      Institute Press, 1993).

46   See generally Thomas J. Sugrue, "The Structures of Urban Poverty: The
      Reorganization of Space and Work in Three Periods of American History," in
      The "Underclass" Debate: Views from History, ed. Michael B. Katz (Princeton:
      Princeton University Press, 1993), p. 85 (reviewing the extensive historical litera-
      ture that examines employment difficulties faced by the nation's urban poor,
      especially African Americans, in labor markets from the nineteenth century
      through the 1960s).

47   *Kerner Report*, pp. 254–5.

48   James P. Smith and Finis R. Welch, *Closing the Gap: Forty Years of Economic Progress for Blacks* (Santa Monica, Calif.: Rand, 1986), pp. viii–ix.

49   Robert D. Mare and Christopher Winship, "Ethnic and Racial Patterns of Educational Attainment and School Enrollment," in *Divided Opportunities: Minorities, Poverty, and Social Policy,* ed. Gary D. Sandefur and Marta Tienda (New York: Plenum Press, 1988), pp. 173, 174.

50   Jaynes and Williams, *Common Destiny,* pp. 348, 350.

51   Gary Orfield, Franklin Monfort, and Melissa Aaron, *Status of School Desegregation, 1968–1986* (Alexandria, Va.: National School Boards Association, 1989), p. 10, tab. 8. According to Orfield and his colleagues, however,

> There [are] clear signs, … that the long-standing achievements in the South and in parts of the Border states [are] beginning to erode. This [is] particularly clear in the cases of Alabama and Mississippi which show major increases in segregation and have joined the list of the nation's most segregated states for black students. Other states, including Florida, are experiencing gradual declines in relatively high levels of integration, declines that may well reflect the failure of many districts in those states to update their desegregation plans in the past fifteen years as vast demographic changes have occurred. The evidence of a significant increase in integration in Missouri, on the other hand, shows the potential value of large-scale city-suburban voluntary exchanges of the sort developed in the metropolitan St. Louis consent agreement in the mid-1980s. (Ibid., p. 29)

52   Robert L. Crain and Rita E. Mahard, "Desegregation and Black Achievement: A Review of the Research," *Law and Contemporary Problems* 42 (Summer 1978), p. 49.

53   *Kerner Report,* p. 269.

54   See, for example, Sylvia Drew Ivie, "Ending Discrimination in Health Care: A Dream Deferred," in *Civil Rights Issues in Health Care Delivery,* by U.S. Commission on Civil Rights (Washington, D.C.: U.S. Commission on Civil Rights, 1980), pp. 282–92 (documenting health disparities between whites and nonwhites at all ages, over a wide range of diseases and conditions); Akwasi Osei, "The Persistence of Differing Trends in African-American Mortality and Morbidity Rates," in Galster and Hill, *Metropolis in Black and White,* p. 128. See generally David P. Willis, ed., *Health Policies and Black Americans* (New Brunswick, N.J.: Transaction, 1989).

55   Average life expectancy among white males in 1991 was 72.9 years; among white females the average was 79.6 years. The 1991 figures for black males and females were 64.6 years and 73.8 years, respectively (Bureau of the Census, *Statistical Abstract: 1994,* 87, no. 114). For a detailed discussion of this phenomenon, see Ronald M. Anderson, Ross M. Mulliner, and Llewellyn J. Cornelius, "Black-White Differences in Health Status: Methods or Substance?," *Milbank Quarterly* 65 (Supp. 1987), p. 72.

56   See William Apgar, Denise Di Pasquale, Jean Cummings, Nancy McArdle, and Marcia Fernald, *The State of the Nation's Housing, 1990* (Cambridge, Mass.: Joint Center for Housing Studies of Harvard University, 1990), pp. 21–2.

57   Ibid., p. 22. In a more recent update, Apgar and his colleagues have noted the arbitrary distribution of federal housing assistance: "Some 1.5 million extremely low-income households (income less than 25% of area median) receive both housing assistance and income assistance; 2.5 million extremely low-income people receive neither" (Joint Center for Housing Studies, *The State of the Nation's Housing, 1993* [Cambridge, Mass.: Joint Center for Housing Studies of Harvard University, 1993], p. 15).

58 Paul A. Leonard, Cushing N. Dolbeare, and Edward B. Lazere, *A Place to Call Home: The Crisis in Housing for the Poor* (Washington, D.C.: Center on Budget and Policy Priorities, 1989), p. 8 (emphasis added).

59 After evaluating data on homeless people in the 1980s, Peter H. Rossi suggested that "based on available information and reasonable assumptions, the most believable national estimate is that at least 300,000 people are homeless each night in this country, and possibly as many as 400,000 to 500,000 if one accepts growth rates in the past few years of between 10 percent and 20 percent" (Rossi, *Down and Out in America: The Origins of Homelessness* [Chicago: University of Chicago Press, 1989], p. 70). See also Christopher Jencks, *The Homeless* (Cambridge, Mass.: Harvard University Press, 1994), p. 13 (estimating that about 350,000 Americans were homeless during March 1987).

60 The total number of renter households receiving federal housing assistance grew from 2.7 million in 1979 to 4.3 million in 1988, representing an increase from a 22 to 29 percent in the proportion of eligible renter households receiving such assistance. Since the number of poor families increased substantially during the 1980s, however, a larger number of eligible households (5.5 million) received no federal assistance in 1987 than in 1979 (4.0 million) Edward B. Lazere and Paul Leonard, *The Crisis in Housing for the Poor: A Special Report on Hispanics and Blacks* (Washington, D.C.: Center on Budget Policy Priorities, 1989), p. 24.

61 *Kerner Report*, p. 457.

62 James T. Patterson, *America's Struggle against Poverty* (New York: Basic Books, 1981), pp. 171–84.

63 Lawrence M. Mead, *Beyond Entitlement: The Social Obligations of Citizenship* (New York: Free Press, 1986) (arguing that public welfare policy has been too permissive and that future policy should make benefits contingent on compliance with minimally acceptable standards of behavior, including a work requirement for employable welfare recipients); Lawrence M. Mead, *The New Politics of Poverty* (New York: Basic Books, 1992) (contending that the underlying dispute over welfare is less about economics than about conduct and public order, with liberals willing to tolerate greater disorder and socially irresponsible, dependent behavior, especially in inner-cities, and conservatives insistent that the inner-city poor must alter their antisocial behavior and attempt to become self-reliant); Charles Murray, *Losing Ground* (New York: Basic Books, 1994) (suggesting that AFDC has contributed to illegitimacy and dependence among the poor). A strong contrary view is offered by many social scientists, most prominently William Julius Wilson, Robert Aponte, and Kathryn Neckerman, "Joblessness versus Welfare Effects: A Further Reexamination," in William Julius Wilson, *The Truly Disadvantaged* (Chicago: University of Chicago Press, 1987), pp. 93–106 (maintaining that structural economic forces have led to the strongly unfavorable economic circumstances presently experienced by the inner-city poor, and that the behaviors and values Mead and Murray condemn are merely symptoms of, and not the causes of, these deteriorating economic circumstances).

64 Gary Burtless, "Public Spending on the Poor: Historical Trends and Economic Limits," in *Confronting Poverty: Prescriptions for Change*, ed. Sheldon H. Danziger, Gary D. Sandefur, and Daniel H. Weinberg (Cambridge, Mass.: Harvard University Press, 1994), pp. 51, 55–8.

65 See, for example, David T. Ellwood, *Poor Support: Poverty in the American Family* (New York: Basic Books, 1988), p. 232; see also Theodore

R. Marmor, Jerry L. Mashaw, and Philip L. Harvey, *America's Misunderstood Welfare State: Persistent Myths, Enduring Realities* (New York: Basic Books, 1990), pp. 35–46, 96–104.

66 Paul Leonard and Robert Greenstein, *The New Budget Reconciliation Law: Progressive Deficit Reduction and Critical Social Investments* (Washington, D.C.: Center on Budget and Policy Priorities, 1993), Appendix II.

67 Krumholz, "The Kerner Commission Twenty Years Later," p. 28.

68 Ibid., p. 29. See also Huey L. Perry, "The Evolution and Impact of Biracial Coalitions and Black Mayors in Birmingham and New Orleans," in *Racial Politics in American Cities*, ed. Rufus P. Browning, Dale Rogers Marshall, and David H. Tabb (New York: Longman's, 1994), p. 140 (offering detailed statistics on black gains in public employment and executive appointments in Birmingham and New Orleans between 1960 and 1985); Raphael J. Sonenshein, "Biracial Coalition Politics in Los Angeles," in Browning et al., *Racial Politics in American Cities*, pp. 33, 41–2 (offering similar statistics on gains in Los Angeles under African American mayor Tom Bradley).

69 Clarence N. Stone, "Race and Regime in Atlanta," in Browning et al., *Racial Politics in American Cities*, pp. 125, 136; see generally Clarence N. Stone, *Economic Growth and Neighborhood Discontent: System Bias in the Urban Renewal Program of Atlanta* (Chapel Hill: University of North Carolina Press, 1976) (examining the systematic neglect of Atlanta's low-income, minority neighborhoods by Atlanta's moderate, pro-development mayoral regimes during the 1960s and early 1970s).

70 Gary Orfield and Carole Ashkinaze, *The Closing Door: Conservative Policy and Black Opportunity* (Chicago: University of Chicago Press, 1991), pp. 49–50 (quoting Robert C. Smith, "Recent Elections and Black Politics: The Maturation or Death of Black Politics?," *Political Science and Politics* 23 [1990], pp. 160–2).

71 Orfield and Ashkinaze, *Closing Door*, pp. 24–5.

72 Douglas S. Massey and Mitchell L. Eggers, "The Ecology of Inequality: Minorities and the Concentration of Poverty, 1970–1980," *American Journal of Sociology* 95 (1990), p. 1153.

73 Douglas S. Massey and Nancy A. Denton, *American Apartheid* (Cambridge, Mass.: Harvard University Press, 1993), p. 126.

74 Michael Katz, "Reframing the 'Underclass' Debate", in Katz, *"Underclass" Debate*, p. 477.

75 Compare William Julius Wilson, "The Hidden Agenda," in Wilson, *Truly Disadvantaged*, pp. 140–64 (arguing for a "fundamental shift from the traditional race-specific approach" toward universal economic programs that draw support from a wider spectrum of American society), and Theda Skocpol, "Targeting within Universalism: Politically Viable Policies to Combat Poverty in the United States," in Jencks and Peterson, *Urban Underclass*, p. 411, with George C. Galster, "The Case for Racial Integration," in Galster and Hill, *Metropolis in Black and White*, pp. 270–82 (insisting that an integrated process is a crucial goal of urban policy); Gary Orfield, "Ghettoization and Its Alternatives," in *The New Urban Reality*, ed. Paul E. Peterson (Washington, D.C.: Brookings Institution, 1985), pp. 161–93 (contending that residential integration is the only serious alternative to continued ghetto formation); and Robert Greenstein, "Universal and Targeted Approaches to Relieving Poverty: An Alternative View," in Jencks and Peterson, *Urban Underclass*, p. 437 (arguing that carefully tailored, class-specific, if not race-specific, economic and social policies are politically viable). See also Anthony Downs, *Opening Up the Suburbs: An Urban Strategy for*

America (New Haven: Yale University Press, 1973) (offering a classic argument in favor of policies that affirmatively promote residential desegregation); Anthony Downs, "Policy Directions Concerning Racial Discrimination in U.S. Housing Markets," *Housing Policy Debate* 3 (1992), p. 685 (reluctantly concluding that, in view of continuing, widespread public resistance to desegregation policies, principal policy efforts should be directed toward reduction of illegal acts of discrimination in housing sales and rental markets).

◆

The Liberal Retreat from Race

Stephen Steinberg

> A moderate is a cat who will hang you from a low tree.
> Dick Gregory, c. 1964

Martin Luther King, Jr.'s 1963 "Letter from Birmingham Jail" has become a part of this nation's political folklore. However, its specific contents have been all but expunged from our collective memory. The letter was not a condemnation of racism. Nor was it, like his celebrated "I Have a Dream" oration – whose contents *are* remembered – an evocation of American ideals or a prophetic vision of better times ahead. King was responding to a letter signed by eight priests, rabbis, and ministers that appeared in the *Birmingham News* while he was imprisoned. The letter spoke sympathetically of "rights consistently denied," but criticized King's tactics as "unwise and untimely" and called for a "constructive and realistic approach," one that would substitute negotiation for confrontation. In his response King acknowledged their sincerity in seeking "a better path," but explained why confrontation and crisis were necessary in order to shake white society out of its apathy and intransigence. Mincing no words, King issued the following indictment of the so-called moderate:

> I have almost reached the regrettable conclusion that the Negro's great stumbling block in the stride toward freedom is not the White Citizens Counciler or the Ku Klux Klanner, but the white moderate who is more devoted to "order" than to justice; who prefers a negative peace which is the absence of tension to a positive peace which is the presence of justice; who constantly says, "I agree with you in the goal you seek, but I can't agree with your methods of direct action"; who paternalistically feels that he can set the timetable for another man's freedom; who lives by the myth of time and who constantly advises the Negro to wait until "a more convenient season."[1]

In his remonstration of "the white moderate," King anticipated the liberal retreat from race that would become a hallmark of the post–civil rights era. By 1963 there were already signs of increasing disaffection on the part of liberals in the North as well as the South. Indeed, this was the subject of a prescient article in the *Atlantic Monthly* entitled "The White Liberal's Retreat." Its author, Murray Friedman, observed that "the liberal white is increasingly uneasy about the nature and consequences of the Negro revolt."[2] According to Friedman, a number of factors contributed to the white liberal retreat. For one thing, after school desegregation came to northern cities, white liberals

Adapted from chapter 5 of Stephen Steinberg, *Turning Back* (Boston: Beacon Press, 1995) and excerpted here from a revised version published in *The House That Race Built*, ed. Wahneema Lubiano (New York: Pantheon Books, 1997), pp. 13–47.

realized that the Negro was not just an abstraction, and not just a southern problem. Second, the rise of black nationalism exacerbated tensions with liberals, especially when white liberals were ejected from some civil rights organizations. Third, the escalating tensions and violence tested the limit of liberal support. "In the final analysis," Friedman wrote, "a liberal, white, middle-class society wants to have change, but without trouble."[3]

As Friedman observed, there was nothing new in the tendency for white liberals to withdraw support from the liberation movement – essentially the same thing had happened during Reconstruction. In both cases advances made by blacks were followed by periods of racism and reaction, each feeding on the other, and liberals capitulated to this white backlash by urging blacks to curb their demands. Friedman described the situation in 1963 in these epigrammatic terms: "to the Negro demand for 'now,' to which the Deep South has replied 'never,' many liberal whites are increasingly responding 'later.'"[4]

It did not take long for the intensifying backlash and the liberal retreat to manifest themselves politically. The critical turning point was 1965, the year the civil rights movement reached its triumphant finale. The 1964 Civil Rights Act – passed after a decade of black insurgency – ended segregation in public accommodations and, at least in theory, proscribed discrimination in employment. The last remaining piece of civil rights legislation – the 1965 Voting Rights Act – was wending its way through Congress and, in the wake of Johnson's landslide victory, was assured of eventual passage. In a joint session of Congress on voting rights in March 1965 – the first such session on a domestic issue since 1946 – President Johnson electrified the nation by proclaiming, in his southern drawl, "And we *shall* overcome." As a senator from Texas, Johnson had voted against antilynching legislation. Now, in the midst of a crisis engineered by a grassroots protest movement, Johnson embraced the battle cry of that movement as he proposed legislation that would eliminate the last and most important vestige of official segregation.

In retrospect, Johnson's speech represented not the triumph of the civil rights movement but its last hurrah. Now that its major legislative objectives had been achieved, not only the future of the movement, but also the constancy of liberal support, were thrown into question. By 1965, leaders and commentators, both inside and outside the movement, were asking, "What's next?" However, this question had an ominous innuendo when it came from white liberals, as King noted in *Why We Can't Wait*, published in 1963. King provides this account of his appearance with Roy Wilkins on *Meet the Press*:

> There were the usual questions about how much more the Negro wants, but there seemed to be a new undercurrent of implications related to the sturdy new strength of our movement. Without the courtly complexities, we were, in effect, being asked if we could be trusted to hold back the surging tides of discontent so that those on the shore would not be made too uncomfortable by the buffeting and onrushing waves. Some of the questions implied that our leadership would be judged in accordance with our capacity to "keep the Negro from going too far." The quotes are mine, but I think the phrase mirrors the thinking of the panelists as well as of many other white Americans.[5]

By 1965 – even before Watts exploded – there was a growing awareness among black leaders that political rights did not go far enough to compensate for past wrongs. Whitney Young epitomized this when he wrote that "there is little value in a Negro's obtaining the right to be admitted to hotels and restaurants if he has no cash in his pocket and no job."[6] As Lee Rainwater and William Yancey have suggested, "The year 1965 may be known in history as the time when the civil rights movement discovered, in the sense of becoming explicitly aware, that abolishing legal racism would not produce Negro equality."[7]

If laws alone would not produce equality, then the unavoidable conclusion was that some form of "special effort" – to use Whitney Young's term – was necessary to compensate for the accumulated disadvantages of the past. By 1965 the words "compensation," "reparations," and "preference" had already crept into the political discourse, and white liberals were beginning to display their disquiet with this troublesome turn of events.[8] In *Why We Can't Wait*, King observed: "Whenever this issue of compensatory or preferential treatment for the Negro is raised, some of our friends recoil in horror. The Negro should be granted equality, they agree; but he should ask nothing more."[9]

*   *   *

Here was an early sign of the imminent breakup of the liberal coalition that had functioned as a bulwark of the civil rights movement. One faction would gravitate to the nascent neoconservative movement. Another faction would remain in the liberal camp, committed in principle to both liberal reform and racial justice. This, however, was to prove a difficult balancing act, especially when confronted with an intensifying racial backlash. Even in the best of times, racial issues tended to exacerbate divisions in the liberal coalition on which Democratic electoral victories depended. As the polity swung to the right, liberals in the Democratic Party came under mounting pressure to downplay or sidestep racial issues.

Thus, the liberal retreat from race was rationalized in terms of realpolitik. The argument ran like this: America is too racist to support programs targeted for blacks, especially if these involve any form of preference, which is anathema to most whites. Highlighting racial issues, therefore, only serves to drive a wedge in the liberal coalition, driving whites from the Democratic Party, and is ultimately self-defeating. That this reasoning amounted to a capitulation to the white backlash did not faze the political "realists" since their motives were pure. Indeed, unlike the racial backlash on the right, the liberal backlash was *not* based on racial animus or retrograde politics. On the contrary, these dyed-in-the-wool liberals were convinced that the best or only way to help blacks was to help "everybody." Eliminate poverty, they said, and blacks, who count disproportionately among the poor, will be the winners. Achieve full employment, and black employment troubles will be resolved. The upshot, however, was that blacks were asked to subordinate their agenda to a larger movement for liberal reform. In practical terms, this meant forgoing the black protest movement and casting their lot with the Democratic Party.

Thus, after 1965 many white liberals who were erstwhile supporters of the civil rights movement placed a kiss of death on race-based politics and race-based public policy. They not only joined the general retreat from race in the society at large, but in fact cited the white backlash as reason for their own abandonment of race-based politics. In this sense the liberal retreat from race can be said to represent the left wing of the backlash.

The Howard Address: A Case of "Semantic Infiltration"

The ideological cleavage that would split the liberal camp was foreshadowed in a commencement address that President Johnson delivered at Howard University on June 4, 1965. The speech, written by Richard Goodwin and Daniel Patrick Moynihan, was riddled with contradictions, and for this very reason epitomizes the political limbo that existed in 1965, as well as the emerging lines of ideological and political division within the liberal camp.[10]

The speech, aptly entitled "To Fulfill These Rights," began with the most radical vision on race that has ever been enunciated by a president of the United States. After reviewing the series of civil rights acts that secured full civil rights for African Americans, Johnson declared: "But freedom is not enough." He continued:

> You do not take a person who, for years, has been hobbled by chains and liberate him, bring him up to the starting line of a race and then say, "you are free to compete with all the others," and still justly believe that you have been completely fair. Thus it is not enough just to open the gates of opportunity. All our citizens must have the ability to walk through those gates.

Johnson's oratory went a critical step further:

> This is the next and more profound stage of the battle for civil rights. We seek not just freedom but opportunity – not just legal equity but human ability – *not just equality as a right and a theory but equality as a fact and as a result.*

With these last words, Johnson adopted the logic and the language of those arguing for compensatory programs that would redress past wrongs. Equality, not liberty, would be the defining principle of "the next and more profound stage" in the liberation struggle.[11]

So far so good. Johnson's speech then took an abrupt detour away from politics to sociology, reflecting the unmistakable imprint of Daniel Patrick Moynihan, who only a month earlier had completed an internal report focusing on problems of the black family. Johnson said:

> ...equal opportunity is essential, but not enough. Men and women of all races are born with the same range of abilities. But ability is not just the product of birth. Ability is stretched or stunted by the family you live with, and the neighborhoods you live in, by the school you go to and the poverty or the richness of your surroundings. It is the product of a hundred unseen forces playing upon the infant, the child, and the man.

Compare the language and logic of this passage with the one that follows:

> Overt job discrimination is only one of the important hurdles which must be overcome before color can disappear as a determining factor in the lives and fortunes of men. … The prevailing view among social scientists holds that there are no significant differences among groups as to the distribution of innate aptitudes or at most very slight differences. On the other hand, differences among individuals are very substantial. The extent to which an individual is able to develop his aptitudes will largely depend upon the circumstances present in the family within which he grows up and the opportunities which he encounters at school and in the larger community.

This latter passage comes from a 1956 book, *The Negro Potential*, by Eli Ginzberg, who was a leading liberal economist of that period.[12] My point is not that Johnson's speechwriters were guilty of plagiarism. Rather it is to take note of their Machiavellian genius. With a rhetorical sleight of hand, Goodwin and Moynihan shifted the discourse away from the radical vision of "equal results" that emanated from the black protest movement of the 1960s back to the standard liberal cant of the 1950s, which held that the black child is stunted by "circumstances present in the family within which he grows up." The conceptual groundwork was being laid for a drastic policy reversal: the focus would no longer be on white racism, but rather on the deficiencies of blacks themselves.

Having planted the seeds of equivocation, the speech then shifted back to a fretful discussion of the "widening gulf" between poor blacks and the rest of the nation, including the black middle class. Johnson cited a litany of statistics on black employment and income. Logically, this might have led to a discussion of policies that would move the nation in the direction of "equal results" in employment and income. However, as Tom Wicker astutely observed in the *New York Times*: "Mr. Johnson did not mention such specific remedies as job quotas or preferential hiring, which some civil rights leaders have advocated."[13] Instead, the speech shifted to more generalities on "the special nature of Negro poverty" and "the breakdown of the Negro family structure." Centuries of oppression, Johnson asserted, had eroded the ability of Negro men to function as providers for their family, and, as a result, fewer than half of Negro children currently live out their lives with both parents. Inasmuch as the family "is the cornerstone of our society," the collapse of the family has dire consequences for individuals and communities alike. "So," Johnson concluded, "unless we work to strengthen the family … all the rest: schools and playgrounds, public assistance and private concern, will never be enough to cut completely the circle of despair and deprivation."

This last comment probably passed over Johnson's audience at Howard as mere political oratory. Only in retrospect can we fully appreciate the dire political implications of suggesting that government programs were futile "unless we work to strengthen the family." With another rhetorical sleight of hand, Johnson (via Goodwin and Moynihan) shifted the focus from "equal results" to the black family which, it was said, was perpetuating "the circle of despair and deprivation." The speech conspicuously avoided any policy pre-scriptions, deferring these to a planned White House conference under the title "To Fulfill These Rights." However, the conceptual groundwork was being laid for policies that would change "them," not "us."

Thus, a presidential speech that began on a progressive note ended up in abysmal political regression. Was this self-contradiction merely the result of careless or muddled thought? Or did it reflect political calculation? There is reason to think that Johnson's advisers acted with deliberation and foresight. In a *New York Times* story on June 5, the day after the Howard speech, unnamed "White House sources" are quoted to the effect that the Howard address was the first major presidential civil rights speech conceived indepen-dently of the direct pressure of racial crisis. Reading between these lines, it would appear that Johnson's political strategists were seeking to wrest control over the troublesome direction that racial politics were headed. Indeed, the Howard speech is a prime example of what Moynihan calls "semantic infiltra-tion."[14] This term refers to the appropriation of the language of one's political opponents for the purpose of blurring distinctions and molding it to one's own political position. In this instance Moynihan invoked the language of "equal results" only to redefine and redirect it in a politically safe direction. When semantic infiltration is done right, it elicits the approbation even of one's political opponents who, as in the case of the audience at Howard, may not fully realize that a rhetorical shill game has been played on them.[15]

*   *   *

The significance of the Howard address was that it drew a line in the politi-cal sand marking how far the Johnson administration would go in supporting the escalating demands of the protest movement. In throwing his support behind the Voting Rights Act, Johnson had gone further than any of his pre-decessors in jeopardizing the Solid South. The rhetoric of "equal results" also threatened to antagonize blue-collar workers, Jews, and other elements of the Democratic coalition. The covert message in the Howard speech was that, as far as the Democratic Party was concerned, the impending Voting Rights Act marked the end of the civil rights revolution ("the end of the beginning," Johnson said disingenuously, quoting Churchill). If blacks were "to fulfill these rights," they would have to get their own house in order. Literally!

Thus, behind the equivocal language in Johnson's address was a key policy issue concerning the role of the state in the post–civil rights era. Would future progress depend on an expansion of antiracist policies – aimed not only at forms of intentional discrimination but also at the insidious forces of institu-tionalized racism that have excluded blacks categorically from whole job sec-tors and other opportunity structures? Or would future progress depend on programs of social uplift that contemplate "the gradual absorption of deserv-ing Negroes one by one into white society"?

These alternative policy options were predicated on vastly different assump-tions about the nature and sources of racism. The one located the problem within "white" society and its major institutions, and called for policies to rapidly integrate blacks into jobs, schools, and other institutional sectors from which they had historically been excluded. The other assumed that racism was waning, but that blacks generally lacked the requisite education and skills to avail themselves of expanding opportunities. This latter school included both traditional liberals who supported government programs that "help blacks to help themselves," and conservatives, including a new genre of black conservatives, who adamantly opposed government intervention, insisting that blacks had to summon the personal and group resources to overcome disabilities of race and class.

* * *

From Infiltration to Subversion: The Moynihan Report

The polarity between antiracism and social uplift became even more sharply defined by the controversy surrounding the publication of the Moynihan Report three months after Johnson's address at Howard University. Officially titled *The Negro Family: The Case for National Action*, the report presented a mound of statistics showing high rates of divorce, illegitimacy, and female-headed households. Although Moynihan paid lip service to the argument that unemployment and low wages contributed to family breakdown, he was practically obsessed with a single statistic showing that Aid to Families with Dependent Children (AFDC) continued to increase between 1962 and 1964, despite the fact that unemployment was decreasing.[16] On this meager empirical basis, Moynihan concluded that poverty was "feeding upon itself," and that the "disintegration of the Negro family" had assumed a dynamic all its own, independent of joblessness and poverty. In yet another leap of faith, he asserted that family breakdown was the *source* of most of the problems that afflict black America. In Moynihan's own words: "...at the center of the tangle of pathology is the weakness of the family structure. Once or twice removed, it will be found to be the principal source of most of the aberrant, inadequate, or anti-social behavior that did not establish, but now serves to perpetuate, the cycle of poverty and deprivation."[17]

Moynihan's critics accused him of inverting cause and effect, and, in doing so, shifting the focus of blame away from societal institutions onto blacks themselves. For example, Christopher Jencks wrote in 1965:

> Moynihan's analysis is in the conservative tradition that guided the drafting of the poverty program (in whose formulation he participated during the winter of 1963–4). The guiding assumption is that social pathology is caused less by basic defects in the social system than by defects in particular individuals and groups which prevent their adjusting to the system. *The prescription is therefore to change the deviants, not the system.*[18]

The regressive implications of Moynihan's report for public policy were also noted by Herbert Gans:

> The findings on family instability and illegitimacy can be used by right-wing and racist groups to support their claim that Negroes are inherently immoral and

therefore unworthy of equality. Politicians responding to more respectable white backlash can argue that Negroes must improve themselves before they are entitled to further government aid. ... Worse still, the report could be used to justify a reduction of efforts in the elimination of racial discrimination and the War on Poverty. ... [19]

Thus, at this critical juncture in race history – when there was political momentum for change and when even the president of the United States gave at least verbal support for "a new phase" that would go beyond political rights to assuring equal results – Moynihan succeeded in deflecting policy debate to a useless dissection of the black family. With his considerable forensic skill as speechwriter for Johnson, Moynihan had brought the nation to the threshold of truth – racial equality as a moral and political imperative – and then, with rhetorical guile, deflected the focus onto the tribulations within black families. By the time that the promised White House conference "To Fulfill These Rights" actually took place, it degenerated into a debate over the Moynihan Report, which by then had become public. Whether by design or not, Moynihan had acted as a political decoy, drawing all the fire to himself while the issue of "equal results" receded into oblivion.[20]

Notwithstanding the efforts of a number of writers, including Moynihan himself, to portray the controversy over the Moynihan Report as fruitless and even counterproductive, it proved to be one of the most formative debates in modern social science. The debate crystallized issues, exposed the conservative assumptions and racial biases that lurked behind mainstream social science, and prompted critics of the report to formulate alternative positions that challenged the prevailing wisdom about race in America. The principal counterposition – encapsulated by psychologist William Ryan's ingenious phrase "blaming the victim" – blew the whistle on the tendency of social science to reduce social phenomena to an individual level of analysis, thereby shifting attention away from the structures of inequality and focusing on the behavioral responses of the individuals suffering the effects of these adverse structures. The controversy also stimulated a large body of research – the most notable example is Herbert Gutman's now classic study *The Black Family in Slavery and Freedom*. This study demolished the myth that "slavery destroyed the black family" – a liberal myth that allowed social scientists and policymakers to blame "history" for the problems in the black family, thus deflecting attention away from the factors in the here and now that tear families apart.[21]

Yet leading liberals today contend that Moynihan was the victim of unfair ideological attack. Moynihan set the tone for this construction of history in an article that was published in *Commentary* (February 1967) under the title "The President and the Negro: The Moment Lost." Again, Moynihan begins on the threshold of truth: "For the second time in their history, the great task of liberation has been left only half-accomplished. It appears that the nation may be in the process of reproducing the tragic events of the Reconstruction: giving to Negroes the forms of legal equality, but withholding the economic and political resources which are the bases of social equality."[22] Moynihan goes on to argue, as I have here, that 1965 represented a moment of opportunity: "The moment came when, as it were, the nation had the resources, and the leadership, and the will to make a *total* as against a partial commitment to the cause of Negro equality. It did not do so."[23]

Why was the opportunity missed? According to Moynihan, the blame lies not with the forces of racism and reaction, and certainly not with himself, but with "the liberal Left" who opposed his initiative to address problems in the black family. Specifically, opposition emanated

> from Negro leaders unable to comprehend their opportunity; from civil-rights militants, Negro and white, caught up in a frenzy of arrogance and nihilism; and from white liberals unwilling to expend a jot of prestige to do a difficult but dangerous job that had to be done, and could have been done. But was not.[24]

Thus, in Moynihan's recapitulation of events, it was his political enemies who, in "a frenzy of arrogance and nihilism," had aborted the next stage in the Negro revolution that Moynihan had engineered as an influential adviser to the president.

Moynihan's account is predicated on the assumption that "the civil-rights movement had no program for going beyond the traditional and relatively easy issues of segregation and discrimination."[25] But this is an inaccurate and patently self-serving construction of events. The civil rights movement was evolving precisely such a program, and it involved a surefire method for achieving equal results: instituting a system of preferences that would rapidly integrate blacks into job markets and other institutions from which they had been excluded historically. Moynihan, as we have seen, was adamantly opposed to such an approach, and he did what he could, as speechwriter for Johnson's duplicitous Howard address and as author of the report on the Negro family, to derail any movement in this direction. Yet he portrays himself sanctimoniously as the innocent victim of "the liberal Left," and shifts the blame for "the moment lost" to his critics. He seems to forget that these critics were only reacting to a political position that he had advanced – one that, despite Moynihan's many disclaimers, did shift the focus of policy away from a concerted attack on racist structures to an inconsequential preoccupation with the black family.

*   *   *

The Intellectual Reincarnation of Daniel Patrick Moynihan

Joyce Ladner's 1973 declaration of "the death of white sociology" turns out to have been premature.[26] A remarkable thing happened: "white sociology" underwent a black reincarnation. In the case of Daniel Patrick Moynihan, his theoretical and political positions were essentially resurrected twenty years later by William Julius Wilson. Indeed, Moynihan would be able to gloat over the fact that Wilson and other black scholars had taken up the very positions for which he had been vilified years earlier. As he commented in his Godkin lectures at

Harvard in 1984: "The family report had been viewed as mistaken; the benign neglect memorandum was depicted as out-and-out racist. By mid-decade, however, various black scholars were reaching similar conclusions, notably William Julius Wilson in his 1978 study, *The Declining Significance of Race*."[27]

In point of fact, Wilson struck a number of themes that were at the heart of Moynihan's political analysis in 1965: that blacks had their political rights, thanks to landmark civil rights legislation; that there was "a widening gulf" between the black middle class, which was reaping the benefits of an improved climate of tolerance, and the black lower class, which was as destitute and isolated as ever; that blacks were arriving in the nation's cities at a time when employment opportunities, especially in the manufacturing sector, were declining; and that future progress would depend less on tearing down racist barriers than on raising the level of education and skills among poor blacks.[28] The underlying assumption in both cases was that the civil rights revolution was a watershed that more or less resolved the issue of "race," but that left unaddressed the vexing problems of "class." By "class," however, neither Moynihan nor Wilson were advancing a radical theory that challenged structures of inequality, or that envisioned a radical restructuring of major political and economic institutions. All they meant was that lower-class blacks needed to acquire the education and skills that are a prerequisite for mobility and that explain the success of the black middle class.

In *The Truly Disadvantaged*, published in 1987, Wilson spelled out the implications of his "declining significance" thesis for politics and public policy. Again, he arrived at a position that Moynihan had articulated in 1965: that there was no political constituency for policies targeted specifically for blacks, and therefore "we have to declare that we are doing it for *everybody*." In the very next sentence, Moynihan added an important caveat: "I think, however, that the problem of the Negro American *is* now a special one, and is not just an intense case of the problem of all poor people."[29] But, he insisted, blacks could be helped only through color-blind programs that defined poverty – not race – as the basis for social action. Here, alas, was the "hidden agenda" that Wilson proposed twenty-two years later.

*   *   *

At first blush, it might appear odd to portray Wilson as a political clone of Moynihan. Wilson, after all, is an ivory-tower scholar and a political outsider who has described himself as a social democrat. Moynihan gave up any pretense of political chastity to become a major entity within the Democratic Party. On closer scrutiny, however, Wilson is far from a detached intellectual. In two national elections he has gone on record, via op-ed pieces in the *New York Times*, to advocate race-neutral politics in order to enhance Democratic electoral prospects.[30] And he has quietly served as President Clinton's exculpation for the administration's failure to develop policies to deal with the plight of the nation's ghettos. Whenever Clinton is confronted with this issue, his stock answer is to defend his do-nothing policy by invoking the name of "the famous African-American sociologist William Julius Wilson," explaining how profoundly influenced he was by his book *The Truly Disadvantaged*, and ending with glowing projections about how blacks stand to benefit from his economic policies.[31] It should come as no surprise that Wilson has been mentioned as a possible cabinet appointee.[32]

Thus, whatever differences exist between Moynihan and Wilson, the factor of overriding importance is that both repudiated race-based politics and race-based public policy. Here we come to the delicate but unavoidable issue concerning the role that the race of a social theorist plays in determining what Alvin Gouldner refers to as "the *social* career of a theory."[33] Not only was Moynihan white, but he wrote at a time of heightened racial consciousness and mobilization, both inside and outside the university. As a white, he was susceptible to charges of racism and of resorting to stereotypes in his depiction of black families. Even the voluble Moynihan was reduced to silence when it came to parrying the charges leveled against him by black scholars and activists.

Wilson, too, has had his critics, but at least he has been immune to charges of "racism." Furthermore, Wilson appeared on the stage of history at a time when racial militancy was ebbing. The nation, including the academic establishment, had grown weary of racial conflict, and was eager, like the Democratic Party, to "get beyond race." Wilson, clearly, was the right person in the right place and the right time, and, as if this were not enough, his book *The Declining Significance of Race* had the right title – one that satisfied the nation's yearning to put race behind, to pretend that racism was no longer the problem it had been in times past.

To be sure, Wilson did not cause the retreat from race that has occurred over the past two decades. He did, however, confer on it an indispensable mark of legitimacy. This is the significance of Wilson's elevation to national prominence and even to celebrity status. It has meant that the retreat from race could no longer be equated with racism and reaction.

Cornel West: The Left Wing of the Backlash

If books could be judged by their titles, one would think that a book entitled *Race Matters* would be the antithesis of a book entitled *The Declining Significance of Race*. But then again, one must beware of semantic infiltration, and the possibility that titles are subversive of meaning.

*   *   *

Any such doubts are seemingly dissipated by the opening sentence [of *Race Matters*]: "What happened in Los Angeles in April of 1992 was neither a race riot nor a class rebellion. Rather, this monumental upheaval was a multiracial, trans-class, and largely male display of justified social rage." With this manifesto, West establishes his credentials as a person on the left. By the end of the same paragraph, however, West says that "race was the visible catalyst, not the underlying cause."[34] Already the reader is left to wonder: does race matter or doesn't it?

In the next paragraph West assumes the rhetorical stance that pervades his book: his is the voice of reason and moderation between liberals and conservatives, each of which is allegedly trapped in rigid orthodoxies that leave us "intellectually debilitated, morally disempowered, and personally depressed."[35] Liberals, West avers, are burdened with a simplistic faith in the ability of government to solve our racial problems. Conservatives, on the other hand, blame the problems on blacks and ignore "public responsibility for the immoral circumstances that haunt our fellow citizens." Both treat blacks as "a problem people." West presents himself as mediator between these ideological poles. He is a leftist who does not resort to a crude economic determinism that denies human freedom and that relieves the poor of moral responsibility for their actions. And he is a theologian who does not use morality to evade public responsibility for social wrongs.

Thus for West racism and poverty are only part of the problem. Of equal concern is the "pervasive spiritual impoverishment" that afflicts ghetto dwellers. With these false dichotomies, West has set the stage for a morality play involving a contest between material and spiritual forces and between left and right. Enter the protagonist: a Man of Vision who sees through the mystifications of both sides, a Great Conciliator who transcends political schism and will point the way to an Eden of racial harmony and social justice.

A captivating tale, to be sure. But the critical issue is this: where does West's laudatory attempt to bridge the ideological chasm lead him? According to West, "the liberal/conservative discussion conceals the most basic issue now facing black America." The reader waits with bated breath: what is this "most basic issue"? West has already conveyed his skepticism of the left's monistic emphasis on issues of racism and political economy. And he claims to reject the conservative emphasis on "behavioral impediments" with its bootstrap morale. The most basic issue now facing black America, according to Cornel West, is "*the nihilistic threat to its very existence.*"[36] West continues:

> This threat is not simply a matter of relative economic deprivation and political powerlessness – though economic well-being and political clout are requisites for meaningful black progress. It is primarily a question of speaking to the profound sense of psychological depression, personal worthlessness, and social despair so widespread in black America.[37]

Now, there can be no doubt that "psychological depression, personal worthlessness, and social despair" abound in ghettos across America. So do "battered identities," "spiritual impoverishment," "social deracination," "cultural denudement," and a host of related afflictions that leave West groping for words to convey the gravity and horror of this situation. Certainly, West should not be faulted for bringing such conditions to light. This point is worth underscoring because Wilson and others have claimed that discussion of ghetto "pathologies" has been taboo ever since Moynihan was clobbered, as they would have it, for reporting some unpleasant statistics on black families. This is a totally unfounded allegation. The only issue, both then and now, concerns the theoretical claims that are advanced concerning the *causes* of these well-known afflictions, together with the related issue of what is to be *done* about them. This was the basis of the attack on Moynihan, and it is on these same issues that West must be judged.

* * *

West's problem, to repeat, is not that he discusses crime, violence, drugs, and the other notorious ills of ghetto life. Rather, the problem is that he presents social breakdown and cultural disintegration as a problem *sui generis*, with an existence and momentum independent of the forces that gave rise to it in the first place. Moynihan, too, had held that centuries of injustice had "brought about deep-seated structural distortions in the life of the Negro American." But he added a remarkable addendum: "At this point, the present pathology is capable of perpetuating itself without assistance from the white world."[38] Similarly, West traces nihilism to centuries of injustice, but goes on to claim that nihilism is so embedded in the life of the ghetto that it assumes a life all its own. At least this is what West implies when he writes that "culture is as much a structure as the economy or politics."[39] Indeed, the whole point of West's critique of "liberal structuralism" is that nihilism is not reducible to political economy. It is precisely because nihilism is so deeply embedded that this "cultural structure" must be addressed as a force in its own right.

It takes hairsplitting distinctions that do not bear close scrutiny to maintain that West's view of nihilism is different from the conservative view of ghetto culture as deeply pathological, and as the chief source of the problems that beset African Americans. Despite his frequent caveats, West has succeeded in shifting the focus of blame onto the black community. The affliction is *theirs* – something we shall call "nihilism."

It is also theirs to resolve. As with the Moynihan Report, the regressive implications of West's theory become clear when one examines his praxis. West calls for "a politics of conversion" – a frail attempt to use radical vernacular as a cover for ideas that are anything but radical. "Like alcoholism and drug addiction," West explains, "nihilism is a disease of the soul."[40] How does one cure a disease of the soul? West's prescription (to paraphrase Jencks) is to change the nihilist, not the system. In West's own words:

> Nihilism is not overcome by arguments or analysis; it is tamed by love and care. Any disease of the soul must be conquered by a turning of one's soul. This turning is done through one's own affirmation of one's worth – an affirmation fueled by the concern of others. A love ethic must be at the center of a politics of conversion.[41]

One can almost hear the national sigh of relief from those who feared that expensive new programs of social reconstruction and a renewed commitment to affirmative action might become necessary to control the disorder emanating from the ghettos of America. Instead, we have an inexpensive palliative: a crusade against nihilism to be waged from within the black community. So much the better that this proposal is advanced not by another black conservative whose politics might be suspect, but by a self-proclaimed socialist. Unfortunately, West, the philosopher and activist, adopts the idiom of the preacher who mounts the pulpit, pounds the lectern, and enjoins his flock to "have the audacity to take the nihilistic threat by the neck and turn back its deadly assaults."[42]

One cannot fault West for trying to bridge the chasm between religion and politics. However, he has not placed himself in the tradition of Martin Luther King, Jr., who invoked religious symbols and appealed to spiritual values in order to mobilize popular support behind a political movement. King did not believe that a love ethic could ever serve as an antidote to spiritual breakdown. The only remedy was a political transformation that eliminated the conditions that eat away at the human spirit. West, on the other hand, offers no political framework for his so-called politics of conversion. Indeed, he explicitly divorces nihilism from political economy, thus implying that moral redemption is to be achieved through some mysterious "turning of one's soul."[43]

West cannot escape the retrograde implications of his position with the disclaimer that "unlike conservative behaviorists, the politics of conversion situates these actions within inhumane circumstances."[44] He ignores his own admonition that "to call on black people to be agents makes sense only if we also examine the dynamics of this victimization against which their agency will, in part, be exercised."[45] And while he is guided by "a vision of moral regeneration and political insurgency for the purpose of fundamental social change for all who suffer from socially induced misery,"[46] he fails to translate this prophetic ideal into a political praxis. On the contrary, the practical implication of West's position is to substitute a vapid and utterly inconsequential "politics of conversion" for a genuine political solution – one that would call upon the power and resources of the national government for what is at bottom a national problem and a national disgrace.

It should come as no surprise that the most prominent convert to West's politics of conversion is President Clinton. In a speech delivered to a Memphis church in 1993, Clinton practically echoed West in asserting that there is a crisis of the spirit. The ramifications for public policy should have been predictable: "Sometimes, there are no answers from the outside in. Sometimes, all of the answers have to come from the values and the stirrings and the voices that speak to us from within."[47] Thus are legitimate spiritual concerns used as a subterfuge for political and moral abdication. The irony is made still more bitter by the fact that Clinton gave his speech in the same Memphis church where Martin Luther King, Jr., delivered his last sermon the night before his 1968 assassination.

Not only does West shift the focus of analysis and of blame away from the structures of racial oppression, but in his chapter entitled "Beyond Affirmative Action" he undercuts the single policy that has gone a decisive step beyond equal rights in the direction of equal results. West is *not* opposed to affirmative action, but he engages in a tortuous reasoning that subverts the whole logic behind it. He begins on the one hand by declaring that in principle he favors a class-based affirmative action (as does William Julius Wilson).[48] On the other hand, he knows that such a policy is politically unrealistic. He also knows that if affirmative action in its present form were abolished, then "racial and sexual discrimination would return with a vengeance."[49] Why, then, all this hairsplitting? Even if a class-based affirmative action could be enacted, few of the benefits would filter down to African Americans, who are not only most in need but also have unique claims for compensatory treatment. Nor would working-class whites who become lawyers and doctors on the basis of affirmative action provide the black community with the professional talent that it sorely needs. Finally, advocates of class-based affirmative action overlook the fact that, unlike blacks, working-class whites do not need governmental protection to assure them of access to working-class jobs.

In short, affirmative action is meant to counteract the evils of *caste*, not of class. It is predicated on a realization that blacks have been victims of a system of oppression that goes far beyond the disabilities associated with class disadvantage, and therefore warrants a special remedy. West's equivocation with respect to race-based affirmative action is the clearest indication of how little race matters in his theoretical framework and in his agenda for change.

Reminiscent of Moynihan and Wilson, West's approach for helping blacks is to help "everybody." Like them, he provides a respectable liberal cover for evading the issue of race, and still worse, backing off from race-targeted policies like affirmative action, all in the name of getting "beyond race." West prides himself on steering "a course between the Scylla of environmental determinism and the Charybdis of a blaming-the-victims perspective."[50] Unfortunately, he ends up in a political never-never land where, as Du Bois once said in his critique of historiography, "nobody seems to have done wrong and everybody was right."[51] And nothing changes.

This nation's ruling elites need to be told that there is no exit from the current morass until they confront the legacy of slavery and resume the unfinished racial agenda. It is *their* nihilism that deserves our condemnation – the crime, the immorality, the self-destructive folly of tolerating racial ghettos and excluding yet another generation of black youth from the American dream.

Conclusion

Was there hyperbole in King's assertion that the great stumbling block in the stride for freedom was not the Council or the Klan but those who seek a middle ground and would settle for a negative peace? Perhaps. As is often argued, liberals are not *the* enemy. However, this "enemy" depends on the so-called liberal to put a kinder and gentler face on racism; to subdue the rage of the oppressed; to raise false hopes that change is imminent; to modulate the demands for complete liberation; to divert protest; and to shift the onus of responsibility for America's greatest crime away from powerful institutions that *could* make a difference onto individuals who have been rendered powerless by these very institutions.

The liberal retreat from race during the post–civil rights era is full of political paradox. When forced to confront the issue, the liberal will argue that in a racist society, race-based politics are not viable precisely because blacks are an isolated and despised minority. As with much race-think, this is upside down and inside out. It is precisely because blacks were an isolated and despised minority that they were forced to seek redress outside of the framework of electoral politics. The civil rights movement was triumphant in part because it tapped the lode of revolutionary potential within the black community, and in part because it galvanized the support of political allies outside the black community, including white liberals. Furthermore, this movement not only achieved its immediate objectives, but also was the major catalyst for progressive change in the twentieth century. As Aldon Morris writes at the conclusion of *The Origins of the Civil Rights Movement*: "The civil rights movement served as a training ground for many of the activists who later organized movements within their own communities. Indeed, the modern women's movement, student movement, farm workers' movement, and others of the period were triggered by the unprecedented scale of nontraditional politics in the civil rights movement."[52]

A common refrain from the right is that advocates of affirmative action are guilty of the very thing that they say they are against – namely, treating blacks as a separate class. Again, this reasoning is upside down and inside out. The truth is that it is the *refusal* to see race – the willful color blindness of the liberal camp – that acquiesces to the racial status quo, and does so by consigning blacks to a twilight zone where they are politically invisible. In this way elements of the left unwittingly join the right in evading any reckoning with America's greatest crime – slavery – and its legacy in the present.

Notes

1   Martin Luther King, Jr., "Letter from Birmingham Jail," in *I Have a Dream: Writings and Speeches That Changed the World*, ed. James Melvin Washington (New York: HarperCollins, 1986), p. 91.
2   Murray Friedman, "The White Liberal's Retreat," *Atlantic Monthly* 211 (January 1963), p. 43.
3   Ibid., p. 44.
4   Ibid., p. 46.
5   Martin Luther King, Jr., *Why We Can't Wait* (New York: Harper & Row, 1963), p. 147.
6   Whitney M. Young, Jr., *To Be Equal* (New York: McGraw-Hill, 1963), p. 54.
7   Lee Rainwater and William L. Yancey, eds., *The Moynihan Report and the Politics of Controversy* (Cambridge, Mass.: MIT Press, 1967), p. 11.
8   In October 1963, the issue of "compensation" was debated in no less public a forum than the *New York Times Magazine*: Whitney M. Young, Jr., and Kyle Haselden, "Should There Be 'Compensation' for Negroes?" *New York Times Magazine* (October 6, 1963), pp. 43ff.
9   King, *Why We Can't Wait*, p. 147.
10 That the speech was written by Goodwin and Moynihan is indicated in Daniel Patrick Moynihan, *Family and Nation* (New York: Harcourt Brace Jovanovich, 1986), p. 30.

11   Johnson's Howard University address is reprinted in Rainwater and Yancey, *The Moynihan Report and the Politics of Controversy*, pp. 125–32 (emphasis added).

12   Eli Ginzberg, *The Negro Potential* (New York: Columbia University Press, 1956), p. 7.

13   Tom Wicker, "Johnson Pledges to Help Negroes to Full Equality," *New York Times*, June 5, 1965.

14   Moynihan ascribes the term to "the world of diplomacy" and has used it in his political sparring over the years. See the *Wall Street Journal*'s "Notable and Quotable" column, April 18, 1985; "'Loose Cannon' Moynihan on a Roll," the *Buffalo News*, July 4, 1993; and *Firing Line*, January 15, 1994.

15   According to the *Washington Evening Star* (June 5, 1965), Johnson was interrupted eighteen times by applause: Orr Kelly, "President Calls Parley 'To Fulfill Civil Rights': 14,000 at Howard Give Him Ovation as Johnson Hails New Era for Negro," *Washington Evening Star*, June 5, 1965. In his retrospective account Moynihan makes a point of "the stunning ovation" that Johnson received at the conclusion of his speech, as if this placed a stamp of black approval on the speech; "The President and the Negro: The Moment Lost," *Commentary* 43 (February 1967), p. 34.

16   It should have been obvious that the burgeoning welfare rolls were an artifact of two factors: the migration of young blacks to cities in the North and West, and the liberalization of eligibility as a response to rising black protest.

17   Daniel Patrick Moynihan, "The Negro Family: The Case for National Action," in Rainwater and Yancey, *The Moynihan Report and the Politics of Controversy*, p. 76.

18   Christopher Jencks, "The Moynihan Report," in Rainwater and Yancey, *The Moynihan Report and the Politics of Controversy*, p. 443 (emphasis added).

19   Herbert J. Gans, "The Negro Family: Reflections on the Moynihan Report," in Rainwater and Yancey, *The Moynihan Report and the Politics of Controversy*, p. 450.

20   As Rainwater and Yancey write, "The controversy was, then, a kind of lucky break for the administration since it served to distract from and conceal the fact that the Administration was not really ready to assume the independent role it had reached for at Howard University"; *The Moynihan Report and the Politics of Controversy*, p. 294.

21   At the very outset of his study, Gutman writes, "This volume...was stimulated by the bitter public and academic controversy surrounding Daniel P. Moynihan's *The Negro Family in America: The Case for National Action* (1965)"; Herbert G. Gutman, *The Black Family in Slavery and Freedom, 1750–1925* (New York: Pantheon, 1976), p. xvii.

22   Moynihan, "The President and the Negro: The Moment Lost," *Commentary* 43 (February 1967), p. 31.

23   Ibid., p. 32 (emphasis in original).

24   Ibid.

25   Ibid., p. 34.

26   Joyce A. Ladner, *The Death of White Sociology* (New York: Vintage Books, 1973).

27   Moynihan, *Family and Nation*, p. 42. Soon after the publication of *The Declining Significance of Race*, Nathan Glazer also commented: "These are not things that haven't been said before. It is the first time that a black social scientist has said them with such strength"; quoted in Hollie West, "Getting Ahead and the Man Behind the Class-Race Furor," *Washington Post*, January 1, 1979.

28   These ideas pervade Moynihan's writing, but are clearly articulated in "Employment, Income, and the Ordeal of the Negro Family," *Daedalus* 94 (Fall 1965), esp. pp. 753–4.

29   Daniel Patrick Moynihan, transcript of the American Academy Conference on the Negro American, May 14–16, 1965, *Daedalus* 95 (Winter 1966), p. 288 (emphasis in original).

30   William Julius Wilson, *New York Times*, March 24, 1990, and March 17, 1992.

31   This reference to Wilson was made by President Clinton in a speech to black ministers in Memphis on November 13, 1993, and cited in a profile on Wilson in *People* magazine (January 17, 1974, p. 81).

32   Gretchen Reynolds, "The Rising Significance of Race," *Chicago* 41 (December 1992), p. 81.

33   Alvin Ward Gouldner, *The Coming Crisis of Western Sociology* (New York: Basic Books, 1970), p. 29 (emphasis in original).

34   Cornel West, *Race Matters* (Boston: Beacon Press, 1993), p. 1.

35   Ibid., p. 2.

36   Ibid., p. 12 (emphasis in original).

37   Ibid., pp. 12–13.

38   Moynihan, "The Negro Family: The Case for National Action," p. 93.

39   West, *Race Matters*, p. 12.

40   Ibid., p. 18.

41   Ibid., p. 19.

42   Ibid.

43   Ibid.

44   Ibid., p. 20.

45   Ibid., p. 14.

46   Ibid., p. 46.

47   "Excerpts from Clinton's Speech to Black Ministers," *New York Times*, November 14, 1993.

48   In Steven A. Holmes, "Mulling the Idea of Affirmative Action for Poor Whites," *New York Times*, August 18, 1991.

49   West, *Race Matters*, p. 64.

50   Ibid., p. 57.

51   W. E. B. Du Bois, "The Propaganda of History," in *Black Reconstruction* (New York: Harcourt, Brace, 1935), p. 714.

52   Aldon Morris, *The Origins of the Civil Rights Movement* (New York: Free Press, 1984), p. 288.

2

The National Conversation on Race

Democracy's Conversation

Lani Guinier

No matter who won the recent midterm elections, the voters all lost. People voted their fears, not their hopes. They voted against candidates, not for solutions. Soundbites eroded deliberation. Hate-mongering seemed to count for more than ever before.

In the rush to take sides, candidates and commentators alike sliced complex issues into noisy bits of sound and fury signifying nothing. "It's like intellectual violence," said a Virginia bookstore owner. "There's so much hatred it scares me. This campaign…appeal[ed] to people's lowest emotions."

Candidates who won often did so by mobilizing the discontent of some voters and demobilizing others whose anger could not be directed at easy scapegoats. This technique has been called "the politics of exclusion" or the "cult of other-ness." Its eventual message is "they" are not like "us," "they" are blameworthy. "We" are the "normal" Americans.

But this discourse of blame hurts Americans of all races. We all lose when negative campaigns with their racial coding about "them" dominate the conversation of democracy. As Kathleen Hall Jamieson, professor and dean of the Annenberg School for Communication at the University of Pennsylvania, observes, "We have now devised a means of campaigning that creates an angry electorate which then vents its anger by voting no, no, no, no." And she adds, "If you go in and just vote no, you're not really licensing someone to govern."

Negative campaigns not only breed lower voter turnout and polarize the electorate, they also mask a deeper malaise. They are the visible sores of a poisoned, winner-take-all political discourse. This winner-take-all election system disproportionately rewards winners and punishes losers. The struggle to prevail at all costs turns language into public relations. Words become bullets in the struggle for advantage. Citizens are buried in a deluge of negative political

Reprinted with permission from the January 23, 1995 issue of *The Nation* magazine, pp. 85–7.

messages. Elections become a spectator sport. People don't think about issues; they choose sides. Inspired by a winner-take-all mentality, institutions designed to foster communication operate to pervert and distort it. The mass media provide conflict-driven coverage, with the focus on controversy and extreme points of view. Within the academic community and among intellectual elites, there is little or no conversation across racial or ideological lines. Officials at the highest levels of decision-making disdain dialogue as a way of resolving or mediating conflict. Politicians distort the views of those they disagree with and attack the caricatures they have drawn. Candidates tout the most simple-minded solutions to complex issues likes crime (three strikes, you're out) or welfare (two years and you're off).

Candidates use race to whip voters' emotions, to get them so excited about some issue or candidate that they will go out and vote. Politicians of all stripes pander to whites' fears of blacks, coding a racial subtext in the language of welfare reform and tough-on-crime policies. Think of the code words whites have for blacks and the black environment: minority, urban, criminal, crime rate, social program participant, special interests, inner city, welfare mother. Think of the codes blacks use for whites: suburban type, Republican, conservative.

Both groups see each other as "them." And many whites express their resentment at "them" in the language of less government, meaning no more subsidies for "them." According to a September *Times-Mirror* poll, 51 percent of whites now agree that "equal rights have been pushed too far in this country." Decoded, this statement means: We have gone too far in pushing for equal rights for "them" in this country.

The American people have learned to see race as an issue of blame and punishment: Who is guilty and who is innocent? Who is at fault for the breakdown of our moral compass on this and other controversial issues: individual bigots or race-obsessed blacks; right-wing zealots or left-wing black nationalists; individual incumbents or their individual opponents; the media, Congress, the American people?

In this polarized, winner-take-all climate, our so-called leaders have lost the political will to do more than simply condemn our problems. Even worse, they have lost the political imagination to do more than censure the victims or blame the victimizers. Many liberals seem overwhelmed by the magnitude of the problems, convinced that they defy solution or that the solutions *are* the problem. Others are in deep denial about the need for collective action and community responsibility to solve the problems. Still others openly accept the formulations of personal responsibility and individual behavior modification that characterize the conservative ideological assault on black people and poor people, who are made out to be victims of their own so-called maladaptive behavior or character flaws. No one offers an approach that gives working-class whites and blacks, poor people of all hues and other political orphans a reason or a way to make common ground. No one tries to frame the debate in terms of how government can be made better, more accountable. No one tries to point out that the interests of minorities and the poor are integral to our collective self-interest.

The public's concerns about welfare dependency and random violence are real, but our elected officials have failed to cast the debates in terms of new or compelling ideas. We are stuck in a 1960s paradigm, in which special government programs help deserving individuals overcome barriers erected by bigotry. The trouble is that talk of "equal rights" has also acquired a winner-take-all connotation, reinforcing the notion that the government takes sides in a zero-sum competition between "us" and "them." It encourages the idea that I and my interests are incompatible with you and your interests. In the name of winning all, it is necessary to disparage as unworthy those who oppose "us."

What can be done? First we must envision a truly "democratic conversation" that permits a range of views to be represented in the sturdy halls of the legislatures and other public spaces constructed to carry on vigorous debate and true deliberation – in order to restore trust, overcome antagonism, regain government's legitimacy and achieve our collective wisdom.

We need to take back the democratic space from which American citizens have been driven by the increasingly angry, bitter and polarizing terms of talk radio, negative political ads, winner-take-all electoral politics and gridlock governance. We need to start looking at democracy as a well-conducted conversation.

This means recognizing the need to talk – to communicate. It means talking differently, talking with reasonableness in a more civilized fashion. It means more people talking. It means reasoned talk, informed talk. It also means talking with, not at, one another. And it means talking to our public leaders and talking with fellow citizens in order to find ways to collaborate, to act together.

Changing demographics, the globalization of our economy and the transformation of information technology make it imperative that we utilize all of America's human resources to meet the challenges of the twenty-first century. The future of "us" depends on understanding and collaborating with "them." By recognizing diversity we will actually be uniting the people of America.

But first we must address America's race problem in a more engaged, more participatory democratic conversation. Race is the great taboo. It is like a giant pothole. If we do not fix it and deny it is there, or simply try to drive around it, it will not go away. One of the arguments I was given for the decision to withdraw my nomination to head the civil rights division of the Justice Department without even a Senate confirmation hearing was that such a hearing would be divisive and polarizing. But I do not believe that talking about race must invariably lead to an us-versus-them debate. Talking, especially if structured to assure reasonable representation of relevant perspectives and the need not just to talk but to listen, may instead reveal points of commonality. Talking can be cathartic rather than chaotic; it can vent and relieve pressure and help identify solutions in which we all win something.

Our goal must be to move beyond the polarizing discourse about race that characterized the 1980s. We need a National Conversation on Race. We need new thinking and new approaches to race and racism that move beyond notions of intentional acts of bigotry and prejudice; beyond the claims of legal racial equality that rallied the civil rights movement in the 1960s; beyond the notion that racial preferences are the only or best way to remedy racial

inequality; away from claims based on individual guilt and individual innocence. We need to disavow the drama of divide and polarize in which some
people are made to feel comfortable with their prejudices and uncomfortable
about "them."

In proposing a National Conversation on Race, I hope to find new ways to
discuss race openly and without partisan rancor. I seek to initiate a broad
public conversation about racial and economic justice to concentrate the
nation's attention on the hard issues that thrash about beneath the surface of
debates over urban crime, minority set-asides or the notion of a color-blind
society. One of the ways to do this is to use racial inequity as a window on the
larger unfairness of distribution of resources.

Let me give an example of how this could work. Lowell High School in San
Francisco is a magnet public school that boasts distinguished alumni, including Supreme Court Justice Stephen Breyer. As a result of a court order to
desegregate the San Francisco public schools, admission to the school is now
supervised by a consent decree. No one ethnic group can make up more than
40 percent of the population of any magnet school.

Consequently, admission to Lowell High School in 1993 was determined on
a sliding scale. Chinese-Americans were initially required to score 66 out of a
perfect 69 to gain admittance; "other whites" and Asian-Americans but not
Chinese-Americans could qualify with a 59; blacks and Latinos a 55. As a
result of pressure from the Chinese-American community, these cut-off scores
were modified somewhat and the entry credentials changed. But the school
still employs race-based quotas to protect diversity.

A group of Chinese-Americans are challenging the consent decree; African-
Americans are defending it. Both groups are proceeding within a winner-take-
all frame that pits minority groups against one another.

Why not escape the false choice of winner-take-all decision-making? Why
not use a lottery that allows anyone with a score over 56 – the lowest the
school now uses – to compete for admission via random selection? If the
school can demonstrate, however, that those with a perfect 69 or close to it
are more likely to do something the school values – such as achieve a seat on
the Supreme Court or win recognition as a Westinghouse Science Finalist or as
a successful candidate to a competitive college – then put their names in the
lottery twice or even three times.

This alternative approach is not perfect, but it might lead to a re-examina-
tion of the school's admissions policy not just for Chinese-Americans or
blacks but for everyone. No one would feel "entitled" to admission; nor
would anyone feel unjustly excluded. Such an approach recognizes that claims
of "merit" and "diversity" are equally legitimate. It does not set "us" against
"them". It does not assume that only one group wins. It avoids a zero-sum
solution in favor of a positive-sum solution that more broadly accommodates
the goals of diversity and genuine merit.

In a National Conversation on Race, we would look for remedies that
do not separate working Americans of all hues into warring factions but
instead help them recognize that they are all excluded or treated arbitrarily by
a status quo that disproportionately rewards winners and stigmatizes losers.

Alternative remedies, such as admissions lotteries with a base-score threshold, might help accomplish a broader consensus on objectives. Similarly, cumulative voting, in which every-one's vote can count toward the election of someone, might be a more palatable and more workable remedy for voting dis-crimination than separate, racially homogeneous districts. The point is not to identify a single solution to a set of complex problems but to locate each problem and its solution within a context that unites or links people around a common goal.

We cannot solve the race problem simply by talking. But a first step to problem-solving is the development of a model of what a successful conversa-tion about race looks like. The next step is to go to churches, workplaces and other institutions where people must interact across barriers of difference and where ordinary people have the opportunity to participate. The next step is to create opportunities within those institutions for ongoing constructive dia-logue and sustained collaboration.

Leadership will come from ordinary men and women grappling with real problems, not from politicians caught up in the sloganeering and mudslinging or winner-take-all election campaigns. Leadership will come from ordinary men and women participating in the conversation of democracy unmediated by the ugly, menacing sounds of campaign consultants telling them how to talk or what to talk about. Leadership will arise when the people become participants, not just spectators, in the democratic process.

Some argue that to govern is to choose. But to govern is also to deliberate. Voting in a winner-take-all paradigm forces complex issues into simple choices; that should be the last, not the first, resort. Voting for a winner who wins all should be secondary to debate and discussion within a repre-sentative body.

Ultimately, collective decision-making must be a well-conducted conversa-tion, a conversation in which we all get a chance to speak, to listen, to be heard and to collaborate to solve *our* problems.

◆

Yackety-Yak About Race

Adolph Reed, Jr.

So what the heck is a "national conversation on race," anyway? Like so much in what passes for public discussion in America these days, the notion soothes and reassures, conveying a sense of gravitas, while at the same time having no clear, practical meaning whatsoever.

I remember hearing calls for this conversation a few years ago, first from former University of Pennsylvania President Sheldon Hackney, then from Lani Guinier and performance artist Anna Deveare Smith. At the time, it seemed to be just a well-intentioned soundbite, a way to express in newschat a concern with racial injustice and anger. As a mass-media metaphor, it seemed harmless enough: a way to evoke a national commitment to honesty and democracy. I couldn't imagine how this call could possibly translate into anything concrete, though. Who would participate in this conversation? Where would it be held? What would the ground rules be? And to what end?

I certainly didn't suspect that the notion would go anywhere; I presumed that it would have the shelf life of slogans from political ads. You know, like "Where's the beef?" or "It takes a village...." Well, I didn't take into account the significance of a New South, psychobabbling baby boomer whose political opportunism comes with cybertechie, New Age flourishes. As it turns out, this national-conversation idea is just Bill Clinton's cup of herbal tea.

Now that Clinton has glommed onto the national conversation, it won't just dissipate through the airwaves over time. He has decided to keep this strange idea alive by formalizing it into a Presidential race-relations advisory board. It just goes to show that Bipartisan Bill has the soul of a talk-show host. But the "conversation" also highlights the profound shift over the last generation in American liberals' ways of talking about racial inequality.

It's impossible, for instance, to imagine Lyndon Johnson using the Presidential bully pulpit to call for a national conversation on race in 1964 or 1965. For all his limitations – the Vietnam War chief among them – Johnson understood that the point in pursuing racial justice is not to stimulate conversation. When people like Everett Dirksen protested that the struggle for black civil rights should rely on efforts to change whites' individual attitudes rather than on changing laws, Johnson made it clear that he was less interested in changing peoples' hearts than their public behavior.

Johnson understood that assertive government action can define acceptable practices and behavior, and ultimately change the world in which attitudes are formed.

Reprinted from *The Progressive*, December 1997, pp. 18–19.

The transformation of the South's racial politics has been incomplete, as the electoral success of governors Kirk Fordice in Mississippi and Fob James in Alabama demonstrate. The region nonetheless has undergone changes that would have seemed unimaginable thirty years ago. Blacks and whites can share public space more or less routinely, interact publicly in ways marked by the civility that presumes social equality, share work stations, and maintain the casual conviviality that normally pertains among co-workers. More than at any point in this century, white elites take for granted the need to take some notion of black interests into account when making public policy.

What made these changes possible was civil-rights law, not attitude adjustment. Presenting white Southerners with a *fait accompli* was the only way to counter the cultural force of white-supremacist ideology. Prohibiting discrimination by law not only enforced blacks' civil and citizenship rights, though that certainly was its intent and most important consequence. It was also the only way to create an environment in which casual contact would occur between blacks and whites as presumptive equals. This interaction has begun to erode racist stereotypes and bigotry by establishing the basis for a shared mundane humanity in workplaces, schools, and other public venues.

In the current anti-statist, market-worshipping climate, it is fashionable to deny that public authority can influence behavior and attitudes. Economists and others who worship market theology contend that slavery and racial discrimination would have been eliminated by the natural workings of the market if abolitionists and civil-rights activists had just been a little more patient. Some even blame attempts to preempt those market forces – through the Civil War and Reconstruction Amendments and 1964 Civil Rights Law and 1965 Voting Rights Law – for creating racism. Public intervention inevitably fails, so this twisted reasoning goes, because its artificiality breeds resentment. Civil-rights laws, and affirmative action in particular, just stir up white hostility, since they are coercive, and an affront to properly market-based notions of justice and equity.

Besides (and here's where this sophistry most clearly approximates religion), the white South would eventually have eliminated slavery on its own because the system was irrational economically. Segregation and other forms of discrimination were already on the decline after World War II for the same reason, say the market moralists. Their argument boils down to this: Had there been no legal abolition of slavery, there would have been no white-supremacist restoration in the South, and had there been no civil-rights legislation, there would be no white racism. If exuberant reformers hadn't gone mucking around with the larger rationality of the system of individual choices and transactions that drive market forces, everything would have turned out fine. Never mind that the Confederacy fought tooth and nail to preserve slavery and that white southerners fought nearly as hard to maintain Jim Crow.

A climate in which this kind of thought is credible makes twaddle like the need for a national conversation about race seem to make sense. It's the norm these days to make public issues a matter of personal feelings, and to separate beliefs from their social context. It is this climate that makes it possible for a supposedly progressive magazine like *Mother Jones* not only to attack affirmative action as divisive, but to call for its demise in order to "reestablish racial healing as a national priority."

This brings us back to Bipartisan Bill's attraction to the conversation. It's an ideal vehicle for him to express his concerns about race, because it's not connected to any real substance. It's just part of the fundamentally empty rhetoric of multiculturalism: diversity, mutual awareness, respect for difference, hearing different voices, and the like.

None of these notions is objectionable on its face, but that's partly because none of them means anything in particular. Several Southern state governments have embraced a brand of multiculturalism that treats foes and advocates of white supremacy as equivalent "voices" equally deserving of respect. So they grant state employees the option to choose either Martin Luther King Jr.'s birthday or Robert E. Lee's as a mid-January holiday.

We should accept the equal humanity of those who support Operation Rescue, the Promise Keepers, the Christian Coalition, or the militia movement, but this cannot mean that we grant the legitimacy of their reactionary political programs. And whether or not we are willing to talk with them about our differences is less important than that we defeat their political objectives and repudiate the larger social vision from which those objectives derive.

No doubt Hackney and Guinier and others calling for this national conversation are well-intentioned. But that doesn't mean the idea is any less vapid – or potentially destructive. As we've seen, opponents of affirmative action also base their argument on their desire to stamp out "racial division." A generation ago, segregationists charged civil-rights activists with creating racial divisiveness. A century earlier, opponents of Reconstruction made the same claim against people who supported black citizenship.

The saccharine language of multiculturalism and respect, diversity, awareness, and healing is wonderfully evanescent; it amounts to a kind of racial-equality lite. Ironically, the "conversation" also reinforces a fundamentally racist assumption: the idea that individuals automatically can articulate the mindset of a group is a vestige of Victorian notions of racial temperament.

The problem isn't racial division or a need for healing. It is racial inequality and injustice. And the remedy isn't an elaborately choreographed pageantry of essentializing yackety-yak about group experience, cultural difference, pain, and the inevitable platitudes about understanding. Rather, we need a clear commitment by the federal government to preserve, buttress, and extend civil rights, *and* to use the office of the Presidency to indicate that commitment forcefully and unambiguously. As the lesson of the past three decades in the South makes clear, this is the only effective way to change racist attitudes and beliefs.

Bill Clinton has absolutely no interest in *that* kind of talk, however, and it's easy to understand why. If he did, he'd have to explain why he and his Administration have repeatedly pandered to the resurgent racist tendencies he purports to bemoan.

He'd have to explain why he made a central prop in his 1992 campaign an element of the lexicon of coded racism – his pledge to "end welfare as we know it" and his constant harping on an invidious distinction between those who supposedly "play by the rules" and those who supposedly don't. He'd have to explain his own half-hearted stand on affirmative action ("mend it, don't end it") and why he refused to provide any support for the mobilization against California's hideous Proposition 209.

He'd have to explain why he proposed and pushed through a draconian crime bill that not only trades on the coded racist rhetoric of the anti-crime hysteria but also disproportionately targets inner-city minorities. (Take, for example, the outrageous disparity in sentencing for possession of crack and powder cocaine. The only difference between the two forms of the drug is the racial breakdown of users.)

He'd have to explain why he signed and supported the odious welfare-reform bill.

He'd have to explain why his Administration resorts to the racialized language of inner-city pathology to justify its attack on the principle of providing public housing for poor people.

It doesn't make sense to feel betrayed by Clinton, however. He's only doing what comes naturally. If progressives don't begin thinking in a more rigorous way about this kind of charade, we'll never stop talking in circles.

3

The Racial Division of Labor

Occupational Apartheid and the Origins of Affirmative Action

Stephen Steinberg

No greater wrong has been committed against the Negro than the denial to him of the right to work.

A. Philip Randolph, *What the Negro Wants*, 1944

The core of the civil rights problem is the matter of achieving equal opportunity for Negroes in the labor market. For it stands to reason that all our other rights depend on that one for fulfillment. We cannot afford better education for our children, better housing, or medical care unless we have jobs.

Whitney M. Young, Jr., *To Be Equal*, 1964

If there is any one key to the systematic privilege that undergirds a racial capitalist society, it is the special advantage of the white population in the labor market.

Robert Blauner, *Racial Oppression in America*, 1972

The essence of racial oppression is *not* the distorted and malicious stereotypes that whites have of blacks. This is the *culture* of oppression, not to be confused with the thing itself. Nor is the essence of racism epitomized by a person having to sit in the back of a bus. In South Africa this was called "petty apartheid," as opposed to "grand apartheid," the latter referring to the political disfranchisement and banishment of millions of blacks to isolated and impoverished "homelands." In the United States, the essence of racial oppression – *our* grand apartheid – is a racial division of labor, a system of occupational segregation that relegates most blacks to work in the least desirable job sectors or that excludes them from job markets altogether.

Adapted from chapters 8 and 9 of Stephen Steinberg, *Turning Back* (Boston: Beacon Press, 1995) and excerpted here from "Occupational Apartheid in America: Race, Labor Market Segmentation, and Affirmative Action," in *Without Justice For All*, ed. Adolph Reed, Jr. (Boulder: Westview Press, 1999), pp. 215–33.

The racial division of labor has its origins in slavery, when some 650,000 Africans were imported to provide cheap labor for the South's evolving plantation economy. During the century after slavery, the nation had the perfect opportunity to integrate blacks into the North's burgeoning industries. It was not southern racism but its northern variant that prevented this outcome. This point is worth emphasizing because it has become customary – part of America's liberal mythology on race – to place the blame for the nation's racist past wholly on the South. But it was not southern segregationists and lynch mobs that excluded blacks from participating in the critical early phases of industrialization. Rather, it was an invisible color line across northern industry that barred blacks categorically from employment in the vast manufacturing sector, except for a few menial and low-paying jobs that white workers spurned. Nor can the blame be placed solely on the doorstep of greedy capitalists, those other villains of liberal iconography. Workers themselves and their unions were equally implicated in maintaining a system of occupational apartheid that reserved industrial jobs for whites and that relegated blacks to the pre-industrial sector of the national economy.[1] The long-term consequences were incalculable, since this closed off the only major channel of escape from racial oppression in the South. Indeed, had the industrial revolution not been "for whites only," this might have obviated the need for a civil rights revolution a century later.

The exclusion of blacks from the industrial sector was possible only because the North had access to an inexhaustible supply of immigrant labor. Some 24 million European immigrants arrived between 1880 and 1930. A 1910 survey of twenty principal mining and manufacturing industries conducted by the U.S. Immigration Commission found that 58 percent of workers were foreign-born. When the commission asked whether the new immigration resulted in "racial displacement," it had in mind not blacks but whites who were native-born or from old immigrant stock. Except for a brief examination of the competition between Italian and black agricultural workers in Louisiana, nothing in the forty-volume report so much as hints at the possibility that mass immigration might have deleterious consequences for blacks, even though black leaders had long complained that immigrants were taking jobs that, they insisted, rightfully belonged to blacks.[2]

If blacks were superfluous so far as northern industry was concerned, the opposite was true in the South, where black labor was indispensable to the entire regional economy. Furthermore, given the interdependence between the regional economies of the South and the North, occupational apartheid had indirect advantages for the North as well. The cotton fiber that Irish, Italian, and Jewish immigrants worked within mills and sweatshops throughout the North was supplied by black workers in the South. In effect, a system of labor deployment had evolved whereby blacks provided the necessary labor for southern agriculture and European immigrants provided the necessary labor for northern industry.

This regional and racial division of labor cast the mold for generations more of racial inequality and conflict. Not until World War I were blacks given significant access to northern labor markets. In a single year – 1914 – the volume of immigration plummeted from 1.2 million immigrant arrivals to only 327,000. The cutoff of immigration in the midst of an economic expansion triggered the Great Migration, as it was called, of southern blacks to the urban North. Industries not only employed blacks in large numbers but in some cases also sent labor agents to the South to recruit black workers. Between 1910 and 1920, there was a net migration of 454,000 southern blacks to the North, a figure that exceeded the volume for the previous forty years combined. Here is historical proof that blacks were no less willing than Europe's peasants to uproot themselves and migrate to cities that offered the opportunity for industrial employment. To suggest that blacks "were not ready to compete with immigrants," as the author of a recent volume on immigration does, is altogether fallacious.[3] The simple truth is that northern industry was open to European immigrants and closed to African Americans. Whatever opprobrium was heaped upon these immigrants for their cultural and religious difference, they were still beneficiaries of racial preference.

It is generally assumed that World War II provided a similar demand for black labor, but this was not initially the case. Because the war came on the heels of the Depression, there was a surfeit of white labor and no compelling need to hire blacks. Indeed, it was blacks' frustration with their exclusion from wartime industries that prompted A. Philip Randolph and his followers to threaten a march on Washington in 1941 unless Franklin Roosevelt took steps to lower racist barriers. Roosevelt pressured black leaders to call off the march (just as John Kennedy did in similar circumstances two decades later), but Randolph persevered until Roosevelt agreed to issue an executive order enunciating a new policy of nondiscrimination in federal employment and defense contracts. The opening up of northern labor markets triggered another mass migration of southern blacks – 1.6 million migrated between 1940 and 1950 – and by the end of the war 1.5 million black workers were part of the war-production workforce. This represented an unprecedented breach in the nation's system of occupational apartheid – one that set the stage for future change as well.

Nevertheless, as recently as 1950 two-thirds of the nation's blacks lived in the South, half of them in rural areas. It was not the Civil War but the mechanization of agriculture a whole century later that finally liberated blacks from their historical role as agricultural laborers in the South's feudal economy. By the mid-1950s, even the harvest of cotton had become mechanized with the mass production of International Harvester's automatic cotton-picking machine. The number of "manhours" required to produce a bale of cotton was reduced from 438 in 1940, to 26 in 1960, to only 6 in 1980.[4] Agricultural technology had effectively rendered black labor obsolete and with it the caste system whose underlying function had been to regulate and exploit black labor.[5] Thus, in one generation white planters went all the way to Africa to import black laborers, and in another century the descendants of those southern planters gave the descendants of those African slaves one-way bus tickets to Chicago and New York.

When blacks finally arrived in northern cities, they encountered a far less favorable structure of opportunity than had existed for immigrants decades earlier.[6] For one thing, these labor markets had been captured by immigrant groups that engaged in a combination of ethnic nepotism and unabashed racism. For another thing, the occupational structures were themselves changing. Not only were droves of manufacturing jobs being automated out of existence, but also a reorganization of the global economy resulted in the export of millions of manufacturing jobs to less developed parts of the world.

The fact that the technological revolution in agriculture lagged nearly a half century behind the technological revolution in industry had fateful consequences for blacks at both junctures. First, blacks were restricted to the agricultural sector during the most expansive periods of the industrial revolution. Second, they were evicted from rural America and arrived in northern cities at a time when manufacturing was in a steep and irreversible decline.

William Julius Wilson has argued that deindustrialization is the principal factor in the genesis of the black underclass in recent decades.[7] According to Wilson, blacks migrating to northern cities not only encountered a shrinking industrial sector, but also lacked the education and skills to compete for jobs in the expanding service sector. For Wilson, this explains why conditions have deteriorated for the black lower classes during the post–civil rights era, a period of relative tolerance that has witnessed the rise of a large and prosperous black middle class.

There can be no doubt that deindustrialization has exacerbated the job crisis for working-class blacks. In the case of New York City, for example, the manufacturing sector was cut in half between 1955 and 1975, involving the loss of some five hundred thousand jobs.[8] As recently as 1990, New York City lost thirty-four thousand jobs over the summer, including fifty-two hundred jobs in manufacturing, fifty-six hundred jobs in construction, and sixty-five hundred jobs in retailing.[9] If these jobs could be magically restored, many blacks would surely benefit.

Nevertheless, there is reason to think that Wilson places far too much explanatory weight on deindustrialization as the reason for the job crisis that afflicts black America. As Norman Fainstein has argued, blacks were never heavily represented in the industrial sector in the first place.[10] Fainstein's data indicate a pattern of "employment ghettoization" involving the exclusion of blacks from whole job sectors – not only job sectors that require the education and skills that Wilson assumes to be lacking among young blacks, but also service-sector jobs that require minimal education and skills. Fainstein concludes that "the economic situation of blacks is rooted more in the character of the employment opportunities in growing industries than in the disappearance of "entry-level" jobs in declining industries."[11]

It is a leap of faith on Wilson's part that, if not for the collapse of the manufacturing sector, blacks would have found their way into these jobs. There is nothing in history to support this assumption, since, as we have seen, the entire thrust of northern racism has been to exclude blacks from blue-collar jobs in the primary sector. Even if three million manufacturing jobs had not disappeared, what basis is there for assuming that they would have gone to blacks, rather than to working-class whites or, as in the past, to the new immigrants who have been pouring into the nation's cities despite the collapse of the manufacturing sector? The lesson of history is that blacks have gained access to manufacturing only as a last resort – when all other sources of labor have dried up. Now we are asked to believe that blacks would have finally gotten their turn, except that the jobs themselves have disappeared.

Wholly absent from Wilson's analysis is any consideration of the role that racism plays in restricting employment opportunities for blacks. In his resolve not to "'trot out' the concept of racism" to explain the job crisis among blacks,[12] he has taken the illogical and dangerous step of eliding racism altogether. Although Wilson's foregrounding of "class" and the role that race-neutral economic forces played in exacerbating inherited racial inequalities had liberal intentions, his theme that racism was of "declining significance" not only constituted a gross distortion of reality but also was seized upon by elites inside and outside the academy that wanted to get "beyond civil rights" and take race off the national agenda.

*   *   *

The civil rights revolution was fundamentally a struggle for liberty, not equality. That is to say, it secured full rights of citizenship for African Americans, but it did little to address the deep-seated inequalities between blacks and whites that were the legacy of two centuries of slavery and another century of Jim Crow. Despite the emergence of a wealthy black elite, there remains an enormous gap in economic condition and living standards between the black and white citizens of this nation. For example, in 1988 the median income for whites was $25,384; for blacks, it was $15,630.[13] Thus, on the whole black income is roughly 60 percent of white income, a ratio that has not changed substantially since 1980.

Furthermore, as Melvin Oliver and Thomas Shapiro have shown in *Black Wealth/White Wealth*, the racial gap in income is far exceeded by the racial gap in wealth (which includes home equity and financial assets).[14] In 1988, the median net worth for white families was $43,800; for black families, it was only $3,700. Whites with a college degree had a net worth of $74,922, whereas blacks with a college degree had a net worth of only $17,437. This latter figure points up the utter precariousness of the so-called black middle class. Insofar as the racial gap in wealth translates into differential access to good housing, schools, and other resources, it provides a rough indication of how unequal the playing field is between blacks and whites.

The disjunction between rights and equality entered public discourse even before the legislative goals of the civil rights movement were attained. A common refrain among civil rights leaders was that "there is little value in a Negro's obtaining the right to be admitted to hotels and restaurants if he has no cash in his pocket and no job."[15] This was the logic for forging a praxis that went beyond the attainment of political rights and attacked the institutional inequalities that were the product of racism, both past and present.

Long before affirmative action entered the political lexicon, black leaders were demanding "compensatory treatment" for blacks in jobs and education. No sooner was this idea broached, however, than it aroused intense opposition.

That opposition emerged initially not from the political right, but from liberals, many of whom had been active supporters of the civil rights movement. Indeed, liberal disaffection with the rhetoric of compensatory treatment precipitated a split within the liberal camp as some prominent liberals declared their opposition to the "radical" direction that the civil rights movement was taking.[16] Here was an early sign that the nation would not go much beyond the grudging passage of civil rights legislation. Thus, it is not surprising that affirmative action policy did not develop through the legislative process. Rather, it evolved through a series of executive orders, court decisions, and administrative policies. At every stage it was liberals, some of whom had defected to the nascent neoconservative movement, who provided the most vocal and adamant opposition.

A key example is the liberal opposition to the Philadelphia Plan. Originally developed in President Lyndon Johnson's Department of Labor, the Philadelphia Plan was shelved after Hubert Humphrey's defeat in 1968. It was Arthur Fletcher, the black assistant secretary of labor during the first Nixon administration, who maneuvered to resurrect the plan. The other unsung heroes of affirmative action are Charles Shultz, then secretary of labor, who gave Fletcher indispensable backing; Attorney General John Mitchell, who successfully defended the plan before the Supreme Court; and Richard Nixon himself, who expended considerable political capital heading off a Democratic challenge to the plan in the Senate. One of the great ironies of racial politics in the post–civil rights era is that the Philadelphia Plan was implemented by Republicans over the opposition of the famed "liberal coalition" and without notable support of the civil rights establishment.[17] Indeed, some black leaders – including Bayard Rustin – sided with labor leaders in opposing the plan.

There has been considerable speculation over the reasons that Nixon, who got elected on the basis of a southern strategy that appealed to popular racism and who later nominated two southern racists to the Supreme Court, was willing to champion the Philadelphia Plan. Contemporaneous opponents of the plan, most notably Rustin, contended that its aim was to split the "progressive" coalition between the labor movement and the civil rights movement. This idea has also been given some credence by Hugh Davis Graham in his history of the civil rights era. According to Graham, as Nixon pondered Shultz's proposal to resurrect the Philadelphia Plan, he was swayed by "the delicious prospect of setting organized labor and the civil rights establishment at each other's Democratic throats."[18] More recently, Graham has been even more explicit in postulating that "Nixon wanted to drive a wedge between blacks and organized labor – between the Democrats' social activists of the 1960s and the party's traditional economic liberals – that would fragment the New Deal coalition."[19]

This "theory" has assumed mythical proportions, invoked by writers on the liberal/left to provide political cover for their retreat from affirmative action. However, there is reason to doubt Graham's account of why Nixon threw his support behind the Philadelphia Plan. One must begin by putting this decision in historical context. In 1969 the Vietnam War was reaching a critical stage, and Nixon had to worry about an escalation of racial protest "on the home front." This was a period when memories of the "riots" following Martin Luther King Jr.'s assassination were still fresh, when black militancy was at its height, and when there were strident job protests in Philadelphia, Chicago, and numerous other cities against racism in the construction trades. Indeed, Graham provides the following account of the job protests during the summer of 1969:

> In Chicago, job protests launched by a coalition of black neighborhood organizations shut down twenty-three South Side construction projects involving $85 million in contracts. ... The demonstrations in Pittsburgh were more violent than in Chicago, but were similarly organized and focused on job discrimination in construction. One clash in Pittsburgh in late August left 50 black protestors and 12 policemen injured. ... Racial violence over jobs also occurred in Seattle, and black coalitions announced job protest drives for New York, Cleveland, Detroit, Milwaukee, and Boston.[20]

This was the context in which Fletcher and Shultz seized the opportunity to resurrect the Philadelphia Plan, whose main objective was to enforce the hiring of blacks in building trades controlled by lily-white unions.[21] From the perspective of the White House, there was little political liability in "sticking it" to the mostly Democratic unions. And there was clear political advantage in neutralizing black protest and in preempting the liberal agenda on civil rights with a policy predicated on contract compliance.

Whatever tangle of motivations were at work, Nixon actively fought off a congressional attempt to pass an anti–affirmative action rider that had the support of many Democrats, and Mitchell successfully defended the Philadelphia Plan before the Supreme Court. Subsequently, the Department of Labor issued a new set of rules that extended the Philadelphia Plan to all federal contractors, including colleges and universities. Thus, the scope of affirmative action policy expanded beyond anything contemplated when the Philadelphia Plan had been disinterred in 1969. Furthermore, the Philadelphia Plan embodied none of the "liberal" elements that were ideologically anathema to Republicans. It envisioned no new government programs, no make-work schemes, no major public expenditures.[22] However, as the backlash against affirmative action mushroomed, Nixon did an about-face and, as Graham points out, railed against the very "quotas" that he had put into place.[23]

Politics aside, affirmative action was unquestionably the most important policy initiative of the post–civil rights era. It drove a wedge into the structure of occupational segregation that had existed since slavery. And affirmative action achieved its principal policy objective, which was the rapid integration of blacks into occupational sectors where they had been excluded historically.

A society with a deep and abiding commitment to racial justice would have celebrated this historic achievement and expanded affirmative action into job sectors and job sites where blacks still have meager representation. Instead, affirmative action has been the object of unrelenting attack. A steady outpouring of books, many of them funded by conservative foundations and think tanks, have found erudite reason for relinquishing the single policy that has been effective in reversing the pattern of occupational apartheid.[24] Political scapegoating assumed a new face as politicians made affirmative action a lightning rod for working-class insecurities over falling wages and corporate downsizing. Liberal equivocation and bad faith served notice that even those proverbial "friends of the Negro" would offer little resistance in defense of affirmative action. As opposition mounted, more liberals threw in the towel, declaring that affirmative action was "too costly" politically.[25] In February 1995, *Newsweek* ran a cover story proclaiming "The End of Affirmative Action." Though President Bill Clinton made a much-publicized stand to "mend it, don't end it," the cynical view was that this only provided a public facade for the quiet dismantling of affirmative action programs and the enforcement mechanisms on which they depend.[26]

Having eviscerated affirmative action policy in a series of rulings, the Supreme Court today seems poised to deliver the coup de grâce. Like *Plessy v. Ferguson* (1896), which marked the end of Reconstruction three decades after the abolition of slavery, the gutting of affirmative action marks the end of the Second Reconstruction. In the first instance, blacks did not go back to slavery, but they lost rights that had been supposedly secured by the Reconstruction Amendments. Today there is no danger of blacks again being relegated to the back of the bus. However, the gutting of affirmative action will certainly lead to a steady erosion of many of the social and economic gains of the post–civil rights era. The sobering lesson of history is that when the First Reconstruction was ended, it took seven decades to recover the ground that had been lost.

Notes

1   The tendency even among labor historians to gloss over union racism has come under challenge, most notably in the work of Herbert Hill. For two recent articles, see Herbert Hill, "Black Workers, Organized Labor, and Title VII of the 1964 Civil Rights Act: Legislative History and Litigation," in Herbert Hill and James E. Jones, *Race in America* (Madison: University of Wisconsin Press, 1993), pp. 263–341; and Herbert Hill, "Meany, Reuther, and the 1964 Civil Rights Act," *New Politics* 25 (Summer 1998), pp. 82–107.

2   See Lawrence H. Fuchs, "The Reactions of Black Americans to Immigration," in *Immigration Reconsidered*, ed. Virginia Yans-McLaughlin (New York: Oxford University Press, 1990), pp. 295–7; and David J. Hellwig, "Patterns of Black Nativism," *American Studies* 23 (Spring 1982), pp. 85–98.

3   Thomas Muller, *Immigrants and the American City* (New York: New York University Press, 1993), p. 91.

4   U.S. Bureau of the Census, *Historical Statistics of the United States* (Washington, D.C.: U.S. Government Printing Office, 1975), p. 500; Gerald David Jaynes and Robin M. Williams Jr., *A Common Destiny* (Washington, D.C.: National Academy Press, 1989), p. 273.

5   See Frances Fox Piven and Richard A. Cloward, *Poor People's Movements* (New York: Vintage Books, 1979), ch. 4.

6   In a paper written for the National Advisory Commission on Civil Disorders in 1968, "Escaping from Poverty: A Comparison of the Immigrant and Black

Experience," in *People, Plans, and Policies* (New York: Columbia University Press, 1991), ch. 18, Herbert Gans debunks the notion that blacks arriving in northern cities were following in the footsteps of earlier immigrants and therefore could anticipate the same beneficial outcomes.

7 William Julius Wilson, *The Truly Disadvantaged* (Chicago: University of Chicago Press, 1987).

8 Karen Gerard, "New York City's Economy: A Decade of Change," *New York Affairs* 8, no. 2 (1984), p. 7.

9 Richard Levine, "New York Lost 34,000 Jobs over Summer," *New York Times*, October 19, 1990.

10 Norman Fainstein, "The Underclass/Mismatch Hypothesis as an Explanation for Black Economic Deprivation," *Politics and Society* 15, no. 4 (1986–7), pp. 403–51.

11 Ibid., p. 439. According to data on New York City compiled by Roger Waldinger, "Ladders and Musical Chairs: Ethnicity and Opportunity in Post–Industrial New York," *Politics and Society* 15 (1986–7), pp. 379–80, 17 percent of whites in 1970 were employed in manufacturing, as compared to 13 percent of blacks. By 1980, there were 38 percent fewer whites employed in manufacturing, whereas the decline for blacks was only 13 percent. In absolute numbers, 115,180 whites lost their jobs, as compared to 7,980 blacks. See also Walter W. Stafford, *Closed Labor Markets: Underrepresentation of Blacks, Hispanics, and Women in New York City's Core Industries* (New York: Community Service Society of New York, 1985).

12 Wilson, *The Truly Disadvantaged*, p. 12.

13 Melvin L. Oliver and Thomas M. Shapiro, *Black Wealth/White Wealth* (New York: Routledge, 1995), p. 86.

14 Ibid., pp. 88, 94.

15 Whitney, M., Young Jr., *To be Equal* (New York: McGraw-Hill, 1963), p. 54. Bayard Rustin, "From Protest to Politics: The Future of the Civil Rights Movement," *Commentary* 39 (February 1964), p. 25, wrote, "What is the value of winning access to public accommodations for those who lack money to use them?" Martin Luther King Jr., "Showdown for Non-Violence," *Look*, April 16, 1968, p. 28, wrote, "What good is it to be allowed to eat in a restaurant if you can't afford a hamburger?"

16 For more detailed examination of the crisis in liberalism, see Stephen Steinberg, *Turning Back* (Boston: Beacon Press, 1995), ch. 4.

17 See John David Skrentny, *The Ironies of Affirmative Action* (Chicago: University of Chicago Press, 1996), chs. 4, 7.

18 Hugh Davis Graham, *The Civil Rights Era* (New York: Oxford University Press, 1990), p. 325.

19 Hugh Davis Graham, "Race, History, and Policy: African Americans and Civil Rights Since 1964," *Journal of Policy History* 6, no. 1 (1994), p. 23.

20 Graham, *The Civil Rights Era*, pp. 334–5.

21 In *The Ironies of Affirmative Action*, ch. 4, Skrentny suggests that crisis management provided the principal rationale behind the Nixon administration's vigorous support of the Philadelphia Plan.

22 Perhaps the most germane account comes from Arthur Fletcher, *The Silent Sell-Out* (New York: Third Press, 1974), p. 65: "I decided to go ahead with the Philadelphia Plan of putting specifications of minority employment goals in all contracts. I did this because my study and experience had convinced me that such targets were essential if we are to measure results in terms of minority

employment. Without such targets, the paper compliance, and the indeterminable ineffectiveness of the government programs would go on. I had not come to Washington to preside over the continuation of the ineffective programs of the past."

23 Graham, *The Civil Rights Era*, pp. 446–7.

24 See Jean Stefancic and Richard Delgado, *No Mercy: How Conservative Think Tanks and Foundations Changed America's Social Agenda* (Philadelphia: University of Pennsylvania Press, 1996), ch. 4, and Amy Elizabeth Ansell, *New Right, New Racism* (New York: New York University Press, 1997), ch. 3.

25 See, for example, Paul Starr, "Civic Reconstruction: What to Do Without Affirmative Action," *American Prospect* 8 (Winter 1992), pp. 7–14; and Jeffrey Klein, "The Race Course," *Mother Jones* 22 (September 1997), pp. 3–5.

26 See Joe Klein, "The End of Affirmative Action," *Newsweek*, February 13, 1995, pp. 36–7.

◆

Bursting the Bubble: The Failure of Black Progress

Sharon M. Collins

Most scholars agree that dramatic progress was made in blacks' access to white-collar occupations over the past three decades. One explanation points to the forces of an impersonal labor market that rewarded improvements in black skills and education with occupational mobility in a growing service economy (see Smith and Welch 1978). And, indeed, both aggregate data and individual cases show that college-educated blacks improved their position when the economy was on the upswing and the need for skilled labor was expanding.

Yet the timing of blacks' attainment as revealed by my study, in conjunction with other research (such as Freeman 1976; Leonard 1984), strongly links this attainment to political pressures on employers exerted by government and by the black community. Since black executives in Chicago entered the job market in an environment dominated by black political activism and governmental intervention, I suggested that the elaboration of the black middle class that has been attributed to their entry into higher-paying white-collar jobs is not grounded solely in their educational attainments and in economic trends. The growing demand for blacks in higher-paying jobs is also a function of a shift in hiring to conform to blacks' demands for increased access to economic resources and to government regulations. I do not mean that education, skills, and related factors such as motivation and hard work are trivial to blacks' gains and greater competitiveness. I mean, rather, that blacks' objective qualifications are still strongly intertwined with racialized processes that continue to operate in the labor market.

Before the 1960s the market economy that spawned the black middle class was dominated by artificial and race-based barriers, not free and impersonal exchange. It was an economy shaped by restrictions that limited interaction between the races and that allowed black business and professional opportunities only in the segregated environment of black ghettos. This economy created opportunities in a narrow range of service areas for a very small number of blacks, such as doctors, morticians, and lawyers. The opportunity structure was broadened somewhat when blacks were able to enter the public sector as teachers or other professionals. But even this somewhat broadened economic system was structured along racial lines: Black professionals distributed services to other blacks, as opposed to the total (i.e., predominantly white) community.

These race-linked occupational restrictions are reflected in executives' descriptions of their labor market experiences. Most college-trained blacks entering the labor market before 1965 went to work for the government. Only the most highly educated broke into the professions in the white private sector. Even in these cases, characteristics ascribed to a free market were not in play; they worked almost exclusively in industries that depended heavily on government contracts for survival.

From the mid-1960s onward, the labor market for educated blacks underwent a transformation. College-educated blacks entered the economic mainstream in jobs similar to those of their white counterparts that better reflected their training and abilities. It appeared that artificial racial barriers had lifted as college-educated blacks captured the incomes and occupations to support the middle-class life-styles previously reserved for whites. For the first time in history, the structure of opportunity for college-educated blacks shifted significantly to include higher-paying white-collar jobs in the central economy.

My study documents this shift in executives' reports of job search experiences, which showed a much broader spectrum of jobs available to them after the mid-1960s than before. After 1965 their rate for going into sales jobs tied to unstable black consumer sectors and into low-paying clerical positions decreased by two-thirds. At the same time, at the other end of the white-collar job spectrum, twice the proportion had access to professional and managerial jobs in the white private sector. Overall, these changes in patterns of employment are consistent with other research showing that the socio-economic status of blacks jumped dramatically when college-educated blacks entered professional-managerial jobs inside government and private industry.

My study reflects the increase in compliance pressures on the part of the EEOC and the OFCCP at the same time that managerial and professional job opportunities in white organizations increased. Executives entering business-related fields credited the activism of black organizations and civil disturbances with helping to create their job opportunities; two-thirds of them who entered business-related fields after 1965 knew of the vulnerability of their company to black consumer boycotts and the vulnerability of company property to urban upheaval, and three-quarters of this group also knew that their employment was a result of a company effort to hire blacks.

Further evidence of a connection between political variables and black employment opportunities appears in employment patterns where blacks fill jobs mediating black demands for white institutions. That is, the alchemy of market and political forces not only influenced new behavior on the part of employers, it also increased demand for blacks by increasing social service and manpower development programs in government and in private industry. Although blacks clearly made gains in a variety of jobs, the new black middle class is grounded in professional and business roles created or reoriented to nullify pressure from black people.

A sizable majority of African American managers in the upper echelons of Chicago's white corporations were channeled into an occupational structure that evolved from the pressures of the civil rights period. Two-thirds of those I interviewed had held at least one job that was oriented toward blacks over the course of their private sector career. One-third of the managers were concentrated in race-oriented jobs throughout their career. This nascent business elite moved, in particular, into personnel areas of corporations to administer affirmative-action policies and into public relations areas to respond to turbulent black communities. One-third of the managers I interviewed who entered the white private sector after 1965 were recruited to fill jobs in one of these two areas; others were enticed to transfer into these jobs by salary increases, better job titles, and promises of future rewards. Even those with incompatible backgrounds and highly technical skills – such as accountants, engineers, and chemists – were tracked into affirmative-action and public relations areas. The forces expanding blacks' economic opportunities were protest related, and the new black middle class is at least in part a politically mediated phenomenon.

My portrayal of the black middle class is both consistent with and different from the dominant theoretical perspectives on race and labor markets. While I agree that unprecedented advancement occurred within the black middle class, I do not agree that attainment among blacks is evidence of the deracialization of labor markets (cf. Wilson 1978). Middle-class attainments among blacks reflect a dependence on employment practices that are sensitive to race. Better job opportunities for blacks are connected to federal legislation and to the expansion of social service bureaucracy and other administrative apparatuses to implement social policies designed to appease disruptive black constituencies.

My observations of the characteristics of jobs that blacks hold contradict the notion that spontaneous market demands in tandem with education and skill lifted the employment barriers faced by talented blacks. Such qualifications are necessary, but they have never been sufficient to ensure the relative success of blacks in the economy. Governmental mandates – not the forces of free markets – are critical to expand and stabilize the black middle class.

Finally, my findings go beyond research that highlights the effects of affirmative-action kinds of government policy on the black middle class to indicate that the intent of such policy is not assimilated by the marketplace. An analysis of the careers of highly successful black executives with great potential as competitors inside the mainstream labor market showed that the economy opened up in only a distinctive and marginalized way. Private employers channeled a group of people with a variety of talent into racialized careers during the 1960s and 1970s. Even the majority of mainstream, that is, nonracialized, careers found in this group have marginalized features. Executives in this study are concentrated in support areas where institutional objectives reflect policy attempts to nullify blacks' potential for disruption, not in the planning and operations functions oriented toward profit that lead to power in an organization. My view of the black middle class is consistent with a conflict model of class relations rather than with traditional status attainment models. Blacks' advancement is a function of protest, and this protest was not resolved by true deracialization in the labor market. Rather, the role of race has been reconfigured in the modern economy and continues to have an impact on blacks' access to middle-class positions.

Implications for Racial Equality

What do a politically mediated model and racialized jobs have to say about blacks' chances for economic equality? The short answer is that they are not likely to eradicate inequality.

Demand is mediated by an interrelationship among economic upswings, political pressures, and a labor supply of qualified workers. The intersection of these three factors created the conditions for some blacks to rise and compete for higher-paying jobs against whites. Yet the processes of attainment reported here show that blacks' new socioeconomic status does not necessarily indicate racial equality in institutions or in labor markets. First, some types of racial segregation and economic inequality are maintained and even facilitated by the mechanisms associated with black middle-class mobility. Second, if the black middle class results from special political and legal conditions, then it can be argued that it occupies a fragile economic position.

Maintaining Inequality

Since the mid-1960s, the black middle class no longer has been relegated strictly to the lower ends of occupation and income hierarchies or restricted by geography. However, a new structure of inequality was created by a system of employment opportunities that channeled some blacks into racialized functions. On the positive side, this system of jobs afforded some blacks a chance to succeed economically and garner unprecedented, albeit temporary, status in white institutions. The negative half of the equation is that this system could not solve the problem of blacks in the long run. Affirmative-action managers, for instance, wrote hiring plans and were in charge of their implementation. But affirmative action was implemented with an eye toward appeasing governmental and public relations requirements, not changing the color of power brokers in white institutions. Data show that black men in particular are underrepresented – even after thirty years of affirmative-action efforts – in managerial jobs and in almost every business-related profession.

Progress was limited because the incumbents of racialized jobs simply did not have the power to change institutional practices. The ability to get things done required access to and persuasiveness with the CEO and other top management. Executives I interviewed who survived in these roles were not individuals likely to risk their jobs by "pushing the envelope" and disrupting the equilibrium of their employing institution. It is logical to presume that they survived in these jobs because of their ability to accommodate whites, not embarrass the company, and not cause trouble.

Their jobs helped companies conform to federal regulations, and programmatic allocations (such as technical assistance, corporate funding of community-based projects and job training) both quelled urban pressures and undermined claims of racism, creating a progressive, more socially conscious, corporate image. But these allocations were too small and were viewed by companies as a short-term atonement for past grievances, rather than as a long-term

commitment to justice. Racialized jobs, therefore, were instrumental in negoti-
ating the needs of the black community and in distributing corporate
resources, but they ultimately maintained inequality by temporarily abating
black pressures and meanwhile marginalizing the incumbent.

At the same time, this study makes it clear that racialized jobs effectively kept
their incumbents from traveling conventional routes up the corporate ladder.
When individuals in this study entered race-oriented and staff positions in white
companies, they assumed career tracks that typically do not lead to line power
in a company. Once in these jobs, many of them were constrained by the perception or the reality that they lacked the necessary skills to contribute in a
mainstream function. Consequently, gains they made over the last three decades
did not – and will not – blossom into meaningful numbers of executives heading
production and planning areas. The tracks their careers took in the 1960s and
1970s diminished the pool of blacks in Chicago corporations who could compete to manage mainstream production units in the 1980s and beyond.

In sum, managers in this study are part of a black middle class that has
occupied a useful but nonadversarial position in white companies. Ultimately
this means that racialized jobs were a factor in reducing competition for
power in organizations along racial lines. And, since they were unable to succeed in policy- and decision-making positions in meaningful numbers, it is
doubtful that the makeup or resource allocation of organizations will change
dramatically. Even current policy decisions to continue affirmative-action programs are contested outside any arena in which blacks exercise power.

What I have found, therefore, is a structure of achievement that preserved
inequality while it carried out its role in reinstating social order, and that
established a class position with obsolete features built in. Executives in this
study were desirable candidates for affirmative-action and public relations
jobs at a time of intense social upheaval; when pressure from blacks abated,
the status of many of these executives tumbled. Specifically, as racial pressures
were ameliorated in Chicago, racialized jobs lost their value. Given the
relationship between these jobs and the political pressures faced by white
corporations during the 1960s and 1970s, one could take the position that
affirmative-action and urban affairs managers did their jobs for companies
too well. In relieving the pressure on companies, they not only helped shut the
window of opportunity through which other blacks could follow but they
undermined the very element that had produced their own positions.

African American Middle-Class Fragility

Although job opportunities for college-educated blacks and whites have converged since the 1960s, class mobility for these two groups stems from different factors. In my view of black attainment, the opportunity to earn income
and maintain middle-class life-styles depended as heavily on blacks' broad
social status and the activity of the state apparatus as on general economic
trends. First, African Americans were viewed by major employers as desirable
candidates for professional and managerial jobs because of governmental

sanctions. Second, meeting the needs of, or solving, the problems of blacks was near the top of the public policy agenda.

Extending this view leads to the conclusion that different factors insure the economic viability of blacks and whites. Thus, if the federal government dismantles strong race-specific programs and affirmative-action mandates, employer effort to create and maintain equal employment opportunities may shrink accordingly. Indeed, this study suggests that the institutional mechanisms for protecting black attainments in the white private sector – affirmative-action and community relations departments – *are* shrinking and becoming watered down. Weakening these areas weakens the race-conscious influence on employment decisions that in the past protected blacks. Moreover, departures from the liberal social thinking that dominated Congress in the 1960s make likely a radically different political agenda and an alteration in the basis for federal policy and spending decisions.

The federal government's incentives and sanctions in the 1960s and the 1970s were not meant to change the intrinsic nature of the economy but only to get employers to respond differently. Two outcomes are possible if these incentives and sanctions are dismantled. First, despite race-conscious political supports, blacks' qualifications and the greater acceptance of blacks in white-dominated settings may enable the same or a larger relative proportion of blacks to move further up the economic ladder. Or, second, the proportion of employed blacks in the next cohort to enter higher-paying white-collar occupations may erode. In the first outcome we would see significant further progress in the black middle class in capturing positions of power within white institutions. In the second outcome, we would see stagnation or vastly diminished rates of change.

Of these two options, the second, I believe, is the more plausible. The link between black class mobility and political pressure predicts the fragility of the middle-class position. Although black protest and government intervention theoretically occur outside the marketplace, they are two of the three ingredients necessary for blacks' economic progress. That is, the status of the economy, the level of black activism, and the public policy agenda all assisted blacks to rise. I believe that gains made in the black middle class will dissolve in the next generation of labor force participants for reasons related to all three of these ingredients.

Changes in public policy

The race-based legislation and spending that assisted blacks to rise is being challenged and dismantled. As a general proposition, as government funding dwindles from social service areas and federal efforts abate in employment legislation, the ability of blacks to maintain and to continue their gains will also erode. If federal antibias employment policy and government spending in social service arenas created the conditions that opened up nontraditional white-collar jobs to blacks, it follows that cutbacks in affirmative-action programs in major companies and cutbacks in government social services would decrease the demand for blacks in specified occupations.

In the national debate, some social critics see blacks' dependence on government as a negative outcome of federal protections. However, I see government dependency as an unavoidable partner in blacks' progress. Because the federal government did not change the intrinsic nature of the economy or of employers, equal employment and color-blind hiring are not institutionalized in the labor market, and fair employment practices would not continue in the government's absence. We must think of affirmative action not only as reparation for past discrimination but also as an instrument necessary to prevent present acts of employment discrimination. And there is plenty of evidence to indicate that racial discrimination, both economic and social, still exists (Cose 1993; Feagin and Sikes 1994; Jones 1986; Kirschenman and Neckerman 1991; Massey and Denton 1993; U.S. Department of Housing and Urban Development 1991).

Black power versus passivity

Within a politically mediated model of middle-class ascendancy, black gains may be fragile for another reason. The rise of the new black middle class is tied to black collective action, but splintered interests and large economic divisions now exist within the black community. In the 1950s, class divisions existed, but segregation forged a racial group consciousness that, in the face of white terrorism, transcended factionalism based on occupational and income differences. In the 1950s, however, the gap caused by the assimilation of a skilled and highly educated black middle class and the dislocation and exclusion of a black underclass may mean that blacks have less ability to form alliances and harness the power of collective action.

The emergence of the new black middle class and blacks' new forms of institutional participation, in part, occurred by siphoning activists and future leaders out of the black community. This siphoning process mirrors that which William Wilson (1987) describes when arguing that desegregation spurred the exodus of middle-class blacks from inner-city neighborhoods. Chicago alderman Bobby Rush, former head of the Black Panther Party, and Chief Justice Thurgood Marshall, the NAACP's chief legal strategist for ending segregation in the South, are prominent individual examples. Much less prominent but still relevant examples are managers in this study who, during the 1960s, were community activists with networks that made them useful recruits for manpower training and development jobs in white corporations. They left behind a dispirited black community increasingly beset by social and economic problems.

At the same time, a new type of black accommodationism and white paternalism emerged. As the new black middle class became dependent on whites for jobs, the raised arms with clenched fists associated with "black power" and solidarity that dominated the 1960s were dropped and sleeved among the middle class in the grey flannel associated with being a "company man" and "fitting in." Integration of this black middle-class vanguard into white corporations set it upon a path of achievement and upward mobility that, having separated it from the black collective, also divests it of both the license and the constituency to argue group claims. Nathan Hare once observed that a vanguard detached from the mass becomes an elite. This reasoning, perhaps, allows whites and black neoconservatives disingenuously to dismiss, as a means to exploit race for its own thinly veiled interests, black middle-class complaints about racial barriers.

The problem blacks confront is whether to attempt to go all the way into the system or to go back to their roots. Assimilation has given rise to a new set of community problems without a corresponding rise in economic power. Put another way, the dilemma is whether to continue to pursue the assimilationist goals embodied by traditional civil rights organizations such as PUSH, the Urban League, and the NAACP or to embrace the separatist ideology exemplified by the Black Muslims.

I predict one of two outcomes. In a politically mediated middle class, when racial pressures on white employers emerged, the system of racialized jobs enabled white bureaucracies to mediate the goals and options open to black communities. If black solidarity, filtered through white bureaucracies, grows weaker, then the power of protest blacks exercised three decades ago is weakened also. African Americans would then find it hard to organize protest strategies on a level impressive enough to protect and provoke further economic gains. Under these conditions advancement among middle-class blacks will erode in the future.

In an alternate scenario, having been exposed to education and the subjective philosophy of merit, the black middle class may become more race conscious. Black executives who played by the rules of the game and now confront glass ceilings may become an angry, alienated middle class that gives birth to new and radicalized black leadership. The broad coalition of disparate organizations that supported the 1995 March on Washington and the antipathy that cuts across class lines against denouncing Louis Farrakhan may cue future coalitions. Limitations to black power inside the system may radicalize the black middle class and spur race-based challenges to institutional practices.

The status of the economy

Finally, blacks gains will erode because of macroeconomic factors. As companies continue to prune functions and excess personnel to be more competitive, and as a global economy and technological advancements sweep away layers of middle managers, the economic positions of both whites and blacks grow more fragile.

Even in the best of times, when the economy is expanding and good jobs are plentiful, blacks make gains but continue to trail their white counterparts. For example, despite the advancement of black men in managerial and business-related professions, they remain greatly underrepresented in jobs at the core of white corporate America. Forecasts of the status of blacks become even gloomier when one considers the predictable effects of economic recessions. That is, in a soft economy, the competition for jobs that secure middle-class life-styles stiffens. Indeed, this may be a reason that race-based employment legislation finds little support among whites, as the *Pollwatcher Letter* columnist suggested in the *New York Times* on May 12, 1992. Thus, while both races are affected by restructuring in the marketplace, the risk, the meaning, and the impact differ considerably for blacks and whites.

In the final analysis, using Christian morality and street militancy to provoke white guilt and embarrassment no longer works. First, these strategies depended in large part on shock value, the contrast between American ideals of justice and equality and the reality of blacks' daily existence, particularly in the South. That contrast alone was powerful enough to give black leadership the moral authority to challenge the economic status quo. Now the degree of poverty among African Americans is no longer shocking, in part because what once was hidden beneath the image of America as a middle-class society now is obvious in urban ghettos. Nor is there national sympathy for the claims of blacks. When race-based demonstrations and appeals arise, they are more likely to provoke disdain in whites, to raise the question, What do those people want from us anyway?

Second, the onus of guilt over what went wrong has shifted. Blame once borne by the national conscience has been placed by economic and cultural conservatives on the poor and "undeserving" blacks doomed by white presumptions of inherent black immorality. Dooming them also is the political expediency of using blacks as scapegoats in an era of economic uncertainty. What remnants of guilt remain have been cleansed away by the rise of a black middle class, and by whites' sense of cultural sacrifice and racial beneficence for implementing thirty years of social welfare programs and affirmative action.

Thus, the controversy once tempered by compassion that began with the passage of the Civil Rights Act in 1964 and with affirmative action has reemerged full blown. Widespread public sentiment among whites increasingly rejects the notion of government intervention, according to a *New York Times* Pollwatcher Letter on May 12, 1992. Given the results of the 1995 congressional elections, it also appears that the white electorate now rejects leaders who have a tradition of supporting black causes. This public resentment appears to bring with it a different political climate for the 1990s and perhaps beyond in which whites' political pressure demands that protective policies oriented toward blacks be retracted and allowed to erode.

As a society we seem to disdain history. We ignore the intransigence, the meaning, and the magnitude of racial inequality, thereby making it easier for social critics to trivialize the need for affirmative action. Ahistorical assessments of the impact of antibias employment legislation, moreover, fail to recognize the potential for future racial conflict in the United States. If affirmative-action and other race-specific legislation are dismantled, no mechanisms exist to replace them. Affirmative action has always been a hotly contested and controversial policy. It was implemented as a last step in a series of escalating antibias policies because racial strife threatened the fabric of the country and because the mechanisms for racial separation in the core economy are tough and enduring.

References

Cose, Ellis. 1993. *The Rage of a Privileged Class: Why Are Middle-Class Blacks Angry? Why Should America Care?* New York: HarperCollins.

Feagin, Joe R., and Melvin P. Sikes. 1994. *Living with Racism: The Black Middle-Class Experience*. Boston: Beacon Press.

Freeman, Richard. 1976. *The Black Elite*. New York: McGraw-Hill.

Jones, Edward W. 1986. "Black Managers: The Dream Deferred." *Harvard Business Review*, May–June, pp. 84–9.

Kirscherman, Joleen, and Kathryn M. Neckerman. 1991. "'We'd Love to Hire Them, But…': The Meaning of Race for Employers." In *The Urban Underclass*, ed. Christopher Jencks and Paul E. Peterson (Washington, D.C.: Brookings Institution), pp. 203–32.

Leonard, Jonathan S. 1984. "The Impact of Affirmative Action on Employment." *Journal of Labor Economics* 2, pp. 439–64.

Massey, Douglas S., and Nancy A. Denton. 1993. *American Apartheid: Segregation and the Making of the Underclass*. Cambridge, Mass.: Harvard University Press.

Smith, James P., and Finis R. Welch. 1978. *Race Differences in Earnings: A Survey and New Evidence*. Santa Monica, Calif.: Rand Corporation.

U.S. Department of Housing and Urban Development. 1991. *Housing Discrimination Study*. Washington, D.C.: U.S. Government Printing Office.

Wilson, William J. 1978. *The Declining Significance of Race*. Chicago: University of Chicago Press.

Wilson, William J. 1987. *The Truly Disadvantaged: The Inner City, the Underclass, and Public Policy*, Chicago: University of Chicago Press.

4

The Race Versus Class Debate

The Case for Class-Based Affirmative Action

Richard D. Kahlenberg

The affirmative action question fascinates, divides, and tears at Americans because neither side of the debate can be easily dismissed. On the one hand, liberals are clearly right to say that the history of discrimination in this country has left a legacy of racial inequality that needs to be addressed proactively – beyond simply outlawing future discrimination. If anyone visits the affluent suburbs in this country, and comes across African Americans or Latinos, the chances are quite good that they are there not as residents but as garbage collectors, gardeners, or child care providers. Such is not a colorblind society.

On the other hand, conservatives make a powerful case that we need to be very, very cautious before employing racial preferences when the long term goal is colorblind society. The casualness with which many advocates of affirmative action now embrace using skin color to decide who should get ahead in society is astonishing. Some advocates say counting race in college admissions is no different than the consideration of other nonacademic factors, such as musical or athletic ability. But these advocates ignore the fundamental reason racial discrimination is morally repugnant in the first place. As a rule, people should be judged by factors within their control. An athlete or violin player can develop her skills through hard work and diligence; skin color is an accident of birth. The color-consciousness of today's left is particularly disturbing as the basis for racial preferences has shifted: where once preferences were justified as a temporary remedy for past discrimination, today preferences are normally supported by the idea that diversity is an overriding and self-justifying goal, and will be forevermore. This vision of unending color-consciousness is highly unappealing to most Americans.

Finally, both liberals and conservatives are noting with increasing frequency the fundamental unfairness of class-blind racial preferences. Since racial affirmative action counts skin color but ignores economic circumstances, it

Reprinted from "Class-Based Affirmative Action: A Natural for Labor," *New Labor Forum*, Spring 1998, pp. 37–43.

necessarily prefers the son of a black doctor over the son of a white garbage collector. With the growth of the black middle class in recent years, the likelihood that race and class will collide in this manner has increased dramatically. When programs promote such patent unfairness, they lose their moral force. These programs begin to look like any other reflection of interest group politics and political power, and cease to claim the mantle of promoting genuine equal opportunity.

The vote of Proposition 209, the California Civil Rights Initiative to ban race and gender preferences, underlines American ambivalence over affirmative action. Californians did vote to abolish such preferences in the public sphere, underlining concerns about the use of race in deciding who will enjoy the American Dream. But the margin was fairly narrow – 54%–46% – which suggests that many Californians were unwilling to simply go "cold turkey."

More recently, a *New York Times/CBS News* poll found that Americans favor affirmative efforts to help disadvantaged minorities, but they reject the use of racial preferences to achieve racial diversity. The poll, published in December 1997, found that 25% of Americans would "do away with" affirmative action preferences, 24% would "leave them as they are" and 43% would "change them."

Is it possible to come up with a compromise on this issue, one that respects the best arguments on both sides of the affirmative action debate? Two possible compromises have emerged to "mend" rather than "end" affirmative action.

Two Possible Compromises

The first possibility – the position embraced by President Clinton – is to say yes to affirmative action preferences, but no to racial quotas. This compromise has been called the "Bakke straddle," named after Justice Lewis Powell's opinion in the famous *Bakke* case from the 1970s. In that Supreme Court decision, four justices said the University of California at Davis Medical School's system of quotas was illegal; four justices said the program was legal; and Justice Powell, casting the deciding vote, tried to split the difference: quotas are illegal, he said, but using race as "one factor" in admissions is permissible. UC Davis could weigh the race of minority candidates in their favor, but it could not set aside a fixed number of seats for people of color.

At first, the Bakke straddle was highly criticized by both sides of the affirmative action debate. In the *Bakke* case itself, the liberal justices were most critical: what is the difference, they asked, between setting aside 16 of 100 seats for minority candidates and using "race as one factor" in admissions with the committee having a pretty good idea of what kind of racial makeup they would like to end up with at the end of the day? Nevertheless, the Bakke straddle has proven a useful rhetorical device, and whenever President Clinton is asked a question about affirmative action, the first thing out of his mouth is that he is opposed to quotas.

But fundamentally the Bakke straddle remains a highly unstable compromise. If the use of skin color is seen as fundamentally unfair, it matters not whether the use of race is a small or large factor. Americans would never tolerate the idea that racial discrimination against people of color is permissible, so long as race is just "one factor" used against a candidate. And in California, and elsewhere, when the issue is posed not as quotas, but as preferences, Americans make clear their opposition to such practices. The courts have become increasingly hostile to the Bakke straddle, and in the 1996 *Hopwood v. Texas* case, the 5th Circuit ruled that preferences are just as illegal as quotas. The Supreme Court declined to take the Hopwood case, but cases involving the University of Michigan and the University of Washington may eventually end up in the Supreme Court, and there is a good chance that the Bakke straddle will not survive.

The second compromise to the affirmative action issue is to provide preferences on the basis of class or socioeconomic status rather than race or color. The roots of the argument lie not in Justice Powell's decision in *Bakke*, but rather in the writings of Dr. Martin Luther King, Jr.

In his 1964 book, *Why We Can't Wait*, King entertained the argument over affirmative action directly. King wrote (as advocates of affirmative action note) that compensation was due: "the nation must not only radically readjust its attitude toward the Negro in the compelling present, but must incorporate in its planning some compensatory consideration for the handicaps he has inherited from the past." At the same time, King had fought too hard and too long for the goal of color-blindness – treating people based on the content of their character not the color of their skin – to casually embrace racial preferences as the optimal means for compensation.

Instead of advocating a new Bill of Rights for the Negro exclusively, King advocated a Bill of Rights for the Disadvantaged. He wrote: "While Negroes form the vast majority of America's disadvantaged, there are millions of white poor who would also benefit from such a bill." In advocating a colorblind program for the disadvantaged, King had two key insights.

First, King saw that a class-based approach would implicitly compensate the victims of discrimination. Because of past discrimination, blacks were disproportionately poor, and would disproportionately benefit from any class-based program. In this way, the program would implicitly take account of history. But at the same time, King saw that fairness demanded the inclusion of poor whites. Discrimination was not the only cause of unequal opportunity, he knew; deprivation also blocked opportunity.

Inequality of opportunity in this country runs far deeper than race and gender discrimination. Sociological studies over the last several decades have demonstrated the degree to which children born into poor families find the deck stacked against them. A child born into the top 10 percent by income is 27 times as likely as a child born into the bottom 10 percent to rise as an adult to earn in the top 10 percent bracket. Poor children – regardless of race – are more likely to grow up in violent neighborhoods, attend inferior schools, and are much less likely to reach their full natural potential. King knew that racial discrimination was but one element of societal unfairness, and he wrote: "It is a simple matter of justice that America, in dealing creatively with the task of raising the Negro from backwardness, should also be rescuing a large stratum of the forgotten white poor."

Secondly, as a matter of politics, King knew that in the matter of preferential treatment, emphasizing class over race was imperative. Toward the end of his life, King was trying to build a multiracial coalition of disadvantaged people culminating in the Poor People's Campaign of 1968. He was assassinated in Memphis as he was helping sanitation workers in a multiracial effort for economic justice. King knew that racial preferences could split that coalition asunder. He wrote: "It is my opinion that many white workers whose economic condition is not too far removed from the economic condition of his black brother, will find it difficult to accept a 'Negro Bill of Rights,' which seeks to give special consideration to the Negro in the context of unemployment, joblessness, etc. and does not take into sufficient account their plight (that of the white worker)."

But if King worried about the divisive effect of a policy of racial preference, division was seen as a plus for Richard Nixon, who, in 1969, instituted the first major federal affirmative action program. Nixon offered the Philadelphia Plan, an effort to impose quotas on the construction industry and trade unions in Philadelphia, in part as a way of dividing King's progressive coalition. Nixon aide John Ehrlichman recalled that Nixon delighted in the Plan's ability to construct "a political dilemma for the labor union leaders and civil rights groups. ... Before long, the AFL-CIO and NAACP were locked in combat over one of the passionate issues of the day."

The great civil rights leader Bayard Rustin, addressing the AFL-CIO in 1969, said the conflict between labor and civil rights groups over the Philadelphia Plan was "a source of tremendous satisfaction to the powerful enemies of the labor movement." The Plan's intent, Rustin said, was to "deliberately throw black and white workers at each other's throats." Years later, Rustin would write: "Any preferential approach postulated on racial, ethnic, religious, or sexual lines will only disrupt a multicultural society and lead to a backlash. However, special treatment can be provided to those who have been exploited or denied opportunities if solutions are predicated on class lines, precisely because all religious, ethnic, and racial groups have a depressed class who would benefit."

What a System of Class-Based Affirmative Action Would Look Like

Using race and gender-based affirmative action as a model, one can easily envision a system of preferences in education, entry-level employment, and government contracting based on economic status. The basic idea is to define preferences in a way that take into account the economic obstacles that poor and working class youth face. If a youth has faced a number of economic disadvantages – and done fairly well despite the odds – the chances are that her long-run potential is greater than a colleague who has a similar record of accomplishment having faced none of the same obstacles.

In the college admissions arena, preferences could be given to students who are disadvantaged by what sociologists say are the three major determinants of life chances: parental income, education, and occupation. That is, students from families with low incomes, whose parents did not attend college, and whose parents work in low status occupations should be given a break.

Today, Bard College provides a leg up to students from low-income families by requiring a notarized copy of IRS form 1040 or letters from a social service agency verifying income. Existing federal guidelines are available to adjust income for family size or even geographic region to reflect the varying value of a given income. Given the importance of a parent's educational level to a student's chances of educational success, Berkeley provides preferences to students whose parents do not have a four-year college degree. And numerous academic studies dating back 80 years have devised sophisticated and consistent ways to rank parental occupations.

In addition, a university might consider factoring in such elements as a family's net worth, the quality of secondary education, neighborhood influences, and family structure. Net worth provides a longer term picture of a family's economic position that goes beyond the snapshot provided by annual income. Counting net worth also uncovers one of the significant differences between blacks and whites in America: even among whites and African Americans of the same income group, blacks tend to have lower net worths, in part because they are less likely to have inherited money from their parents. The quality of secondary education can be measured by objective standards such as median high school test scores or graduation rates. If a particular student does quite well even though he attends an underachieving high school, that student probably has a great deal to offer in the long term. Neighborhood influences can be measured by such factors as the poverty or unemployment rate in the applicant's census tract. This factor reflects strong sociological evidence that it is a disadvantage to be born into a poor family, but it is doubly disadvantageous to be born into a poor family living in concentrated poverty. This factor will, in the aggregate, tend to benefit people of color, who are generally more likely to live in concentrated poverty than whites. Finally, a school could consider whether the applicant was raised in a single parent family. Numerous studies show that even after controlling for income, growing up without two parents presents an independent obstacle to success.

Many of these factors – such as income and net worth – are already known to college admissions officers through financial aid offices. Parental education levels are normally supplied as well. And in recent years schools like the University of California and Los Angeles Law School have succeeded in devising workable class-based affirmative action programs which go beyond the information normally available to financial aid and admissions officers.

Because large numbers of low income youth are not in a position to pursue college, similar preferences could be provided in entry-level employment to students entering the workforce directly from high school. The federal government currently provides such hiring preferences to low income workers who build new public housing. Likewise, federal contractors could be required to provide entry level opportunities to disadvantaged youth as a condition for receiving federal funds, much as such contractors are now required to take account of race in hiring. Class-based preferences in promotions down the line make less sense in part because individuals are more responsible for their economic position as they grow older, and in part because highly skilled jobs are less amenable to flexibility in hiring.

In government contracting, preferences can be provided to small firms (irrespective of the owner's race) which agree to employ individuals from high poverty census tracts. In May 1996, for example, President Clinton issued an executive order directing the Commerce Department to provide preferences to government contractors employing significant numbers of residents from census tracts with poverty rates of 20% or more. In New York City, Mayor Ed Koch instituted a similar program in the 1980s based on economic status rather than race or gender. The program set aside contracts for small firms that did at least 25% of their business in depressed areas or employed economically disadvantaged workers as 25% of their work-force.

All these types of affirmative action will disproportionately benefit people of color, but will do so on the unifying basis of class rather than the dividing basis of race.

It should be emphasized that class-based preferences should supplement, rather than supplant, strict enforcement of civil rights laws. Such laws include not only those aimed at eliminating intentional discrimination (the Civil Rights Act of 1964) but also those aimed at hiring practices which result in a statistical racial imbalance and cannot be justified on nonracial grounds (the Civil Rights Act of 1991). These are powerful tools and should be backed up with increased funding for government enforcement.

Prospects for Class-Based Affirmative Action

What is the likelihood that a class-based affirmative action will be put into place? The chances increase every day. The attacks on affirmative action have led both liberals and conservatives to begin talking seriously about class-based alternatives.

Racial preferences are under heavy attack from the most democratic institution (the ballot initiative) and the least democratic (the judiciary). Passage of Proposition 209 in California has spawned similar efforts to cut back on affirmative action in 1998 in Ohio, Colorado, Florida, and Washington. More severe threats come from the courts. Proponents of affirmative action dodged a bullet when civil rights groups settled the case of *Piscataway v. Taxman*, but new cases are making their way up to the High Court, and new restrictions are likely.

The legal and political attacks have raised the salience of the class-based alternative as the left begins contingency planning, and the right searches for something positive to say. Among conservatives, Jack Kemp argues affirmative action "should be done on the basis of income and socioeconomic status such as an enterprise zone instead of just giving a tax break to someone based on color." And Newt Gingrich argues racial preferences should be replaced with special help for people "who come out of poor neighborhoods, who come out of poor backgrounds, who go to school in poor counties." These statements, underreported by the mainstream press, constitute a not insignificant development, considering the inattention conservatives have historically given to issues of class inequality.

Among Democrats, President Clinton has flirted on and off with class-based affirmative action. In March 1995, Clinton made headlines by declaring that, instead of emphasizing racial preferences "I want us to emphasize need-based programs where we can, because they work better and have a bigger impact and generate broader support." Clinton quickly backed off that statement after Jesse Jackson threatened to run for president, but in late 1997, Clinton returned to the concept of need-based preferences. In the Akron, Ohio town hall meeting, Clinton said "the real issue" is whether a "class-based affirmative opportunity agenda" should supplement or replace race-based affirmative action. "I think that's the question," he stressed; "that's the nub of the affirmative action debate." The president continued: "politically and substantively you'll help more people and build more unity by having an economic basis for social policy now."

Public support for class-based affirmative action continues to grow. In the December 1997 *New York Times/CBS* poll, Americans supported preferences for people from poor families by 53%–37%. When asked, "Is it a good idea to select a person from a poor family over one from a middle-class or rich family if they are equally qualified?," Americans favored the idea by 2:1 (56%–27%).

What is particularly interesting is the attention younger people have given to the idea of class-based affirmative action. The younger generation is generally more racially tolerant, and for that reason sees less need for racial preferences in coming years. During the debate over affirmative action in California, the Berkeley student newspaper came out in favor of paying "special attention to economic status" rather than to race or gender. When students at Berkeley find common cause with Newt Gingrich, it is time to take note.

A Natural for Labor

In particular, it is time for labor to take note. In the debate over race vs. class-based affirmative action, what Clinton calls the "nub" of the affirmative action debate, labor has been astonishingly quiet. There can be little question where the interests and values of labor historically lay: in multiracial approaches which benefit working-class people generally. Where racial preferences have spawned division, class-based affirmative action would unite various races, and remind the ranks of labor who their true friends are.

Big business has turned out to be a great champion of affirmative action, which in itself should give labor reason for pause. Under the current legal regime, business can use preferences to achieve racial balance as a way of fending off suits from people of color, secure in the knowledge that "reverse discrimination" suits from whites will rarely prevail. If affirmative action policies are altered, business will be equally subject to lawsuits for unfair treatment from all sides. Because business does not want that kind of accountability, it fought an anti-preference initiative in Houston, Texas in 1997, and it put the bulk of the money up to prevent the Supreme Court from hearing the arguments in the Piscataway affirmative action layoff case.

With the notable exception of the late Albert Shanker, labor has done very little to support the class-based alternative to racial preferences. In another era, labor would surely have been at the forefront: policies which polarize workers by race, labor knew, always give management an advantage.

Class-based affirmative action tries to address the historic wrongs high-lighted by proponents of racial preferences but uses means not offensive to the majority of Americans who oppose racial preferences. More importantly, class-based preferences are firmly rooted in an American sense of fairness – giving a break to those who need it – in a way that unites rather than divides. This is a natural for the American labor movement. It will be a lasting shame if the Republicans manage to figure all of this out first.

◆

Should Public Policy Be Class Conscious Rather than Color Conscious?

Amy Gutmann

We have yet carefully to consider a proposal that promises to go a long way toward securing fair opportunity for black Americans while avoiding the pitfalls of color consciousness by shifting the focus of public policy from race to class. One advocate of "class, not race" argues that "it was clear that with the passage of the Civil Rights Act of 1964, class replaced caste as the central impediment to equal opportunity."[1] If class is the central impediment to equal opportunity, then using class as a qualification may be fairer to individuals than using race. Counting poverty as a qualification – on grounds that it is highly correlated with unequal opportunity, with untapped intellectual potential, and with life experience from which more affluent individuals can learn – would help blacks and nonblacks alike, but only those who are poor. In addition to being fairer, its advocates claim, class preferences would be politically more feasible and therefore potentially more effective in addressing racial as well as class injustice. The apparently rising tide of resentment and distrust between blacks and whites in the Unites States makes the call to leave race preferences behind all the more appealing.

Advocates most often look to university admissions as the realm in which class should supplant color as a qualification, so it makes sense to focus on the promise of "class, not race" in this extensive and familiar realm. University admissions policies would be fairer if considerations of color were left behind, advoctes argue, while considerations of class took their place. Why? Because poverty accompanied by academic accomplishment is, generally speaking, a sign of uncommon effort, untapped intellectual potential, and unusual life experiences from which more affluent students can learn.

One advocate of "class, not race" notes that "we rarely see a breakdown of [SAT] scores by class, which would show enormous gaps between rich and poor, gaps that would help explain differences in scores by race."[2] After breaking down average SAT scores by class and race, we see enormous gaps between rich and poor students. If this were all that we observed, then the shift from class to race could provide fair opportunity for black Americans, since black Americans are disproportionately poor. But when average SAT scores are broken down by class and race, we also see enormous gaps between black and white students *within* the same income groups. Moreover, the very same argument that "class, not race" advocates invoke for counting poverty as a qualification in admissions also supports the idea that being black is a similarly important qualification. The same evidence of a significant gap in SAT scores between groups – whether identified by class or color – lends support to the idea that both poor students and black students face distincitive educational disadvantages. The educational disadvantages faced by black students are not statistically accounted for by the income differentials between white and black students. This is what we should expect if (and only if) color is an independent cause of injustice in this country.

The evidence from SAT scores alone is of course insufficient to provide a full picture of either class or racial injustice, let alone its causes. But the very same kind of evidence that advocates take as sufficient to support class as a consideration for university admissions also supports color as a consideration. There is a significant gap between the average SAT scores of groups, whether those groups are defined by class, color, or both. The average combined SAT scores for black students whose parents earn between $10,000 and $20,000 is 175 points lower than the average combined score for white students whose parents fall in the same income category. The gap between the average SAT scores of black and white students within this income category narrows by only 21 points out of the 196 point gap between all black and white students taking the test.

As long as such gaps persist, a "class, not race" policy in university admissions will do far less to increase the higher educational opportunity of blacks than nonblacks. If selective colleges and universities reject color in order to adopt class as a consideration in admitting disadvantaged students, their student bodies would become almost entirely nonblack. For colleges and universities committed to educating future leaders, this result should be as alarming as the image of an affulent, multicolored society without well-educated black leaders. It is just as doubtful that nonblack leaders in such a society could be well educated, for their education would have taken place in almost entirely nonblack universities.

Proportional representation by color in selective universities is not an ultimate goal of a just society. Fair equality of opportunity is. The problem in universities' focusing on class considerations to the exclusion of color is not disproportionality of results but unfairness, as indicated by the inconsistency in the reasoning that supports the proposed shift from color to class. The statistical evidence of lower average SAT scores by income categories is taken to indicate that low-income students are disadvantaged in a way that warrants making low income a qualification. But the analogous statistical evidence of lower average SAT scores by the U.S. Census's racial categories is not taken to indicate that black students are disadvantaged in a way that warrants making color a qualification.

The same statistical evidence that is used to establish the case for class as a consideration in admissions is either ignored or discounted when considering color as a consideration, and for no good reason. Some critics say that individual responsibility is undermined when black students who have lower SAT scores than nonblack students are admitted, but precisely the same argument could be made against admitting students from poor families who score lower than their more affluent peers. In both cases, the argument is extremely weak.

Holding individuals responsible for their educational achievement is completely consistent with counting class *and* color as qualifications, as long as class and color are not the *only* qualifications, and individuals are not held to be *exclusively* responsible for their educational successes or failures.

The situation is therefore more complex than the "class, not race" perspective admits. In order to be admitted to a selective university, all applicants – whether they be poor, middle-class, rich, black, white, or some other color – must demonstrate unusual educational accomplishment relative to their similarly situated peers. They must also demonstrate the capacity to succeed academically, once admitted. These prerequisites to admission to a selective university ensure that individual applicants are held responsible for educational achievement. But social institutions, including universities, also share responsibility with individuals for overcoming the obstacles associated with color and class in our society. Why? Because to be responsible for accomplishing something entails having the effective power to do so. Individuals often do not have the power to overcome all the obstacles associated with being poor or black. Nor is responsibility a zero-sum quantity. Just because individuals are responsible for working hard does not mean that institutions are not responsible for coming to their aid, when they can thereby help equalize opportunity. It is therefore both unrealistic and unfair to expect individuals alone to overcome all the obstacles that are associated with being black or poor in our society.

The "class, not race" perspective admits half as much by urging universities to consider low income as a qualification for university admission – not the only qualification, to be sure, but a legitimate one that can justify admitting some applicants with lower SAT scores and lower high school grades and passing over other applicants with higher SAT scores and high school grades. Universities fall short of providing fair equality of educational opportunity, according to the "class, not race" perspective, to the extent that their admission policies neglect low income as an obstacle to educational achievement, and therefore refuse to pass over some applicants who score higher on these conventional indices (which do not predict future educational performance past the freshman year, let alone future career success or social leadership). The very same thing can be said about neglecting the extent to which being black is an obstacle to educational achievement in our society. The refusal to count being black as one qualification among many entails falling short of providing fair equality of educational opportunity for black students who demonstrate unusual educational achievement relative to the obstacles that they have faced. The best available evidence suggests that color and class are both obstacles, with interactive effects in the lives of a majority of black Americans.

Why, then, shift from color to class, rather than use both class and color, as independently important considerations in university admissions? The inconsistency and unfairness in substituting class for color as a qualification becomes vivid when we imagine what universities that adopt the "class, not race" perspective would effectively be saying to their applicants. To the average low-income white student, they would say – "Giving you a boost in admissions is consistent with our expectation that you have worked hard to get where you are and will continue to work hard to earn your future success."

To the average low-income black student, they would say – "If we give you an added boost in admissions over the average low-income white student, we will be denying your responsibility for your lower scores and decreasing your incentive to work hard and earn your success." To average middle-income black students, they would say: "We cannot give you any boost in admissions over average middle-income white students because you no more than they have any special obstacles to overcome."

Universities could achieve consistency by refusing to consider any of the educational obstacles faced by applicants, whether they be poor or black or physically handicapped. But the price of this policy would be forsaking fair equality of educational opportunity as well as overlooking the potential for intellectual accomplishment and social leadership of individuals who have faced far greater than average obstacles to academic achievement, as conventionally measured. Yet another price of a policy of "neither class nor color" would be discounting the values – associational as well as educational – of cultural diversity on university campuses. Consistency would also require giving up all the other, nonacademic factors that the most selective universities have traditionally considered relevant in admissions, such as geographical diversity and athletic ability.

Were citizens of this society engaged in designing our system of higher education from scratch, a case might be made for counting only intellectual accomplishment in admissions. But few if any critics of counting color as a consideration in university admissions propose such a radical redesigning of our college and university system. In any case, the fairest way to such radical restructuring would not begin by giving up on color as a consideration in admissions. There are many reasons to doubt whether such a radical redesign would produce a better system of higher education than the one we now have, and there is no reason to believe that this society would democratically support such a restructuring. In this context, we cannot justify rejecting color while accepting class as one among many legitimate considerations for admissions.

What about the critics' claim that when universities give a boost to applicants above and beyond their actual educational achievements, they fostser in that group of applicants a sense of irresponsibility for their (relative lack of) educational achievements? This argument from the value of individual responsibility cannot be sustained for two reasons. First responsibility is not zero-sum. If universities assume some responsibility for helping applicants who have faced unusually great obstacles to educational achievement, they are not denying the responsibility of those applicants to work hard and demonstrate their capacity to succeed once they are admitted. (Perhaps the critics are objecting to universities that admit a high proportion of black students who cannot graduate, in which case the critics are pointing to a correctable problem, and not one that besets the strongest case for counting color as a qualification.) Second, the same argument from responsibility is rarely if ever invoked in opposition to giving a boost to low-income or physically handicapped students, even though it applies with the same (weak) force. The force of the argument is weak because responsibility for educational accomplishment is both institutional and individual. When universities share responsibility for helping students overcome educational obstacles, they do not therefore relieve them of the responsibility to succeed academically. Students who are given a boost in an admissions process still must compete for admissions, work for their grades, and compete for jobs on the basis of their qualifications.

The case for both class *and* color as considerations in university admissions is therefore strong: stronger than either consideration taken to the exclusion of the other. The "class, not race" proposal, by contrast, fails by the color blind test of fairness; it does not treat like cases alike. It discriminates against blacks by giving a boost only to students who score low because of disadvantages associated with poverty, but not to students who score low because of disadvantages that are as credibly associated with their color.

A more complex way of counting class as a qualification, some critics say, would avoid these inequities and thereby obviate the need to take color into account. A "complex calculus of advantage" would take into account not only parental income, education, and occupation but also "net worth, the quality of secondary education, neighborhood influences and family structure." The complex calculus of class is fairer than the simple one, which counts only income, because it considers more dimensions of disadvantage. Since blacks "are more likely than whites to live in concentrated poverty, to go to bad schools and live in single-parent homes," the complex calculus would "disproportionately" benefit blacks.[3] Its advocates say that the complex calculus not only is fair but also has a decisive political advantage over any color conscious policy: it would go almost as far toward fair equality of educational opportunity as would explicit considerations of color without calling attention to the enduring racial divisions in our society.

But the political strength of the complex calculus of disadvantage is also its weakness. By not calling attention to enduring divisions of color in our society, some suggest, we may be better able to overcome them. But it is at least as likely that we will thereby fail to make much progress in overcoming them. It is impossible to say on the basis of available evidence – and the enduring imperfections of our self-understanding – which is more likely to be the case. What we can say with near certainty is that if blacks who live in concentrated poverty, go to bad schools, or live in single-parent homes are also stigmatized by racial prejudice as whites are not, then even the most complex calculus of *class* is an imperfect substitute for also taking color explicitly into account. Perhaps the disadvantages of color can be adequately addressed by remedies that do not explicitly take color into account, but the adequacy of the complex calculus of disadvantage will then be closely related to the intention of its designers to come as close as possible to achieving the justice demanded by color as well as class consciousness.

Fairness speaks in favor of taking both class and color into account as qualifications. If politics precludes considerations of color, then we are far better off, morally speaking, with a complex calculus of class than with a simple one. But we would be better off still with policies that at least implicitly recognize the independent dimension of color as an obstacle to educational achievement in our society. The color blind principle of fairness has these inclusive implications. It encourages employers and universities to consider both class and color dimensions of disadvantage (along with other dimensions, such as gender) and also to consider a wider range of qualifications for jobs and places in a university.

Even color, class, *and* gender considerations, taken together, however, would not adequately address the problem of racial injustice. None of these considerations, as commonly defended, addresses a more urgent problem: the deprivation experienced by the poorest citizens, over 30 percent of whom are black. The poorest citizens are not in a position to benefit from admissions or hiring policies that count either class or color as added qualifications. This is a weakness shared by all kinds of policies that focus on giving a boost to individuals – whatever their skin color and relative advantage to one another – who are already among the more advantaged of our society. Millions of citizens, a vastly disproportionate number of them black, suffer from economic and educational deprivations so great as to elude the admittedly incomplete and relatively inexpensive remedies of affirmative action. Policies aimed at increasing employment, job training, health care, child care, housing, and education are desperately needed for all these individuals, regardless of their color. These policies, like the admissions policies we have been considering, would not give *preferential* treatment to anyone. They would treat the least advantaged citizens as civic equals who should not be deprived of a fair chance to live a good life or participate as equals in democratic politics because of the bad luck of the natural lottery of birth or upbringing.

Social welfare and fair workfare policies – which provide jobs that pay and adequate child care for everyone who can work – are a necessary part of any adequate response to racial injustice. They are also far more expensive than admissions and hiring policies that treat class and color as qualifications, and far more expensive than policies of preferential treatment, at least in the short run. Over time, these policies would in all likelihood more than pay for themselves. They would alleviate the increasingly expensive and widespread problems of welfare dependency, unemployment, and crime in this country. Moreover, without fair workfare and welfare policies, we cannot be a society of civic equals. Citizens will be fighting for their fair share of a social pie that cannot provide fairness for everyone; many men and women who are willing and able to work will not be able to find work that pays, and others will work full-time only to earn less, or little more than they would on welfare, while they are also unable to ensure adequate care for their children.

The political fights in such a context will invariably divide us by groups since effective democratic politics is by its very nature group politics. To build a society in which citizens both help themselves by helping each other and help each other by helping themselves, we must be committed not only to making the economic pie sufficiently large but also to dividing it in such a way that every person who is willing to work can find adequate child care and decent work that pays.

As urgent as social welfare, workfare, and child care policies are they would not by themselves constitute a sufficient response to racial injustice in the short run. We have seen that color conscious programs are also part of a comprehensive response to injustice, although not the most urgent (or most expensive) part. Suppose that a more comprehensive, color conscious perspective is fair. Is it feasible? An eye-opening study entitled *The Scar of Race* shows that mere mention of the words "affirmative action" elicits negative attitudes about black Americans from white Americans. After affirmative action is mentioned in the course of an interview with white citizens, the proportion of respondents who agree with the claim that "blacks are irresponsible" almost doubles, increasing from 26 percent to 43 percent. (The proportions grow from 20 percent to 31 percent for the claim that "blacks are lazy" and from 29 percent to 36 percent for the claim that "blacks are arrogant.") White Americans' "dislike of particular racial policies," the authors conclude, "can provoke dislike of blacks, as well as the other way around."[4]

"Provoking dislike" is importantly ambiguous between *producing* dislike and *triggering* the open expression of it (where the dislike already preceded the mere mention of affirmative action). It is doubtful that the mere mention of affirmative action *creates* racial prejudice. More likely, it *releases greater oral expression* of preexisting racial animosity. Many white Americans seem to take the mention of affirmative action, particularly in a matter-of-fact question that opens up the possibility of their criticizing affirmative action policies, as a signal that it is acceptable to be critical not only of affirmative action but also of blacks. This is cause for concern, but the concern cannot be effectively addressed simply by relabeling affirmative action policies as something else. A good reason to avoid the term "affirmative action" is the massive confusion that surrounds its meaning. An effective and appropriate response to this confusion would be to go beyond simple sound bites, which rarely serve justice well, and distinguish between morally better and worse policies that are color conscious. The negative reaction to the mere mention of the term "affirmative action" surely is not a sufficient reason to abandon affirmative action programs – whatever we call them – that are otherwise fair and beneficial to blacks.

Another finding of this same study suggests why it would be a mistake to oppose affirmative action only on these grounds. The popularity of programs that are perceived to help blacks is highly volatile, shifting with citizens' perception of the state of the law and the moral commitments of political leadership. When white citizens are asked for their views on a set-aside program for minorities – "a law to ensure that a certain number of federal contracts go to minority contractors," 43 percent say they favor it. But when they are told that the set-aside program for minorities is a law passed by both houses of Congress, the support significantly increases to 57 percent.[5]

Not only does the force of law seem to have the capacity to change people's minds on race matters, so does the force of moral argument. When exposed to counterarguments to their expressed positions on various policy responses to racial problems, many people switch their position in the direction of the counterarguments. This tendency is greatest for social welfare policies, such as government spending for blacks, but the tendency is also significant for affirmative action policies, where an even greater proportion of whites shift to favoring a pro–affirmative action position than switch to an anti–affirmative action position when exposed to counterarguments to their original positions. Twenty-three percent of white respondents shift from a negative to a positive position on affirmative action, compared to 17 percent who shift in the opposite direction.[6]

Moral argument and political leadership, as this study vividly indicates, make a significant difference in public opinion on race matters. This is potentially good news for deliberative democracy. Were we to make our politics more deliberative, we would also – in all likelihood – increase the potential for bringing public policy and color consciousness more in line with the force of moral arguments. There are no guarantees, of course, about where the force of argument will lead citizens and public officials on these complex issues. But as long as the potential exists for changing minds through deliberation, citizens and public officials alike have good reason – moral as well as prudential – not to endorse public policies merely because they conform to public opinion polls. "New majorities can be made – and unmade," Paul Sniderman and Thomas Piazza conclude. "The future is not foreordained. It is the business of politics to decide it."[7]

All the more reason to approach the political morality of race with renewed openness, at least as much openness as ordinary citizens evince in extended discussions of racially charged issues, which include most issues of our public life. Unless we keep the aim of overcoming racial injustice at the front of our minds and at the center of our democratic deliberations, we shall not arrive at an adequate response to racial injustice. I do not pretend to be able to provide that response, or even anything close to it in this essay. But there is value in keeping democratic doors open to exploring new possibilities and to changing minds, including our own, as our deliberations on these issues continue. Only if we keep the aim of overcoming racial injustice at the center of our deliberations about social justice can we realistically hope to develop into a democracy with liberty and justice for all.

Notes

1   Richard Kahlenberg, "Class, Not Race," *New Republic*, April 3, 1995, p. 21.
2   Ibid., p. 24.
3   Ibid., p. 25.
4   Paul M. Sniderman and Thomas Piazza, *The Scar of Race* (Cambridge, Mass.: Harvard University Press, 1993), p. 104.
5   Ibid., pp. 131–2.
6   Ibid., p. 148.
7   Ibid., p. 165.

5

The Future of Affirmative Action

When Preferences Disappear

Peter Schrag

By now, there can no longer be much doubt that the days of formal race preference programs, at least in the public sector, are numbered. On November 5
[1997], California voters did what everyone had long expected, approving
Proposition 209, the California Civil Rights Initiative, which prohibits any
consideration of race or gender in California public education, employment,
and contracting. The vote was narrower than had once been expected (and
might have been narrower still had CCRI opponents not used an inflam-
matory and offensive television commercial, complete with a burning KKK
cross, in the last weeks of the campaign). But, with a margin of 54 percent to
46 percent, it was decisive enough.

CCRI is only the most recent assault on affirmative action measures. And
while Proposition 209 still faces legal challenges in federal court that may take
years to resolve fully, the drift is clear. In the summer of 1995, the regents of
the University of California, under heavy pressure from a governor with over-
weening presidential ambitions, voted to end race and gender preferences in
all UC admissions and employment. In March 1996, in *Hopwood v. Texas,* a
three-judge panel of the U.S. Fifth Circuit Court of Appeals struck down practices giving preferences to blacks and Latinos in admissions to the University
of Texas Law School. In issuing its decision, the Fifth Circuit Court perpetrated an unprecedented act of judicial chutzpah, dismissing the Supreme
Court's 1978 *Bakke* decision, which had allowed consideration of race as one
"plus factor" in university admissions, as if it had never really existed. Justice
Lewis Powell, the Fifth Circuit panel held, had been alone in articulating the
Bakke standard in the Court's divided decision; subsequent high court decisions
had conspicuously ignored it; and "it is not binding precedent on this issue." In
response to the Fifth Circuit decision, Colorado abandoned its race-based

Reprinted with permission from *The American Prospect* 30 (January–February 1997),
pp. 38–41. Copyright © 1997 The American Prospect, P.O. Box 383080, Cambridge, MA
02138. All rights reserved.

scholarship program, and a number of other state university systems began reexamining their use of race preferences in admissions.

In the meantime, in a series of increasingly emphatic decisions, the U.S. Supreme Court has cast growing doubt on its willingness to uphold any race-based policy other than those narrowly tailored to remedy a specific instance of prior discrimination. It has severely restricted racial set-asides in federal contracting (*Adarand v. Pena*) and racial gerrymandering in drawing Congressional and legislative districts (*Shaw v. Hunt*). The high court also declined to review a Fourth Circuit decision (*Kirwin v. Podberesky*) striking down a University of Maryland scholarship program for African Americans as a denial of equal protection, and it deferred review of the *Hopwood* decision, even though it left federal law confused and inconsistent in a highly volatile arena – and even though the Fifth Circuit decision was a direct challenge to the high court's own *Bakke* precedent. If one of its conservatives retires and is replaced by a Clinton appointee, the Court may respond to these challenges. But for the moment, it appears likely that the Court declined review because the liberal-to-moderate justices – Breyer, Ginsburg, Souter, Stevens – on this closely divided court are not confident they have the fifth vote necessary to overturn lower court rejections of affirmative action.

It's easy enough to dismiss any one of these developments as limited – by geography or subject or political scope or by the cynicism of the political act (and cynical was what California Governor Pete Wilson's exploitation of affirmative action certainly was). In his call to "mend it but don't end it," President Clinton vowed to protect the principle of affirmative action, and even Republican governors like George Pataki in New York, Christine Todd Whitman in New Jersey, and George Bush, Jr., in Texas, along with Jack Kemp in the years before the 1996 election, defended affirmative action programs. Still the trend is clear enough, whether one looks at the courts, which once helped advance affirmative action, at the opinion polls, or at the demographic complexities in states like California, where the growing number of minorities of all shades makes it increasingly difficult to favor one group without explicitly discriminating against another.

It's also revealing that despite the surprising failure of people like Pete Wilson and Newt Gingrich to make race preferences a hot-button political issue, which is certainly what they had been hoping to do last year, there was no significant counterforce defending race-based preferences, either among the nation's leaders or the public at large. The opponents of Proposition 209 in California, fearing a low turnout of minority voters despite the upsurge of newly naturalized Latino citizens, tried to base their campaign not on the measure's impact on minorities but on what they warned would be the damage it would do to women. But that strategy, too, fell flat: on November 5, women split almost evenly on the issue, while men supported it overwhelmingly.

Race and Merit

And yet, if the winding down of race-based affirmative action represents one declaration of social priorities – even, perhaps, the end of an era of public policy – it runs counter to another developing set of priorities, particularly in higher education, and raises a host of new questions about what, other than test scores and grades, should replace race and ethnicity in choosing candidates for admission to selective public institutions. Even as state policymakers and voters appear to be asking higher education to become more meritocratic in its admissions and hiring and as the courts increasingly insist on strict scrutiny of race-based policies in all public-sector activities, the trend in much of higher education seems to be toward broader, less objective – and sometimes more squishy – standards.

The most obvious examples of this trend are the attacks, often backed by the Department of Education's Office of Civil Rights, on objective testing – and in particular the attacks on the SAT and PSAT (which is used as one of the primary screens for National Merit Scholars) – as biased against women and minorities. In its effort to deflect the attacks and to raise the scores of women, the College Board, which designs and runs these testing programs, has already revised the PSAT by doubling the weight given to the verbal sections on the test (thereby reducing the weight of the math portion, on which men have consistently done better), and, in an agreement with OCR, will now revise it further to include items designed to test the writing skills of applicants, on which women generally do better. (College Board officials say they were going to institute the writing items anyway, but they don't deny that the timing of the announcement was advanced by federal pressure.) These revisions of standardized testing may, in themselves, be welcome reforms, but coming, as they do, in response to government pressure to make the scores of women match those of men, it suggests that the battle over affirmative action is far from over. It is merely being carried on under other names on other fronts. In the meantime, a growing number of institutions, including the whole Maryland system, are de-emphasizing the use of the SAT in admissions, or vowing to abandon it altogether.

From Race to Class?

The alternatives most favored by politicians and other critics of race-based affirmative action are "outreach" and class-based preferences for those who have suffered economic disadvantage. Many institutions have been employing this approach for years, either by using straight income or welfare criteria or through programs that give preferences to children from families where no one had ever gone to college. Class-based affirmative action is part of the new regents' formula in California – which, in a strange bow to current fads of victimology, also calls for extra consideration for those who have lived in "an abusive or otherwise dysfunctional home." (The most thorough treatment of the idea of class-based affirmative action is probably Richard D. Kahlenberg's recent book, *The Remedy: Class, Race, and Affirmative Action.*)

The problem is that in places like California, replacing race with class doesn't do much to maintain, much less increase, the percentage of blacks and Latinos on campus. It will merely bring in more poor Asians – Chinese,

Vietnamese, Koreans – to replace the middle-class blacks and Hispanics who will be lost (most of them to private institutions) when race preferences end this year. There has been a florid array of proposals for programs that are not explicitly aimed at blacks and Latinos but that would effectively give them preferential treatment anyway. For example, the University of California at San Diego is considering a plan that would give extra credit to graduates of the state's worst high schools. But admission to the nation's handful of highly selective public institutions – the University of Texas Law School, for example, or Berkeley's Boalt Law School, or any undergraduate program at Berkeley or UCLA – is so competitive that, as long as other criteria are not changed, no device other than overt race preferences can achieve the ethnic diversity that the institutions would like. In this process there is, as Dennis Galligani, UC's assistant vice president for admissions, put it, "no surrogate for ethnicity."

For different reasons, the same is even more true in civil service employment and public-sector contracting. By definition, most of the people who apply for jobs as truck drivers, firefighters, and meter readers are already working class. More to the point, there is not much justification for class preferences in contracting or in hiring for civil service jobs: the only real rationale for establishing an ethnically diverse public-sector workforce is to increase its effectiveness and legitimacy. Sending a poor white boy to patrol Watts or Harlem is not the same as sending a black. A contractor working a street job in a big city with only white heavy-equipment operators will not enhance the social morale of the minority community even if every backhoe and tractor is driven by a poor boy. Having only white judges in courtrooms dealing mainly with minority criminal defendants is, as we have so painfully learned, no way to persuade the community that the legal system is fair, even if some of the whites come from the wrong side of the tracks.

The bigger question that follows – as much in hiring for the police department or the road crew as in choosing candidates for college or graduate school – is whether, race preferences aside, the old criteria really made sense in the first place. What, beyond minimal competence to meet the technical requirements of the task, should be required? Some positions, it is true, clearly require more formally meritocratic standards than others; but for most positions, this question is a valid one. In some respects, race preferences have always been an inadequate way of compensating for the larger shortcomings that large public systems use in selecting applicants: how well does the Law School Admissions Test or the Medical College Admissions Test predict who will be a good lawyer or a good doctor? Unlike Amherst or Princeton, where admissions officers professedly pore over applicants' folders bulging with their letters of recommendation, autobiographical essays, and descriptions of extracurricular activities (from the chess club to the volunteer summer with African refugees), admissions offices at places like the University of Texas Law School or the University of California proceed almost entirely by numbers. In the 1970s, when it became plain that grade point averages and SAT scores left the entering classes at Berkeley and UCLA embarrassingly white and Asian in a surrounding society that was increasingly Latino, the system (to oversimplify this history only slightly) simply added another set of numbers to raise the percentage of what it calls URMs (underrepresented minorities). Anything that's not quantifiable is more or less ignored. (UC does ask for essays from applicants but rarely reads them.) Which is to say that, with some glaring exceptions (friends of politicians, children of big donors) the admission system at most large public universities has always been more like a civil service system than like the admission procedures (themselves highly imperfect) that the more selective private colleges ostensibly use.

Toward Relevant Standards

The question now is whether these numbers-based admission systems will be rationally reexamined, or whether most of the gatekeepers will simply look for new labels to put on the old dodges and keep the number system more or less intact. In the higher reaches of academic and professional selectivity, the selection criteria may be relatively self-evident, but at the lower levels, they're not easy to agree upon, especially in view of the great American ambivalence between merit and inclusion.

What should be easy to agree upon is that there is room for reform in admissions practices in most of higher education: placing more emphasis on demonstrated performance instead of seat time, credits earned, grade point average, and test scores would be a good place to start. There is even more room in public contracting, where old-boy networks still dominate, and in blue-collar civil service, where high scores on a paper-and-pencil test may be of far less relevance than good judgment, honesty, and a host of other intangibles. That those qualities are hard to measure hardly justifies abandoning them as selection criteria. Making selection and promotion criteria really relevant to the job might do more to open jobs for minorities and women in civil service – and indeed has already done so in the many instances where artificial criteria have been scrapped (such as in the cases of irrelevant height and weight thresholds for candidates for firefighters' jobs; unnecessary paper-and-pencil tests for laborers in public utility jobs; and artificial barriers to women in a variety of combat and combat-support roles in the military). Striking down more of these barriers and better aligning entrance criteria with the jobs they select for are likely to do more for diversity than all the overt race and gender preferences in the world. One of the reasons that race-based preferences are so vehemently defended is that few minorities believe that genuine equal opportunity, the other half of the race-blind promise, will ever really be provided.

Still, the gradual rollback of race preferences provides opportunities to create more relevant standards that are long overdue. Those opportunities go beyond the long litany of arguments about fairness and racism that have been made in the course of the debate over affirmative action. What it surely will not do is end the fight between the meritocrats and the inclusivists; in America that fight is almost as old as the Republic, and it will continue.

◆

Is Affirmative Action Doomed?

Ronald Dworkin

Is affirmative action unconstitutional? Does it violate the Fourteenth Amendment's guarantee of "equal protection of the laws" for universities to give preference to blacks and other minorities in the fierce competition for student places, as the best of our universities have done for thirty years? In 1978, the late Justice Lewis Powell, in his opinion in the Supreme Court's famous *Bakke* decision, ruled that racial preferences are permissible if their purpose is to improve racial diversity among students, and if they do not stipulate fixed minority quotas, but take race into account as one factor among many. Since four other justices in that case would have upheld even a quota system, five of the nine agreed that plans meeting Powell's tests were constitutional.

Many lawyers fear that the Supreme Court will soon reconsider its *Bakke* ruling, however, and declare that any racial preference in an admissions process is, after all, unconstitutional. In 1996, the Fifth Circuit Court of Appeals, in the *Hopwood* case, struck down the Texas Law School's affirmative action plan, and two of the three judges in the panel declared that recent Supreme Court decisions about affirmative action policies in areas other than education have already in effect overruled *Bakke,* so that all university affirmative action is now unconstitutional.

The Fifth Circuit's decision had immediate and, in the view of the Texas Law School's faculty, disastrous results: that school had admitted thirty-one black students in 1996, but it enrolled only four in 1997. The Supreme Court refused to review the decision, but the Center for Individual Rights, a Washington, D.C.-based organization that had facilitated the *Hopwood* litigation, has already filed a new lawsuit in Michigan challenging the University of Michigan's affirmative action plan, and other suits can be expected in other jurisdictions. The Supreme Court will have to rule on the matter soon.

It will be not only ironic but sad if the Court reverses its own longstanding ruling now, because dramatic evidence of the value of affirmative action in elite higher education has just become available. Critics of the policy have long argued, among other things, that it does more harm than good, because it exacerbates rather than reduces racial hostility, and because it damages the minority students who are selected for elite schools where they must compete with other students whose test scores and other academic qualifications are much higher than their own. But a new study – *The Shape of the River* by William G. Bowen and Derek Bok – draws on a huge database of information about student records and histories, and on sophisticated statistical techniques,

Reprinted from *The New York Review of Books*, November 5, 1998, pp. 56–60, with permission from The New York Review of Books. Copyright © 1998 NYREV, Inc.

not only to refute those claims but to demonstrate the contrary.[1] According to the *River* study, affirmative action has achieved remarkable success: it has produced higher rates of graduation among black college students, more black leaders in industry, the professions, and community and neighborhood service, and more sustained interaction and friendship among different races than would otherwise have been possible. If the Supreme Court declares affirmative action unconstitutional, the study declares, black enrollment in elite universities and colleges will be sharply reduced, and scarcely any black students will be admitted to the best law and medical schools. That would be a huge defeat for racial harmony and justice. Will the Supreme Court rule that the Constitution requires us to accept that defeat?

The Fifth Circuit judges are convinced that it will, and if we are to understand why they think so, and why so many commentators fear that they are right, we must explore the apparatus of legal doctrines and distinctions that the Court has developed, over the last several decades, to assist it in applying the equal protection clause I mentioned; for this is one of those instances, created by our constitutional system, in which America's social and political future hinges on careful legal analysis.

The equal protection clause does not, of course, protect citizens from all legal distinctions or classifications that work to their disadvantage. Government must decide which medical research to support, which art to subsidize, which industries or products to protect by tariffs or other trade policy, which businesses to regulate for environmental reasons, where to locate a new army base or airport or a new nuclear waste dump, and thousands of other matters that will affect the fates and fortunes of different citizens very differently. Officials make such decisions for a variety of reasons. In principle, they should aim at decisions that, though they benefit some citizens and disadvantage others, are in the general interest of the community as a whole. In practice, interest-group politics often play a crucial part: an industry that is denied protection or selected for regulation may have lost its legislative battle, not because a different decision would have been less in the public interest, but because it lacked the political power, on this occasion, to force that different decision.

The equal protection clause is violated, not whenever some group has lost an important decision on the merits of the case or through politics, but when its loss results from its special vulnerability to prejudice or hostility or stereotype and its consequent diminished standing – its second-class citizenship – in the political community. The clause does not guarantee each citizen that he will benefit equally from every political decision; it guarantees him only that he will be treated as an equal – with equal concern and respect – in the political processes and deliberations that produce those decisions.

But the Fourteenth Amendment therefore poses a special difficulty for the courts that must enforce it: it requires them to judge not merely the consequences of legislation for different groups, but the motive behind that legislation. Was the law that injures this or that group the product of a forbidden, prejudiced attitude toward that group, or of more benign motives? It is extremely difficult to attribute motives and attitudes to general legislation, not just because it is difficult to identify the psychological states of different individual legislators and other officials, but for the deeper reason that it is often unclear how we should translate those individual motives – and the motives and attitudes of the constituents in whose interests the legislation has supposedly been adopted – into an overall motive that we can attribute to the legislation itself.

In some cases, that judgment seems easy, at least in retrospect. The Court rightly decided, in 1954, that racial school segregation violated the equal protection rights of black children, because segregation signaled their inferiority and exclusion. It rightly decided, in 1996, that a Colorado state constitutional amendment forbidding any local antidiscrimination protection for homosexuals violated the equal protection rights of members of that group, because, as Justice Anthony Kennedy said, "the amendment seems inexplicable by anything but animus toward the class it affects … ."[2]

Other cases, however, are much more difficult to assess. Does a local rent-control ordinance, for example, express a theory about wise and fair housing management or a special hostility toward landlords as a class? It seems silly to invite judges to review the political sociology of every piece of legislation that anyone challenges, because they have neither the time nor the equipment for such studies. It also seems dangerous to democracy, because judges might overrule democratic decisions on the barest speculation of improper motives.

The courts have instead tried to approach the question of motive indirectly, through doctrines intended to "smoke out" improper motives by concentrating on the apparently more objective question of a law's actual effects. They subject all political decisions that are challenged on equal protection grounds to an initial threshold classification. If a decision imposes serious disadvantages on what the Supreme Court has called a "suspect" class – a class, according to one prominent definition, that is "saddled with such disabilities, or subjected to such a history of purposeful unequal treatment, or relegated to such a position of political powerlessness as to command extraordinary protection from the majoritarian political process" – then the decision is to be subject to "strict scrutiny." This means that it must be rejected as violating the equal protection clause unless the disadvantage can be shown to be essential in order to protect some "compelling" governmental interest. But if those whom a law disadvantages do not form such a "suspect" class – if they are only the members of a particular business or profession or the residents of a particular area, and are not different from their fellow citizens in any way historically associated with prejudice or antipathy – then that law is subject to only a "relaxed" scrutiny: it is constitutional unless it can be demonstrated to serve no purpose or point at all.

The initial assignment of any particular law or decision to one or the other of these "levels of scrutiny" has almost always proved final. As one leading commentator put it long ago, strict scrutiny is "'strict' in theory and fatal in fact,"[3] because almost no interest has seemed sufficiently "compelling" to justify imposing further disadvantage on a suspect class, and "relaxed" scrutiny is in effect no scrutiny at all, because some purpose or other can always be attributed to even the most inane legislation.

So lawyers considering the constitutionality of affirmative action programs naturally begin by asking whether such programs should be initially classified as requiring strict or only relaxed scrutiny. But they have great difficulty answering that question, because neither choice seems fully appropriate. On the one hand, affirmative action plans seem entitled to relaxed scrutiny, because though they use racial classifications, the group they mainly disadvantage – white applicants to colleges and universities – do not constitute a "suspect class," that is, a class that has been the victim of prejudice. But race is so closely associated with bias and favoritism that some racial classifications which seem benign on the surface might turn out, after a closer look, to be constitutionally offensive. Black municipal councils might conceivably have acted to favor black businesses out of racial solidarity, for example, or to punish innocent whites for the past racial crimes of their ancestors; a university admissions scheme that gives preference to blacks might conceivably have been constructed to reduce the number of Asian-Americans or Jews admitted.

Careful inspection would almost always disclose such improper motives – statistics could show whether any such group was disproportionately represented among the applicants displaced by affirmative action – but relaxed scrutiny would not permit that inspection. On the other hand, subjecting racial classifications that benefit "suspect" groups to the same standards of strict scrutiny as those classifications that impose further damage on those groups seems insensitive to the important moral differences between those two aims. It also seems perverse because, as the *River* study apparently demonstrates, affirmative action is one of the most effective weapons we have against the racism that strict scrutiny is designed to thwart.

So affirmative action presents a great challenge to the conventional doctrine, and lawyers and judges have suggested different responses to that challenge. The most direct – and I believe the most appealing – response would be to declare the level-of-scrutiny strategy inapposite to the problem. That strategy, as it has historically been understood and used, is designed to identify types of legislation that by their nature involve either so high a risk of invidious discrimination that invidiousness should be nearly irrevocably presumed or so low a risk that its possibility should be nearly irrevocably dismissed. Race-sensitive programs that are, on their face, designed to help a disadvantaged racial group fall into neither of these categories, and it is procrustean to try to force them into one or the other.

Instead, I believe, judges should inspect such plans, when they are challenged in litigation, on a more case-by-case basis: they should use, as Justice Thurgood Marshall once recommended, a "sliding-scale" approach in order to decide whether there is any convincing evidence that the racial classification actually does reflect prejudice or hostility of the kind forbidden by the equal protection clause.[4] Such an approach would take into account, among other pertinent factors, the character of the groups benefited and disadvantaged by the program, the racial or other character of the officials who have designed and will administer the plan, and whether the plan aims at a goal – like educational diversity, for example – that has historically been recognized as appropriate for the institution in question. It is true that this case-by-case approach to the affirmative action problem would require more judicial work and provide less predictability and guidance for lower courts, at least initially, until new rules of thumb and doctrinal strategies began to emerge. But any initial loss in predictability would be more than outweighed by the more accurate discrimination between valuable and invidious policies that greater flexibility would allow.

Supreme Court justices have disagreed for many years about whether to abandon the levels-of-scrutiny approach for affirmative action and, if not, about which level to choose. In two cases, the Court tried to solve the problem by defining an "intermediate" level of scrutiny, which requires that an affirmative action plan be shown to serve an "important" but not necessarily a "compelling" interest. But in recent cases, chiefly through a series of opinions written by Justice O'Connor, the Court has decided that all racial classifications, including those that are apparently designed to favor rather than injure suspect groups, are subject to strict scrutiny. In 1986, in the *Croson* case, the Court struck down a Richmond, Virginia, city council plan that required city contractors to subcontract at least 30 percent of the dollar amount of any contract to minority-owned firms. Richmond called its plan "remedial," and said it had adopted the plan "for the purpose of promoting wider participation by minority business enterprises in the construction of public projects."

O'Connor ruled that Richmond could properly claim a "compelling" interest in rectifying the continuing effects of past discrimination only if it had itself been the author of the injustice, either directly, by its own discriminatory practices, or "as a 'passive participant' in a system of racial exclusion practiced by elements of the local construction industry"; and she held that the city had not shown that its plan was carefully tailored to rectify only the effects of its own direct or passive discrimination. It could not satisfy strict scrutiny, she said, by claiming an interest in achieving a racially more diverse local construction industry, because there might be many reasons, other than the continuing effects of past discrimination, why a particular race was underrepresented in a particular industry, and it was not a permissible aim of government to pursue racial diversity or proportionality for its own sake.

The Fifth Circuit judges, in their *Hopwood* opinion striking down the Texas Law School plan, relied mainly on the Supreme Court's *Croson* decision to justify their claim that university affirmative action plans are now unconstitutional. The Texas Law School argued that its affirmative action plan was justified, even under a strict scrutiny test, because, among other things, affirmative action was necessary in order to produce a racially diverse student body – the goal that Powell had approved in *Bakke*. But the judges said that *Croson* and other cases had in effect overruled Powell's principle. These decisions had established the new rule that no state institution may use a racial classification for any purpose except to remedy the continuing effects of its own direct or indirect discrimination. The law school could not satisfy that test, the judges said, because it had ceased discriminating against minorities many years ago. Are those judges right that *Croson* and later cases have had that dramatic and devastating consequence? That is a crucial question for the future of American education and society, and it is important that the public understand the actual force of these Supreme Court precedents.

* * *

Universities are in a much stronger position than Richmond or the FCC was to dispel any suspicion that they seek racial diversity for improper underlying motives or on stereotypical assumptions. University admissions policies are not set by politicians, who might hope to court the votes of a racial bloc, but by faculty members, who are not running for office. Their interest in diversity is not novel or unusual, as Richmond's was, but traditional and recognized: no one disputes that large, mainly white, universities have a social and educational responsibility to seek a student body that is diverse in many ways, and any such university that abandoned that aim altogether would be behaving irresponsibly. Elite universities believe that it would now be irrational to seek diversity in geographical origin, in social class, and in cultural orientation, and not also to seek racial diversity.

Indeed, their failure to seek the latter dimension of diversity as well would make their general concern with diversity seem arbitrary. They have decided, and the *River* study amply confirms their view, that they cannot achieve racial diversity indirectly by relying on economic class as a proxy for race, or by using otherwise less efficient means to the hoped-for end. Any such policy would be not only disingenuous but harmful. Nor do universities rely, as O'Connor said the FCC did, on any presumed connection between race and belief, conviction, taste, culture, or attitude.

They seek racial diversity because race is itself important, unfortunately but inescapably, in contemporary America: it is vital that students of each race meet and work with, not just other students with other attitudes or culture, but students who are in fact of a different race. Nor would the courts be risking open-ended and indiscriminate racial preferences by continuing to permit affirmative action on the *Bakke* model. Universities have used such programs judiciously for a third of a century, with no tendency to expand them beyond sensible proportions.

These institutions have, moreover, a crucial stake in their academic reputations, both absolutely and relative to other comparable institutions, that would check any desire significantly to expand an admissions policy or curriculum that might threaten that reputation. Nor is there any genuine risk that race-sensitive admissions programs will be used as a pretense for disfavoring any other particular group of applicants. Any suspicion of that could be tested, as I said, using statistical means like those used in the *River* study, by analyzing the retrospectively rejected students to see whether they were disproportionately members of any suspect group.

There is ample evidence, moreover, that O'Connor, as well as several other members of the present Court, has already accepted that the search for racial diversity among students is a compelling interest that survives strict scrutiny. In 1986, in the *Wygant* case, the Supreme Court struck down a Michigan school board's collective bargaining agreement that gave minority schoolteachers special protection against layoffs: it rejected the school board's claim that its interest in correcting the effects of past discrimination in the community at large, or in providing black faculty "role models" with whom black students might identify, justified this racial classification. O'Connor wrote a separate opinion in which she noted that the board had not claimed that it had acted to protect racial diversity on its faculty, and that the Court was therefore not to be understood to have ruled out that interest as compelling. "Although its precise contours are uncertain," she said, "a state interest in the promotion of racial diversity has been found sufficiently 'compelling,' at least in the context of higher education, to support the use of racial considerations in furthering that interest."

O'Connor has several times, moreover, cited Powell's *Bakke* opinion, which declared diversity in higher education a compelling interest, as authority for her view that any racial classification must be subjected to strict scrutiny. She would hardly rely on that opinion with such force if she thought that Powell did not himself understand the implications of his strict scrutiny approach, or intended to lay down, under that name, a different doctrine from the one for which she cited his authority.

The argument is therefore strong that the *Bakke* principle, in force for over twenty years, remains good constitutional law, and that American colleges and universities may continue to rely on that principle to justify using race-sensitive admissions policies to secure a diverse student body. If I were defending such schemes in the courts, I would certainly emphasize that interest in student diversity, which seems enough, on its own, to ensure that the programs survive strict scrutiny. I must add, however, that I believe that the other institutional interest I mentioned – helping to redress the still-deplorable absence of blacks from key positions in government, politics, business, and the professions – is at least an equally important one that should also be recognized as sufficiently compelling to sustain race-sensitive admissions policies. One of the gravest problems of American society is the de facto racial stratification that has largely excluded blacks and other minorities from the highest ranks of power, wealth, and prestige; and past racial discrimination, as well as the vicious circle that robs black children of successful black leaders to emulate, has contributed substantially to that stratification.

Nevertheless, many statements sprinkled throughout the various Supreme Court opinions I have been discussing might well be read as hostile to that further, and different, justification of race-sensitive admissions policies, including Powell's statement, in *Bakke,* that medical schools may not use affirmative action just in order to increase the number of black doctors.

Several of the justices have declared that racial classifications cannot be justified as helping to cure the lingering effects of past "societal discrimination," and the *Wygant* decision rejected the claim that they can be justified as providing "role models" for black children. It might be, however, that these statements have not paid sufficient attention to the distinction that Justice Stevens has several times made – between backward-looking justifications of racial classifications as compensatory and forward-looking justifications that argue that such classifications may, in some circumstances, be in the general interest of the community as a whole.

Compensatory justifications suppose that affirmative action is necessary, as Scalia put it, to "make up" to minorities for damage done to their race or class in the past, and he was right to point out the mistake in supposing that one race "owes" another compensation. But universities do not use race-sensitive admission standards to compensate either individuals or groups: affirmative action is a forward-looking, not a backward-looking, enterprise, and the minority students whom it benefits have not necessarily been victims, as individuals, of any distinct injustice in the past. Great universities hope to train more blacks and other minority students not to repay them for past injustice, but to make the future better for everyone by helping to lift a curse that the past laid on us all.

O'Connor and other justices have worried that any broad and general remedial justification for affirmative action is too "amorphous" and "open-ended" because it would license racial preferences until every industry or social or professional stratum had the same racial and ethnic composition as the nation as a whole. But however genuine or inflated that concern might be as a worry about the consequences of government-imposed hiring or contracting regulations, it is distinctly out of place as an objection to university affirmative action plans. If any branch of government – whether Congress or a local city council – requires employers or contractors to hire a quota of black employees, or to set aside a quota of contracts for black firms, its decision ensures a particular racial representation in some segment of employment or industry. No more natural process of decision-making can alter or shape that racial structure so long as the government's program is in place. In such cases, government, and only government, decides how many members of each of the racial or ethnic groups it designates will fill which jobs in which sectors or roles or offices. Judges who are particularly sensitive to the danger that some of these decisions might be made out of improper motives will be reluctant to accept so broad a justification for them as the claim that they are necessary to prevent excluding one or another race from power, wealth, and prestige.

But colleges, universities, and professional schools use race-sensitive standards not in response to any central government mandate but through individual decisions by individual schools. They act, not to fix how many members of which races will occupy what roles in the overall economy and polity, which is in any case beyond their power, but only to increase the number of blacks and other minorities who are in the pool from which other citizens – employers, partners, patients, clients, voters, and colleagues acting in their own interests and for their own purposes – will choose employees, doctors, lawyers, and public officials in the normal way.

The distribution of position and power that affirmative action helps to achieve, that is, flows and changes naturally in accordance with millions of choices that people make for themselves. If the policy works to improve the overall position of any minority – as the *River* study suggests it has helped to improve the position of blacks – it does so only because other people have chosen to exploit the results of that policy: the greater range and variety of graduates with the motive, self-respect, and training to contribute effectively to their lives. Affirmative action in universities, in that way, makes the eventual economic and social structure of the community not more artificial but less so; it produces no balkanization, but helps to dissolve the balkanization now sadly in place.

If the justices recognize this aspect of what our best universities aim to do, as well as their academic need for educational diversity, then they will have served us particularly well. They will have acted not just as judges allowing a crucial educational initiative to continue, but as teachers helping to explain to the nation the true and continuing costs to everyone of our racist past, and the distinct promise of an educational policy that can help us all to achieve, if we really want it, a more perfect union.

Notes

1 William G. Bowen and Derek Bok, *The Shape of the River: Long-Term Consequences of Considering Race in College and University Admissions* (Princeton, N.J.: Princeton University Press, 1998).
2 *Romer v. Evans*, 116 S. Ct. 1620.
3 Gerald Gunther, "The Supreme Court, 1971 Term – Foreword: In Search of Evolving Doctrine on a Changing Court: A Model for a Newer Equal Protection," 86 *Harvard Law Review* 1, at 8 (1972).
4 Marshall endorsed the "sliding-scale" approach in his dissent in *San Antonio Independent School District v. Rodriguez*, 411 U.S. 1, at 98–99 (1973), *Furman v. Georgia*, 408 U.S. 238, 330 (1972), and *Dandridge v. Williams*, 397 U.S. 471, at 520–521 (1970).

6

Should the Ghetto Be "Dismantled"?

The Future of the Ghetto

Douglas S. Massey and Nancy A. Denton

The isolation of Negro from white communities is increasing rather than decreasing...Negro poverty is not white poverty. Many of its causes...are the same. But there are differences – deep, corrosive, obstinate differences – radiating painful roots into the community, the family, and the nature of the individual.

President Lyndon Johnson,
address to Howard University,
June 4, 1965

After persisting for more than fifty years, the black ghetto will not be dismantled by passing a few amendments to existing laws or by implementing a smattering of bureaucratic reforms. The ghetto is part and parcel of modern American society; it was manufactured by whites earlier in the century to isolate and control growing urban black populations, and it is maintained today by a set of institutions, attitudes, and practices that are deeply embedded in the structure of American life. Indeed, as conditions in the ghetto have worsened and as poor blacks have adapted socially and culturally to this deteriorating environment, the ghetto has assumed even greater importance as an institutional tool for isolating the byproducts of racial oppression: crime, drugs, violence, illiteracy, poverty, despair, and their growing social and economic costs.

For the walls of the ghetto to be breached at this point will require an unprecedented commitment by the public and a fundamental change in leadership at the highest levels. Residential segregation will only be eliminated from

American society when federal authorities, backed by the American people, become directly involved in guaranteeing open housing markets and eliminating discrimination from public life. Rather than relying on private individuals to identify and prosecute those who break the law, the U.S. Department of Housing and Urban Development and the Office of the Attorney General must throw their full institutional weight into locating instances of housing discrimination and bringing those who violate the Fair Housing Act to justice; they must vigorously prosecute white racists who harass and intimidate blacks seeking to exercise their rights of residential freedom; and they must establish new bureaucratic mechanisms to counterbalance the forces that continue to sustain the residential color line.

Given the fact that black poverty is exacerbated, reinforced, and perpetuated by racial segregation, that black-white segregation has not moderated despite the federal policies tried so far, and that the social costs of segregation inevitably cannot be contained in the ghetto, we argue that the nation has no choice but to launch a bold new initiative to eradicate the ghetto and eliminate segregation from American life. To do otherwise is to condemn the United States and the American people to a future of economic stagnation, social fragmentation, and political paralysis.

Race, Class, and Public Policy

In the United States today, public policy discussions regarding the urban underclass frequently devolve into debates on the importance of race versus class. However one defines the underclass, it is clear that African Americans are overrepresented within it. People who trace their ancestry to Africa are at greater risk than others of falling into poverty, remaining there for a long time, and residing in very poor neighborhoods. On almost any measure of social and economic well-being, blacks and Puerto Ricans come out near the bottom.

The complex of social and economic problems that beset people of African origin has led many observers to emphasize race over class in developing remedies for the urban underclass.[1] According to these theories, institutional racism is pervasive, denying blacks equal access to the resources and benefits of American society, notably in education and employment. Given this assessment, these observers urge the adoption of racial remedies to assist urban minorities; proposals include everything from special preference in education to affirmative action in employment.

Other observers emphasize class over race. The liberal variant of the class argument holds that blacks have been caught in a web of institutional and industrial change.[2] Like other migrants, they arrived in cities to take low-skilled jobs in manufacturing, but they had the bad fortune to become established in this sector just as rising energy costs, changing technologies, and increased foreign competition brought a wave of plant closings and layoffs. The service economy that arose to replace manufacturing industries generated high-paying jobs for those with education, but poorly paid jobs for those without it.

Just as this transformation was undermining the economic foundations of the black working class, the class theorists argue, the civil rights revolution opened up new opportunities for educated minorities. After the passage of the 1964 Civil Rights Act, well-educated blacks were recruited into positions of responsibility in government, academia, and business, and thus provided the basis for a new black middle class.[3] But civil rights laws could not provide high-paying jobs to poorly educated minorities when there were no jobs to give out. As a result, the class structure of the black community bifurcated into an affluent class whose fortunes were improving and a poverty class whose position was deteriorating.[4]

The conservative variant of the class argument focuses on the deleterious consequences of government policies intended to improve the economic position of the poor.[5] According to conservative reasoning, federal antipoverty programs implemented during the 1960s – notably the increases in Aid to Families with Dependent Children – altered the incentives governing the behavior of poor men and women. The accessibility and generosity of federal welfare programs reduced the attractiveness of marriage to poor women, increased the benefits of out-of-wedlock childbearing, and reduced the appeal of low-wage labor for poor men. As a result, female-headed families proliferated, rates of unwed childbearing rose, and male labor force participation rates fell. These trends drove poverty rates upward and created a population of persistently poor, welfare-dependent families.

Race- and class-based explanations for the underclass are frequently discussed as if they were mutually exclusive. Although liberal and conservative class theorists may differ with respect to the specific explanations they propose, both agree that white racism plays a minor role as a continuing cause of urban poverty; except for acknowledging the historical legacy of racism, their accounts are essentially race-neutral. Race theorists, in contrast, insist on the primacy of race in American society and emphasize its continuing role in perpetuating urban poverty; they view class-based explanations suspiciously, seeing them as self-serving ideologies that blame the victim.[6]

By presenting the case for segregation's present role as a central cause of urban poverty, we seek to end the specious opposition of race and class. The issue is not whether race *or* class perpetuates the urban underclass, but how race *and* class *interact* to undermine the social and economic well-being of black Americans. We argue that race operates powerfully through urban housing markets, and that racial segregation interacts with black class structure to produce a uniquely disadvantaged neighborhood environment for African Americans.

If the decline of manufacturing, the suburbanization of employment, and the proliferation of unskilled service jobs brought rising rates of poverty and income inequality to blacks, the negative consequences of these trends were exacerbated and magnified by segregation. Segregation concentrated the deprivation created during the 1970s and 1980s to yield intense levels of social and economic isolation. As poverty was concentrated, moreover, so were all social traits associated with it, producing a structural niche within which welfare dependency and joblessness could flourish and become normative. The expectations of the urban poor were changed not so much by generous AFDC payments as by the spatial concentration of welfare recipients, a condition that was structurally built into the black experience by segregation.

If our viewpoint is correct, then public policies must address both race and class issues if they are to be successful. Race-conscious steps need to be taken to dismantle the institutional apparatus of segregation, and class-specific policies must be implemented to improve the socioeconomic status of minorities. By themselves, programs targeted to low-income minorities will fail because they will be swamped by powerful environmental influences arising from the disastrous neighborhood conditions that blacks experience because of segregation. Likewise, efforts to reduce segregation will falter unless blacks acquire the socioeconomic resources that enable them to take full advantage of urban housing markets and the benefits they distribute.

Although we focus in this chapter on how to end racial segregation in American cities, the policies we advocate cannot be pursued to the exclusion of broader efforts to raise the class standing of urban minorities. Programs to dismantle the ghetto must be accompanied by vigorous efforts to end discrimination in other spheres of American life and by class-specific policies designed to raise educational levels, improve the quality of public schools, create employment, reduce crime, and strengthen the family. Only a simultaneous attack along all fronts has any hope of breaking the cycle of poverty that has become deeply rooted within the ghetto. Before discussing policies to end residential segregation, however, we take a quick look at preliminary data from the 1990 Census to see if there is any hint of progress toward integration under current policies.

Segregation in the 1980s

As this [essay] was being completed, early data from the 1990 Census had just become available to update the segregation patterns we observed for the 1970s. Although a complete analysis of the 1990 data is beyond the scope of this brief section, a general sense of trends can be gleaned from table 1, which presents indices of black-white residential dissimilarity computed for the thirty largest metropolitan black communities in 1970, 1980, and 1990. These indices give the relative percentage of blacks who would have to change their census tract (i.e., neighborhood) of residence in order to achieve an even, or desegregated, residential pattern.[7]

Little of the information presented in earlier chapters leads us to expect significant declines in black-white segregation during the 1980s, and segregation indices computed for northern metropolitan areas confirm our pessimistic expectations. In the north, the prevailing pattern during the 1980s was one of stasis: the average index changed by only 2.3 percentage points (compared with 4.4 points during the prior decade), and of the eighteen northern metropolitan areas shown, thirteen had 1990 indices within 3 points of their 1980 values (five were actually a little higher). Only Boston, Columbus, Kansas City, Los Angeles, and St. Louis displayed declines worth mentioning; but at the average rate of change they displayed, it would take northern areas

Table 1   Trends in black-white segregation in thirty metropolitan areas with largest black populations, 1970–90

Metropolitan area	1970	1980	1990
Northern areas			
Boston	81.2	77.6	68.2
Buffalo	87.0	79.4	81.8
Chicago	91.9	87.8	85.8
Cincinnati	76.8	72.3	75.8
Cleveland	90.8	87.5	85.1
Columbus	81.8	71.4	67.3
Detroit	88.4	86.7	87.6
Gary–Hammond–E. Chicago	91.4	90.6	89.9
Indianapolis	81.7	76.2	74.3
Kansas City	87.4	78.9	72.6
Los Angeles–Long Beach	91.0	81.1	73.1
Milwaukee	90.5	83.9	82.8
New York	81.0	82.0	82.2
Newark	81.4	81.6	82.5
Philadelphia	79.5	78.8	77.2
Pittsburgh	75.0	72.7	71.0
St. Louis	84.7	81.3	77.0
San Francisco–Oakland	80.1	71.7	66.8
Average	84.5	80.1	77.8
Southern areas			
Atlanta	82.1	78.5	67.8
Baltimore	81.9	74.7	71.4
Birmingham	37.8	40.8	71.7
Dallas–Ft. Worth	86.9	77.1	63.1
Greensboro–Winston Salem	65.4	56.0	60.9
Houston	78.1	69.5	66.8
Memphis	75.9	71.6	69.3
Miami	85.1	77.8	71.8
New Orleans	73.1	68.3	68.8
Norfolk–Virginia Beach	75.7	63.1	50.3
Tampa–St. Petersburg	79.9	72.6	69.7
Washington, D.C.	81.1	70.1	66.1
Average	75.3	68.3	66.5

Sources: For 1970 and 1980: Douglas S. Massey and Nancy A. Denton, "Trends in the Residential Segregation of Blacks, Hispanics, and Asians: 1970–1980," *American Sociological Review* 52 (1987), pp. 815–16. For 1990: Roderick J. Harrison and Daniel H. Weinberg, "Racial and Ethnic Segregation in 1990," presented at the annual meetings of the Population Association of America, April 30–May 2, 1992, Denver, Co.

another twenty-eight years just to reach the upper bound of the moderate range (about 60). At the average rate of change across all northern areas, this threshold would not be reached for another seventy-seven years. As of 1990, eight northern metropolitan areas (Buffalo, Chicago, Cleveland, Detroit, Gary, Milwaukee, New York, and Newark) had segregation indices above 80, indicating an extreme separation of the races.

Segregation trends in southern metropolitan areas are more complex. Although average segregation levels did not change much between 1980 and 1990 (the mean dropped by only 1.8 percentage points), this overall stability was achieved by counterbalancing several different trends. Modest but significant declines in segregation occurred in six of the twelve southern metropolitan areas, but these were offset by a 5-point increase in Greensboro, and a very marked increase of 31 points in Birmingham, Alabama (where blacks were unusually integrated in earlier years). Segregation levels showed no significant change in Houston, Memphis, New Orleans, and Tampa (where the total change was under 3 points).

In general, southern metropolitan areas appear to be converging to a level of black-white segregation in the range of 65 to 70: with one exception, those areas with indices lying below this range in 1980 increased their segregation, whereas those with indices above it decreased; and those with segregation levels in that range stayed roughly constant. An average segregation index of 67 would put southern metropolitan areas about 10 points below their northern counterparts, yielding a north–south differential close to the historical average. This level of racial segregation remains well within the high range, and at the average level of change recorded during the 1980s it would take southern areas another thirty-six years to cross into the moderate range of segregation.

Thus there is little in recent data to suggest that processes of racial segregation have moderated much since 1980, particularly in the north, where segregation remains high and virtually constant. Among the thirty areas we examined, eighteen had indices above 70 in 1990, seventeen experienced no significant change over the prior decade, and twenty-nine displayed 1990 indices that could be described as high according to conventional criteria. Given that these thirty areas contain 60% of all urban blacks in the United States, we conclude that the ghetto remains very much a part of the urban black experience. Racial segregation still constitutes a fundamental cleavage in American society.

*   *   *

Dismantling the Ghetto

Public policies to end racial segregation must attack racial discrimination in private housing markets, where 98% of all dwellings are allocated. In particular, they must interrupt the institutionalized process of neighborhood racial turnover, which is the ultimate mechanism by which the ghetto is reproduced and maintained. Racial turnover is built into the structure of urban housing markets through a combination of white prejudice and racial discrimination, which restrict black access to most white neighborhoods and systematically channel black housing demand to a few black or racially mixed areas.

The elimination of racial barriers in urban housing markets requires the direct institutional involvement of the federal government. To an unprecedented degree the U.S. Department of Housing and Urban Development, in particular, must fully commit itself to fair housing enforcement.

First, HUD must increase its financial assistance to local fair housing organizations to increase their ability to investigate and prosecute individual complaints of housing discrimination. Grants made to local agencies dedicated to fair housing enforcement will enable them to expand their efforts by hiring more legal staff, implementing more extensive testing programs, and making their services more widely available. In the early history of fair housing, many testers and legal assistants were funded by federal programs such as the Comprehensive Education and Training Act and the Office of Economic Opportunity. The elimination of these programs by the Reagan Administration undercut the ability of local organizations to enforce fair housing law, and these cuts must be restored if racial discrimination is to be overcome.

But spirited individual prosecution, even when federally assisted, is not enough. As a second step, HUD must establish a permanent testing program capable of identifying realtors who engage in a pattern of discrimination. A special unit dedicated to the regular administration of large-scale housing audits should be created in HUD under the Assistant Secretary for Fair Housing and Equal Opportunity. Audits of randomly selected realtors should be conducted annually within metropolitan areas that have large black communities, and when evidence of systematic discrimination is uncovered, the department should compile additional evidence and turn it over to the Attorney General for vigorous prosecution.

Neither of these two proposals requires significant changes in fair housing law. Indeed, the 1988 Fair Housing Amendments, in making it easier to pursue discriminations and increasing the costs for those who are caught, make the 1990s a particularly opportune time to redouble enforcement efforts. The new law authorized a Fair Housing Initiatives Program at HUD to fund state and local governments and nonprofit corporations seeking to carry out programs to prevent or eliminate discriminatory housing practices. The amendments empowered HUD to initiate investigations on its own, without a prior complaint of discrimination, clearing the way for a bureaucratically based testing program.

Racial discrimination is a problem not only in real estate transactions, however, but also in the home loan industry, where blacks are rejected at rates considerably above those of whites. Congress therefore has required financial institutions to compile detailed racial data on their lending practices. The 1974 Equal Credit Opportunity Act requires them to tabulate the race of clients they accept and reject for home loans; the 1975 Home Mortgage Disclosure Act requires them to report which neighborhoods receive mortgage funds; and the 1977 Community Reinvestment Act requires them to demonstrate that they have provided credit to areas that have been unable to secure capital in the past.

But despite these requirements, little has been done with these data to monitor lender compliance with fair housing statutes. As a third policy initiative, a staff should be created under the Assistant Secretary for Fair Housing and Equal Opportunity to scrutinize lending data for unusually high rates of rejection among minority applicants and black neighborhoods. When the rejection rates cannot be explained statistically by social, demographic, economic, or other background factors, a systematic case study of the bank's lending practices should be initiated. If clear evidence of discrimination is uncovered, the case should be referred to the Attorney General for prosecution, and if not, an equal opportunity lending plan should be conciliated, implemented, and monitored.

Because HUD continues to play a large role in overseeing federally subsidized housing, a fourth policy initiative must be a more vigorous promotion of desegregation under the affirmative mandate of the Fair Housing Act. Given the reality of intense opposition to the construction of projects outside the ghetto, significant desegregation is unlikely to occur by building new projects. More promise has been shown through the use of subsidized rental vouchers that enable poor blacks to obtain units through the private market. In one evaluation of the remedy arising from the *Gautreaux* decision, blacks who moved into integrated settings through the use of rental vouchers experienced greater success in education and employment than did a comparable group who remained behind in the ghetto; and, significantly, participants did not encounter the kind of white hostility commonly experienced by project inhabitants.[8] Funding for housing certificate programs authorized under Section 8 of the 1974 Housing and Community Development Act should therefore be expanded, and programs modeled on the Gautreaux Demonstration Project should be more widely implemented.

Finally, effective enforcement of the Fair Housing Act requires prompt judicial action and timely relief. Since 1968, fair housing enforcement has been a long, drawn-out, expensive, and emotionally draining process for plaintiffs, even if they ultimately prevail. Congress recognized this problem in 1988 when it passed amendments to create an administrative process for adjudicating fair housing cases; but acting on a motion by Senator Orrin Hatch of Utah, Congress also granted defendants the right to request a trial in federal court.

Most accused discriminators elect to have their cases heard in federal court, which slows down the judicial process considerably and defeats the new administrative hearing process. Because defendants are usually realtors or developers with significant financial resources, a long trial provides them with a decided advantage over plaintiffs, whose resources are generally more modest. In order to expedite fair housing judgments and grant more timely relief to victims of discrimination, Congress should amend the Fair Housing Act to require that initial trials be held before an administrative law judge and to provide access to federal courts only upon appeal.

Even if these five policy initiatives are successful in lowering racial barriers in urban housing markets, however, they are not likely to end racial segregation unless black demand is simultaneously allowed to spread more evenly around metropolitan housing markets. To a great extent, blacks are reluctant to enter white neighborhoods because they fear becoming victims of racial hate crimes.[9] These fears can only be allayed by vigorous and swift punishment of those who commit crimes against minority families seeking to integrate white neighborhoods.

Given the overriding importance of residential mobility to individual well-being, and in view of the great social and economic harm done to the nation by segregation, hate crimes directed against black in-migrants must be considered more severe than ordinary acts of vandalism or assault. Rather than being left to local authorities, they should be prosecuted at the federal level as violations of the victim's civil rights. Stiff financial penalties and jail terms should be imposed, not in recognition of the severity of the vandalism or violence itself, but in acknowledgment of the serious damage that segregation does to the nation's well-being.

Black housing demand is also geographically skewed by racial segregation within the real estate industry itself. Most real estate brokers depend on the cooperation of other agents for sales and referrals, a fact that is formalized through multiple listing services (MLS). These services provide extensive listings of properties for sale or rent throughout a metropolitan area, and when MLS transactions are completed, the commission is divided between the participating agents. But these listings typically cover only white suburbs and select city neighborhoods, and are available only to agents serving those areas; brokers serving black communities generally do not have access to these services. Moreover, access is typically controlled by local real estate boards, and in some instances suburban brokers who sell to blacks have been denied membership on the board and hence prevented from using multiple listing services.[10]

Under prevailing marketing practices in the real estate industry, therefore, homeseekers living in segregated black neighborhoods do not have full access to information about wider housing opportunities, and black housing searches are consequently much less efficient than those of whites. Frequently blacks are forced to rely on drives through neighborhoods in search of "For Sale" signs.[11] If black demand is ever to be expressed naturally and widely, realtors serving black clients must be given complete access to multiple listing services. Congress should adopt legislation removing monopoly control of multiple listing services from local realty boards; access to the service should be open to all agents willing to pay a standard membership fee, irrespective of their race or that of their clients.

HUD should also establish new programs, and expand existing programs, to train realtors in fair housing marketing procedures. Agents catering primarily to white clients should be instructed about advertising and marketing methods to ensure that blacks in segregated communities gain access to information about housing opportunities outside the ghetto; agents serving the black share of the market should be trained to market homes throughout the metropolitan area and should be instructed especially in how to use multiple listing services. HUD officials and local fair housing groups should carefully monitor whether realtors serving blacks are given access to the MLS.

Such programs should be implemented in concert with a strengthening of the Voluntary Affirmative Marketing Agreement. In strengthening the terms of the agreement, the list of realtors that signed it should once again be made public, the use of testers should be encouraged, and the responsibilities of realtors to enforce the Fair Housing Act should be spelled out explicitly.

Although it is important for HUD to work with the National Association of Realtors and local real estate boards, efforts should also be made to monitor realtor compliance with Title VIII. Ultimately the Assistant Secretary for Fair Housing and Equal Opportunity at HUD must take a more active role in overseeing real estate advertising and marketing practices, two areas that have received insufficient federal attention in the past. Realtors in selected metropolitan areas should be sampled and their advertising and marketing practices regularly examined for conformity with federal fair housing regulations. HUD should play a larger role in ensuring that black homeseekers are not being systematically and deliberately overlooked by prevailing marketing practices.

The Case for National Action

For the most part, the policies we have recommended do not require major changes in legislation. What they require is political will. Given the will to end segregation, the necessary funds and legislative measures will follow. But political will is precisely what has been lacking over the past several decades, and resistance to desegregation continues to be strong. For each proposal that is advanced to move the fair housing agenda forward, there are other efforts to set it back.

At the time the 1988 Fair Housing Amendments were being debated, for example, Senator Orrin Hatch of Utah introduced a bill endorsed by the National Association of Realtors to limit the filing of fair housing suits to parties actually intending to rent or buy real estate (as opposed to testers, fair housing staff members, or others harmed by discriminatory practices), thereby attempting to undo twenty years of court decisions that had broadened the question of standing and made fair housing enforcement easier. The Hatch bill also would have banned the hearing of fair housing cases before administrative law judges and relied instead on secret conciliation as the principal means of fair housing enforcement.

After the Hatch bill was discarded in favor of legislation sponsored by Senators Kennedy and Specter, the Reagan Administration offered regulations implementing the amendments that could have banned a variety of affirmative marketing strategies used by fair housing organizations. In addition, the National Association of Realtors attempted to limit funding for the Fair Housing Initiatives Program, which was intended to support local antidiscrimination efforts; and in 1991, a House banking subcommittee quietly added a provision to pending legislation that would have exempted more than 85% of U.S. banks from the 1977 Community Reinvestment Act, which required financial institutions to meet the credit needs of low-income minority areas.

Later that year the Bush Administration proposed abolishing the U.S. Commission on Civil Rights, which for years had kept pressure on HUD to improve fair housing enforcement.[12]

Although race has become embroiled in partisan politics during the 1980s and 1990s, residential desegregation is not intrinsically a cause of either the right or the left; it is neither liberal nor conservative, democrat nor republican. Rather it is a bipartisan agenda in the national interest. The ghetto must be dismantled because only by ending segregation will we eliminate the manifold social and economic problems that follow from its persistence.

For conservatives, the cause of desegregation turns on the issue of market access. We have marshaled extensive evidence to show that one particular group – black Americans – is systematically denied full access to a crucial market. Housing markets are central to individual social and economic well-being because they distribute much more than shelter; they also distribute a variety of resources that shape and largely determine one's life chances. Along with housing, residential markets also allocate schooling, peer groups, safety, jobs, insurance costs, public services, home equity, and, ultimately, wealth. By tolerating the persistent and systematic disenfranchisement of blacks from housing markets, we send a clear signal to one group that hard work, individual enterprise, sacrifice, and aspirations don't matter; what determines one's life chances is the color of one's skin.

For liberals, the issue is one of unfinished business, for residential segregation is the most important item remaining on the nation's civil rights agenda. In many areas of civil life, desegregation has occurred; in the south, Jim Crow is dead, and throughout the country blacks are accepted in unions, sports, entertainment, journalism, politics, government, administration, and academia. Many barriers have fallen, but still the residential color line remains – and from residential segregation follows a host of deadly social ills that continue to undercut and overwhelm the progress achieved in other areas.

Residential desegregation should be considered an effort of national unity; any other course of action is politically indefensible. For conservatives, turning away from the task means denying the importance of markets and individual enterprise; for liberals it means sweeping the last piece of unfinished civil rights business under the rug. Ultimately, however, residential desegregation requires a moral commitment and a bipartisan leadership that have been lacking among politicians for the past two decades. Without a willingness to lead and take risks on the part of elected officials, and without a will to change on the part of the American people, none of the legal changes and policy solutions we propose will succeed.

For America, the failure to end segregation will perpetuate a bitter dilemma that has long divided the nation. If segregation is permitted to continue, poverty will inevitably deepen and become more persistent within a large share of the black community, crime and drugs will become more firmly rooted, and social institutions will fragment further under the weight of deteriorating conditions. As racial inequality sharpens, white fears will grow, racial prejudices will be reinforced, and hostility toward blacks will increase, making the problems of racial justice and equal opportunity even more insoluble.

Until we face up to the difficult task of dismantling the ghetto, the disastrous consequences of residential segregation will radiate outward to poison American society. Until we decide to end the long reign of American apartheid, we cannot hope to move forward as a people and a nation.

Notes

1   See Douglas G. Glasgow, *The Black Underclass: Poverty, Unemployment, and Entrapment of Ghetto Youth* (San Francisco: Jossey-Bass, 1980); Alphonso Pinkney, *The Myth of Black Progress* (Cambridge: Cambridge University Press, 1984); Charles V. Willie, "The Inclining Significance of Race," *Society* 15 (1978), pp. 10, 12–15.

2   See Theodore Hershberg, Alan N. Burstein, Eugene P. Ericksen, Stephanie W. Greenberg, and William L. Yancey, "A Tale of Three Cities: Blacks, Immigrants, and Opportunity in Philadelphia, 1850–1880, 1930, 1970," in *Philadelphia: Work, Space, Family and Group Experience in the 19th Century*, ed. Theodore Hershberg (New York: Oxford University Press, 1981), pp. 461–91; John D. Kasarda, "Caught in the Web of Change," *Society* 21 (1983), pp. 41–7; John D. Kasarda, "Urban Change and Minority Opportunities," in *The New Urban Reality*, ed. Paul E. Peterson (Washington, D.C.: Brookings Institution, 1985), pp. 33–68; John D. Kasarda, "Jobs, Migration, and Emerging Urban Mismatches," in *Urban Change and Poverty*, ed. Michael G. H. McCeary and Lawrence E. Lynn, Jr. (Washington, D.C.: National Academy Press, 1988), pp. 148–98; John F. Kain, "Housing Segregation, Negro Employment, and Metropolitan Decentralization," *Quarterly Journal of Economics* 82 (1968), pp. 175–97; William Julius Wilson, *The Declining Significance of Race* (Chicago: University of Chicago Press, 1978); William Julius Wilson, *The Truly Disadvantaged* (Chicago: University of Chicago Press, 1987).

3   Bart Landry, *The New Black Middle Class* (Berkeley: University of California Press, 1987).

4   Douglas S. Massey and Mitchell L. Eggers, "The Ecology of Inequality: Minorities and the Concentration of Poverty, 1970–1980," *American Journal of Sociology* 95 (1990), pp. 1153–88.

5   See Lawrence M. Mead, *Beyond Entitlement: The Social Obligations of Citizenship* (New York: Free Press, 1986); Charles Murray, *Losing Ground: American Social Policy, 1950–1980* (New York: Basic Books, 1984).

6   William Ryan, *Blaming the Victim* (New York: Random House, 1971); Willie, "The Inclining Significance of Race."

7   See David R. James and Karl E. Taeuber, "Measures of Segregation," in *Sociological Methodology 1985*, ed. Nancy Tuma (San Francisco: Jossey-Bass, 1985), pp. 1–32; Douglas S. Massey and Nancy A. Denton, "The Dimensions of Residential Segregation," *Social Forces* 67 (1988), pp. 281–315.

8   James E. Rosenbaum, Marilynn J. Kulieke, and Leonard S. Rubinowitz, "White Suburban Schools' Responses to Low-Income Black Children: Sources of Success and Problems," *Urban Review* 20 (1988), pp. 28–41; James E. Rosenbaum and Susan J. Popkin, "Employment and Earnings of Low-Income Blacks Who Move to Middle Class Suburbs," in *The Urban Underclass*, ed. Christopher Jencks and Paul E. Peterson (Washington, D.C.: Brookings Institution, 1991), pp. 342–56.

9   Reynolds Farley, Suzanne Bianchi, and Diane Colasanto, "Barriers to the Racial
    Integration of Neighborhoods: The Detroit Case," *Annals of the American
    Academy of Political and Social Science* 441 (1979), pp. 97–113.
10 John Yinger, "The Racial Dimension of Urban Housing Markets in the 1980s,"
    in *Divided Neighborhoods: Changing Patterns of Racial Segregation*, ed. Gary A.
    Tobin (Newbury Park, Calif.: Sage Publications, 1987), pp. 43–67.
11 Robert W. Lake, "The Fair Housing Act in a Discriminatory Market: The
    Persisting Dilemma," *Journal of the American Planning Association* 47 (1981),
    pp. 48–58.
12 See U.S. Commission on Civil Rights, *A Report of the Racial and Ethnic Impact
    of the Section 235 Program* (Washington, D.C.: U.S. Government Printing Office,
    1971); U.S. Commission on Civil Rights, *Equal Opportunity in Housing*
    (Washington, D.C.: U.S. Government Printing Office, 1974): U.S. Commission on
    Civil Rights, *The Federal Fair Housing Enforcement Effort* (Washington, D.C.:
    U.S. Government Printing Office, 1979).

◆

The Complexities of a
Public Housing Community

Larry Bennett and Adolph Reed, Jr.

Cabrini-Green has achieved legendary status among public housing projects in the United States. For many years, Chicago-based newspaper reporters and television news crews have visited the neighborhood to examine its physical decay or to post updates on its periodic waves of gang violence. In 1981, during Mayor Byrne's brief stay in Cabrini-Green, the neighborhood won a flash of national attention. More recently, a number of widely publicized violent criminal incidents, notably the Dantrell Davis shooting in 1992 that set in motion Vincent Lane's redevelopment campaign, have occurred on Cabrini-Green's grounds. Since the Davis murder, the project has received ongoing national news coverage as a barometer of the efforts to regenerate public housing in major American cities.

Invariably, the journalists and public figures who have sought to characterize Cabrini-Green have emphasized its physically appalling, socially deviant features. For example, Vincent Lane once vowed that his Hope VI redevelopment proposal would substitute a "normal neighborhood" for the existing public housing complex.[1] In the more carefully bureaucratic prose of the CHA's 1993 Hope VI proposal to HUD, Lane's view is elaborated: "This isolation, over time, is also reflected in an absence of external public, private and social service resources available to the community. Like many of Chicago's public housing and low income communities, the Cabrini-Green area and families are chronically underserved."[2]

Another characteristic view of Cabrini-Green was expressed by journalist Steve Bogira, who in the mid-1980s visited a number of Cabrini-Green families touched by gang violence and titled his resulting article in the *Chicago Reader* "Prisoners of the War Zone." Kevin Coyle, author of *Hardball*, a book chronicling the fortunes of a Cabrini-based Little League baseball team, emphasized the project's physical harshness in his initial description of Cabrini-Green: "From afar, each building appears to have been formed out of a single gargantuan brick and shoved endlong into the earth. The only signs of life come from the windows, many of which display shades, greenery, or in a few cases, lace curtains. Many others, however, are burned out, empty, hollow. It is the empty windows, particularly those on the upper floors, to which the eye is instinctively drawn."[3]

Excerpted from *Without Justice For All*, ed. Adolph Reed, Jr. (Boulder: Westview Press, 1999), pp. 195–202 and 207–8. Copyright © 1999 by Westview Press, a member of Perseus Books, L.L.C. Reprinted by permission of Westview Press.

Abnormality, danger, emptiness: these are the terms that key most Chicagoans' understanding of Cabrini-Green. Aside from the consistently negative quality of these depictions, they share another feature: each is the product of a visitor to Cabrini-Green – possibly a well-intentioned visitor – but nonetheless someone who spends a limited time in the neighborhood and then withdraws.

A survey of the poems, stories, and essays that appeared in the local newspaper *Voices of Cabrini* (VOC), which was produced from early 1993 until mid-1994 (and briefly revived the following year), communicates another sense of Cabrini-Green. For example, in "A Mother's Prayer," Margaret Smith begins:

> I raised my children
> with a smile, hugs, love,
> and lots of good food.
> We sing and dance
> and swing our hair to
> the beat of our favorite raps.
> O' Lord I pray that they
> finish school that's the hope
> I have for them that it
> will become a reality one day ...[4]

However, *Voices of Cabrini* is not simply a compendium of warm sentiments. In "Untitled," another Cabrini-Green mother, Gloria Corkrell, observes:

> I live in the ghetto, But I won't
> let the ghetto live in me.
> Through the bullets, the drugs, and the
> crime trying to raise a family of kids ... three.
> Alone and on my own without a man
> raising my children as a single Parent I know I can.
> Though my job is tough, hard and a heavy load,
> All I can do is my best to keep my children
> On the right road ...[5]

Cabrini-Green residents require no reminder of the hazards offered by their surroundings, as well by some of the other tenants in the public housing complex. Nevertheless, CHA and city of Chicago decisionmakers should not suppose that there are not thousands of family-oriented, law-abiding residents of Cabrini-Green or that these Cabrini-Green residents have not fashioned a working community.

Social Networks and Neighborhood Institutions

The residents of Cabrini-Green, and most assuredly their social networks, their institutions, and their neighborhood's physical environment, do indeed bear the marks of the project's turbulent circumstances. Nevertheless, Cabrini-Green is a community dense in social ties and the home of many committed residents. Without the material affluence of middle-class people, Cabrini-Green's low-income residents routinely depend on relatives and neighbors for short-term use of household items and articles of clothing, child care, shopping assistance, and advice and companionship. As one of our informants (who, though wishing to remain in Cabrini-Green, recently moved into an apartment a few blocks away) put it: "It was a family.... If somebody died, family would come and see about you; if you're hungry, they feed your kids; if the kids are outside and they're getting their kid a popsicle, they'll get all of them a popsicle; if you come upstairs with your hands full of groceries, everybody'll help to take your groceries in. That's in Cabrini ... PERIOD."[6] Another informant estimated that he had about fifty local relatives in Cabrini-Green, "plus their kids." This same individual, who is the father of seven, emphasized how important it is for him to be able to depend on neighbors to watch after his children – a favor that he is more than willing to return when he has the time.

Beyond the family and friendship networks that give structure to the lives of many Cabrini-Green residents, the neighborhood – quite contrary to the depiction offered in the 1993 Hope VI proposal – is served by a variety of churches and social service agencies. Among the *Voices of Cabrini* features was a church directory, which included as many as twenty local congregations. Some of these churches represent very small congregations, but others, such as Saint Joseph's Roman Catholic Church on North Orleans Street, play a significant role in the larger community's life. There are ten to fifteen social service agencies operating in and near Cabrini-Green. Table 1 identifies some of the more important agencies and congregations in the neighborhood.

Table 1   Selected Cabrini-Green area social service agencies, religious congregations, and community-based organizations

Organization	Main program/services
Chicago Center for Law and Justice	Legal services
Al Carter Youth Foundation	Youth sports
Fellowship of Friends	Tutoring, college preparation
Fourth Presbyterian Church	Center for Whole Life (pre-school)
Holy Family Lutheran Church	Day care, legal services, Cabrini Alive!
Lasalle Street Church	Day care, tutoring, family counseling
Lower North Center	Youth recreation, leadership development, Project Lead
St. Joseph's Roman Catholic Church	Youth and after-school programs
St. Matthews United Methodist Church	Girl Scouts, community meeting space
Montgomery Ward Tutoring Program	Primary- and secondary-level tutoring
Winfield Moody Drop-in Center	Family counseling, drug/AIDS awareness, pregnancy prevention, youth field trips
Winfield Moody Health Center	Health and social services

Sources: CHA documents; Cabrini-Green LAC

Locally based agencies offer a wide array of services: medical treatment, youth-oriented sports programming, individual and family counseling, and legal assistance. Bounding the Cabrini-Green area on the north, the New City YMCA's LEED Council offers a variety of educational and workforce preparation programs. The staffs of most (possibly all) of these organizations would agree that the local demand for their services stretches their resources to the limit, but this is quite a different situation from the one presented in the 1993 Hope VI proposal: that the current Cabrini-Green is "isolated" and lacking in social service resources.

The Cabrini-Green area's institutional network is not simply the consequence of programs developed to serve the public housing population or of coincidence – agencies located in the area before the arrival of public housing. Cabrini-Green's Local Advisory Council dates from the 1970s, and over the past quarter century it has dealt with issues such as management of building laundry rooms, architectural modifications (including the closing in of the high-rise building open-air corridors, or "ramps"), home appliance orders, and, in recent years, the evolving plans to redevelop the project and its adjoining neighborhood.

Since the 1980s, several groups of tenants have been working to develop the Resident Management Corporations (RMCs) that will soon provide most building services throughout the Cabrini-Green complex. The president of the Cabrini Rowhouse RMC estimates that a group of approximately twenty residents has worked to build that organization, which has taken shape, in part, through work accomplished at weekly meetings dating back to 1993. Since the spring of 1996, the four Cabrini-Green RMCs have been producing and distributing a newsletter.

Despite the Cabrini-Green LAC's growing distrust of CHA/city redevelopment plans for the neighborhood, many local residents have developed proposals or participated in initiatives associated with the Hope VI process. The residents' Human Capital Development Committee has funded an array of programs involving Cabrini-Green tenants in community service–oriented efforts. Cabrini Alive! predates the Hope VI era, bringing together Near North Ministerial Alliance volunteers and Cabrini-Green residents to rehabilitate project apartments. For several years in the early 1990s, Cabrini Greens, whose participants were mainly local teenagers, raised produce for sale to neighborhood residents and at a local farmers' market. Since 1994, several dozen Cabrini-Green teenagers have participated in Project Lead, a program that emphasizes youth decisionmaking and action to address community problems. Project Peace, which is directed by a team of local residents, offers conflict resolution training in two local schools. Also funded by Hope VI have been the training/licensing of a number of Cabrini-Green residents as professional day care workers and the training of volunteer tenant patrols. Participation in the Human Capital Development Committee has itself represented a significant commitment for its half-dozen members, who have attended weekly (and more recently, monthly) meetings since 1994.

Table 2 identifies ongoing tenant initiatives at Cabrini-Green. In the future, this list of projects is likely to expand. For instance, the RMCs are in the process of opening five laundromats. In addition, the Cabrini Rowhouse RMC

Table 2 Cabrini-Green resident initiatives

Program	Start-up date	No. of participants
Cabrini-Green Textile Works	Early 1996	11
CADRE (Combating Alcohol and Drugs Through Rehabilitation and Education)	Late 1995	7
CHA Works job training	August 1995	45
Child care training	1996	14
Project Lead	1994	206
Project Peace	1996	5
Resident safety monitors	Early 1997	80
Volunteer tenant patrolling	1989	150

Sources: CHA documents; Cabrini-Green LAC

will train and hire a team of energy auditors who will visit individual apartments to assess how efficiently residents' heat and other utilities are working and, when appropriate, suggest needed repairs.

Cabrini-Green and the Near North Side

Physical descriptions of Cabrini-Green – particularly those, such as Kevin Coyle's, that emphasize the Green Homes and Cabrini-Extension buildings – typically highlight the incongruence of the complex and its neighborhood environment. This is not an implausible way of viewing Cabrini-Green. If one sets out to the east of the complex, soon enough after passing under the Chicago Transit Authority elevated track – just as in Harvey Zorbaugh's time – one has left the slum for the Gold Coast. Heading north, west, or south of Cabrini-Green, one would – until very recently – encounter open space (south of North Avenue), deteriorating industrial sites (along Halsted Street and the Chicago River's North Branch), and an obsolete commercial street (Chicago Avenue). In short, Cabrini-Green seemed to be isolated. One consequence of this way of viewing Cabrini-Green is to suppose that there is nothing there within the project. In the previous section of this chapter, we have highlighted what is there, in so doing noting a set of varied and well-established neighborhood social patterns and institutions quite like what is present in many inner-city areas.

There is a second consequence of viewing Cabrini-Green as a physical anomaly within its neighborhood context, which is to suppose that its residents are cut off from the surrounding area. This is not a point of view expressed by Cabrini-Green residents, though what they have to say about their neighborhood in relation to the larger Near North Side tells us much about the evolving character of this portion of Chicago. In the first place, our informants frequently characterize their neighborhood as including areas well beyond

Cabrini-Green's boundaries. For one informant it was "North Avenue to Chicago, from Sedgwick all the way to Halsted." Another individual expanded the neighborhood far beyond these bounds by mentioning that he had lived in different parts of the city and that he had friends in each of these areas.

When we asked residents about community amenities, there was a comparable apportioning of items. Among the very local sites or facilities of note are Stanton and Seward Parks (but not in the evening), the public library, and the New City YMCA (just north-west of Cabrini-Green). However, the larger area includes amenities that are frequently visited by local people: Water Tower Place's movie theaters, the lakefront, and Lincoln Park (with several individuals mentioning the zoo's special attraction for Cabrini-Green youths). One informant noted the convenience offered by the number 29 bus, which allows her to go to the Loop for shopping or to use the Harold Washington Library. Nor is this more expansive sense of neighborhood defined only in terms of what a person can take from the larger community. In discussing the area adjoining Cabrini-Green, one informant noted that she often volunteered at Saint Joseph's school. In short – and even while noting various Cabrini-Green physical and social shortcomings – Cabrini-Green residents often think of their part of Chicago as a good place to live.

Aside from the Cabrini-Green area's amenities, there is another environmental point about which local residents tend to agree. At present, the Cabrini-Green area is not awash in economic opportunity. Some long-standing local employers, such as Montgomery Ward, have reduced hiring. Others, notably the Oscar Mayer plant that stood just to the east of Cabrini-Green, have shut down altogether. In essence, the economic and geographic restructuring of the Chicago metropolitan region since the 1960s has yielded a series of destabilizing changes in the Cabrini-Green area: relatively well-paying manufacturing and warehousing jobs in the Near North Side and along the North Branch of the Chicago River have been lost; during the 1970s and 1980s considerable physical deterioration and building abandonment resulted from the downturn of the "old" local economy; and in the 1990s up-scale residential development (promising few, if any, jobs for incumbent low-income residents) has become the engine of economic change.[7] For many Cabrini-Green residents, the much-heralded revival of the Near North Side is a bitter-tasting remedy for the neighborhood's various ills. Having persevered through decades of CHA mismanagement, and having learned to make the best of their neighborhood, many long-time residents expect that they will be pushed to another part of the city now that real estate developers have taken an interest in the Cabrini-Green area.

*   *   *

The Real Costs of Relocation

The CHA/city of Chicago Near North Redevelopment Initiative proposes to reduce the Cabrini-Green housing stock from thirty-six hundred to twenty-three hundred units. Approximately seven hundred new units scattered through the NNRI area have been promised to displaced Cabrini-Green residents. Beyond these local relocations to "hard units" (that is, CHA-owned dwellings), the CHA proposes to offer Section 8 rent assistance to additional displaced Cabrini-Green residents for use in obtaining private-sector housing. The philosophy animating the Section 8 rental assistance program – offering market choice to low-income families, and permitting them to seek housing outside of racial ghettos – is certainly convergent with the rhetoric driving the NNRI. However, the empirical features of Chicago's real estate market and the local record of the Section 8 program suggest that for Cabrini-Green relocatees "market choice" will be more illusion than reality. Furthermore, their dispersal via Section 8 certificates or vouchers is viewed by many Cabrini-Green residents as an exercise in community seeking via community destruction.

For low-income families, the housing market in the Chicago area is very tight. In a 1994 report on rental housing in Chicago, the Metropolitan Tenants Organization noted that the number of rental apartments in the city had decreased by 10 percent between 1980 and 1990. Furthermore, demand pressures especially drive up rents for apartments suited to large families, just the kinds of family groups that the NNRI will move from Cabrini-Green. The result of these market conditions is that landlords, particularly when screening larger families, can be very choosy in selecting their tenants. The Metropolitan Tenants Organization report comments, "Discrimination based on familial status is often coupled with gender, marital status, and racial discrimination."[8] The acuity of this observation is borne out by two features of the Chicago-area experience with Section 8 vouchers and certificates. First, approximately three in ten Section 8 recipients are unable to use their certificates or vouchers.[9] That is, they simply cannot find housing to suit their needs, coupled with a landlord willing to rent to Section 8–assisted tenants. Second, the bulk of Section 8 recipients locate housing in city neighborhoods or suburban communities that are quite racially segregated.[10] For example, among Chicago's six community areas with the greatest concentrations of Section 8 tenants are South Shore, Austin, West Englewood, and Woodlawn – each with an African American population approaching or exceeding 90 percent.[11]

These problems with the Section 8 program are well known to Cabrini-Green residents. The Voorhees Center (University of Illinois–Chicago) report on the Section 8 program and Cabrini-Green redevelopment, released in May 1997, notes that residents already displaced by the vacating of Cabrini-Green buildings have experienced considerable difficulty in using Section 8 assistance. These residents have complained not just about the difficulties of using Section 8 vouchers or certificates in the Chicago rental market, but also about ineffective relocation advice and counseling by the firm hired by the CHA to assist relocation.[12]

The local record of the Section 8 program cautions against high expectations that displaced Cabrini-Green residents will be well served in finding new places to live. At the same time, the rationale driving the NNRI's tenant relocation provisions rests on the most dubious of foundations. Moving residents from Cabrini-Green presumes that they suffer from an absence of the institutions and other social supports essential for satisfactory community living. Yet the wholesale displacement of residents has the immediate effect of pulling apart the very networks of social and family ties that allow the low-income population of Cabrini-Green to survive. As we have documented in the preceding pages, there is a vital Cabrini-Green community; and as is typically the case in low-income inner-city neighborhoods, the quality of local life is largely sustained by informal, friendship- and family-defined social networks.[13] The NNRI fails to recognize this feature of the real Cabrini-Green. Instead, it proposes a strategy of neighborhood upgrading via upscale real estate investment that promises to destroy the neighborhood's intricate network of community-sustaining ties, practices, and commitments.

Notes

1   Patrick Reardon, "Cuts Imperil CHA Plans for Cabrini," *Chicago Tribune*, February 10, 1994.
2   Chicago Housing Authority, "The Urban Revitalization Demonstration Program" (Chicago: Chicago Housing Authority, May 5, 1993), p. 19.
3   Kevin Coyle, *Hardball: A Season in the Projects* (New York: Putnam's, 1993), p. 23.
4   Margaret Smith, "A Mother's Prayer," *Voices of Cabrini*, April 24, 1994.
5   Gloria Corkrell, "Untitled," *Voices of Cabrini*, December 19, 1993.
6   This quotation, as well as subsequent quotations from Cabrini-Green residents, are drawn from interviews that were conducted between July and December 1997.
7   Wim Wiewel, "Industries, Jobs, and Economic Development Policy in Metropolitan Chicago: An Overview of the Decade," in *Creating Jobs, Creating Workers: Economic Development and Employment in Metropolitan Chicago*, ed. Lawrence B. Joseph (Champaign: University of Illinois Press, 1990), pp. 27–59; Nikolas C. Theodore and D. Garth Taylor, "The Geography of Opportunity: The Status of African Americans in the Chicago Area Economy" (Chicago: Chicago Urban League, March 1991).
8   Metropolitan Tenants Organization, "Children + Female-Headed Households + African American/Latino: Nowhere to Live in Chicago" (Chicago: Metropolitan Tenants Organization, March 1994), p. 2.
9   Nathalie P. Voorhees Center for Neighborhood and Community Development, "The Plan to Voucher Out Public Housing: An Analysis of the Chicago Experience and a Case Study of the Proposal to Redevelop the Cabrini-Green Public Housing Area" (Chicago: Nathalie P. Voorhees Center for Neighborhood and Community Development, University of Illinois–Chicago, May 1997), p. 9.
10 Paul B. Fischer, "A Racial Perspective on Subsidized Housing in the Chicago Suburbs" (Chicago: South Suburban Housing Center, 1992).
11 Voorhees Center, "The Plan to Voucher Out Public Housing," p. 14.
12 Ibid., pp. 20–3.
13 Carol B. Stack, *All Our Kin: Strategies for Survival in a Black Community* (New York: Harper Collophon, 1975); Kathryn Edin and Laura Lein, *Making Ends Meet: How Single Mothers Survive Welfare and Low-Wage Work* (New York: Russell Sage Foundation, 1997), pp. 149–67.

7

School Desegregation

Turning Back to Segregation

Gary Orfield

Four decades after the civil rights revolution began with the Supreme Court's unanimous 1954 school desegregation decision, *Brown v. Board of Education*, the Supreme Court reversed itself in the 1990s, authorizing school districts to return to segregated and unequal public schools. The cases were part of a general reversal of civil rights policy, which included decisions against affirmative action and voting rights. After decades of bitter political, legal, and community struggles over civil rights, there was surprisingly little attention to the new school resegregation policies spelled out in the Court's key 1990s decisions in *Board of Education of Oklahoma City v. Dowell*,[1] *Freeman v. Pitts*,[2] and *Missouri v. Jenkins*.[3] The decisions were often characterized as belated adjustments to an irrelevant, failed policy. But in fact, these historic High Court decisions were a triumph for the decades-long powerful, politicized attacks on school desegregation. The new policies reflected the victory of the conservative movement that altered the federal courts and turned the nation from the dream of *Brown* toward accepting a return to segregation.

Dowell, *Pitts*, and *Jenkins* spelled out procedures for court approval of the dismantling of school desegregation plans – plans that, despite the well-publicized problems in some cities, have been one of the few legally enforced routes of access and opportunity for millions of African American and Latino schoolchildren in an increasingly polarized society. Though now showing clear signs of erosion, the school desegregation *Brown v. Board of Education* made possible had weathered political attacks better than many had predicted it would.

But *Dowell*, *Pills*, and *Jenkins* established legal standards to determine when a local school district had repaid what the Court defined as a historic debt to its black students, a debt incurred during generations of intentional racial segregation and discrimination by state and local policies and practices. Under these decisions, districts that, in the eyes of a court, had obeyed their court

Reprinted from Gary Orfield and Susan E. Eaton, *Dismantling Desegregation* (New York: The New Press, 1996), chapter 1.

orders for several years could send students back to neighborhood schools, even if those schools were segregated and inferior. With the 1995 *Jenkins* decision, the Court further narrowed educational remedies.

This is a troubling shift. *Brown* rested on the principle that intentional public action to support segregation was a violation of the U.S. Constitution. Under *Dowell* and *Pitts*, however, public decisions that re-create segregation, sometimes even more severe than before desegregation orders, are now deemed acceptable. These new resegregation decisions legitimate a deliberate return to segregation. As long as school districts temporarily maintain some aspects of desegregation for several years and do not express an intent to discriminate, the Court approves plans to send minority students back to segregation.

Dowell and *Pitts* embrace new conceptions of racial integration and school desegregation. These decisions view racial integration not as a goal that segregated districts should strive to attain, but as a merely temporary punishment for historic violations, an imposition to be lifted after a few years. After the sentence of desegregation has been served, the normal, "natural" pattern of segregated schools can be restored. In just two years in the early 1990s, *Dowell* and *Pitts* had reduced the long crusade for integrated education to a formalistic requirement that certain rough indicators of desegregation be present briefly.

These resegregation decisions received little national attention, in part because their most dramatic impact was on the South, the region that became the most integrated after *Brown*. The Supreme Court's 1974 *Milliken* decision had already rendered *Brown* almost meaningless for most of the metropolitan North by blocking desegregation plans that would integrate cities with their suburbs. Resegregation decisions made no difference to Washington and New York City since there were no desegregation plans in place.

In this chapter, we analyze the effects of the *Dowell, Pitts,* and *Jenkins* decisions and describe the social and political forces that shaped their underlying philosophy. These three cases largely displace the goal of rooting out the lingering damage of racial segregation and discrimination with the twin goals of minimizing judicial involvement in education and restoring power to local and state governments, whatever the consequences.

The Supreme Court handed down the first of the three resegregation decisions in 1991. *Board of Education of Oklahoma City v. Dowell* outlined circumstances under which courts have authority to release school districts from their obligation to maintain desegregated schools.[4] A previously illegally segregated district whose desegregation plan was being supervised by a court could be freed from oversight if the district had desegregated its students and faculty, and met for a few years the other requirements laid out in the Supreme Court's 1968 *Green v. School Board of New Kent County* decision.[5] *Green* ordered "root and branch" eradication of segregated schooling and specified several areas of a school system – such as students, teachers, transportation, and facilities – in which desegregation was mandatory. Under *Dowell*, a district briefly taking the steps outlined in *Green* can be termed "unitary" and is thus freed from its legal obligation to purge itself of segregation. Unitary might best be understood as the opposite of a "dual" system, in which a school district, in essence, operates two separate systems, one black and one white. A unitary district is assumed to be one that has repaired the damage caused by generations of segregation and overt discrimination.

Under *Brown*, proof of an intentionally segregated dual system triggers desegregation mandates. But once the formerly dual system becomes unitary, according to the decisions of the 1990s, minority students no longer have the special protection of the courts, and school districts no longer face any requirement to maintain desegregation or related education programs.

In 1992, a year after *Dowell*, the *Freeman v. Pitts*[6] decision went even further, holding that various requirements laid out in *Green* need not be present at the same time. This meant, for example, that a once-segregated system could dismantle its student desegregation plan without ever having desegregated its faculty or provided equal access to educational programs.

The Court's 5–4 decision in the 1995 case, *Missouri v. Jenkins*, found the Court's majority determined to narrow the reach of the "separate but equal" remedies provided in big cities after the Supreme Court blocked city-suburban desegregation in 1974. Its 1995 decision prohibited efforts to attract white suburban and private school students *voluntarily* into city schools through excellent programs. Kansas City spent more than a billion dollars upgrading a severely deteriorated school system. The goal here was to create desegregation by making inner city schools so attractive that private school and suburban students would choose to transfer to them. Because possible desegregation was limited within the city system by a lack of white students, the emphasis was put on upgrading the schools. When the district court said that it would examine test scores to help ensure that the remedy actually helped the black children who had been harmed by segregation, the Supreme Court said no, emphasizing the limited role of the courts and the need to restore state and local authority quickly, regardless of remaining inequalities. Ironically, the conservative movement that claimed it would be more productive to emphasize choice and "educational improvement" over desegregation, won a constitutional decision in *Jenkins* that pushed desegregation in big cities toward simple, short-term racial balancing within a city, even where the African American and Latino majority is so large that little contact with whites is possible.

Under *Dowell*, *Pitts*, and *Jenkins*, school districts need not prove actual racial equality, nor a narrowing of academic gaps between the races. Desegregation remedies can even be removed when achievement gaps between the races have widened, or even if a district has never fully implemented an effective desegregation plan. Formalistic compliance for a time with some limited requirements was enough, even if the roots of racial inequality were untouched.

This profound shift of judicial philosophy is eerily compatible with philosophies espoused by the Nixon, Reagan, and Bush administrations. This should not be much of a surprise, since the Supreme Court appointees of these presidents generally shared conservative assumptions about race, inequality, and schooling with the presidents who appointed them. Furthermore, under the Reagan and Bush administrations, even the federal civil rights agencies actively undermined desegregation while embracing a "separate but equal" philosophy. Clarence Thomas, first named by President Reagan to begin dismantling enforcement activities in the civil rights office at the Education Department, was appointed by President Bush to the Supreme Court and became the deciding vote on the Supreme Court in the 1995 *Jenkins* decision.

Civil rights groups, represented by only a handful of lawyers, had little money to resist powerful dismantling efforts by local school districts and their legal teams. The fiscal and organizational crises that in the 1990s plagued the NAACP, the most visible and important civil rights organization, compounded the problem. Local school boards seeking to dismantle their desegregation plans were allied in court not only with powerful state officials but also, in the 1980s, with the U.S. Department of Justice.

After *Dowell* and *Pitts*, many educational leaders thought that, with courts out of the way, racial issues might be set aside and attention would shift from the divisiveness of imposed desegregation plans to educational improvement for all children. With this idea in mind, many school systems, including some of the nation's largest, have filed or are now considering filing motions for unitary status that will make it easier for them to return to neighborhood schools. Living under antidesegregation rhetoric and loosening desegregation standards, still other school districts have adopted policies based on "separate but equal" philosophies. Such policies pledge to do what *Brown* said could not be done – provide equality within segregated schools. Some have tried new and fashionable approaches that focused less and less on desegregation and incorrectly view segregation and its accompanying concentration of poverty as irrelevant to educational quality.

Development of Law Before the Resegregation Cases

The school desegregation battle was for a lasting reconstruction of American education, not for desegregation as a temporary punishment for the quickly absolved sin of racial segregation. The significance of the *Dowell*, *Pitts*, and *Jenkins* decisions, in fact, is best understood within the historical context of this long, difficult and yet unfinished post-*Brown* struggle toward desegregated schooling. The quiet, gradual movement from the holdings of *Brown* to those of *Dowell*, *Pitts*, and *Jenkins*, expressed allegiance to *Brown* while chipping away at its spirit and its power. In many communities, *Brown* is left intact today in theory only.

The path toward *Brown* and the movement away from it reflect the larger social and political contexts in which the Supreme Court makes its decisions. It handed down the *Brown* decision less than a decade after the end of a world war against a racist Nazi dictatorship. Both the Truman and Eisenhower administrations had explicitly urged the High Court to act against racial segregation in the South.

Harry Truman, in fact, was the first president since Reconstruction to propose a serious civil rights program. In 1947, the Truman-appointed Committee on Civil Rights issued "To Secure These Rights," which called for ending segregation in American life. The report offered forty suggestions for eliminating segregation, among them a proposal for the Justice Department to enter the legal battle against segregation and discrimination in housing. Later that year, Truman called on Congress to prohibit lynching, the poll tax, and segregation in all interstate transportation.[7]

Dwight D. Eisenhower desegregated the military. His Justice Department urged the Supreme Court to end school segregation in the South, and he appointed a chief justice, Earl Warren, who wrote the Brown decision.[8] Although Eisenhower never publicly endorsed the *Brown* decision, the civil rights tradition of the party of Abraham Lincoln still had important echoes in his administration.

The Supreme Court justices who handed down the *Brown* decision were appointed by Presidents Franklin D. Roosevelt, Truman, and Eisenhower. The Court that later expanded and crystallized *Brown*'s mandate through the 1968 *Green* decision and the *Keyes* and *Swann* decisions of the early 1970s, which expanded desegregation requirements to the North and approved student transportation as a means for integration, had been changed by the appointments made by Presidents John F. Kennedy and Lyndon B. Johnson.

After 1968, however, no Democratic president would make a Supreme Court appointment for nearly twenty-five years; all appointees in the 1970s and 1980s were chosen by presidents whose campaigns had promised a more conservative judiciary and weaker civil rights policies. Perhaps the starkest symbol of reversal was the appointment of Clarence Thomas, a staunch critic of civil rights policy, to the chair of Justice Thurgood Marshall, who had argued *Brown* as an NAACP Legal Defense Fund lawyer.

Amid all the changes, the central constitutional provision of the Fourteenth Amendment – the guarantee of "equal protection of the laws" – remained unaltered. The broad policy changes generally reflected the political views of the presidents who appointed the justices.

Brown and Its Unanswered Questions

The *Brown* decision had tremendous impact upon the consciousness of the country and was an important catalyst and support for the civil rights movement. It challenged the legitimacy of all public institutions embracing segregation. The decision established a revolutionary principle in a society that had been overtly racist for most of its history. But the statement of principle was separated from the commitment to implementation, and the implementation procedures turned out not to work. For this reason, *Brown* and its implementation decision, *Brown II*, might most accurately be viewed as flawed compromises that combined a soaring repudiation of segregation with an unworkable remedy.

Brown announced, in no uncertain terms, that intentional segregation was unconstitutional; unanimity was obtained, however, by putting off the decision about how to enforce the new constitutional requirement.[9] In order to win a unanimous vote, the High Court diluted the subsequent 1955 *Brown II* decision on enforcement. The enforcement decision was so weak that it could not overcome resistance from the Southern political leaders who were prepared to close public education to resist desegregation. The 1955 decision on enforcement, *Brown II*, ordered desegregation with "all deliberate speed." The Court did not define what either "desegregation" or "all deliberate speed" meant. *Brown II's*, ambiguity left decisions about implementing *Brown* to the federal district courts in the South, which were without clear guidance from either the High Court or the federal government for more than a decade.[10]

Under fierce local political pressure, most Southern federal courts reacted to the vague mandates by delaying desegregation cases for long periods and then, in the end, ordering limited changes. Often these plans amounted to allowing a few black schoolchildren to attend a few grades in white schools, while maintaining a school district's essentially segregated character. Sometimes this meant that no whites were ever transferred to the previously all-black schools, faculties remained segregated, and black-and-white schools offered educational programs that differed in content and quality.[11]

The Southern segregated school system remained largely intact a full decade after *Brown*. By 1964, only one-fiftieth of Southern black children attended integrated schools. Northern segregation, meanwhile, was virtually untouched until the mid-1970s. Most Northern districts even refused to provide racial data that could be used to measure segregation. For nearly two decades following *Brown*, the Supreme Court denied hearings to school desegregation cases from the North.

After the rise of the civil rights movement, Congress passed the 1964 Civil Rights Act, the first major civil rights law in ninety years. It was only when serious executive enforcement was tied to the principles of *Brown* that the revolutionary potential of the constitutional change became apparent. The 1964 law, which barred discrimination in all schools and other institutions receiving federal dollars, forced rapid and dramatic changes on the South. Under President Johnson, the federal government vigorously enforced desegregation. Federal rules and sanctions took hold in 1965, backed by cutoffs of federal aid to school districts and extensive litigation by Justice Department civil rights lawyers.[12] This commitment lasted for only about three years, dying shortly after Richard Nixon was elected president in 1968.

Just a few years of intensive enforcement was enough to transform Southern schools and create much stricter and clearer desegregation standards. Following the enactment of the 1964 Civil Rights Act and the issuance of executive branch desegregation standards, the Supreme Court established a clear obligation for rapid and thorough desegregation of the South. The guiding principle here was that far-reaching desegregation must be accomplished by immediate change in an unequal opportunity structure. Finally, districts were told what they must do to eliminate segregation, how their progress toward a unitary, nonsegregated system would be measured, and what would be done to force change if they resisted.[13] By 1970, the schools in the South, which had been almost totally segregated in the early 1960s, were far more desegregated than those in any other region. The few years of active enforcement had had huge impacts.

Even when the mandates for action were clear, some key questions remained unanswered. No one really knew how long it would take to repair the corrosive damage caused by many generations of segregation or when the courts' responsibility for oversight would be fulfilled. By the late 1970s, lawyers, educators, and politicians were asking when a court order would cease and what obligations to desegregate would continue once judicial super-vision ended. In what would become an increasingly important question well into the 1990s, they asked: Would courts view a return to neighborhood schools, a move with the foreseeable effect of recreating segregation, as a "neutral" act, or as another constitutional violation? Through the 1980s, the Supreme Court justices left these questions unanswered.

A Turn to the Right: Nixon and His Court

Civil rights politics turned sharply to the right following the triumph of Nixon's "Southern strategy" in the 1968 presidential election, a strategy that wooed the Southern vote by attacking early busing policies and other targets of Southern conservatives.[14]

Following Nixon's election, H. R. Haldeman, Nixon's chief of staff, recorded in his diary the President's directives to staff to do as little as possible to enforce desegregation. An excerpt from early 1970 is typical of comments found throughout Haldeman's diary:

> Feb. 4 ... he plans to take on the integration problem directly. Is really concerned about situation in Southern schools and feels we have to take some leadership to try to reverse Court decisions that have forced integration too far, too fast. Has told Mitchell [Attorney General] to file another case, and keep filing until we get a reversal.[15]

Early on in his first term, Nixon had fired Leon Panetta, then director of the Department of Health, Education, and Welfare's civil rights office, because Panetta had enforced school desegregation requirements. Nixon supported strong congressional action, even a constitutional amendment, to limit urban desegregation.[16]

Against the strong opposition of the Nixon administration, the Supreme Court's 1971 *Swann* decision ruled that busing was an appropriate means of achieving desegregation. That same year, President Nixon named the deeply conservative Justice Department lawyer, William Rehnquist, to the Supreme Court. During his tenure, Nixon appointed four Supreme Court justices. Rehnquist, elevated to chief justice by Ronald Reagan fifteen years later, became the member of the Supreme Court most hostile to desegregation issues. In Rehnquist's first twelve years on the Court, a law review analysis concluded, he had "never voted to uphold a school desegregation plan."[17] When the Rehnquist Court was firmly installed by the end of the 1980s, the stage would be set for dismantling desegregation.

Rehnquist had been a clerk at the Supreme Court during the *Brown* case, and he wrote a memo expressing approval for the "separate but equal" doctrine established by the 1896 *Plessy v. Ferguson* decision, which was the very doctrine that *Brown v. Board of Education* overturned. (Rehnquist later claimed that the memo did not express his views, but was actually an expression of Justice Jackson's early views on the *Brown* case.)[18]

The Rehnquist memo said:

> I realize that it is an unpopular and unhumanitarian position, for which I have been excoriated by "liberal" colleagues, but I think *Plessy* v. *Ferguson* was right and should be reaffirmed.[19]

Professor Sue Davis's analysis of Rehnquist's actual decisions on the Supreme Court in the 1970s and early 1980s showed that, although Rehnquist accepted *Brown* in theory, he gave it a narrow interpretation and disagreed with many of the later Supreme Court decisions that spelled out *Brown*'s mandate.[20] Rehnquist was the first clear dissenter on school desegregation in the eighteen years after *Brown*. In the 1973 *Keyes* decision, Rehnquist argued against extending desegregation law to the North, calling the decision a "drastic extension of *Brown*." In a 1975 dissent, he attacked a decision from Wilmington, Delaware, which provided a metropolitan-wide desegregation remedy, calling it "more Draconian than any ever approved by this Court" and accused his colleagues of "total substitution of judicial for popular control of local education."[21]

In a 1979 case in which the Court decided to continue to desegregate entire urban districts rather than just individual schools, Rehnquist accused the majority of favoring a policy of "integration *über alles*," suggesting a parallel with the Nazi anthem, "*Deutschland über alles*."[22] By the time of the resegregation decisions of the 1990s, Rehnquist's views, long expressed in lonely dissents, would become the majority view of the Supreme Court. Rehnquist himself wrote the 1995 *Jenkins* decision.

Accepting segregation in the North: the turning point in Detroit

The impetus of *Brown* and the civil rights movement for desegregating American schools hit a stone wall with the 1974 *Milliken v. Bradley* decision. The metropolitan Detroit decision, known as *Milliken I*, represented the first major Supreme Court blow against school desegregation. With *Milliken*, the Supreme Court was forced to grapple with the basic barrier to achieving urban school desegregation. After the Second World War, the pattern of white suburbanization in Northern cities intensified; many districts were left with too few white students to achieve full and lasting desegregation. In response to this demographic pattern, lower courts hearing the *Milliken* case approved a desegregation plan that would include not only Detroit's central city, but the predominantly white suburbs around it. But, in the face of intense opposition from the Nixon administration and many state governments, the High Court rejected the metropolitan remedy by a 5–4 vote.

This decision was particularly devastating to civil rights advocates, because only the year before, the Court in *Rodriguez* had ruled that children had no constitutional right to equal school expenditures.[23] Taken together, *Rodriguez* and *Milliken* meant that illegally segregated minority students in school districts with high numbers of minority students had a right to neither equalization nor desegregation.

Milliken viewed desegregation as unfairly punishing the suburbs. The Court ruled that unless it could be shown either that suburban communities or discriminatory state action created the pattern of all-white suburbs and heavily black city schools, Detroit would have to desegregate by mixing its dwindling white enrollment with its huge and rapidly growing black majority. Chief Justice Warren Burger cited the "deeply rooted tradition" of local control of public schools as the legal rationale for denying a metropolitan remedy and allowing segregated schools to persist. Since the minority population in the industrial North is much more concentrated in a few big cities than it is in the South, this decision guaranteed that segregation would be limited and temporary in much of the North.

In his dissent, Justice Byron White challenged Burger, noting that school districts and municipal governments are not sovereign. State governments and state law created and empowered these districts; thus states have the power to change or dissolve them, White said. The basic tradition of U.S. law is not the independence of local government and school systems, but their existence as subdivisions of state government. He argued that the Supreme Court had ample authority to order the state to craft an interdistrict remedy. Justice William O. Douglas argued in his dissent that "metropolitan treatment" of various problems, such as sewage or water, is "commonplace" and that regional approaches could be used to accomplish the basic constitutional mandate of desegregation.[24]

Justice Thurgood Marshall challenged his colleagues about what he thought was the Court's real reason for denying the suburban-city remedy: suburban political and racial resistance.

The Court did not even consider the ways in which suburban governments around Detroit had perpetuated and contributed to the segregation of housing that led to the segregated schools across Detroit's metropolitan area.

Three years later, in the second Detroit case, *Milliken II*, the Court approved a plan ordering the state to pay for compensatory programs to redress the harms of segregation. But as the judge who later presided over the monetary remedies in Detroit said in 1993, *Milliken II* has been a "limited form of reparations." In Detroit and other cities…, the *Milliken II* remedy has not been implemented successfully.[25]

Rejection of city-suburban desegregation brought an end to the period of rapidly increasing school desegregation for black students, which began in 1965. No longer was the most severe segregation found among schools within the same community; the starkest racial separations occurred between urban and suburban school districts within a metropolitan area. But *Milliken* made this segregation almost untouchable. By 1991, African Americans in Michigan were more segregated than those in any other state. When the Supreme Court, through *Milliken I*, slammed the door on the only possible desegregation strategy for cities with few whites, it shifted the attention of urban educators and civil rights lawyers away from desegregation and toward other approaches for helping minority children confined to segregated and inferior city schools.

The outcome in *Milliken v. Bradley* reflected Nixon's goal of weakening desegregation requirements. His four appointees made up four of the five votes to protect the suburbs. *Milliken* was consistent with Nixon's fervent attacks on busing and on efforts to open up suburban housing to black families. He had derided suburban housing initiatives as "forced integration of the suburbs" just before firing the leading advocate for the initiatives, Housing and Urban Development Secretary George Romney. John Ehrlichman, Nixon's top domestic policy advisor, said the strategy was based on politics and on Nixon's conviction that blacks were *genetically inferior* to whites.[26]

Writing to his chief of staff early in 1972, the year of his reelection campaign, Nixon called for emphasis on three domestic issues in the campaign: inflation, the drug problem, and his opposition to busing.[27] Writing two months later to Ehrlichman, Nixon said it was time for the administration to abandon "the responsible position" on desegregation and "come to a Constitutional Amendment" in order to express a clear difference with the Democrats.[28] "We are not going to gain any brownie points whatsoever by being so responsible that we appear to be totally ineffective," he wrote.[29]

Nixon repeatedly declared that mandatory measures to achieve desegregation were unnecessary, and that Congress must stop courts from imposing "complicated plans drawn up by far-away officials in Washington, D.C." Fearing a constitutional crisis if Congress tried to override the authority of the Supreme Court to interpret the Constitution, the Senate narrowly blocked Nixon's attempt to limit judicial power by statute.[30] After he was reelected, the Watergate crisis diverted his attention from the desegregation issue.

By the mid-1970s, the United States had become an increasingly suburban country with a corresponding powerful suburban political perspective. Presidential elections were largely about the suburban vote, reapportionment was about expanding suburban representation, and older suburbs themselves were struggling with the problems of aging facilities and an antitax, antigovernment mood.

After the sudden changes of the civil rights era, the country denied the need to deal with race and income differences. White suburbanites were increasingly isolated from, and more fearful of, rapidly declining central cities. Between the mid-1960s and the early 1970s, Gallup Polls showed that racial inequality and race relations fell from the top concern of Americans to one of their lowest priorities.[31]

But although Nixon's triumph in the *Milliken* case did lock millions of minority schoolchildren into inferior, isolated schools, it did not resegregate the South. In a handful of cases outside the South – in Louisville, Wilmington, and Indianapolis – federal courts found grounds to mandate city-suburban desegregation in spite of *Milliken*. Civil rights advocates crushed by the *Milliken* defeat could at least celebrate the fact that millions of African American and Latino schoolchildren were enrolled in Southern school districts where desegregation was feasible and an increasingly accepted part of community life. This enduring desegregation was the special target of the 1990s resegregation decisions.

The South's Comparative Success in Desegregation

The South was the target of the most aggressive and persistent desegregation enforcement. In the late 1960s, the Justice Department had launched a full-scale attack on Southern segregation under *Green*'s "root and branch" mandate. In the early 1970s, after the Supreme Court's *Swann* decision rejected the Nixon administration's efforts to ban busing, the Justice Department reluctantly enforced urban desegregation. In a compromise between Congress and the Nixon administration, a substantial federal aid program for desegregated schools – the Emergency School Aid Act – was passed in 1972.[32] After the Nixon White House halted administrative enforcement of urban school desegregation, federal courts in Washington found the administration in violation of the 1964 Civil Rights Act, which mandated cutoff of federal funds to school districts not complying with desegregation law, and ordered that enforcement resume. As a result, scores of Southern school districts were required to end local desegregation.[33]

The *Green* and *Swann* decisions, which required full and immediate desegregation, had more impact on the South than they did in the North. First of all, there were already hundreds of school districts in the South that had been required, by *Brown* and the 1964 Civil Rights Act, to adopt some kind of desegregation plan. Even though many of these strategies were inadequate – they often consisted of "freedom of choice" transfer options that did not lead to desegregation – there was at least some plan in existence. This was not the case in much of the North. In the South, plans were already on the books and districts were under court jurisdiction or federal administrative supervision. Thus it was a simple matter to file motions or issue regulations to have a plan updated to the newer standards required by *Green* and *Swann*. After *Swann*, more than a hundred districts rapidly implemented new desegregation plans, imposing a move to districtwide orders for immediate and total desegregation of students, faculties, and transportation.

It had been easy to find school districts in the South guilty of segregation, but the question of guilt in the North was always more ambiguous. The South had overt segregation laws requiring separate schools; reading the state laws was enough to prove that government had imposed segregation, which itself was linked to many government actions. Northern segregation was compounded by many complex school policies such as the drawing of attendance zones or the construction of schools serving residentially segregated areas. This meant that civil rights lawyers in the North often had a more arduous task and a less certain outcome in their school desegregation cases. It would take years to prove guilt before anyone even began to talk about a remedy. By the time a plan could be drawn up, shifting demographics often made full, lasting desegregation within the city school system impossible.

Where a northeastern or midwestern metropolitan area had dozens of separate school districts, many metropolitan areas in some Southern states were contained within a single school district. Therefore, the South was much better equipped to institute long-term desegregation within single districts. Florida was an excellent example of this, with countrywide districts including cities and suburbs across the state. The Supreme Court's decision against crossing district lines was much more damaging to Northern desegregation.

Many areas of the booming Sunbelt were experiencing white immigration from the North. This trend was in stark contrast to the declining cities and some metropolitan areas of the North that were losing white residents rapidly.

After *Milliken I*, desegregation law remained relatively stable through the 1980s, and the South maintained the relatively high levels of school integration achieved under *Green*, *Swann*, and civil rights regulations through 1988. The struggle over the meaning of the law was ongoing. In two 1970s cases originating in the Ohio cities of Dayton and Columbus, Justice Rehnquist failed in his attempt to roll back the citywide desegregation requirements laid out in *Keyes*, which had ruled that once intentional segregation was found in one part of a school system, lower courts should presume that segregation found in other parts of that system was also unconstitutional. This presumption meant that desegregation plans would be drawn for entire districts rather than for just a few schools. Trying to reverse the *Keyes* requirement, Rehnquist, on his own initiative, blocked the desegregation of 43,000 Columbus students just before school opened in 1978. The next year, in the Ohio cases, however, the Supreme Court reaffirmed its citywide desegregation stand.[34]

President Jimmy Carter expressed reservations about busing policies both as governor of Georgia and during his presidential campaign. Griffin Bell, Carter's attorney general, also had a record of opposition.[35] Once Carter was in office, however, he appointed civil rights officials who favored school desegregation, and a few important cases were filed by the Justice Department. These included the Indianapolis case, resulting in a metropolitan-wide desegregation remedy despite the *Milliken* constraints. In fact, the first successful lawsuit to link school and housing desegregation in a single city (Yonkers, N.Y.) was filed under Carter's presidency.

During this time, though, Congress voted to limit mandatory desegregation by prohibiting the use of the federal fund cutoff sanction in the 1964 Civil Rights Act to enforce civil rights compliance if busing was needed. Without this enforcement power, there was no potential for a nationwide executive branch desegregation policy. By the end of its term, however, the Carter administration was trying to craft coordinated school and housing desegregation policies. But the belated effort was aborted by President Reagan's election. Carter did not have the opportunity to appoint a Supreme Court justice.

The Reagan Era and the Movement to Dismantle

Opposition to mandatory desegregation reached a new intensity during the Reagan administration. Although desegregation orders were still sufficiently well-rooted to prevent a clear trend toward resegregation, the shift toward a "separate but equal" philosophy manifested itself at the end of the 1980s. Not even the South's favorable demographics and enforcement history could withstand the dismantling policies and court appointments of the Reagan administration.

In its first months, the administration won congressional action to rescind the Emergency School Aid Act of 1972, cutting off the only significant source of public money earmarked for the educational and human relations dimensions of desegregation plans. This was the largest federal education program deleted in the vast Omnibus Budget Reconciliation Act, which slashed hundreds of programs with a single vote.[36] Only the part that provided funds to specialized "magnet schools" was later restored. This restoration reflected the administration's desire to focus on choice. (Magnet schools relied upon parent's choosing to send their children to a particular school in an effort to achieve desegregation.) The Reagan administration also tried to eliminate Desegregation Assistance Centers, the only federally funded organizations that provide even limited assistance to desegregating school districts. Congress refused wholesale elimination, but funding cuts meant that the number of centers declined by three-fourths during this time.

During President Reagan's administration, the Justice Department, under the direction of Assistant Attorney General for Civil Rights William Bradford Reynolds, supported some of the school districts the Justice Department had once sued for intentional segregation, but failed to file any new desegregation lawsuits.[37] The administration proposed reliance on voluntary parental "choice" measures, like those the Supreme Court had rejected as inadequate in 1968 in *Green*. The administration also shut down research on ways to make desegregation more effective, took control of the formerly independent U.S. Civil Rights Commission, and used it to assail urban desegregation and other civil rights policies.

In 1981, Assistant Attorney General Reynolds told a congressional committee that "compulsory busing of students in order to achieve racial balance in the public schools is not an acceptable remedy." This position, Reynolds said, "has been endorsed by the President, the Vice President, the Secretary of Education, and me." At that time, however, Reynolds said that the administration would not try to apply the anti-desegregation principle to end desegregation plans already in force. He said: "Nothing we have learned in the 10 years since *Swann* leads to the conclusion that the public would be well-served by reopening wounds that have long since healed."[38] This resolve was quickly abandoned. Soon Reynolds and others intervened in older cases in an effort to dismantle settled desegregation plans.

As early as 1982, the administration called on the Supreme Court to restrict busing in metropolitan Nashville.[39] The Justice Department also supported an ultimately successful move in Norfolk, Virginia, to dismantle desegregation and become the first district to get court approval to return to segregated neighborhood schools. The department actively encouraged similar moves toward dismantling in other cities.

By the mid-1980s, educators and policymakers in a number of cities were actively discussing the option of dismantling their desegregation plans. This discussion picked up steam in 1986, soon after the Rehnquist Supreme Court refused to hear the Norfolk case, thus allowing a federal court to permit a return to racially segregated schools.

During this period, the Justice Department insisted that the plans were failures, unfair to whites and to local school systems. The plans should be seen as temporary punishments only, and districts should be allowed to return to segregated neighborhood schools. The department supported neighborhood schools, even in cities with no history of neighborhood schools, where the pre-desegregation policy had sent students to black or white schools, often well outside their neighborhoods.

For most of the 1980s, however, desegregation was surprisingly persistent. In contrast to the widespread belief that desegregation was a fragile, self-destructing policy, school desegregation endured year after year of attacks. Although the Reagan administration continually denounced desegregation as a failure, segregation levels for black students declined slightly during the Reagan years, showing the durability of many local plans, even in the face of opposition from Washington. Public opinion became more supportive of desegregation, even of busing. As the notion that widespread desertion of public schools was caused by integration won favor, the proportion of U.S. students attending public schools actually rose during the decade. Between 1984 and 1991, public school enrollment rose 7.1 percent, while enrollment in private schools dropped 8.9 percent.[40] The political leadership had succeeded in creating the false impression that desegregation policy had failed and families were deserting public education.

The Reagan administration's campaign against desegregation was successful after Reagan left because it was built upon appointments to the Supreme Court and the lower federal courts. Presidents Reagan and Bush appointed a new majority in the Supreme Court, and President Reagan elevated Justice William Rehnquist, the Court's leading opponent of school desegregation, to chief justice. With this new elevation, Rehnquist gained power to assign opinions, thereby gaining tremendous influence within the Court, and became the nation's leading legal figure. A full 60 percent of sitting federal judges in 1995 had been appointed by Presidents Reagan and Bush.[41] They had been screened for ideology to an unprecedented degree with elaborate investigations by the Justice Department and the White House.[42] This is significant because lower federal court judges have extensive power to decide whether a school district is unitary, whether it has complied "in good faith" with the desegregation order, and, finally, whether the district can return to segregated schooling.

The impact of the conservative agenda was finally clear when the Supreme Court handed down the 1991 *Dowell* decision that spelled out the process by which districts could resegregate schools. *Dowell*, and then *Pitts* in 1992, created the means by which even the South might return to segregated education. *Milliken* had blocked desegregation in the North and Midwest; now the South, where rigorous enforcement had led to better levels of desegregation, was vulnerable.

The 1990s' Definition of Unitary Status

The Court expressed its philosophical shift away from *Brown*'s principles most clearly by redefining the legal term "unitary status." In doing so, the Court managed to invent a kind of judicial absolution for the sins of segregation. Under the new resegregation decisions, if a court declared a school district "unitary," that school district could knowingly re-create segregated schools with impunity

This new use of unitary status represented an important change. Ironically, unitary status had been first used by the Court in its 1968 *Green* decision as a standard that segregated school districts should strive to attain. *Green* posited a unitary school system with equitable interracial schools as a long-term, permanent goal, viewing any school board action that worked against or ignored the goal of total desegregation to be impermissible.

By 1990, unitary status in that sense – discrimination-free, racially integrated education – was no longer the objective; it became merely a method of getting out of racial integration. The Court rejected not only the ideal of lasting integration, but also the idea that elements of a desegregation plan were part of an inseparable package necessary to break down the dual school system and create desegregated education.

Thus unitary status decisions now have profound consequences for racial integration in U.S. schools. A court-supervised district that has never been declared unitary is obligated under the law to avoid actions that create segregated and unequal schools. But after a declaration of unitary status, the courts presume any government action creating racially segregated schools to be innocent, unless a plaintiff proves that the school officials intentionally decided to discriminate. This burden of proof is nearly impossible to meet, as contemporary school officials can easily formulate plausible alternative justifications. They certainly know better than to give overtly racist reasons for the policy change. With local authorities expressing innocence and the courts inclined to accept any professed educational justification regardless of consequences, minority plaintiffs face overwhelming legal obstacles when they try to prevent resegregation and other racial inequalities. Many of the very same actions that were illegal prior to a unitary status declaration become perfectly legal afterward.

The unitary status ruling assumes two things: that segregation does not have far-reaching effects and that a few years of desegregation, no matter how ineffective, could miraculously erase residual "vestiges" or effects of segregation. In this way, the courts implied that generations of discrimination and segregation could be quickly overcome through formal compliance with *Green* requirements for just one-tenth or one-twentieth as much time as the segregation and discrimination had been practiced.

Many courts do not even investigate whether or not vestiges of segregation are ever remedied. For example, under *Pitts*, *Dowell*, and *Jenkins*, school districts do not need to show that education gains or opportunities are equal between minority and white children. Nor do courts require solid evidence that discriminatory attitudes and assumptions growing out of a history of segregation have been purged from the local educational system.

In practice, the shift in the burden of proof that results from the unitary status declaration may be the key difference that allows a system to resegregate its schools. For example, after an Austin, Texas Independent School District was declared unitary in 1983, the federal district court relinquished jurisdiction completely in 1986; one year later, the school board redrew attendance zones to create segregated neighborhood schools. By 1993, nearly one-third of the elementary schools had minority enrollments of more than 80 percent non-white in a district that still had a white majority.[43] The judge allowed this segregation, though the student reassignments created the segregation in fourteen of the nineteen imbalanced schools.[44] Since the school district had been officially proclaimed unitary, actions that created segregation were assumed to be nondiscriminatory as long as the school leaders claimed an educational justification for the new plans. In contrast, an attendance plan in Dallas, then a nonunitary system, was rejected because it would have created too many one-race schools.[45] (Dallas has since been declared unitary.)

After the *Dowell* and *Pitts* decisions of 1991 and 1993, the road to resegregation seemed to be wide open. Teams of lawyers and experts were available, usually at steep fees, to help school districts fight for a return to segregated schools.

By the mid-1990s, several large systems had already moved to reinstitute segregated neighborhood schools, at least for the elementary school grades, by going into court to win unitary status. In some cases, civil rights lawyers, desperate to hang on to whatever remedies they could, simply settled these cases for fear that a trial would result in courts ending all desegregation immediately.

By 1995, courts had granted unitary status in a number of cases. Oklahoma City had been allowed to operate segregated neighborhood schools with only perfunctory consideration of the issues in the Supreme Court guidelines. Austin, Texas, had been allowed to reinstate segregated elementary schools. In Savannah-Chatham County, the district was declared unitary after implementing a purely voluntary plan that failed to meet the guidelines of a 1988 order. In that case, District Judge B. Avant Edenfield's language expressed the views of many judges now supervising desegregation cases. He praised the district's "momentous efforts," claiming that requiring more would be "imposing an exercise in futility." His ruling terminated all supervision of the system.[46] Older central city desegregation plans were closed with settlement agreements. Such agreements were adopted in such cities as Cincinnati and Cleveland.[47] In September 1995, the plan that produced the first Supreme Court decision in the North (Denver) was dissolved and the plan that had made metropolitan Wilmington the most integrated urban center on the east coast was dropped the month before.[48]

Today, a great many school districts remain under desegregation orders and have not filed motions to dissolve their plans. Some, including many in Florida, have plans that are increasingly ineffective because of the tremendous growth of white suburbs and the expansion of city ghettos without any adjustment of attendance areas set up in the old court order.

Many communities are on the brink of initiatives to dissolve plans that had provided an important, if imperfect, route of access for minority schoolchildren. Even in the regions that integrated most successfully and stably in the decades following the *Brown* decision, school systems were debating a return to segregation.

Themes about the "failure" or irrelevance of desegregation echo in public debates in city after city. Proposals for resegregation and attacks on desegregation often sail smoothly through school boards without objection, not because they will produce gains or because they represent the goals of the public, but because the civil rights side has been weakened, poorly funded, and struggling for survival in an increasingly conservative society with deepening racial and economic divisions.

The NAACP, by far the largest civil rights organization and the one with the most influential local chapters, has been in decline during the mid-1990s. It has experienced bitter internal struggles, the removal of its executive director and board chairman, division, and bankruptcy, all of which threaten its viability. With all of the major civil rights programs and many substantive programs crucial to the black community under political and legal attack, weakened civil rights groups have been overwhelmed.

Does It Matter?

All this might be of only academic interest if it really were true that school desegregation had "failed," or had already been dismantled, or if the country had learned how to make separate institutions truly equal in a racially divided and extremely unequal society.

The truth, however, is that although urban desegregation has never been popular with whites, it is viewed as a success by both white and minority parents whose children experienced it. In the 1990s, there remains a widely shared preference in the society for integrated schools, though there is deep division about how to get them. Meanwhile, there is simply no workable districtwide model that shows that separate schools have actually been made equal in terms of outcomes or opportunities. A return to "separate but equal" is a bet that some unknown solution will be discovered and successfully implemented, and that local politics will now be sufficiently responsive to the interests of African American and Latino students that they can safely forgo the protection of the courts before ever actually experiencing equal education.

Notes

1   *Bd. of Educ. of Oklahoma City v. Dowell*, 498 U.S. 237 (1991).
2   *Freeman v. Pitts*, 112 S. Ct. 1430 (1992).
3   *Missouri v. Jenkins*, 115 S. Ct. 2038 (1995).
4   *Bd. of Educ. of Oklahoma City v. Dowell*, 498 U.S. 237 (1991).
5   *Green v. Sch. Bd. of New Kent County*, 391 U.S. 430 (1968).
6   *Freeman v. Pitts*, 112 S. Ct. 1430 (1992).
7   Richard Kluger, *Simple Justice* (New York: Vintage Books, 1975), p. 253.
8   Herbert Brownell with John P. Burke, *Advising Ike: The Memoirs of Attorney General Herbert Brownell* (Lawrence: University of Kansas Press, 1993);

Mark Stern, "Presidential Strategies and Civil Rights: Eisenhower, the Early Years, 1952–54," *Presidential Studies Quarterly* 19, no. 4 (Fall 1989), pp. 769–95.

9 G. Edward White, *Earl Warren: A Public Life* (New York: Oxford University Press, 1982), pp. 166–8.

10 J. W. Peltason, *58 Lonely Men: Southern Federal Judges and School Desegregation* (New York: Harcourt, Brace and World, 1961).

11 Ibid.; Reed Sarratt, *The Ordeal of Desegregation* (New York: Harper and Row, 1966).

12 Gary Orfield, *The Reconstruction of Southern Education: The Schools and the 1964 Civil Rights Act* (New York: John Wiley, 1969).

13 *Green v. Sch. Bd. of New Kent County*, 391 U.S. 430 (1968).

14 Harry S. Dent, *The Prodigal South Returns to Power* (New York: John Wiley & Sons, 1978).

15 H. R. Haldeman, *The Haldeman Diaries: Inside the Nixon White House* (New York: G. P. Putnam's Sons, 1994), p. 126.

16 Ibid., pp. 126–30, 142, 183–4, 276; Leon Panetta and Peter Gall, *Bring Us Together: The Nixon Team and the Civil Rights Retreat* (Philadelphia: Lippincott, 1971).

17 Sue Davis, "Justice Rehnquist's Equal Protection Clause: An Interim Analysis," *University of Nebraska Law Review* 63 (1984), pp. 288, 308.

18 Senate Committee on the Judiciary, *Hearings on the Nomination of Justice William Hobbs Rehnquist*, 99th Cong. 2d. Sess., 1986, pp. 161–2.

19 Ibid., p. 325.

20 Davis, "Equal Protection," pp. 308–9.

21 *Delaware State Bd. of Educ. v. Evans*, 446 U.S. 923 (1975).

22 *Columbus Bd. of Educ. v. Penick*, 443 U.S. 449 (1979).

23 *San Antonio Indep. Sch. Dist. v. Rodriguez*, 541 U.S. 1 (1973).

24 *Milliken v. Bradley*, 94 S. Ct. 3112, 3134–41 (1974).

25 Judge Avram Cohn, letter to author, May 4, 1994.

26 Bruce Oudes, ed., *From: The President: President Nixon's Secret Files* (New York: Harper and Row, 1989), p. 399.

27 Oudes, *From: The President*, Nixon to John Ehrlichman, May 19, 1972, p. 451.

28 Ibid.

29 Ibid.

30 Gary Orfield, *Congressional Power: Congress and Social Changes* (New York: Harcourt Brace Jovanovich, 1975), pp. 182–4; G. Orfield, *Must We Bus? Segregated Schools and National Policy* (Washington, D.C.: Brookings Institution, 1978), pp. 247–54.

31 George H. Gallup, *The Gallup Poll: Public Opinion 1935–1971* (New York: Random House, 1972), pp. 1934, 2009.

32 Orfield, "Desegregation Aid and the Politics of Polarization," *Congressional Power*, ch. 9.

33 *Adams v. Richardson*, 356 F. Supp. 92 (D.D.C. 1973), was the first of many orders.

34 *Columbus Bd. of Educ. v. Penick*, 443 U.S. 449 (1979); *Dayton Bd. of Educ. v. Brinkman*, 443 U.S. 526 (1979).

35 "What Carter Believes: Interview on the Issues," *U.S. News & World Report*, May 24, 1976, pp. 22–3; Bell record is summarized in 95th Cong. 1st sess., *Congressional Record* daily ed., (January 25, 1977), pp. S1301–6.

36 See John Ellwood, ed., *Reductions in U.S. Domestic Spending* (New Brunswick, N.J.: Transaction Books, 1982), pp. 191–8.

37 Ibid., p. 35.
38 House Committee on the Judiciary, Subcommittee on Civil and Constitutional Rights, *Hearings on School Desegregation*, 97th Cong. 1st sess., 1981, pp. 614, 619.
39 *Education Week*, November 24, 1982.
40 U.S. National Center for Education Statistics, *The Condition of Education* (Washington, D.C.: U.S. Government Printing Office, 1993), p. 100. The trends had shown falling public and rising private enrollment in the 1970–84 period. (Ibid.)
41 Herman Schwartz, *Packing the Courts: The Conservative Campaign to Rewrite the Constitution* (New York: Charles Scribner's Sons, 1988); *New York Times*, November 30, 1995.
42 Edwin Meese III, *With Reagan: The Inside Story* (Washington, D.C.: Regnery Gateway, 1992), pp. 316–17.
43 P. Karatinos, "*Price v. Austin Indep. Sch. Dist.*: Desegregation's Unitary Tar Baby," 77 W. *Educ. L. Rep.* 15 (1992); see also *Price v. Austin Indep. Sch. Dist.*, 729 F. Supp. The Austin Independent School District, Planning and Development Office, March 1994.
44 Karatinos, "*Price v. Austin.*"
45 *Tabsy v. Wright,* 713 F. 2d 90 (5th Cir. 1993).
46 *Stell v. Board of Public Education*, 860 F. Supp. 1563 (S.D. Ga. 1994).
47 *Cleveland Plain Dealer*, August 25, 1994, p. 6-B.
48 Patrice M. Jones, "School District Seeks Release From Edict on Cross-Town Busing," *Cleveland Plain Dealer*, January 5, 1995, p. 1-B; "Court Oversight of Denver Schools Is Ended," *New York Times*, September 13, 1995, p. B7; Peter Schmidt, "U.S. Judge Releases Wilmington Districts from Court Oversight," *Education Week*, September 6, 1995, p. 9.

Integration Dilemmas in a Racist Culture

Doris Y. Wilkinson

Since the demise of the institution of slavery in the United States, the last leading industrialized country to relinquish this inhumane system, economic and social integration of Americans of African descent has been exceedingly problematic. As various forms of racial interaction have unfolded throughout history, principally "black versus white" (e.g., slavery, Jim Crowism, desegregation), a language to accompany them has been cultivated. The vocabulary of resistance to the inherently contradictory structural phenomenon of school integration has included an array of political concepts such as "states' rights," "desegregation," "reverse discrimination," "quotas," "affirmative action," "preferential treatment," and, more recently, the seductive language of "diversity" and "multiculturalism." During its evolution, racial integration has been fraught with complexities and has been the target of sustained opposition by Americans of European ancestry at all levels of the economic class hierarchy.

With the waning of the twentieth century, among the central questions that remain in the United States are those involving interracial relations. Specifically: (1) Was the dismantling of the black segregated school a "necessary and sufficient" condition for structural integration? (2) What have been the behavioral, psychological, academic, and cultural consequences of a judicial decree targeted at the constitutionality of racially disparate public schools on a heretofore ecologically isolated and economically powerless yet close-knit and communal population? (3) How does a governing stratum in a democracy incorporate descendants of slaves in its educational institutions in relatively equal ways without erasing the traditions, values, and customs of the marginalized group? Rather than addressing the last question, which has not been resolved since the Emancipation Proclamation or the overturning of Jim Crow laws, I will briefly explore the consequences of a "facilities" emphasis on children.

To illustrate the theme of this exploration into the cultural and social psychological effects of forced public school integration on African American children, my personal observations and experiences under segregation and the voices of two teachers of African descent will be introduced. This supporting information renders a profile of the contemporary integration crisis and the myth of the benefits of racial association in the elementary, middle, and secondary grades.

The paradoxical character of racially based structural integration in the public school context is evident. This integration dilemma emanates from a race-conscious society and a judicial declaration regarding the constitutionality of dual systems and the presumed negative impact of the all-black school. With respect to this, it is the thesis of this discussion that public school integration and the associated demolition of the black school has had a devastating impact on African American children – their self-esteem, motivation to succeed, conceptions of heroes or role models, respect for adults, and academic performance. Racial animosities have also intensified. Unless rational alternatives are devised that take into account the uniqueness of the African American heritage, busing and compulsory school integration will become even more destructive to their health and ultimately to the nation as a whole.

Rethinking *Brown I* and *Brown II*

Whatever one's ideological orientation, it is not unreasonable to accept the notion that the constitutionality of segregation could have been questioned on grounds other than its psychological effects. For in constitutionally framing the racially entrenched fiction that "any school that is black is inferior and that blacks cannot succeed without the benefit of the company of whites," the Supreme Court reflected the potency of racialistic thinking. It is demonstrably true that in the South and in the Northern urban communities, the African American public school was inferior in the quality of its buildings, facilities, and textbooks.

Nevertheless, this did not apply to the dedication and capabilities of teachers, the unbiased learning environment, or the opportunities for developing healthy self-attitudes. What was unanticipated by the Court in the two *Brown v. Board of Education of Topeka* cases was the pervasive and irreversible damage that might be inflicted on poor black children reared in stable yet ecologically constructed social worlds.

Before the Supreme Court's *Brown* decision, racial discrimination and structural segregation in public and private schools, in colleges and universities, and in all facets of daily life in the southern United States were normative and legal. Arguing the substance of the desegregation case, the Court asserted that "racial discrimination in public education is unconstitutional and all provisions of federal, state or local law requiring or permitting such discrimination must yield to this principle." Separate educational facilities were declared to be "inherently unequal." The revolutionary nature of this decision resonated in its profound influence on centuries-old social customs, on class arrangements, on the rigid racial hierarchy, and on fundamental dimensions of African American life that had solidified under segregation. In rearguing the question of community relief, the Supreme Court affirmed that District Courts were to act in accordance with the opinion and "to admit the parties to these cases to public schools on a racially nondiscriminatory basis with all deliberate speed." The Court's insistence was anchored in constitutional precepts and in a demarcated set of beliefs about the interconnections between social structure and collective psychology. This resulted in the assumption that segregation was harmful to children of African ancestry principally because "it had the sanction of law."

Taking into account community circumstances, the need for "practical flex-ibility in shaping remedies" was specified in *Brown II*. The follow-up pronouncement stipulated replacing the dual system within a sensible time frame. The Court reasoned that what was "at stake is the personal interest of the plaintiffs in admission to public schools as soon as practicable on a non-discriminatory basis." Since spatially distinct educational systems had been entrenched for centuries, the Court alluded to potential organizational difficulties. Nonetheless, it failed to grasp or predict the profound cultural significance of what was evolving. The pronouncement was an amalgam of structural psychology mirroring the political ethos of the times. Thus, in the historic 1954 decision, the cardinal principle was that segregated schools were not only unconstitutional but that the black school was fundamentally deficient. Racial isolation from whites was construed as permanently harm-ful to the self-feelings of African American children. The possibility of socially disruptive outcomes from unwarranted racial contact and the demo-lition of the black school was neither incorporated in any arguments nor anticipated.

Coming of Age in a Segregated Town

In the city of Lexington, Kentucky, a relatively quiet family-oriented town, where residential segregation and employment and social discrimination still exist, I attended all-black elementary and secondary neighborhood schools. At that time, in the late 1940s and 1950s, there was no awareness of the prospect of integration nor of alternatives to racial separation. My family could not shop in the department stores, sit at the lunch counters, use rest rooms in a service station, live in any neighborhood that they chose, drink at any water fountain, vote without fear, eat in downtown restaurants, enter the front door of hospitals or theaters, attend the local university, or even sit in the front of buses used for local and interstate transportation. I am a product of this form of inflexible and degrading structural, social, and economic discrimination. However, I grew up at a time when African American children had two par-ents in the home, the extended family was prominent, neighborhoods were safe, teachers taught basic literacy skills, drugs and violence were virtually unknown, and families were secure in their communities.

In contradistinction to the aftermath of imposed public school integration, within the structurally and culturally unique African American school, motivation was high and the quality of the learning environment was con-structive. The positive communal features emerging out of ecological apartheid counteracted myths of "racial inferiority." African American children could become champions in speech contests, valedictorians, artists, captains of the football and basketball teams, class president, editor of the student news-paper, or homecoming queen; and black boys dated black girls. Taught by African American teachers, mostly women, who were often their neighbors and Sunday school teachers, children learned to read, to write, and to do arithmetic in the first grade. Those born in the post-Depression and World

War II years also grew up with healthy self-images and high achievement aspirations.

Out of racist segregation and discrimination, the African American neighborhood molded a set of cohesive values, beliefs, legends, customs, and family lifestyles. Across the country, the schools for Americans of African descent were named after creative warriors in the struggle for freedom – Paul Lawrence Dunbar, Booker T. Washington, Frederick Douglass, and George Washington Carver. These names symbolized a rich heritage and provided models for historical continuity. Racial integration of public schools drastically transformed all of this. Dr. Robert Douglas, Professor of Pan-African Studies at the University of Louisville, has stated that integration "tore the underlying fabric of black communities apart."

With the implementation of the 1954 decision in the South, many schools designed for African American children were closed. The names that once embraced the halls of these virtually "natural institutions" were erased or reassigned to predominantly white schools, depriving them of their historical and cultural relevance. Teachers were either transferred or lost their jobs. And the African American principal – often a male hero and community leader – became obsolete. The loss of this black role model and parental figure has had far-reaching ramifications.

Because residential separation has remained as the most virulent social indicator of racist attitudes and practices, busing was invented as the tool to enforce the Court's judgment. At the time of its introduction, there were no apparent options. Transporting children thus became the technique for dismantling the historically segregated school. As the process of racial integration unraveled across the country, new types of organizational and adjustment problems surfaced. Beginning with removing children from their neighborhoods, busing constituted an expensive remedy that affected mostly poor children and families. Those transported remain primarily African Americans who must leave home in the early-morning hours for long bus trips to attend schools with strangers – other children who are not members of their neighborhood, racial group, or social class. Not only were poor and working-class children used as the agents of change, but the African American school was gradually disassembled across the country. What could be more harmful than taking children away from familiar environments for the purposes of implementing a dominant-sector philosophy?

Segregation within Integration: An Ironic Outcome

To address the challenge of documenting and critically evaluating the impact of forced school integration on African American children, I interviewed two of my first cousins who have taught in public schools for more than twenty-five years. Products of rigid discrimination and a segregated school system, both women are competent and effective teachers. They have also experienced profound transformations in the social organization of elementary and secondary schools. Their voices are representative of others across the country.

The first, who has taught for over thirty years, offers critical insights into the integration quandary. When asked to describe how school desegregation has affected African American children, she stated:

> The black child has gotten cheated through integration with lots of whites. [The] black child has to prove himself [or herself]. With integration, [we] got more money, better facilities, better text books. [But] what is missing is nurturing and the caring. This has had negative effects. Kids who could have been leaders are pretty much ignored. [You] can't ignore somebody and expect them to behave, to fit in.

She expressed deep concern about one practice that harms the learning potential of African American students: frequently and disproportionately issuing them hall passes. Such permissions are excuses to "get in the hall" and out of the classroom. Unfortunately, there is a tendency for teachers to approve hall passes "just to get rid of them." On the other hand, "to say 'no' indicates caring." She noted that since African American students often do not receive positive feedback in the classroom, those who congregate in the halls tend to be loud because "they're seeking negative attention." In the middle-class white environment, this attention-seeking behavior ultimately crystallizes animosity and racist stereotypes.

Another cousin, who has also taught for over twenty-five years in different grades as well as in special education, was asked: "What has integration done for or to African American children?" With wisdom and understanding of elementary and secondary school cultures, she observed irony in the fact that integration has actually "separated our black kids. It has divided them." Racial stratification and separation permeate the integrated school.

> The ones they bus to schools are from the projects. Integration prevents these kids from participating in extracurricular activities. They have to ride the bus and can't participate in clubs, organizations. As far as the parents are concerned, they are from the projects and don't have access to transportation.

> You get a few of these kids in one school; they group together. They want to be seen; they become behavior problems. Then, they're put in special education classes; [or] they're put in behavior disorder classes. They congregate. They don't do their work, [thus] they're labeled as slow. Then they're tracked. What happens as a result of that? Low self-esteem. "I'm slow any way, so why try?"

> It's interesting that black kids are a minority in the [white] school but a majority in the special education and behavior disorder classes.

> [At meal time,] they go by classes to the cafeteria. They go in and look for each other. They get together and become noisy. Then, they are put on school suspension.

I then asked if she thought this peculiar form of integration could work. Her immediate response was no. She stated that what has evolved is not interracial desegregation but racial exclusion.

> I don't think it's integration. I think it's separation. The kids live in the projects across from each other. [However], in the morning, they're separated by busing. That's why when they get to school, they look for people like themselves.

Additionally, the social life of African American teenage girls has been affected severely by the breakup of the communal black high school. "They don't have any black guys to date. [But] black guys will date white girls." Thus, few African American youth participate in student activities. From this alienating social world, it is highly probable that the cycle of alienation experienced in the middle and high school years may be a prime factor in dropout rates, interracial tension, teenage pregnancy, and the number of female-headed households.

My final question to these women centered on what could be a resolution to the integration dilemma. Both feel that the only answer is "neighborhood schools."

> I don't think the solution is integration of schools. The solution is integration of neighborhoods. When they started integration, black kids were bused out of the inner city into white schools.

> The neighborhood school is a fallacy. Let there be only magnet schools. They [local and state governments] integrated by closing black schools. Black teachers were sent to white schools. ... Black students were bused out of the neighborhood and bused out of similar economic conditions. [They] were used for numbers – to meet quotas.

Integration as "Reverse Discrimination"

The views of two talented teachers – who experienced segregation and the changing character of public schools – reveal the multiple human costs associated with displacing the black school and forcing children to integrate. Presently, children and adolescents in the United States, who live in familiar enclaves, are the victims of structurally based philosophies that have not taken into account the intergenerational fragmentation and psychological impairment of African American children's identities and hopes. Integration in elementary, middle, and high schools across the country is simply not working. Racial animosities are at an all-time high. African American children are not developing in constructive and unbiased environments. As many middle-class teachers enter the classroom with negative attitudes toward them and their parents, their feelings of self-worth and academic potential are damaged.

Where busing has been used to propel integration, when there are few black students in a classroom, they experience prolonged isolation in a predominantly white setting. Excluded from learning opportunities, they are also disengaged from student social circles that result in the cultivation of leadership skills and lasting friendships. Furthermore, minimal communication transpires between white teachers and African American parents. One disturbing result is that too often the Parent Teacher Association tends not to represent a cohesive and meaningful bond between the family and the neighborhood. Because parents lack an understanding of what occurs in the classroom, they feel a loss of control.

Essentially, in a historically race-conscious country founded on the ideology of white supremacy, separate facilities, amenities, and services in all institutional spheres will always be unequal. Even in a "desegregated" or partially integrated society, the economically deprived and politically disenfranchised will never be treated fairly. The destruction of the healthy aspects of African American family life that flowed from the sense of community under segregation will have a permanent influence on African Americans and the larger society. Although segregated schools were "separate and unequal," within their boundaries African American children were not exposed to denigrating racial imagery from the teachers, tracking, low expectations, or race hatred. Hence, the constitutional and structural benefits gained from obligatory school integration do not outweigh the immeasurable cultural and psychological losses. As Chicago attorney Thomas Hood stated at a meeting of the Kentucky African American Heritage Commission, "the same people in charge of desegregation had been in charge of segregation. Instead of integrating, they disintegrated." Such an occurrence epitomizes genuine "reverse discrimination." Therein rests a principal contradiction associated with the mandatory transformation of the public school.

At this political moment, integration of the schools has been an abysmal failure. Although this mandated change was a necessary prerequisite for granting access to public accommodations and all other institutions in the United States, in the school setting, it is malfunctioning. One is thus compelled to ask what the rationale is for maintaining the philosophy and practice of compulsory school integration. The data are sparse and inconsistent on the benefits of busing and school "integration." It is known, however, that African American children are failing, dropping out at alarming rates, and graduating without basic literacy skills. In addition, their developmental and cultural needs are not being met. Suppressed motivation, low achievement, poor test performance, and attrition rates for these children are major signals of the failure of school integration. Also, in the desegregated school, racial hostility and "hate speech" have reached an all-time high. Similarly, violence is a frequent mode of conflict resolution.

While the guiding supposition of the 1954 Supreme Court ruling – that racially separate educational facilities are inherently unequal – was accurate, the assumption of a direct link between structural inequality, in the case of the black school, and intellectual and psychological deficiencies is questionable. What has been neglected in integration history over the past forty to forty-five years has been a rational assessment of the emotional, motivational, learning, and community impact of abolishing the black school on poor and working-class African American children. Few performance and behavioral outcomes were of concern or envisioned in the Court's edict to desegregate "with all deliberate speed" and to concomitantly dismantle schools set aside for Americans of African descent. Especially ignored was the cultural chaos that would ensue for a disenfranchised and disempowered population accustomed to surviving under absolute ecological and institutional segregation. This extraordinary dilemma permeates the entire social and political fabric of the United States at the culmination of the twentieth century.

8

Racial Districting

Groups, Representation, and Race Conscious Districting

Lani Guinier

[N]ow that the first round of reapportionment has been accomplished, there is need to talk "one man-one vote" a little less and to talk a little more of "political equity," and of functional components of effective representation. *A mathematically equal vote which is politically worthless because of gerrymandering or winner-take-all districting is as deceiving as "emperor's clothes."*[1]

With voices pitched in the high decibel range, critics of race-conscious districting[2] are blasting the Voting Rights Act and its 1982 amendments. A recent *Wall Street Journal* headline declares that voting is now "rigged by race."[3] Ethnic activists, the writer asserts, are collaborating with GOP operatives in an unholy political alliance to herd minorities into their own convoluted urban districts in order to improve GOP prospects in majority white suburban areas. According to such critics, this is a "political one-night stand" made possible by misguided federal courts and Department of Justice officials construing the 1982 Act to create majority minority districts, the newest form of "racial packaging."[4]

My students inform me that Cokie Roberts, as part of ABC News's election night coverage, dramatically illustrated the concerns of critics when she traced on a map of the Chicago area the "earmuff" district, allegedly carved out of two noncontiguous Chicago neighborhoods joined by a narrow rod to maximize the possibility that the Latino residents would be able to elect a representative of their choice to Congress.[5] And in June 1993, the Supreme Court discovered a new constitutional right enabling white voters in North Carolina to challenge, based on its odd and irregular shapes, a "highway" district that narrowly tracks the path of an interstate, creating a swatch of voters on either side of the highway from one end of the state to the other.

Excerpted from Lani Guinier, *The Tyranny of the Majority* (New York: The Free Press, 1994), chapter 5.

This fifty-four percent black district, the most integrated in the state, elected Melvin Watt, one of the first two blacks elected to Congress from that state in this century.

The Voting Rights Act codified the right of protected minority groups to an equal opportunity to elect candidates of their choice, although its language disclaims the right to racial representation by members of the racial group in direct proportion to population. The critics now claim this is special and unwarranted protection for racial and language minority groups. In the name of liberal individualism, these critics assert that the statute effected a radical transformation in the allocation and nature of representation.

Although race-conscious districting is their apparent target, these critics have fixed their aim on a deeper message – that pressing claims of racial identity and racial disadvantage diminish democracy. We all lose, the theory goes, when some of us identify in racial or ethnic group terms.

In my view, critics of race-conscious districting have misdirected their fire. Their emperor has no clothes. Their dissatisfaction with racial-group representation, and representation ignores the essentially group nature of political participation. In this regard, the critics fail to confront directly the group nature of representation itself, especially in a system of geographic districting. Perhaps unwittingly they also reveal a bias toward the representation of a particular racial group rather than their discomfort with group representation itself. In a society as deeply cleaved by issues of racial identity as ours, there is no one race. In the presence of such racial differences, a system of representation that fails to provide group representation loses legitimacy.

Yet these critics have, in fact, accurately identified a problem with a system of representation based on winner-take-all territorial districts. There is an emperor wearing his clothes, but not as they describe. Rather than expressing a fundamental failure of democratic theory based on group representation per se, the critics have identified a problem with one particular solution. It is districting in general – not race-conscious districting in particular – that is the problem.

Winner-take-all territorial districting imperfectly distributes representation based on group attributes and disproportionately rewards those who win the representational lottery. Territorial districting uses an aggregating rule that inevitably groups people by virtue of some set of externally observed characteristics such as geographic proximity or racial identity. In addition, the winner-take-all principle inevitably wastes some votes. The dominant group within the district gets all the power; the votes of supporters of nondominant groups or of disaffected voters within the dominant group are wasted. Their votes lose significance because they are consistently cast for political losers.

The essential unfairness of districting is a result, therefore, of two assumptions: (1) that a majority of voters within a given geographic community can be configured to constitute a "group"; and (2) that incumbent politicians, federal courts, or some other independent set of actors can fairly determine which group to advantage by giving it all the power within the district. When either of these assumptions is not accurate, as is most often the case, the districting is necessarily unfair.

Another effect of these assumptions is gerrymandering, which results from the arbitrary allocation of disproportionate political power to one group. Districting breeds gerrymandering as a means of allocating group benefits; the operative principle is deciding whose votes get wasted. Whether it is racially or politically motivated, gerrymandering is the inevitable byproduct of an electoral system that aggregates people by virtue of assumptions about their group characteristics and then inflates the winning group's power by allowing it to represent *all* voters in a regional unit.

Given a system of winner-take-all territorial districts and working within the limitations of this particular election method, the courts have sought to achieve political fairness for racial minorities. As a result, there is some truth to the assertion that minority groups, unlike other voters, enjoy a special representational relationship under the Voting Rights Act's 1982 amendments to remedy their continued exclusion from effective political participation in some jurisdictions. But the proper response is not to deny minority voters that protection. The answer should be to extend that special relationship to *all* voters by endorsing *the equal opportunity to vote for a winning candidate* as a universal principle of political fairness.

I use the term "one-vote, one-value" to describe the principle of political fairness that as many votes as possible should count in the election of representatives. Each voter should be able to choose, by the way she casts her votes, who represents her. One-vote, one-value is realized when everyone's vote counts for someone's election. The only system with the potential to realize this principle for *all* voters is one in which the unit of representation is political rather than regional, and the aggregating rule is proportionality rather than winner-take-all. Semiproportional systems, such as cumulative voting, can approximate the one-vote, one-value principle by minimizing the problem of wasted votes.

One-vote, one-value systems transcend the gerrymandering problem because each vote has an equal worth independent of decisions made by those who drew district lines. Votes are allocated based on decisions made by the voters themselves. These systems revive the connection between voting and representation, whether the participant consciously associates with a group of voters or chooses to participate on a fiercely individual basis. Candidates are elected in proportion to the intensity of their political support within the electorate itself rather than as a result of decisions made by incumbent politicians or federal courts once every ten years.[6]

My project in this chapter is to defend the representation of racial groups while reconsidering whether race-conscious districting is the most effective way of representing these groups or their interests.[7] My claim is that racial-group representation is important, but it is only imperfectly realized through the electoral system based on territorial districting or through the limited concept of racially "descriptive" representation.

*   *   *

Race in this country has defined individual identities, opportunities, frames of reference, and relationships. Where race has been of historical importance and continues to play a significant role, racial-group membership often serves as a political proxy for shared experience and common interests At least to the extent that an overwhelming majority of group members experience a common "group identity," those who are group members are more likely to represent similar interests. Group members also may share common cultural styles or operating assumptions.[8]

Group members also are more likely to be perceived by their constituents as representing them. This definition of representative as descriptive likeness or racial compatriot has a psychological component. Just as the flag stands for the nation, the presence of racial group members symbolizes inclusion of a previously excluded group. The symbolic role results from both the personal characteristics of the racial-group member and the assumption that, because of those characteristics, the racial-group member has had experiences in common with her constituents. As Hanna Pitkin writes in her groundbreaking work on representation, "We tend to assume that people's characteristics are a guide to the actions they will take, and we are concerned with the characteristics of our legislators for just this reason."[9] Thus, many racial minorities do not feel represented unless members of their racial group are physically present in the legislature.

As a result, traditional voting rights advocates comfortably rely on race as a proxy for interests. For example, in conventional voting rights litigation, election contests between black and white candidates help define the degree of racial polarization, *i.e.*, the degree to which blacks and whites vote differently. The idea is that the outcome would be different if elections were held only in one community or the other. The assumption of difference extends explicitly to the specific candidate elected, and implicitly to the issues that the candidate, once elected, would emphasize.

The assumption of this difference between races rests in part on the claim that where black candidates enjoy protection from electoral competition with whites, black voters can ratify their choices to hold their representatives accountable. In this way, the association between race and interests is modified to the extent that voters are given a meaningful choice in both initiating *and* terminating a representational relationship. Voting rights advocates assume that minority group sponsorship is critical. It is only where minority voters exercise electoral control, or have a meaningful opportunity to retire their representative that race functions as a representational proxy. Thus, majority-black single-member districts take advantage of segregated housing patterns to use geography as a proxy for racial choice, racial control, and racial representation.

*   *   *

Where voting is racially polarized, white voters and black voters vote differently. Where blacks are a numerical minority, racial bloc voting means that the political choices of blacks rarely are successful. To remedy this problem of being a permanent loser, black political activists and voting rights litigants have sought majority black districts in which the electoral choices of a majority of blacks determined the electoral winner.

Yet some commentators challenge race-conscious districting on the grounds that special protection throughout the political process for the rights of minority groups is unnecessary as long as individual minority group members have a fair chance to participate formally by voting in an election.[10] For these commentators, race-conscious districting is illegitimate because the right to vote is individual, not group-based.[11] Relying again on assumptions about fungibility and access, these observers challenge the right of minority groups to representative *or* responsive government.[12]

Given the prominence of racial group identities, I am not persuaded by this criticism to abandon the concept of group representation. I am aware of, but not in accord with, those critics of race-conscious districting who object on moral grounds to the drawing of districts along racial lines. As I suggested earlier, representation is a bottom-up process that ideally recognizes the importance of influencing public policy decisions on behalf of constituency interests. Accordingly, we cannot define political fairness merely as electoral fairness that guarantees nonbiased conditions of voting eligibility and equally counted votes. Nor do I think the only issues are whether blacks have special claims for protection or whether whites can or should represent blacks, although I think they can and and do.

Yet, in making the argument that racial groups deserve representation, I do not rely primarily on the political, sociological, or cultural claims involved in racial-group identity, or even on the historic context of group disfranchisement. My principal argument rests on the distinction within the political process between a claim for group rights and a claim for group representation. I argue for the latter based on the historic evidence that representation within territorial districts is implicitly about recognition of group interests, not just individual access. However, the future of such group representation – like the future of the group itself – lies less inside geographic boundaries and more within the cultural and political community forged by group consciousness and group identity. Empowerment – for a group as well as for an individual – comes from active assertion of self-defined interests. A group is represented where it has the opportunity to speak out and not just to be spoken for.

* * *

An illustration of this fractal problem is a 1992 New York City congressional plan that included a Brooklyn/Queens district to represent the interests of a Latino minority. This district concentrated Latinos in a new 12th Congressional District. Several Latino activists filed as candidates in the Democratic primary. So did Representative Stephen Solarz, a white incumbent whose previous district was consolidated within one-fifth of the new "Latino" district.

The entry of a well-financed, nine-term incumbent from a largely Jewish section of Brooklyn shifted the political expectations. The primary, which had been expected to focus on issues of interest to a poor Latino constituency, turned into a debate over whether a minority group could be represented by someone of a different ethnicity. According to a Latino community organizer, "The community is saying, 'Why is it that this Jewish person who has always represented other interests than ours, comes in now saying he's going to be our savior?'"[13] This complaint – that the white incumbent should not enter the race – rested on a complex, but misinformed, understanding of group representation.

The group is deemed represented where it has electoral control over the winner. The organizer's concern was that the sixteen percent white minority in the district – not the Latino majority – could have electoral control by consolidating their votes and converting their minority status into a plurality win. Since there were at least four Latino candidates, the white candidate would most likely win if the Latino vote were split, even though Latinos are fifty-five percent of the district's voting-age population. If the Latino majority was disaggregated into factions supporting different Latino candidates, it could have been white voters who chose the representative for the new district.

Latino activists complained that this did not give their community the choice they deserved. "The whole idea was to give our community some degree of choice, Latinos or non-Latinos who have some connection with the community.... [The well-financed white incumbent] doesn't fit that bill at all."[14] The white candidate answered, "The other candidates fear that I'll win, which somewhat belies their notion that the purpose of this district was to empower the people to make a choice."[15]

*   *   *

In fact, the successful candidate was Nydia Velazquez, a former representative of Puerto Rico to New York, who polled thirty-three percent of the vote, compared to twenty-seven percent for Mr. Solarz. According to the *New York Times*, Ms. Velazquez's margin of victory came from over-whelming Latino support in Brooklyn and from strong support from the black community.[16] She reportedly benefited from an endorsement by the city's black mayor, David Dinkins, and from the "firestorm" of criticism that erupted when Mr. Solarz decided to run in the newly drawn district.[17]

Four other Latino candidates competed in the primary. Elizabeth Colon polled twenty-six percent; Ruben Franco polled eight percent; Eric Ruano Mèlendez and Rafael Mendez each received three percent of the vote. Although I do not have the actual precinct totals, these figures do not rebut the possibility that a majority of Latino voters (especially those living in Queens) actually preferred someone other than Ms. Velazquez. Similarly, they do not deny the possibility that blacks, who are only eight percent of the District, may have supported Ms. Velazquez, but Asians and whites may have preferred someone else.

*   *   *

Indeed, over the ten-year term of the District, the Latino majority may act cohesively and return the Latina incumbent to office. Re-election of the incumbent may occur with decreasing turnout as a percentage of all the District's population, but with increasing support among those who do vote simply because she is the incumbent. This is consistent with evidence that minority candidacies generate relatively high voter turnout the first time a viable minority group member competes. Turnout, however, tends to go down when constituents realize that the election of a single minority incumbent changes very little of their day-to-day lives.

But the fact that the Latina is now an incumbent gives her tremendous resource advantages over any future opponents. Some may argue that her continued re-election reduces polarization within the district, as the other non-Latina voters see Ms. Velazquez work on their behalf. On the other hand, her predictable re-election success may exacerbate rather than reduce intergroup conflict. The District's complicated racial, ethnic, and linguistic mix is not reflected in the ethnic or racial group membership of its representative. The fact that the district winner in a multi-ethnic district has a psychological, cultural, and sociological connection primarily to one ethnic or racial group may alienate other groups over time.

If Asians, for example, feel consigned to permanent minority status within the minority district, they may bide their time until redistricting in the year 2000, when the legislature decides how many minority districts should be created and who should control them. The fight to be "the group" who gets the district, and with it all the power, pits minorities against each other. The fact that some members of the other minority groups in the 12th District can only cast wasted votes for ten years encourages each group ultimately to think in terms of its own moral, historical, and pragmatic claims to exclusive or primary district representation. Where representation becomes the lottery of competing oppression, no one wins.

*   *   *

The courts, however, have been hesitant to employ a one-vote, one-value system as a remedy under the Voting Rights Act. In Granville County, North Carolina, black voters challenged the at-large method of electing the county commissioner. Blacks, who comprised forty-four percent of the county's population, had never been able to elect any person to the five-member commission. The defendant-commissioners conceded that black voters were not represented on the county's at-large commission. They also admitted that if the county were districted, *and if two additional commissioner seats were added*, blacks would be able to elect one of seven commissioners, giving the forty-four percent black population "electoral control" over fourteen percent of the commission. The single-member districting remedy failed to capture much of the black community, which was dispersed throughout the county.

The plaintiffs proposed, and the district court approved, retention of the staggered term, at-large method of election with a threshold lowering, semiproportional modification that allowed voters to cast only three votes for the five open seats. When the modified system was employed, three blacks were elected to the seven-person commission.

The Fourth Circuit in *McGhee v. Granville* reversed and restricted the relief granted based on a narrow definition of the causal relationship between what the plaintiffs challenged and the available relief. The court ruled that single-member districts were the only appropriate remedy. Since the plaintiffs challenged at-large elections that prevented black candidates from getting elected, the exclusive remedy was to create single-member districts in which black candidates were likely to get elected. Even if all or many black voters did not reside in the newly configured majority-black districts, their remedy was limited to the "virtual" representation they received from districts that enjoy black electoral success.

*   *   *

I do not mean to denigrate concerns that the proliferation of political interest constituencies may undermine consensus, exacerbate tension, and destabilize the political system. These concerns reflect a preference for conflict resolution that camouflages rather than identifies political differences. My preference, however, is first to recognize salient differences and then to work with those differences to achieve positive-sum solutions. My idea is that politics need not be a zero-sum game in which those who win, win it all. My idea is that where everyone can win something, genuine consensus is possible.

*   *   *

Conclusion

The controversy over racial-group representation offers us an opportunity to re-examine the political fairness of our district-based electoral system. I posit that a system is procedurally fair only to the extent that it gives each participant an equal opportunity to influence outcomes. I call this principle one-vote, one-value. This is a measure of procedural, not substantive, legitimacy. According to this principle, outcomes are relevant only to the extent that they enable us to measure degrees of input, not to the extent they achieve some objective, substantive notion of distributive justice.

The challenge to racial-group representation is actually a criticism of a different kind of group representation: representation based on homogeneous geographic constituencies. Race-conscious districting is simply one expression of a larger reality: winner-take-all districting. Both justify wasting votes with often unstated assumptions about the group characteristics of district voters. In other words, the criticism of racial-group representation is, at bottom, a criticism of winner-take-all districting in which the district boundaries and the incumbent politicians define the interests of the *entire* district constituency.

I conclude that group representation is as American as winner-take-all districting; that the two are conflated in criticisms of race-conscious districting; and that consideration of alternative means of representing racial groups can shift the debate about political fairness. By directly confronting the problem of wasted voting, we may make the system more legitimate from the perspective of previously disenfranchised groups, and more fairly representative of issue-based groups who previously have been aggregated and silenced within the majority.

Notes

1   Robert G. Dixon, Jr., *Democratic Representation: Reapportionment in Law and Politics* (New York: Oxford University Press, 1968), p. 22 (emphasis added).

2   I use the term "race-conscious districting" to describe the practice of consolidating the number of minority group members in a single or a few winner-take-all subdistricts.

3   Jim Sleeper, "Rigging the Vote by Race," *Wall Street Journal*, August 4, 1992, at A14.

4   Ibid.

5   See *ABC News Special: The '92 Vote* (ABC television broadcast, Nov. 3, 1992), available in LEXIS, CMPGN Library, ABCNEW File. It may be worth noting for the record that Ms. Roberts's mother, Lindey Boggs, was arguably "redistricted" out of a seat in Congress in response to a successful lawsuit under the Voting Rights Act. See *Major v. Treen*, 574 F. Supp. 325 (E.D. La. 1983).

6   A recent example is Chilton County, Alabama, where the first Republican and the first black were elected to the county commission when the county implemented a modified at-large system of election using cumulative voting. Jim Yardley, "1 Voters, 7 votes? County Boosts Minority Clout," *Atlanta Journal/Atlanta Constitution*, October 23, 1992, at G5. Because the balance of power on the commission is now closely divided between white Republicans and white Democrats, even if voting is racially polarized the black Democrat may become an influential swing vote.

7   By representation of racial groups, I do not mean to suggest that only members of a group can represent its interests, that members of a group are necessarily racially similar, or that racial group members are necessarily homogeneous in thinking or interest.

8   Studies of black and female politicians do show that they have somewhat different agendas. See Rufus P. Browning et al., "Racial Politics in American Cities: Blacks and Hispanics in the U.S.," in *Political Mobilization, Power and Prospects* (New York: Longman, 1990); see also R. W. Apple, Jr., "Steady Local Gains by Women Fuel More Runs for High Office," *New York Times*, May 24, 1992, §4, at 5 (reporting on a survey of approximately half of all state legislatures which found that "even when men and women shared the same party affiliation and ideology, women were much more likely to expend their energies on health care, children's and family questions and women's rights issues; survey also found that women public officials tend more than their male counterparts of the same party and ideology to involve private citizens in governmental process to focus on needs of the poor, and to conduct public business in the open rather than behind closed doors"); Gwen Ifill, "Female Lawmakers Wrestle with New Public Attitude on 'Women's' Issues," *New York Times*, November 18, 1991, at B7 (describing a study done by the Center for American Women and Politics at Rutgers University which found huge gaps between male and female legislators over issues involving women's rights, health care, and children).

9   Hanna F. Pitkin, ed., *The Concept of Representation* (Berkeley: University of California Press, 1967), p. 89.

10 Cf. James F. Blumstein, "Defining and Proving Race Discrimination Perspectives on the Purpose vs. Results Approach from the Voting Rights Act," 69 *Virginia Law Review* 633, 636 (1983) (concluding that while minorities have the right to ballot access, there is no corresponding entitlement to racial group representation).

11   Ibid., at 712 n. 378; see also Michel Rosenfeld, "Affirmative Action, Justice, and
     Equalities: A Philosophical and Constitutional Appraisal," 46 *Ohio State Law
     Journal* 845, 912 (1985) ("The right to vote is a paradigmatic individual right.
     Each individual has only one vote, and absent any discrimination or unfair proce-
     dures, no group of voters has a right to complain that its candidate lost."); cf.
     Brian K. Landsberg, "Race and the Rehnquist Court," 66 *Tulane Law Review*
     1267, 1305 (1992) (asserting that proponents of the individual-based model tend
     to oppose race-conscious affirmative action).
12   Of course, some commentators challenge race-conscious districting on grounds
     unrelated to group representation principles. To some of these critics, require-
     ments to maximize minority representation are a quota system that awards bene-
     fits, *i.e.*, votes, through a racial entitlement. They view the arguments for
     minority representation in proportion to minority population ominously because
     the arguments rely on the implicit belief that maximizing minority representation
     means accepting the assumption that only minorities should represent minorities.
     Abigail Thernstrom, for example, is quoted as denouncing this assumption
     because it reflects the divisive notion that "this is a deeply divided society of sep-
     arate nations." Ronald Brownstein, "Minority Quotas in Elections?" *Los Angeles
     Times*, August 28, 1991, at A1, A14. Similarly, Judge Eisele asks. "Do we really
     believe in the idea of one political society or should this be a nation of separate
     racial, ethnic, and language political enclaves?" *Jeffers v. Clinton*, 730 F. Supp.
     196, 227 (E. D. Ark, 1989) (Eisele, C. J., dissenting), *aff'd*, 498 U.S. 1019 (1991).
        My response to this criticism is twofold. First, to some extent I agree that the
     current approach is divisive. Nevertheless, the right to vote is not a benefit but an
     essential element of our system's political legitimacy. Therefore, those who take
     issue with current approaches have a responsibility not just to criticize but to pro-
     pose alternative solutions that protect the right of the minority to have its voice
     represented and heard in the legislative debate. Second, in light of recent events in
     Los Angeles, concerns about *unnecessarily* dividing society do not seem consistent
     with the divided society, in which we already find ourselves. These concerns fail
     to acknowledge the prediction from twenty years ago of the Kerner Commission
     Report, that unfortunately we *are* becoming two nations, separate and unequal.
     See National Advisory Commission on Civil Disorders, *Report of the National
     Advisory Commission on Civil Disorders* 1 1968); see also Samuel Issacharoff,
     "Polarized Voting and the Political Process: The Transformation of Voting Rights
     Jurisprudence," 90 *Michigan Law Review* 117 (1992) (documenting and analyz-
     ing the significance of racially polarized voting in contemporary political dis-
     course). While concerns about balkanization are real, the solution to the problem
     of racial division is not to ignore the divisions but to attempt to heal them.
13   Alison Mitchell, "In Politics, There Is Only One Language," *New York Times*,
     July 19, 1992, at A29 (quoting David Santiago).
14   Ibid. (quoting Angelo Falcon, President of the Institute for Puerto Rican Policy).
15   Sam Roberts, "Does Politics of Fairness Mean Only Those From Minorities
     Should Apply?" *New York Times*, July 27, 1992, at B4 (quoting Rep. Steven J.
     Solarz). Others suggest that politics, not principles of choice, motivated Solarz's
     decision. "When his polls showed he couldn't win against any incumbent," he
     ran in an open district created to enhance the power of Latino residents. Ibid.
     (quoting Fernando Ferrer, President of the Bronx Borough). Still others suggested
     that Solarz had an unfair advantage based not on his ethnic background but his
     financial foreground. "It's not a question of what background he is. It's the color
     of his money," said Herman Badillo, the city's first Latino congressman. Ibid.

16 Mary B. W. Tabor, "Loyalty and Labor," *New York Times*, September 17, 1992, at B6.

17 See Lindsey Gruson, "For Solarz, A Career Ends in Grief and Relief," *New York Times*, October 7, 1992, at B3 (attributing Ms. Velazquez's 1869-vote margin primarily to criticism of Solarz's decision to run in a "Hispanic district"); "New York: The Race for the House," *New York Times*, September 16, 1992, at B8 (listing the final election returns from the Democratic primary for the 12th district). Incidentally, Ms. Velazquez was heavily outspent. Solarz spent $2 million in the race, about $220 for each of the 9138 votes he won. Alison Mitchell, "Rep. Solarz Loses in a New District," *New York Times*, September 16, 1992, at A1 (noting that Solarz had a "campaign fund of $2 million, more than all the other candidates combined").

The Future of Black Representation

Carol M. Swain

The Supreme Court has "eviscerated" the Voting Rights Act, a *New York Times* editorial declared on June 30, the day after the Court ruled five to four that it is unconstitutional to use the race of voters as the "predominant" factor in drawing the lines of congressional districts. A dejected Cynthia McKinney, whose Georgia district was the focus of the Court's scrutiny. warned that the decision in *Miller v. Johnson* might lead to the "ultimate bleaching of the U.S. Congress." Some melodramatic critics even likened the *Miller* decision to *Dred Scott*, the 1857 Court ruling that blacks were not citizens of the U.S. and "had no rights which the white man was bound to respect."

If the critics of *Miller* are right, the future of black political representation in Congress is grim, and blacks ought to mobilize to salvage what they can of racial districting. But another interpretation suggests a different response. The Court's decision may not diminish black influence in congressional elections, and it may not doom black candidates for Congress. And rather than diminishing the legislative strength of minorities, the decision may well enhance minority influence in Congress by enabling liberal candidates with agendas more friendly to African Americans to get elected in districts adjacent to some of the current black-majority districts. The Supreme Court handed down a decision; it didn't hand down the future. Much of what happens now depends on how the Congressional Black Caucus and other black leaders respond to new judicial and political realities.

Why *Miller* Isn't Fatal

Critics of the *Miller* decision have greately overstated its likely impact on minority representatives. The redrawing of the offending district lines does not mean that current black and Latino incumbents will automatically lose their re-election bids.

Most current black incumbents will not be fatally affected by the *Miller* ruling. Racial gerrymandering is not an issue for the numerous black representatives of geographical areas with large compact minority populations. The growing number of black politicians elected from districts without black majorities will also have little cause for concern over the Court's ruling. Black Democrats Ronald Dellums, Alan Wheat, and Bill Clay and black Republicans

Gary Franks and J. C. Watts have shown that white voters in congressional elections will support black candidates. Similarly, the elections of Illinois Senator Carol Moseley Braun, former Virginia Governor L. Douglas Wilder, Ohio Treasurer J. Kenneth Blackwell, and New York Comptroller Carl McCall show that race is no longer an insurmountable barrier to black electoral success at the state level as well. Carl McCall's victory was especially significant as he was the only New York Democrat to win statewide in 1994.

Many black incumbents, moreover have been anticipating that the Supreme Court would rule against race-conscious districting since last year's decisions in two earlier cases, *Johnson v. DeGrandy* and *Holder v. Hall*, and have been gathering resources in anticipation of more competitive campaigns. Georgia's McKinney and North Carolina's Mel Watts, for example, have reached out to white voters and eagerly sought to build biracial coalitions. They will now be in a stronger position to gain white votes than in previous elections.

Critics of *Miller* are also missing two other important facts. First, the Court did not authorize white officials to return to the old practice of breaking up compact minority populations into separate districts to dilute their voting power. *Miller* does not overturn *Beer v. United States* (1976), which led to a no-retrogression policy interpreted by the courts to mean that a redistricting plan or an electoral change cannot leave minority voters worse off. Thus, while partisan gerrymanders are certainly possible, black incumbents in compact minority districts have some protection against regressive redistricting plans.

Second, even if the Court had approved race-conscious districting, the strategy of grouping together black voters in the same district to elect blacks to Congress has nearly been exhausted. Today there are few places where African Americans are concentrated enough to create more black-majority districts. Philadelphia's 1st district, New York's 16th and 17th, and Mississippi's 4th are among the last remaining areas where such a strategy has any hope for increasing black representation. If black interests are to be better represented in Congress, racial gerrymandering is not the way.

Putting Color Before Substance

Most people would agree that African Americans lost substantive representation in 1994: the new Republican Congress represents their interests less than the previous Democratic one even though the new Congress has more black members. What went wrong? One answer is that the strategy to enhance minority representation through racial gerrymandering had the unintended consequence – unintended, that is, by most voting-rights advocates – of increasing Republican strength.

It was clearly the intention of the architects of the minority districts to give greater voting power to both African Americans and Latinos, two predominantly Democratic groups. Indeed, 13 blacks and 5 Hispanics were elected in the 18 newly created minority districts in 1992. The newly elected blacks, all Democrats, were reelected in 1994, but other members of their party did not fare as well. The Democrats' loss of 52 House seats in 1994 gave the Republicans 12 more than they needed for control. Race-conscious redistricting, the evidence suggests, cost of the Democrats enough seats to shift the balance of power in the House. By concentrating liberal voting strength in a few minority districts with supermajorities of Democratic voters, Democratic candidates in nearby districts were deprived of allies in their contests with more conservative Republicans.

Moreover, some white Democrats at the state and local level lost because minority voters failed to turn out for the general elections in districts where congressional black incumbents had no serious competition. In several congressional districts, Republicans declined even to run candidates against black incumbents. Since the elections in these districts were not actively contested, some black voters stayed home and failed to cast votes for white Democratic candidates running for other offices.

Some critics have disputed this analysis. Soon after the election, the Legal Defense Fund (LDF) of the NAACP issued a detailed analysis of what was then thought to be a Democratic loss of 54 seats (later narrowed to 52 after a couple of cliff-hangers were resolved). That analysis showed that Republicans captured 24 seats in states where there were no nonwhite-majority districts and 15 seats in white-majority districts surrounded by other white-majority districts. Of the remaining 15 districts, 8 gained minority voters and 6 remained the same. According to the LDF report, far from impeding the re-election rate of white Democrats in the South, race-conscious districting helped save Democrats in such states as Mississippi and Georgia. The report concludes that Democrats lost seats for the simplest of reasons: a majority of white voters shifted to the Republican Party.

But the LDF report fails to provide a satisfactory account of such states as Georgia, where two black-majority districts were added to the one that previously existed. The Georgia plan was largely designed to unseat Newt Gingrich by obliterating his old district and forcing him to move his residence. As it turned out, race-conscious redistricting gave him a safer Republican constituency, cutting black voters from 14 percent of his district in 1990 (when he won by only 974) votes to 6 percent in 1992 and after.

The dismemberment of Gingrich's former district contributed directly to the defeat of 12-term Democrat Richard Ray, and redistricting led three other white Democrats to retire. Since redistricting, a nine-to-one seat Democratic advantage has turned into a seven-to-three Republican advantage (with Republicans picking up one seat when white Democrat Nathan Deal switched parties). Now Georgia's only Democrats in the House are blacks representing districts where the voting-age population is over 57 percent black.

North Carolina, which created two black majority congressional districts, is another case that illustrates how redistricting backfired. Although its six Democratic incumbents survived the 1992 elections, they were decimated in 1994 when Democrats lost two incumbents and three open seats. Before redistricting, North Carolina Democrats held an eight-to-four advantage; after 1994 the Republicans had a seven-to-four advantage. Two of the state's four Democrats are black, and one of the white Democrats, Charlie Rose, was barely re-elected. The time may come when southern officeholders primarily consist of black Democrats and white Republicans.

North Carolina's second district was the one most directly affected by the concentration of black voters in nearby districts. Before redistricting, blacks made up 37 percent of the voting-age population; after redistricting, they constituted only 20 percent. Tim Valentine, the six-term Democratic incumbent, retired after his re-election margin dropped from 75 percent in 1990 to 54 percent in 1992. His Republican successor David Funderburk, a former U.S. ambassador to Romania, won the district with 56 percent of the vote. Commenting on Funderburk's qualifications, Valentine said, "He was an attractive candidate, a smart articulate man who had written several books. He's also probably to the right of Jesse Helms."

Other Democrats whose losses related to redistricting include Joan Kelley Horn of Missouri, who was barely elected in 1990 and then defeated in 1992 after losing more than 8,000 black voters to the district of a 13-term black Democrat, Bill Clay. Alabama's five-term Ben Erdreich, Maryland's three-term Tom McMillen, and Louisiana's ten-term Jerry Huckaby are among the other casualties of redistricting.

These results should scarcely be surprising. After all, the coalition to racialize voting districts included not only blacks and Hispanics, but also Republicans. Why should a party otherwise opposed to affirmative action have advocated quotas in the electoral system by supporting specially drawn racial districts that would surely elect Democrats? Could it be that the Republicans knew something about the effect of concentrating their opponents' strength in a few nonwhite-majority districts that escaped less discerning analysts?

Defending the strategy of race-conscious redistricting, the Reverend Jesse Jackson declared, "These new districts are beneficial because they've made the U.S. Congress look more like America. It's white, it's black, it's Hispanic, it's Asian, it's Native American, it's male, and it's female." And "it's also Republican," as Steven Holmes of the *New York Times* pointed out after the election.

Racial districting has had an impact not only on the makeup of Congress, but on the disposition of white representatives after black voters were stripped from their districts. In a study of the voting patterns of the white Democrats in the last Congress who had lost black voters through redistricting, political scientists L. Marvin Overby and Kenneth Cosgrove found that they became more conservative and less supportive of policies preferred by African Americans.

Although a number of analysts had predicted that the black and Hispanic empowerment strategy would backfire, voting-rights activists and minority-group leaders, almost all Democrats, forged ahead with their unholy alliance with the Republicans. The upshot was that black voters lost power and influence. Black politicians gained safer seats in a hostile Congress where many now consider themselves under siege. With the Republican capture of the House of Representatives, all but two of the African American representatives in Congress have become minority members of the minority party. African Americans lost 3 chairmanships of full committees and 17 chairmanships of subcommittees as well as other important leadership posts.

The Republican Agenda and the Black Caucus

Blacks in America are bound to suffer in the new political milieu of the mid-1990s, as Republicans advance their ambitious agenda to eliminate affirmative action, curtail social programs such as free school lunches, and reduce taxes. The Democratic Party has traditionally represented the policy preferences of African Americans much more effectively than have the Republicans, and the power of the Congressional Black Caucus depends on Democratic control.

During the last Congress, the Black Caucus became a major player in shaping the budget, the crime bill, the space program (which passed by a single vote), and other legislation. Caucus members were prominent in debates on health care, NAFTA, the ban on assault weapons, welfare reform, and environmental policy. The caucus provided the margin of victory on 16 of 87 key votes during the first session of the last Congress.

In the Republican Congress, caucus members represent 19 percent of the Democratic membership (an increase of 4 percent over the 103rd), but the change in party power has effectively marginalized them. One of Newt Gingrich's first acts as Speaker was to eliminate funds for 28 legislative caucuses, including the Congressional Black Caucus and the Congressional Hispanic Caucus. The Republican also abolished three standing committees, two of which, the Post Office and Civil Service Committee, and the District of Columbia Committee, had many black members. (During the last Congress, blacks constituted 47 percent of the Democratic membership of the Post Office Committee and 62 percent of the District of Columbia Committee.)

The Republican decision to reduce the size of all standing committees meant that under seniority rules, the most junior Democrats lost their assignments on the more prestigious committees. Blacks and Hispanics who had been in Congress for less than two terms were disproportionately affected. Carrie Meeks of Florida, with the lowest seniority, lost her place on the Appropriations Committee. Mel Reynolds and Cleo Fields lost their seats on Ways and Means. Bobby Rush of Illinois lost his seats on Banking and Financial Services and on the Science Committee. Before the 1994 elections, blacks were represented on all standing committees except Natural Resources. Ron Dellums of California chaired the Armed Services Committee, John Conyers of Michigan chaired Government Operations, and Bill Clay of Missouri chaired the Post Office and Civil Service Committee. (Clay had also been in line to chair the important Education and Labor Committee.) After the 1994 election, blacks lost all these positions and many others as well.

The resurgent Republicans also eliminated more than 600 committee staff jobs, many of which were held by blacks. Hundreds of personal staffers of defeated Democrats lost their jobs; many of these too were black, since Democrats in recent years have often reached out to hire more blacks.

The Congressional Black Caucus must bear some responsibility for what has happened. Bolstered by its increased size during the 103rd Congress, the caucus under Chairman Kweisi Mfume of Maryland took highly publicized aggressive stances against President Clinton and the Democratic congressional leadership. Caucus members publicly chastised the president over such issues as the withdrawal of Lani Guinier's nomination as head of the Civil Rights Division of the Justice Department, the racial justice provisions of the crime bill, and U.S. policy toward Haiti. Perhaps because caucus members often represent poorer-than-average congressional districts, they fought vigorously against provisions to ban contributions from political action committees, a key element of campaign reform.

A combination of factors, including the group's larger size, its aggressiveness, and the increased media attention paid to race-conscious districting, worked in concert to ensure that the caucus received more press coverage than ever before. On more than one occasion President Clinton was portrayed as kow-towing to the caucus's demands. The CBS Show *60 Minutes*, for instance, portrayed the caucus as goading President Clinton to intervene militarily in Haiti to restore power to exiled president Jean-Bertrand Aristide. Although some caucus members opposed the invasion, the segment suggested the group was a monolithic far-left power bloc with substantial influence over the president. Conservative talk-show host John McLaughlin, after criticizing Mfume for trying to direct the military efforts in Haiti, referred to him as "General Mfume."

The media also focused on the conflict between the caucus and its lone Republican member, Representative Gary Franks of Connecticut. At issue was Franks's desire to participate fully in Black Caucus meetings and the organization's desire to make plans without having a member of the opposition party present. The group received still more attention when Franks threatened to resign and had to be cajoled into staying.

But the most costly public mistake made by the group was probably its apparent embrace of Louis Farrakhan at its annual legislative weekend, which was aired on C-SPAN and coincidentally occurred during the historic week when Israel signed its peace agreement with the Palestine Liberation Organization. After a number of groups denounced the caucus's action, individual members placed the blame on Mfume, who they said acted without their authority. Two months later Khalid Muhammad, a disciple of Farrakhan, delivered a venomous speech at Kean College attacking Jews, Catholics, and other groups. The ensuing public outrage was so great that it led the Congress, for the first time in history, to pass a resolution condemning the speech of a private citizen. Twenty caucus members voted for the resolution, eleven voted against, four voted present, and three failed to vote as the measure passed the House 361 to 34. Mfume later reported that during 1994 the caucus had received thousands of racist threats and "buckets of hate mail." A more reflective and circumspect Congressional Black Caucus could have avoided that response.

"Black people have no permanent friends, no permanent enemies ... just permanent interests," runs the Black Caucus motto. To pursue those interests, blacks in Congress need more friends and fewer enemies. In response to *Miller*, black Democrats need to reach out across partisan and racial lines to form coalitions with those who share their values. In some cases, they may have to work with sympathetic Republicans to craft new policies that depart from traditional approaches to the problems that perennially affect African Americans.

Rather than constitute a disaster, the *Miller* ruling is good for the Democratic Party, good for the Congressional Black Caucus, and good for the vast majority of African Americans who need more representation of their liberal views of policy than they need people who look like them. Minority-group leaders have encouraged voters to confuse increased black and brown faces in legislative assemblies with greater power and influence, but the two are obviously not the same. African Americans can succeed politically only when they build broader coalitions. As a result of *Miller*, a more dispersed black population may enable enough Democrats to defeat Republicans to recapture the House of Representatives. More blacks in white-dominated districts will have a moderating influence on many Democrats and Republicans. So rather than decrease African American representation, the *Miller* decision may actually serve to increase it and to get Congress to become more solicitous of black interests, whatever the count of black faces.

Part II

The Politics of Diversity

Introduction to Part II:
The One and the Many

"What is the American, this new man?" This question, which reverberates through all of American history, was posited in 1782, by J. Hector St. John Crevecoeur, a French immigrant, in a volume entitled *Letters from an American Farmer*. Long before American social scientists began to track marriage patterns among ethnic groups, Crevecoeur observed: "I could point out to you a family whose grandfather was an Englishman, whose wife was Dutch, whose son married a French woman, and whose present four sons have now four wives of different nations." "From this promiscuous breed," he concluded, "that race now called Americans have arisen."[1]

There was a political subtext to Crevecoeur's treatise. The prevailing view in the American colonies at that time, articulated by John Jay in the *Federalist* papers, was that Americans were "one united people – a people descended from the same ancestors, speaking the same language, professing the same religion, attached to the same principles of government, very similar in their manners and customs."[2] Crevecoeur's position was that Americans were not merely transplanted Englishmen, but were an amalgam of many peoples who had converged on American soil, to forge a truly "new nation."

Yet it would be a mistake to see Crevecoeur as the original multiculturalist. Though he challenged *English* hegemony, his conception of "this new man" was itself hegemonic. Aside from the unwitting elision of women, Crevecoeur's "new man" was not meant to include Native Americans, who would be pushed to the brink of extinction by the invaders from Europe. Nor did it encompass the people of African descent who arrived on slave galleys and who constituted one-fifth of the population at the time that Crevecoeur wrote. Nor, finally, could Crevecoeur anticipate the great waves of immigration from non-European nations that would change the face of America.

Still, Crevecoeur's question was a prescient one. The reason that it reverberates through all of American history is that it has never lent itself to an answer that is fixed for all time. Just as the presence of non-English in the American colonies prompted Crevecoeur's famous question, each successive wave of immigration from yet other quadrants of the globe, injecting yet other peoples onto American soil, has raised the question anew. As in Crevecoeur's case, the tendency has been to broaden the prevailing conception of what it means to be "American."

For example, the arrival of hundreds of thousands of Irish during the "famine migration" beginning in the 1840s constituted the first mass influx of non-Protestants. For quite some time the Irish were reviled as the vanguard of a papal invasion, and their concentration in cities like Boston, New York, and Chicago presented the first challenge to the Protestant elements that permeated public education. Political elites were thus confronted with a choice: either they must provide funding for parochial schools (as is done in Canada, for example) or they must forgo Protestant influences in public education. The latter course of action was taken, less out of devotion to the idea that there should be "a wall of separation" between religion and schools (there never had been!) than out of aversion to promoting sectarianism in general and Catholicism in particular. Later Jews and other religious minorities raised similar objections to remaining Christian elements in the public schools (such as the morning prayer and Christmas celebrations). The answer, once again, was to close whatever gaps remained in the wall of separation between religion and the schools, and to insist that schools be scrupulously secular.

Thus the paradox: as America became more ethnically and religiously diverse, the nation's public institutions came under pressure to adopt universal principles that transcended the claims of any of the nation's constituent groups, beginning with the hegemonic claims of the dominant majority. No longer is the United States held to be "a white Christian nation," except in the ravings of a few extremist groups. On the contrary, the idea of the United States as "a nation of nations" seems to have taken root both in official ideology and in popular consciousness.

The image and reality of the United States as "a nation of nations" has been magnified by the arrival of some 20 million immigrants over the past several decades. Furthermore, this "new immigration" is far more diverse than earlier waves of immigration, thanks to the 1965 Hart-Celler Act which abolished the national origins system favoring groups from northern and western Europe. Now all nations, regardless of region or size, were placed on an equal footing. The consequences, though unanticipated, have been enormous. Two-thirds of post-1965 immigrants originate from Asia and Latin America. There are also very large flows from Africa, the Middle East, and the Caribbean. According to demographers, if present trends continue, whites will constitute only 52 percent of the national population in the year 2050.[3] America is becoming more diverse than ever, a truly inclusive nationality encompassing the spectrum of the world's population.

This new immigration has ignited old debates concerning "the one and the many" – how to balance the imperatives of "nation" with the fact of racial and ethnic "difference." These debates, however, are not exact replicas of the debates earlier in the century. For one thing, the new immigrants do not resemble the "huddled masses" of yore: many arrive with education, skills, and sometimes capital as well. Others, of course, lack these resources, and like earlier immigrants, are concentrated in the lowest and most exploitative job sectors. However, the fact that immigrants are so diverse in their class origins goes a long way toward explaining not only the variable experiences of the newcomers, but also the variable treatment accorded them by the receiving society.

A second point of difference is that today's immigrants enter a society with a far more favorable climate of tolerance. It is easily forgotten that the Irish, Italians, Poles, Jews, and others from European extraction were once regarded as "races" whose destiny was predetermined by their inbred cultures, if not their genes. Thanks in large part to the civil rights movement, which was itself the catalyst for immigration reform, "race" does not carry the same stigma that it did in times past. Furthermore, the ongoing struggle of African Americans and other minorities for justice and equality means that new immigrants are entering an ideological and political context that is conducive to their assertiveness and mobilization as well.

For these reasons current debates over the new immigration are on the whole less strident, and less saturated with racist animus, than the immigration debates of the past. Nevertheless, debate and controversy abound, and the purpose of Part II is to present recent writing on a range of issues concerning "the one and the many."

We begin with two thoughtful but divergent perspectives on the meaning of American nationality. In "What Does It Mean to Be an 'American'?" Michael Walzer explores the ways in which citizenship and nationality are compatible with the preservation of ethnic identity, culture, and community. On the other hand, David Hollinger takes a more skeptical view of ethnic pluralism, and asks whether the "ethno-racial pentagon" – consisting of African Americans, Euro-Americans, Native Americans, Asian Americans, and Hispanic Americans – is little more than a sanitized version of the old-fashioned division between black, white, red, yellow, and brown.

The next pair of readings deals with the perennial issue of assimilation. In "Assimilation's Quiet Tide," Richard Alba reviews evidence suggesting that descendants from early waves of immigration at the turn of the century are actually at an advanced stage of assimilation. Joel Perlmann and Roger Waldinger then ask "Are the Children of Today's Immigrants Making It?" They conclude that the overall picture is quite favorable, despite the fact that many immigrants languish in poverty and have fewer channels of escape than existed for past immigrants.

After these "framework" readings, we explore a number of specific issues:

The immigration debate   In "The Immigrant Contribution to the Revitalization of Cities," Thomas Muller examines the many ways in which immigrants have helped to resuscitate the urban economies of cities of high immigrant concentration. A far less sanguine analysis, however, is presented by Vernon Briggs in his article on "Immigration Policy and the U.S. Economy." Briggs argues that low-skilled immigrants increase competition and lower wages, and while immigrants who do have skills fill short-term needs, this comes at the cost of training and upgrading natives and new immigrants alike.

Multicultural education   Historically, the public schools have been the battleground for "culture wars" involving racial and ethnic diversity. Diane Ravitch presents a trenchant critique of multiculturalism, under the ironic title "E Pluribus Plures" ("from many, many"). Though conceding the importance of acknowledging and celebrating "diversity," Ravitch insists that the overarching mission of the schools is to emphasize values and ideas that will promote national unity. This viewpoint is challenged by Gary Nash in "The Great Multicultural Debate." Though there are areas of agreement between the two authors, Nash argues forcefully for a multicultural curriculum that confronts the historical cleavages that still divide America along lines of race, ethnicity, gender, and class.

Language politics   In "Lingo Jingo," Geoffrey Nunberg contends that the English-only movement is "a bad cure for an imaginary disease," in that it is trying to stamp out languages that are rapidly disappearing anyway. Donaldo Macedo, on the other hand, bemoans "The Tongue-Tying of America," and argues that the loss of native languages deprives groups of the cultural tools that they need in order to "become actors in the reconstruction of a more democratic and just society."

Self-segregation on college campuses   As colleges have become more ethnically diverse, the tendency of minorities to segregate themselves socially has been the subject of controversy. Two such cases are examined. Peter Beinart adopts a critical stance with respect to the demands of Orthodox Jewish students at Yale for separate housing. Troy Duster, however, suggests that critics of balkanization err by treating this as a question of either/or. According to Duster, the synergy that develops from different approaches – some integrationist, others separatist – redounds to the advantage of the community as a whole.

The debate over "identity politics"   Todd Gitlin is a prominent critic of so-called "identity politics" – the tendency of such groups as women, blacks, Latinos, Asians, and gays to pursue their special agendas. Arguing from a left perspective, Gitlin criticizes these groups for abandoning the universal principles that previously bound the left, allowing it to function more effectively as an instrument for political change. Robin Kelley, on the other hand, rejects the argument that "identity politics" is incompatible with a left agenda, or is responsible for the current debility of the left. Instead of unrealistically "transcending" difference, he argues for developing coalitions and building unity "by supporting and perhaps even participating in other people's struggles for social justice."

As is readily apparent from these annotations, the debates over "the one and the many" constitute an intellectual minefield. Indeed, the format of two readings on each issue is intended to convey to you, as readers, that these are contested areas where you are challenged to think through the issues and arrive at your own conclusions.

One word of caution. In a multicultural society all of us are actors in the drama that is being played out on the ground and debated in the academy. However, the fact that these debates tap your personal life experience can be either a boon or a detriment to learning. You should, of course, bring your observations and life experiences to bear (after all, the authors of the selections have done so!). On the other hand, if one is too bound by personal experience and self-interest, this can get in the way of seeing issues in a new and different light. By being confronted with divergent viewpoints, you will be challenged to reexamine your own assumptions, to don a different set of lenses, to transcend the personal domain, and to reach for a larger understanding of the socially ideal relationship between "the one and the many."

Notes

1 Quoted in Milton M. Gordon, *Assimilation in American Life* (New York: Oxford University Press, 1964), p. 116.
2 Quoted in John Higham, *Send These to Me* (New York: Atheneum, 1975), p. 3.
3 Philip Martin and Elizabeth Midgley, "Immigration to the United States: Journey to an Uncertain Destination," *Population Bulletin* (Washington, D.C.: Population Reference Bureau, 1994), p. 9. Assuming that present trends of immigration continue, the white proportion is projected to decline from 74 percent in 1993 to 52 percent in 2050. Comparable figures for blacks are 12 and 14 percent; for Hispanics, 10 and 22 percent; for Asians, 3 and 10 percent.

9

The Meaning of American Nationality

What Does It Mean to Be an "American"?

Michael Walzer

There is no country called America. We live in the United States *of America*, and we have appropriated the adjective "American" even though we can claim no exclusive title to it. Canadians and Mexicans are also Americans, but they have adjectives more obviously their own, and we have none. Words like "unitarian" and "unionist" won't do; our sense of ourselves is not captured by the mere fact of our union, however important that is. Nor will "statist," even "united statist," serve our purposes; a good many of the citizens of the United States are antistatist. Other countries, wrote the "American" political theorist Horace Kallen, get their names from the people, or from one of the peoples, who inhabit them. "The United States, on the other hand, has a peculiar anonymity."[1] It is a name that doesn't even pretend to tell us who lives here. Anybody can live here, and just about everybody does – men and women from all the world's peoples. (The *Harvard Encyclopedia of American Ethnic Groups* begins with Acadians and Afghans and ends with Zoroastrians.)[2] It is peculiarly easy to become an American. The adjective provides no reliable information about the origins, histories, connections, or cultures of those whom it designates. What does it say, then, about their political allegiance?

Patriotism and Pluralism

American politicians engage periodically in a fierce competition to demonstrate their patriotism. This is an odd competition, surely, for in most countries the patriotism of politicians is not an issue. There are other issues, and this question of political identification and commitment rarely comes up; loyalty to the *patrie*, the fatherland (or motherland), is simply assumed. Perhaps it isn't

Excerpted from *Social Research* 57, no. 3 (Fall 1990), pp. 591–614.

assumed here because the United States isn't a *patrie*. Americans have never spoken of their country as a fatherland (or a motherland). The kind of natural or organic loyalty that we (rightly or wrongly) recognize in families doesn't seem to be a feature of our politics. When American politicians invoke the metaphor of family they are usually making an argument about our mutual responsibilities and welfarist obligations, and among Americans, that is a controversial argument. One can be an American patriot without believing in the mutual responsibilities of American citizens – indeed, for some Americans disbelief is a measure of one's patriotism.

Similarly, the United States isn't a "homeland" (where a national family might dwell), not, at least, as other countries are, in casual conversation and unreflective feeling. It is a country of immigrants who, however grateful they are for this new place, still remember the old places. And their children know if only intermittently, that they have roots elsewhere. They, no doubt, are native grown, but some awkward sense of newness here, or of distant oldness, keeps the tongue from calling this land "home." ...

Nor is there a common *patrie*, but rather many different ones – a multitude of fatherlands (and motherlands). For the children, even the grandchildren, of the immigrant generation, one's *patrie*, the "native land of one's ancestors," is somewhere else. The term "Native Americans" designates the very first immigrants, who got here centuries before any of the others. At what point do the rest of us, native grown, become natives? The question has not been decided; for the moment, however, the language of nativism is mostly missing (it has never been dominant in American public life), even when the political reality is plain to see. Alternatively, nativist language can be used against the politics of nativism, as in these lines of Horace Kallen, the theorist of an anonymous America:

> Behind [the individual] in time and tremendously in him in quality are his ancestors; around him in space are his relatives and kin, carrying in common with him the inherited organic set from a remoter common ancestry. In all these he lives and moves and has his being. They constitute his, literally, *natio*, the inwardness of his nativity.[3]

But since there are so many "organic sets" (language is deceptive here: Kallen's antinativist nativism is cultural, not biological), none of them can rightly be called "American." Americans have no inwardness of their own; they look inward only by looking backward.

According to Kallen, the United States is less importantly a union of states than it is a union of ethnic, racial, and religious groups – a union of otherwise unrelated "natives." What is the nature of this union? The Great Seal of the United States carries the motto *E pluribus unum*, "From many, one," which seems to suggest that manyness must be left behind for the sake of oneness. Once there were many, now the many have merged or, in Israel Zangwell's classic image, been melted down into one. But the Great Seal presents a different image: the "American" eagle holds a sheaf of arrows. Here there is no merger or fusion but only a fastening, a putting together: many-in-one.

Perhaps the adjective "American" describes this kind of oneness. We might say, tentatively, that it points to the citizenship, not the nativity or nationality, of the men and women it designates. It is a political adjective, and its politics is liberal in the strict sense: generous, tolerant, ample, accommodating – it allows for the survival, even the enhancement and flourishing, of manyness.

On this view, appropriately called "pluralist," the word "from" on the Great Seal is a false preposition. There is no movement from many to one, but rather a simultaneity, a coexistence – once again, many-in-one. But I don't mean to suggest a mystery here, as in the Christian conception of a God who is three-in-one. The language of pluralism is sometimes a bit mysterious – thus Kallen's description of America as a "nation of nationalities" or John Rawls's account of the liberal state as a "social union of social unions" – but it lends itself to a rational unpacking.[4] A sheaf of arrows is not, after all, a mysterious entity. We can find analogues in the earliest forms of social organization: tribes composed of many clans, clans composed of many families. The conflicts of loyalty and obligation, inevitable products of pluralism, must arise in these cases too. And yet, they are not exact analogues of the American case, for tribes and clans lack Kallen's "anonymity." American pluralism is, as we shall see, a peculiarly modern phenomenon – not mysterious but highly complex.

In fact, the United States is not a "nation of nationalities" or a "social union of social unions." At least, the singular nation or union is not constituted by, it is not a combination or fastening together of, the plural nationalities or unions. In some sense, it includes them; it provides a framework for their coexistence; but they are not its parts. Nor are the individual states, in any significant sense, the parts that make up the United States. The parts are individual men and women. The United States is an association of citizens. Its "anonymity" consists in the fact that these citizens don't transfer their collective name to the association. It never happened that a group of people called Americans came together to form a political society called America. The people are Americans only by virtue of having come together. And whatever identity they had before becoming Americans, they retain (or, better, they are free to retain) afterward. There is, to be sure, another view of Americanization, which holds that the process requires for its success the mental erasure of all previous identities – forgetfulness or even, as one enthusiast wrote in 1918, "absolute forgetfulness."[5] But on the pluralist view, Americans are allowed to remember who they were and to insist, also, on *what else they are*.

They are not, however, bound to the remembrance or to the insistence. Just as their ancestors escaped the old country, so they can if they choose escape their old identities, the "inwardness" of their nativity. Kallen writes of the individual that "whatever else he changes, he cannot change his grandfather."[6] Perhaps not; but he can call his grandfather a "greenhorn," reject his customs and convictions, give up the family name, move to a new neighborhood, adopt a new "life-style."

He doesn't become a better American by doing these things (though that is sometimes his purpose), but he may become an American simply, an American and nothing else, freeing himself from the hyphenation that pluralists regard as universal on this side, though not on the other side, of the Atlantic Ocean. But, free from hyphenation, he seems also free from ethnicity: "American" is not one of the ethnic groups recognized in the United States census. Someone who is only an American is, so far as our bureaucrats are concerned, ethnically anonymous. He has a right, however, to his anonymity; that is part of what it means to be an American.

For a long time, British-Americans thought of themselves as Americans simply – and not anonymously: they constituted, so they would have said, a new ethnicity and a new nationality, into which all later immigrants would slowly assimilate. "Americanization" was a political program designed to make sure that assimilation would not be too slow a process, at a time, indeed, when it seemed not to be a recognizable *process* at all. But though there were individuals who did their best to assimilate, that is, to adopt, at least outwardly, the mores of British-Americans, that soon ceased to be a plausible path to an "American" future. The sheer number of non-British immigrants was too great. If there was to be a new nationality, it would have to come out of the melting pot, where the heat was applied equally to all groups, the earlier immigrants as well as the most recent ones. The anonymous American was, at the turn of the century, say, a place-holder for some unknown future person who would give cultural content to the name. Meanwhile, most Americans were hyphenated Americans, more or less friendly to their grandfathers, more or less committed to their manyness. And pluralism was an alternative political program designed to legitimate this manyness and to make it permanent – which would leave those individuals who were Americans and nothing else permanently anonymous, assimilated to a cultural nonidentity.

*   *   *

Hyphenated Americans

Good it certainly was to be an American citizen. Horace Kallen was prepared to call citizenship a "great vocation," but he clearly did not believe (in the 1910s and '20s, when he wrote his classic essays on cultural pluralism) that one could make a life there. Politics was a necessary, but not a spiritually sustaining activity. It was best understood in instrumental terms; it had to do with the arrangements that made it possible for groups of citizens to "realize and protect" their diverse cultures and "attain the excellence appropriate to their kind."[7] These arrangements, Kallen thought, had to be democratic, and democracy required citizens of a certain sort – autonomous, self-disciplined, capable of cooperation and compromise. "Americanization" was entirely legitimate insofar as it aimed to develop these qualities; they made up Kallen's version of civic virtue, and he was willing to say that they should be common to all Americans. But, curiously perhaps, they did not touch the deeper self. "The common city-life, which depends upon like-mindedness, is not inward, corporate, and inevitable, but external, inarticulate, and incidental … not the expression of a homogeneity of heritage, mentality, and interest."[8]

Hence Kallen's program: assimilation "in matters economic and political," dissimilation "in cultural consciousness."[9] The hyphen joined these two processes in one person, so that a Jewish-American (like Kallen) was similar to other Americans in his economic and political activity, but similar only to other Jews at the deeper level of culture. It is clear that Kallen's "hyphenates," whose spiritual life is located so emphatically to the left of the hyphen, cannot derive the greater part of their happiness from their citizenship. Nor, in a sense, should they, since culture, for the cultural pluralists, is far more important than politics and promises a more complete satisfaction. Pluralists, it seems, do not make good republicans – for the same reason that republicans, Rousseau the classic example, do not make good pluralists. The two attend to different sorts of goods.

Kallen's hyphenated Americans can be attentive and conscientious citizens, but on a liberal, not a republican model. This means two things. First, the various ethnic and religious groups can intervene in political life only in order to defend themselves and advance their common interests – as in the case of the NAACP or the Anti-Defamation League – but not in order to impose their culture or their values. They have to recognize that the state is anonymous (or, in the language of contemporary political theorists, neutral) at least in this sense: that it can't take on the character or the name of any of the groups that it includes. It isn't a nation-state of a particular kind and it isn't a Christian republic. Second, the primary political commitment of individual citizens is to protect their protection, to uphold the democratic framework within which they pursue their more substantive activities. This commitment is consistent with feelings of gratitude, loyalty, even patriotism of a certain sort, but it doesn't make for fellowship. There is indeed *union* in politics (and economics) but union of a sort that precludes intimacy. "The political and economic life of the commonwealth," writes Kallen, "is a single unit and serves as the foundation and background for the realization of the distinctive individuality of each *natio*."[10] Here pluralism is straightforwardly opposed to republicanism: politics offers neither self-realization nor communion. All intensity lies, or should lie, elsewhere.

Kallen believes, of course, that this "elsewhere" actually exists; his is not a utopian vision; it's not a case of "elsewhere, perhaps." The "organic groups" that make up Kallen's America appear in public life as interest groups only, organized for the pursuit of material and social goods that are universally desired but sometimes in short supply and often unfairly distributed. That is the only appearance countenanced by a liberal and democratic political system. But behind it, concealed from public view, lies the true significance of ethnicity or religion: "It is the center at which [the individual] stands, the point of his most intimate social relations, therefore of his intensest emotional life."[11] I am inclined to say that this is too radical a view of ethnic and religious identification, since it seems to rule out moral conflicts in which the individual's emotions are enlisted, as it were, on both sides. But Kallen's more important point is simply that there is space and opportunity *elsewhere* for the emotional satisfactions that politics can't (or shouldn't) provide. And because individuals really do find this satisfaction, the groups within which it is found are permanently sustainable: they won't melt down, not, at least, in any ordinary (noncoercive) social process. Perhaps they can be repressed, if the repression is sufficiently savage; even then, they will win out in the end.

Kallen wasn't entirely unaware of the powerful forces making for cultural meltdown, even without repression. He has some strong lines on the effectiveness of the mass media – though he knew these only in their infancy and at a time when newspapers were still a highly localized medium and the foreign-language press flourished. In his analysis and critique of the pressure to conform, he anticipated what became by the 1950s a distinctively American genre of social criticism. It isn't always clear whether he sees pluralism as a safeguard against or an antidote for the conformity of ethnic-Americans to that spiritless "Americanism" he so much disliked, a dull protective coloring that destroys all inner brightness. In any case, he is sure that inner brightness will survive, "for Nature is naturally pluralistic; her unities are eventual, not primary. ..."[12] Eventually, he means, the American union will prove to be a matter of "mutual accommodation," leaving intact the primacy of ethnic and religious identity. In the years since Kallen wrote, this view has gathered a great deal of ideological, but much less of empirical, support. "Pluralist principles ... have been on the ascendancy," writes a contemporary critic of pluralism, "precisely at a time when ethnic differences have been on the wane."[13] What if the "excellence" appropriate to our "kind" is, simply, an American excellence? Not necessarily civic virtue of the sort favored by nativists, republicans, and contemporary communitarians, but nonetheless some local color, a brightness of our own?

Peripheral Distance

This local color is most visible, I suppose, in popular culture – which is entirely appropriate in the case of the world's first mass democracy. Consider, for example, the movie *American in Paris*, where the hero is an American simply and not at all an Irish- or German- or Jewish-American. Do we drop our hyphens when we travel abroad? But what are we, then, without them? We carry with us cultural artifacts of a quite specific sort: "*une danse americaine*," Gene Kelly tells the French children as he begins to tap dance. What else could he call it, this melted-down combination of Northern English clog dancing, the Irish jig and reel, and African rhythmic foot stamping, to which had been added, by Kelly's time, the influence of the French and Russian ballet? Creativity of this sort is both explained and celebrated by those writers and thinkers, heroes of the higher culture, that we are likely to recognize as distinctively American: thus Emerson's defense of the experimental life (I am not sure, though, that he would have admired tap dancing), or Whitman's democratic inclusiveness, or the pragmatism of Peirce and James.

"An American nationality," writes Gleason, "does in fact exist."[14] Not just a political status, backed up by a set of political symbols and ceremonies, but a full-blooded nationality, reflecting a history and a culture – exactly like all the other nationalities from which Americans have been, and continue to be, recruited. The ongoing immigration makes it difficult to see the real success of Americanization in creating distinctive types, characters, styles, artifacts of all sorts which, were Gene Kelly to display them to his Parisian neighbors, they would rightly recognize as "American." More important, Americans recognize one another, take pride in the things that fellow Americans have made and done, identify with the national community. So, while there no doubt are people plausibly called Italian-Americans or Swedish-Americans, spiritual (as well as political) life – this is Gleason's view – is lived largely to the right of the hyphen: contrasted with real Italians and real Swedes, these are real Americans.

This view seems to me both right and wrong. It is right in its denial of Kallen's account of America as an anonymous nation of named nationalities. It is wrong in its insistence that America is a nation like all the others. But the truth does not lie, where we might naturally be led to look for it, somewhere between this rightness and this wrongness – as if we could locate America at some precise point along the continuum that stretches from the many to the one. I want to take the advice of that American song, another product of the popular culture, which tells us: "Don't mess with mister in-between." If there are cultural artifacts, songs and dances, styles of life and even philosophies, that are distinctively American, there is also an idea of America that is itself distinct, incorporating oneness and manyness in a "new order" that may or may not be "for the ages" but that is certainly for us, here and now.

The cultural pluralists come closer to getting the new order right than do the nativists and the nationalists and the American communitarians. Nonetheless, there is a nation and a national community and, by now, a very large number of native Americans. Even first- and second-generation Americans, as Gleason points out, have graves to visit and homes and neighborhoods to remember *in this country*, on this side of whatever waters their ancestors crossed to get here.[15] What is distinctive about the nationality of these Americans is not its insubstantial character – substance is quickly acquired – but its nonexclusive character. Remembering the God of the Hebrew Bible, I want to argue that America is not a jealous nation. In this sense, at least, it is different from most of the others.

Consider, for example, a classic moment in the ethnic history of France: the debate over the emancipation of the Jews in 1790 and '91. It is not, by any means, a critical moment; there were fewer than 35,000 Jews in revolutionary France, only 500 in Paris. The Jews were not economically powerful or politically significant or even intellectually engaged in French life (all that could come only after emancipation). But the debate nonetheless was long and serious, for it dealt with the meaning of citizenship and nationality. When the Constituent Assembly voted for full emancipation in September 1791, its position was summed up by Clermont-Tonnerre, a deputy of the Center, in a famous sentence: "One must refuse everything to the Jews as a nation, and give everything to the Jews as individuals. ... It would be repugnant to have ... a nation within a nation."[16] The Assembly's vote led to the disestablishment of Jewish corporate existence in France, which had been sanctioned and protected by the monarchy. "Refusing everything to the Jews as a nation" meant withdrawing the sanction, denying the protection. Henceforth Jewish communities would be voluntary associations, and individual Jews would have rights against the community as well as against the state: Clermont-Tonnerre was a good liberal.

But the Assembly debate also suggests that most of the deputies favoring emancipation would not have looked with favor even on the voluntary associations of the Jews, insofar as these reflected national sensibility or cultural difference. The future Girondin leader Brissot, defending emancipation, predicted that Jews who became French citizens would "lose their particular characteristics." I suspect that he could hardly imagine a greater triumph of French *civisme* than this – as if the secular Second Coming, like the religious version, awaited only the conversion of the Jews. Brissot thought the day was near: "Their eligibility [for citizenship] will regenerate them."[17] Jews could be good citizens only insofar as they were regenerated, which meant, in effect, that they could be good citizens only insofar as they became French. (They must, after all, have some "particular characteristics," and if not their own, then whose?) Their emancipators had, no doubt, a generous view of their capacity to do that but would not have been generous in the face of resistance (from the Jews or from any other of the corporate groups of the old regime). The price of emancipation was assimilation.

This has been the French view of citizenship ever since. Though they have often been generous in granting the exalted status of citizen to foreigners, the successive republics have been suspicious of any form of ethnic pluralism. Each republic really has been "one and indivisible," and it has been established, as Rousseau thought it should be, on a strong national oneness. Oneness all the way down is, on this view, the only guarantee that the general will and the common good will triumph in French politics.

America is very different, and not only because of the eclipse of republicanism in the early nineteenth century. Indeed, republicanism has had a kind of afterlife as one of the legitimating ideologies of American politics. The Minute Man is a republican image of embodied citizenship. Reverence for the flag is a form of republican piety. The Pledge of Allegiance is a republican oath. But emphasis on this sort of thing reflects social disunity rather than unity; it is a straining after oneness where oneness doesn't exist. In fact, America has been, with severe but episodic exceptions, remarkably tolerant of ethnic pluralism (far less so of racial pluralism). I don't want to underestimate the human difficulties of adapting even to a hyphenated Americanism, nor to deny the bigotry and discrimination that particular groups have encountered. But tolerance has been the cultural norm.

Perhaps an immigrant society has no choice; tolerance is a way of muddling through when any alternative policy would be violent and dangerous. But I would argue that we have, mostly, made the best of this necessity, so that the virtues of toleration, in principle though by no means always in practice, have supplanted the singlemindedness of republican citizenship. We have made our peace with the "particular characteristics" of all the immigrant groups (though not, again, of all the racial groups) and have come to regard American nationality as an addition to rather than a replacement for ethnic consciousness. The hyphen works, when it is working, more like a plus sign. "American," then, is a name indeed, but unlike "French" or "German" or "Italian" or "Korean" or "Japanese" or "Cambodian," it can serve as a second name. And as in those modern marriages where two patronymics are joined, neither the first nor the second name is dominant: here the hyphen works more like a sign of equality.

We might go farther than this: in the case of hyphenated Americans, it doesn't matter whether the first or the second name is dominant. We insist, most of the time, that the "particular characteristics" associated with the first name be sustained, as the Know-Nothings urged, without state help – and perhaps they will prove unsustainable on those terms. Still, an ethnic American is someone who can, in principle, live his spiritual life as he chooses, *on either side of the hyphen*. In this sense, American citizenship is indeed anonymous, for it doesn't require a full commitment to American (or to any other) nationality. The distinctive national culture that Americans have created doesn't underpin, it exists alongside of, American politics. It follows, then, that the people I earlier called Americans simply, Americans and nothing else, have in fact a more complicated existence than those terms suggest. They are American-Americans, one more group of hyphenates (not quite the same as all the others), and one can imagine them attending to the cultural aspects of their Americanism and refusing the political commitment that republican ideology demands. They might still be good or bad citizens. And similarly, Orthodox Jews as well as secular (regenerate) Jews, Protestant fundamentalists as well as liberal Protestants, Irish republicans as well as Irish Democrats, black nationalists as well as black integrationists – all these can be good or bad citizens, given the American (liberal rather than republican) understanding of citizenship.

One step more is required before we have fully understood this strange America: it is not the case that Irish-Americans, say, are culturally Irish and politically American, as the pluralists claim (and as I have been assuming thus far for the sake of the argument). Rather, they are culturally Irish-American and politically Irish-American. Their culture has been significantly influenced by American culture; their politics is still, both in style and substance, significantly ethnic. With them, and with every ethnic and religious group except the American-Americans, hyphenation is doubled. It remains true, however, that what all the groups have in common is most importantly their citizenship and what most differentiates them, insofar as they are still differentiated, is their culture. Hence the alternation in American life of patriotic fevers and ethnic revivals, the first expressing a desire to heighten the commonality, the second a desire to reaffirm the difference.

At both ends of this peculiarly American alternation, the good that is defended is also exaggerated and distorted, so that pluralism itself is threatened by the sentiments it generates. The patriotic fevers are the symptoms of a republican pathology. At issue here is the all-important ideological commitment that, as Gleason says, is the sole prerequisite of American citizenship. Since citizenship isn't guaranteed by oneness all the way down, patriots or superpatriots seek to guarantee it by loyalty oaths and campaigns against "un-American" activities. The Know-Nothing party having failed to restrict naturalization, they resort instead to political purges and deportations. Ethnic revivals are less militant and less cruel, though not without their own pathology. What is at issue here is communal pride and power – a demand for political recognition without assimilation, an assertion of interest-group politics against republican ideology, an effort to distinguish this group (one's own) from all the others. American patriotism is always strained and nervous because hyphenation makes indeed for dual loyalty but seems, at the same time, entirely American. Ethnic revivalism is also strained and nervous, because the hyphenates are already Americans, on both sides of the hyphen.

In these circumstances, republicanism is a mirage, and American nationalism or communitarianism is not a plausible option; it doesn't reach to our complexity. A certain sort of communitarianism is available to each of the hyphenate groups – except, it would seem, the American-Americans, whose community, if it existed, would deny the Americanism of all the others. So Horace Kallen is best described as a Jewish (-American) communitarian and a (Jewish-) American liberal, and this kind of coexistence, more widely realized, would constitute the pattern he called cultural pluralism. But the different ethnic and religious communities are all of them far more precarious than he thought, for they have, in a liberal political system, no corporate form or legal structure of coercive power. And, without these supports, the "inherited organic set" seems to dissipate – the population lacks cohesion, cultural life lacks coherence. The resulting "groups" are best conceived, John Higham suggests, as a core of activists and believers and an expanding periphery of passive members or followers, lost, as it were, in a wider America.[18] At the core, the left side of the (double) hyphen is stronger; along the periphery, the right side is stronger, though never fully dominant. Americans choose, as it were, their own location; and it appears that a growing number of them are choosing to fade into the peripheral distances. They become American-Americans, though without much passion invested in the becoming. But if the core doesn't hold, it also doesn't disappear; it is still capable of periodic revival.

At the same time, continued large-scale immigration reproduces a Kallenesque pluralism, creating new groups of hyphenate Americans and encouraging revivalism among activists and believers in the old groups. America is still a radically unfinished society, and for now, at least, it makes sense to say that this unfinishedness is one of its distinctive features. The country has a political center, but it remains in every other sense decentered. More than this, the political center, despite occasional patriotic fevers, doesn't work against decentering elsewhere. It neither requires nor demands the kind of commitment that would put the legitimacy of ethnic or religious identification in doubt. It doesn't aim at a finished or fully coherent Americanism. Indeed, American politics, itself pluralist in character, *needs* a certain sort of incoherence. A radical program of Americanization would *really* be un-American. It isn't inconceivable that America will one day become an American nation-state, the many giving way to the one, but that is not what it is now; nor is that its destiny. America has no singular national destiny – and to be an "American" is, finally, to know that and to be more or less content with it.

Notes

1   Horace M. Kallen, *Culture and Democracy in the United States* (New York: Boni & Liveright, 1924), p. 51.

2 *Harvard Encyclopedia of American Ethnic Groups*, ed. Stephan Thernstrom (Cambridge, Mass.: Harvard University Press, 1980).
3 Kallen, *Culture and Democracy*, p. 94.
4 Ibid., p. 122 (cf. 116); John Rawls, *A Theory of Justice* (Cambridge, Mass.: Harvard University Press, 1971), p. 527.
5 Quoted in Kallen, *Culture and Democracy*, p. 138; the writer was superintendent of New York's public schools.
6 Kallen, *Culture and Democracy*, p. 94.
7 Kallen, *Culture and Democracy*, p. 61.
8 Ibid., p. 78.
9 Ibid., pp. 114–15.
10 Kallen, *Culture and Democracy*, p. 124.
11 Ibid., p. 200.
12 Ibid., p. 179.
13 Stephen Steinberg, *The Ethnic Myth: Race, Ethnicity, and Class in America* (Boston: Beacon Press, 1981), p. 254.
14 Philip Gleason, "American Identity and Americanization," in *Harvard Encyclopedia*, p. 32.
15 Gleason, "American Identity," p. 56.
16 Quoted in Gary Kates, "Jews into Frenchmen: Nationality and Representation in Revolutionary France," *Social Research* 56 (Spring 1989); p. 229. See also the discussion in Arthur Hertzberg, *The French Enlightenment and the Jews: The Origins of Modern Anti-Semitism* (New York: Schocken, 1970), pp. 360–2.
17 Kates, "Jews into Frenchmen," p. 229.
18 John Higham, *Send These to Me* (New York: Atheneum, 1975), p. 242.

◆

The Ethno-Racial Pentagon

David Hollinger

"If Alex Haley had traced his father's bloodline, he would have traveled twelve generations back to, not Gambia, but *Ireland*," Ishmael Reed has observed of Haley's *Roots*.[1] Haley's choice of roots is an emblem for three points that drive this [essay]: the United States is endowed with a *non*ethnic ideology of the nation; it is possessed by a predominantly *ethnic* history; and it may now be squandering an opportunity to create for itself a *post*ethnic future in which affiliation on the basis of shared descent would be more voluntary than prescribed.

The national ideology is nonethnic by virtue of the universalist commitment – proclaimed in the Constitution and the prevailing political discourse – to provide the benefits of citizenship irrespective of any ascribed or asserted ancestral affiliations. This commitment lies behind our sense that Haley had a real choice, and one that was his to make: individual Americans are to be as free as possible from the consequences of social distinctions visited upon them by others. Yet the decision Haley made was driven by a history predominantly ethnic in the extent to which each American's individual destiny has been determined by ancestrally derived distinctions. These distinctions have been flagged, at one time or another, by such labels as Negro, Jewish, Indian, Caucasian, Hispanic, Indigenous, Oriental, Irish, Italian, Chinese, Polish, white, black, Latino, Euro-American, Native American, Chicano, and African American. That any person now classified as black or African American might see his or her own life as more the product of African roots – however small or large a percentage of one's actual, biological genealogy and cultural experience – than of European roots reflects this history.

Hence Haley's choice is the Hobson's choice of genealogy in America. Haley could choose to identify with Africa, accepting, in effect, the categories of the white oppressors who had determined that the tiniest fraction of African ancestry would confer one identity and erase another. Or, Haley could choose to identify with Ireland, denying, in effect, his solidarity with people who most shared his social destiny. The nature of this choice is further illuminated by an experience reported by Reed, whose ancestry is also African and Irish, and who has flirted with the other option in the structured dilemma I am calling Haley's choice. Reed mentioned his "Irish-American heritage" to a "Professor of Celtic Studies at Dartmouth," who "laughed."[2]

In a postethnic America someone of Reed's color could march in a St. Patrick's Day parade without anyone finding it a joke. A postethnic America

Excerpted from "Haley's Choice and the Ethno-Racial Pentagon," in David A. Hollinger, *Postethnic America* (New York: Basic Books, 1995), pp. 19–50.

would offer Haley a choice more real than the one Hobson gave visitors to his stable when he told them that they could take any horse they wanted as long as it was the one nearest the door. And postethnicity would enable Haley and Reed to be both African American and Irish American without having to choose one to the exclusion of the other. Postethnicity reacts against the nation's invidiously ethnic history, builds upon the current generation's unprecedented appreciation of previously ignored cultures, and supports on the basis of revocable consent those affiliations by shared descent that were previously taken to be primordial.

Although this ideal gains some credibility in the context of the recent efforts of mixed-race Americans to defy traditional classifications, the notion of a postethnic America is deeply alien to many features of American and world history. This notion exists in uneasy tension, moreover, with a contemporary system of entitlements predicated on clear, enduring, and monolithic ethno-racial identities. Hence the exploration of the postethnic ideal needs to begin by underscoring the inequalities that have dominated the historical record and recognizing that these inequalities lend credibility to claims made on behalf of communities defined by descent.

Not every citizen's fortunes have been influenced to the same degree, or in the same direction, by America's notorious failure to act on its universalist aspirations. Being classified as Euro-American, white, or Caucasian has rarely been a basis for being denied adequate employment, housing, education, or protection from violence. One response to the patently unequal consequences of ethno-racial distinctions has been to invoke and sharpen the nation's official, Enlightenment-derived commitment to protect all its citizens from them. What this commitment means has been contested, of course, from the day a committee of the Second Continental Congress deleted from the Declaration of Independence Thomas Jefferson's denunciation of slavery to the most recent decisions of the United States Supreme Court concerning the limits of affirmative action. The commitment is plain enough, however, to make obvious the gap between the theory and the practice of American nationality. Indeed, the magnitude and persistence of this gap have inspired a second, very different response: pressure from the gap's other side, its ethnic side.

This alternative strategy for closing the gap asks public authority to facilitate and actively support affiliation on the basis of ancestry. By promoting the development of communities defined by descent, one might reasonably hope for more equal treatment of every descendant of every tribe. After all, the results produced by the long-preferred method of closing gaps – invoking and sharpening the nonethnic ideological tradition – remain disappointing even to most people who believe progress has been substantial. The nonethnic character of the ideological tradition can be construed as part of the problem rather than part of the solution. That tradition treats as irrelevant to citizenship the very distinctions that, in this newer view, need to be asserted, reinforced, and celebrated. Policies that ignore the distinctions now called "ethnic" or "racial" may place at a disadvantage people whose physical appearance, social behavior, or cultural tastes lead others to classify them ethno-racially, and then to discriminate against them in keeping with prevailing prejudice.

This feeling – that the goal of equality demands for America a future even more ethnic than its past – has encouraged the nation to accept a distinctive system of classification by descent-defined communities. This is the set of categories Americans most often confront when asked to identify themselves by a multitude of public and private agencies. On application forms and questionnaires, individuals are routinely invited to declare themselves to be one of the following: Euro-American (or sometimes white), Asian American, African American, Hispanic (or sometimes Latino), and Indigenous Peoples (or sometimes Native American). To gain a clearer understanding of this five-part demographic structure and of the pressures now being brought against it is the chief concern of this chapter.

The ethno-racial pentagon, as we might call it, is a remarkable historical artifact, distinctive to the contemporary United States. The five specified blocs are not equally populated or empowered, but the five-part structure itself is supposed to embrace us all. This structure might also be called a "quintuple melting pot," replacing the "triple melting pot" made famous by Will Herberg's book of 1955, *Protestant-Catholic-Jew*.[3] The distinctions between white Jews, white Catholics, and white Protestants that Herberg and his contemporaries thought so important have now diminished. The elements in each segment of the new structure do "melt" to some extent, but the old figure of the melting pot does not capture the process by which individuals are assigned space on the basis of their perceived communities of descent. Today's device for classification is not even a guide to lines along which genealogical interaction and merging are taking place; rather, it is a framework for politics and culture in the United States. It is an implicit prescription for the principles on which Americans should maintain communities; it is a statement that certain affiliations matter more than others.

Although this ethno-racial pentagon is now visible in many places, it is not the only demographic blueprint now being used. One competitor is defined by the term *people of color*. In this view, white and nonwhite are the two relevant categories, and all distinctions between various "colored" peoples are less significant than the fact that they are nonwhite. But it is the ethno-racial pentagon, not the color–noncolor dichotomy, that public and private agencies most often ask residents of the United States to locate themselves within. A major difference between the two systems of classification concerns culture. The white-colored dichotomy does not have a strong cultural content, but the ethno-racial pentagon does, and increasingly so, especially for educational purposes. An example is the widely publicized decision made in 1989 by the faculty of the University of California at Berkeley to require undergraduates to take a course involving the comparative study of at least three of five American cultures. The three were to be selected from the five blocs in the ethno-racial pentagon.[4]

The pentagon, in its capacity as guide to the cultural life of the United States, has symbolically erased much of the cultural diversity within the Euro-American bloc. The category of Euro-American, observed a journalist concerned with Irish American identity, has accomplished in short order a task that centuries of British imperial power could not complete: making the Irish indistinguishable from the English. Jewish identity, too, receded in significance when all Americans of predominantly European stock were grouped together. To be sure, a value of the pentagon is its capacity to call attention to a certain range of social and cultural diversity. But as is so often the case when the virtues of difference are contrasted to the vices of sameness, at issue is not really difference in general but the highlighting of certain differences at the expense of others.

Indeed, this diminution of the differences between various groups of Euro-Americans has dramatized the contingent, contextual character of the entire process by which differences and similarities are created, perpetuated, and altered. A New Hampshire resident of French Canadian ethnicity may learn, by moving to Texas, that he or she is actually an Anglo. Many European immigrants of the nineteenth century did not come to see themselves as significantly Italian or German until these identities were thrust upon them by the novel demographic conditions of the United States, which rendered obsolete the local identities into which they had been acculturated in Sicily and Swabia. Distinctions between Protestants, Catholics, and Jews of European extraction were once taken as seriously in the United States as are the distinctions now made between Euro-Americans and Asian Americans. Although the insight that ethno-racial distinctions are socially constructed is rapidly gaining ground, it is still obliged to struggle against popular, deeply entrenched assumptions that ethno-racial groups are primordial in foundation.

The sudden transformation of a great number of distinctive ethnic identities into Euro-America ought to make white Americans more sensitive to the comparable erasures of diversity that attend on the other four, pseudoprimal categories, some of which have been sanctioned by longer use. Tribal and linguistic distinctions among Native American peoples have long been lost on many non-Indian observers. The identity one attributes to Americans whose ancestors were Koreans, Cambodians, Chinese, Vietnamese, and Japanese by calling them all Asian Americans (or, in the older usage, Orientals) is obtained by diminishing the differences between them and other Americans of Asian extraction. The Hispanic, or Latino, bloc has more linguistic cohesion than does the Asian American or the Indigenous Peoples bloc, but it, too, can be broken down into subgroups defined, for example, by such points of origin as Argentina, Cuba, El Salvador, Mexico, and Puerto Rico.

The internal diversity of the African American bloc may be the least obvious, as measured by linguistic distinctions and national origins. Nothing, however, illustrates the selective suppression of diversity and the socially constructed character of these ethno-racial blocs more tellingly than the historic denial, by generations of empowered whites, that they share with black Americans a substantial pool of genes. As historian Barbara Fields has put the point, we still have a convention "that considers a white woman capable of giving birth to a black child but denies that a black woman can give birth to a white child."[5] The persistence of the "one-drop rule" deprives those with any hint of black skin of any choice in their ethno-racial affiliation. It makes a mockery of the idea that the ethno-racial pentagon is simply a realistic response to the facts of genealogical life, a set of five gardens each providing natural and sustaining roots. Hence, Haley's choice.

And it is choice, so highly valued by the postethnic perspective, that is so severely limited by this pentagon. A Cambodian American does not have to remain Cambodian, as far as non–Asian Americans are concerned, but only with great difficulty can this Cambodian American cease to be an Asian American. So, too, with Japanese Americans or Chinese Americans. As was implicitly asked by the white autoworker from Detroit who in 1989 clubbed to death the Chinese American Victor Chin, thinking him Japanese, "What's the difference, anyway?" The same applies to the other blocs: indigenous peoples might care who is a Cherokee and who is a Kwakiutl, but outside that section of the pentagon, an Indian is usually an Indian. Some Jewish Americans might take great pride in their particularity as Jews, but from the viewpoint of many African Americans – returning an old favor – it is the whiteness of the whole lot of them that counts. And so on. Moreover, the Bureau of the Census allows the selection of one ethno-racial category and prohibits the choice of more than one.

The lines between the five unequally inhabited sides of the ethno-racial pentagon mark the limits of individual movement, as set by prevailing convention. The several lines distinguishing one segment of the pentagon from another are not resistant in exactly the same degree to intermarriage and other types of border crossing and category mixing. Yet, all are strong enough to function as "racial" as opposed to "ethnic" boundaries. Two kinds of lines are, in fact, being drawn, and they are widely accepted, at least for now: fainter lines distinguish the ethnicities found *within* each of the five blocs (Swedes, Filipinos, Pawnees, etc.), while bolder, thicker lines render the five blocs themselves into races, or race equivalents.

The ethno-racial pentagon is a highly particular creation of recent American history, although it draws upon traditional races. Some of the blocs owe much more than others do to classical race theory of the nineteenth century. Two "races" included in most of those old, now anachronistic schemas – some of which posited the existence of only three or four races, and others of which listed dozens – were called Mongoloid and Negroid, obviously prefiguring the Asian American and African American blocs. But the American adherence to the one-drop rule renders the African American bloc a distinctive formation, unlike the categories traditionally employed in Brazil, South Africa, and elsewhere to recognize racial mixture. Moreover, Mongoloid was generally taken to encompass only the peoples of east Asia, not those of south Asia now routinely included in the Asian American segment of the pentagon. When Mongoloid was construed by race theorists as a broader category, it embraced not the Hindus of south Asia or the Persians of central Asia but the original population of the Western Hemisphere, who, according to some other schemes, were a separate American race. The latter prefigured the Native American or Indigenous bloc.

The Euro-American bloc is obviously derived from the white category, but the American sense of whiteness was not simply an application of the Caucasian of classical race theory. Immigrants from India were undoubtedly Caucasians according to physical anthropologists in the early twentieth century, but the United States Supreme Court ruled in 1923 that south Asian immigrants and their descendants were sufficiently "nonwhite" to be ineligible for naturalization as whites.[6] Jews from Europe and elsewhere were sometimes said to be a separate race. Even European immigrant groups whose whiteness was not legally contested – those from Ireland, Italy, and Poland, for example – were long considered so different that the significance of their whiteness diminished except in contexts when black-skinned people were present. The category of "white people" was articulated in the modern United States primarily in relation to black people and secondarily in relation to people of other colors. It took on greater significance as more and more European immigrant groups consolidated their political and economic connections with the Anglo-Protestant population so obviously in control of American institutions.[7]

"White" is a dehistoricized and culturally vacant category, while "Euro-American" invokes something at least slightly more specific. When voices representing the nonwhite affiliations placed greater emphasis on the cultural component of each of these groups in keeping with the multiculturalism of the 1980s and 1990s, the notion that whites should be comparably particularized as Euro-Americans made better and better sense. The linguistic move from *white* to *Euro-American*, inspired in part by the increasing popularity of *African American* to replace *black* and even *Afro-American*, symbolically cut down to size the whites who would otherwise continue to be anomalously unhistoricized. Whites, too, were migrants from elsewhere to what is now the United States, and thus deserving of a hyphen indicating their point of origin. The transition from "white" to "Euro-American" thus partakes of the particularizing dynamic that has made the ethno-racial pentagon a more sharply defined feature of American life.

The bloc that owes the least to classical race theory is the Hispanic, or Latino, bloc. The various peoples now grouped in this bloc were usually considered white, or Caucasian, until only the last two decades. Also, they were commonly designated by country of origin – Mexico, Cuba, Puerto Rico, etc. – much the way European ethnics were associated with either Italy or Poland or Denmark. "Brown" remained only a colloquial designation, although it served to mark lines of discrimination in many communities, especially in California and Texas. As late as the 1990 census, more than half of the Mexican American population continued to classify itself as white. This notion of the whiteness of Hispanic ethnics has prevailed despite the recognition that the ancestry of the people of Mexico was heavily indigenous and that the population of Puerto Rico consisted largely of a mixture of white and black ancestry in a combination anomalously exempted from the American one-drop rule. A sign of the consolidation of the ethno-racial pentagon, however, is the increasing frequency with which the people in this Latino bloc are being called a "race" in popular discourse.

This gradual racialization of Latinos completes, in turn, the process by which the blocs of the pentagon, whatever their shifting labels, have come to replicate the popular color-consciousness of the past: black, white, red, yellow, and brown. If the classical race theory of the nineteenth century is not directly behind the pentagon, this structure's architecture has its unmistakable origins in the most gross and invidious of popular images of what makes human beings different from one another.

Yet it was enlightened antiracism that led to the manufacturing of today's ethno-racial pentagon out of old, racist materials. The most immediate force behind the creation of the pentagon has been the antidiscrimination and affirmative action policies of the federal government. Reliable statistics were required to enforce the Voting Rights Act of 1965. It was difficult to protect black people from being disenfranchised without census data revealing the extent and exact location of their exclusion from voting. The same dynamic applied to employment discrimination; pools of candidates identified by ethno-racial category had to be available to facilitate enforcement of Title VII of the Civil Rights Act of 1964. Affirmative action runs on numbers. In this context, the single event most responsible for the lines that separate one bloc from another was the issuing in 1977 of what seemed to be a modest directive by the Office of Management and Budget designed to enable government workers to collect needed information.

Statistical Directive 15 of this office of the federal bureaucracy instructed federal agencies to classify people racially as white, black, American Indian, and Asian or Pacific Islander, and to distinguish within the white race between those of Hispanic and those of non-Hispanic origin. Although the words commonly used to denote these groups have shifted somewhat during the years since 1977, and still vary somewhat from context to context, the five blocs of the pentagon are clearly visible in this administrative directive. That it makes sense to call these blocs race equivalents is borne out by the demand of the National Council of La Raza that the Census Bureau reclassify Hispanics as a race rather than merely an ethnic group for the census to be taken in the year 2000.[8]

Exactly where ethnicity ends and race begins has been much contested in our time, when zoologists and anthropologists have found so little scientific utility in the concept of race,[9] and when humanists and social scientists have found so much evidence for the socially constructed character of race as well as ethnicity. Classifying people by the physical marks that distinguished the races, the philosopher Anthony Appiah has pointed out, was "like trying to classify books in a library" on the basis of size and shape.[10] Only a tiny fraction of a person's genetic inheritance, like a tiny fraction of a book's character, is taken into account by such a mode of classification. Yet the term *race* continues to have great currency, even among people who deny that races exist as anthropological entities and who know that genetic variation from one race to another is scarcely greater than genetic variation within the races. Two of the most eloquent of these nonbelievers in race, Henry Louis Gates, Jr., and Tristan Todorov, have carried on a vehement debate over whether the word *race* should be placed in quotation marks within the pages of a book about the role of race in literature, the contributors to which agreed that there was no such thing as race.[11]

*   *   *

When it is said that race affects one's destiny more than ethnicity does, the reference usually turns out to be to different degrees of mistreatment within a social system, not to different degrees of cultural particularity and group enforcement of norms. Some of the various ethnic groups within the Euro-American bloc have had their share of suffering, but it is dwarfed, according to our common if not always stated understanding, by the suffering inflicted on races. Moreover, the Chinese American suffers less as a Chinese than as an Asian, just as the Crow suffers not as a Crow but as an Indian. Although Japanese Americans were interned during World War II as Japanese rather than as Asians, that Asianness made the difference is proven by the less harsh treatment afforded Americans of highly visible German or Italian affiliations. This distinction between degrees of victimization is the key to the place of Latinos in the ethno-racial pentagon and to the assertion of a racial status on their behalf.[12]

Since the 1970s, Latinos have won more widespread recognition as a historically disadvantaged minority that has suffered wrongs comparable to those suffered by the minority groups earlier called races. These wrongs include discriminatory acts by whites in the twentieth-century United States, but in the background is a slavery equivalent. This is the annexation of what is now the southwestern section of the United States from Mexico in 1848. This conquest is said to confer upon even recent immigrants from parts of Mexico not conquered by the United States the status of an American-oppressed minority. Hence the logic of racial distinctions comes to embrace Latinos – including, by indirection, immigrants from El Salvador and Venezuela, countries that felt the force of American imperialism even less directly – despite the traditional Latino self-conception as non-Anglo white. Even if the victimization is symbolic, it is the victimization that counts.

*   *   *

Hence, the blocs of the pentagon get their integrity not from biology, nor even from culture, but from the dynamics of prejudice and oppression in U.S. history and from the need for political tools to overcome the legacy of that victimization. *Race* may be a word we are stuck with, but there are sound reasons to resist its continued use as an unmodified noun. The notion of race was originally developed to refer to the deeply structural differences between human groups; these differences were understood to be both highly determinative of human character and immutable, as in the old figure of speech, "the leopard cannot change his spots." Yet now, paradoxically, we rely upon the word *race* to mark something virtually antithetical: identities created by patterns in human *conduct* that we take to be *changeable*, indeed, exactly the ones we would *most* like to change, namely, the patterns of unequal treatment according to perceived descent. The word *racism* still works splendidly to indicate this pattern of unequal treatment.

The parties to this interaction that are still commonly called races I prefer to subsume under the more general category ethno-racial blocs.[13] This phrasing better reflects our understanding of the contingent and instrumental character of the categories, acknowledges that the groups traditionally called racial exist on a blurred continuum with those traditionally called ethnic, and more easily admits the renunciation, once and for all, of the unequal treatment in America of human beings on the basis of the marks of descent once called racial. Changing our vocabulary will not do much to diminish unequal treatment, but it might at least keep us aware of the direction in which antiracists want to be heading. Racism is real, but races are not.

Real, too, are differences from bloc to bloc in the degree of freedom individuals have to choose how much or how little emphasis to place on their community of descent. Nowhere within the entire ethno-racial pentagon do individuals have more of this freedom than within the Euro-American bloc. The ease with which American whites can affirm or ignore their ethnic identity as Italians, Norwegians, Irish, and so on has often been noted by sociologists, and was convincingly documented by Mary C. Waters in her 1990 book, *Ethnic Options: Choosing Identities in America*. Many middle-class Americans of third- or fourth-generation immigrant descent get a great deal of satisfaction out of their ethnic affiliations, which, in the current cultural and political environment, cost them little.[14] Waters found that these white ethnics tended to avoid aspects of communal life that imposed obligations and intruded on their privacy and individuality. They affirmed what the sociologist Herbert Gans calls "symbolic ethnicity." They take pleasure in a subjective feeling of ethnic identity, but shy away from the more substantive ethnicity that demands involvement in a concrete community with organizations, mutual commitments, and some elements of constraint.[15]

Although Waters found abundant evidence for the voluntary character of the ethnicity affirmed by middle-class whites, she also encountered among these manifestly voluntary ethnics the persistent notion that ethnicity is a primordial, biological status. Her subjects' denial of the voluntary character of their own ethnic identities rendered them, in turn, insensitive to the difference between their own situation and that of Americans with non-European ethno-racial identities. These whites see a formal "equivalence between the African-American and, say, Polish-American heritages." Thus, they deny, in effect, the depth and durability of the racism that has largely constructed and persistently bedeviled the African American and rendered that heritage less voluntary than an affirmation of Polishness.[16] Waters's subjects do not understand, one might say, the distinction between the blocs of the pentagon and the ethnicities nested within the blocs.

Waters's book is intended, in part, to liberate white Americans from these blindnesses, which help to prevent many nonwhite Americans from enjoying the freedom now experienced by whites to affiliate and disaffiliate at will. When Waters argues for such a consummation – a time when "all Americans" are equally "free to exercise their 'ethnic option' " – she upholds the ideal I am calling postethnic.[17] In such a consummation, the vividly etched lines that define the five sections of the ethno-racial pentagon would be fainter, more like the lines internal to each of the five segments. By contrast, an ethnic America would present us with what we have already had, only more so: the lines now vivid would become even more sharply drawn, and the lines now faint would become more bold.

Uncertain as the future is, there is no doubt that the ethno-racial pentagon is now being placed under severe pressure by the rate of intermarriage and by the greater visibility of mixed-race people. The conventional term *mixed race* perpetuates the anachronism of race I quarreled with above. But here the retention of the word *race* actually serves to convey more dramatically than *bloc* the depth of the challenge presented to the system by people whose proclaimed descent lies in more than one of the segments of the pentagon. Between a quarter and a third of all marriages involving Japanese Americans are now out-group marriages. More indigenous people marry outside the Indigenous bloc than marry within it. Even marriages between African Americans and whites, prohibited in some states as late as the 1960s, have increased by 300 percent since 1970.[18] A society long hostile to racial mixture, and exceptionally skilled at denying its reality, now confronts a rapidly increasing population of avowedly mixed-race families and individuals.

And it is the avowal that matters, even more than the numbers. Organizations advancing the distinctive interests of mixed-race peoples have multiplied in recent years and often lobby the Bureau of the Census to recognize them as a distinctive ethno-racial group of their own. The significance of the increase in cross-bloc mixtures consists also in the specific kinds of mixtures that now demand public acceptance. Asian European mixtures are highly visible because the society does not have a long-standing convention of concealing them by automatically consigning them to the Asian side of the descent, as it consigns black-white mixtures to the black side. Moreover, Asians have been more widely understood to be a race than Latinos have been, with the result that Asian European mixtures are, again, more dramatic challenges to the system than have been Latino European mixtures. Mexican Americans, in particular, have long embodied and taken for granted a mixed ancestry. Yet in the present climate this tradition of mixture, as it is reaffirmed and proclaimed, also contributes to the challenge being mounted against the constraints of the pentagon. "By merely reaffirming their heritage," suggests Carlos Fernandez, Mexican Americans are "uniquely positioned to upset the traditional Anglo-American taboo" against mixing.[19]

The most potent threat to the ethno-racial pentagon is probably the increase in avowed double minorities and multiple minorities. People whose descent is divided between African American and one or more of the other non-Euro-American blocs represent a special challenge to the terms of Haley's choice. The phenomenon of the double minority is not new. But persons of mixed African American and either indigenous or Latino descent were traditionally classified as belonging to any one or another of these three blocs, depending on the immediate social environment. The one-drop rule was sometimes quietly compromised when non-Euro-American people were involved. But this compromise has become less quiet in the wake of two developments.

First, the greater pride taken in indigenous and Latino as well as African American descent in recent years has made more compelling the claims of each descent on any individual who happens to be heir to more than one of them. If the affirmation of a white heritage has traditionally risked bringing upon anyone of partially African American descent the charge of denying solidarity with black people and "wanting to be white," this difficulty diminishes with double minorities. The difficulty is not altogether absent in the case of affirmation of Latino descent, but now that Latinos, whether white or not, are in possession of their own race-equivalent bloc in the pentagon, the problem is smaller. Nor does the difficulty raised by "wanting to be white" loom large in the affirmation of safely nonwhite indigenous descent.

Second, there has recently emerged for the first time on a demographically significant scale a new kind of double minority: Asian African. The mixed-race individuals who lobby the most adamantly for a new census category to accommodate them are often Asian-African-Americans.

If the one-drop rule ever falls, it is mostly likely to do so under the specific pressure brought upon it by double and multiple minorities, who may then create an atmosphere in which this rule can weaken elsewhere, even where it now serves to separate the Euro-American and the African American segments of the pentagon. Even now, this strongest of all ethno-racial barriers is being chipped away as individuals of white and African American mixture are heard more frequently in public hearings trying to defy the one-drop rule.[20]

While the demand to add mixed race to the federal census can be construed as merely an effort to turn the pentagon into a hexagon, the logic of mixed race actually threatens to destroy the whole structure. A concern for the political cohesion of the African American bloc, in particular, has led a number of scholars and activists to resist this innovation. "Instead of draining the established categories of their influence," a writer for the *New Yorker* recently found some African American intellectuals in the process of concluding, "it would be better to eliminate racial categories altogether."[21] The various blocs of the pentagon are literally filled with mixed-race people.[22] Although this fact is noted the most often in regard to the African American bloc for which Alex Haley is so convenient a symbol, it is also visible in the Indigenous bloc, where it has reached the point of a statistical apocalypse.

Tribal governments, which are legally empowered to decide who shall be counted as a member of any given tribe, apply radically divergent standards. At least one tribal government will enroll "those with 1/256 Indian blood heritage," reports Terry Wilson, while other tribal governments demand "one-half quantum from the *mother's* heritage," and still others follow an old practice of the U.S. government, classifying as Indian anyone with one-quarter indigenous ancestry.[23] In the meantime, no individual needs to obtain tribal authorization to self-identify on a census form as a member of the American Indian race. Thousands of Americans who had never before declared themselves to be indigenous peoples have done so in recent censuses in response, presumably, to the promise of entitlements and to the cultural reality of more positive public attitudes toward Indians. The number of Americans who identified themselves as American Indians on federal census forms increased by 259 percent between 1960 and 1990.[24]

Some whites, in the meantime, have insisted that they are black. Opportunities for self-identification have produced a statistically tiny but administratively portentous effort to enter the African American bloc for the purpose of exploiting entitlement programs designed for minorities. The most notorious case involves two brothers – Paul and Philip Malone – who obtained employment in the Boston fire department in 1977 by self-identifying as black even though, as the state supreme court of Massachusetts ruled in 1989, they had declared themselves to be black solely for the purpose of gaining employment for which their test scores as whites had been too low to qualify.[25] Although such cases might seem to be easily resolvable at the level of common sense, the question of who is a real minority can be highly frustrating when it comes to establishing clear and equitable legal rules for making the determination.

To what extent should self-identification be supplemented by the opinions of a larger community? And should that community consist of obvious members of the entitlement-targeted population in question, or of members of the groups most likely to be guilty of the discrimination against which the entitlement programs are directed? Legal scholar Christopher Ford finds these questions demanding of much more attention than American jurisprudence has so far provided. It makes some sense to let each group decide who is in and who is out, but there are limits to this approach. "Since the distribution of racial disadvantage is presumably keyed by how the *rest of society* perceives the claimant," Ford observes, the standards for identifying a black person that obtain outside the black community would

> appear the most likely to target remedy to wrong: preference would be given an individual, for example, not according to Blacks' feelings of solidarity with her but rather to whether or not the majority of the White population – the presumptive wrong-allocators – perceive her to be Black. It would certainly seem a poor remedial system which denied someone an anti-discrimination remedy because she was not felt "Black" by Blacks, if at the same time the rest of the population treated her as if she were.[26]

Other administrative systems have given more attention to developing clear and consistent rules for making such determinations. Yet these particular systems are not ones from which we today are eager to learn. Ford points out: "It would be ironic indeed if for the intelligible administration of modern anti-discrimination law we borrowed our models of procedural rectitude in part from our own segregationist past or from the *apartheid* state of South Africa," but "if we must administer a race-conscious public policy ... we have to understand that categorization requires method."[27]

Malone v. Haley and the movement to add mixed race to the federal census exemplify two extremely different kinds of pressure on the ethno-racial pentagon. The problem of keeping whites like the Malone brothers from taking unfair advantage of entitlement programs is nested firmly in the political-economic matrix out of which arose the entitlement programs that consolidated the ethno-racial pentagon in the 1970s. Yet the problem of meeting the demand for multiple identity on the part of mixed-race Americans is located instead in a cultural matrix. The people who lobby the Census Bureau for recognition as mixed race have followed the multiculturalist movement's use of the ethno-racial pentagon as a basic guide to cultural identity in the United States. San Francisco residents asked on a street corner how many racial categories should be listed in the census answered as often as not in strictly cultural terms. They took for granted that the reporter's question was about the public recognition of cultures, not about facilitating entitlements for victims of racism.[28]

Thus the routine, public attribution of cultural significance to the blocs of a pentagon originally designed for the purposes of economic and political equality has brought to a point of tragic contradiction two valuable impulses in contemporary America: the impulse to protect historically disadvantaged populations from the effects of past and continuing discrimination, and the impulse to affirm the variety of cultures that now flourish within the United States and that flourish even within individual Americans. Whatever we as a society decide to do with our ethno-racial pentagon, we will do well to remember both the tragic character and the depth of this contradiction. David Harvey has wisely reminded us that a "politics which seeks to eliminate the processes which give rise" to racism may turn out to look very different from a "politics which merely seeks to give full play to differentiated identities once these have arisen."[29]

Just how prescriptively ethnic American society should be is but one of a legion of questions about affiliation that have intensified during the past generation. A prominent characteristic of our era is a preoccupation with affiliation: when the term "we" is invoked, what community is implied? Affiliation has come to the fore in discussions of scientific knowledge, moral values, nationalism, human rights, and the physical health of the earth. In a multitude of discourses, the claims of particular, historically specific communities have been advanced against claims made on behalf of all humankind. The ethno-racial pentagon is a vivid artifact of a sweeping movement from species to ethnos. Within this larger movement in recent and contemporary intellectual history the multiculturalist debates can be addressed most productively, and a postethnic perspective elaborated most clearly.

Notes

1 Ishmael Reed et al., "Is Ethnicity Obsolete?" in *The Invention of Ethnicity*, ed. Werner Sollors (New York: Oxford University Press, 1989), p. 227, commenting on Alex Haley, *Roots: The Saga of an American Family* (New York: Dell, 1976).

2 Ibid., p. 229.

3 Will Herberg, *Protestant-Catholic-Jew: An Essay in American Religious Sociology* (Garden City, N.Y.: Anchor Books, 1955). Although Herberg's book popularized and developed this notion, it was introduced by Ruby Jo Reeves Kennedy, "Single or Triple Melting Pot," *American Journal of Sociology* 49 (1944), pp. 331–9.

4 "Each course will take substantial account of groups drawn from at least three of the following: African Americans, American Indians, Asian Americans, Chicano/Latinos, and European Americans." Regulation 300, *Regulations of the Berkeley Division of the Academic Senate of the University of California*, adopted April 1989.

5 Barbara J. Fields, "Ideology and Race in American History," in *Region, Race, and Reconstruction*, ed. Morgan Kousser et al. (New York: Oxford University Press, 1982), p. 149.

6 *United States v. Bhagat Singh Thind*, 261 U.S. 206 (1923).

7 The work of the historian David Roediger has been especially valuable in tracing the growth in political and economic significance of the category of whiteness. See his *The Wages of Whiteness: Race and the Making of the American Working Class* (New York: Verso, 1991); and *Toward an Abolition of Whiteness: Essays on Race, Politics, and Working Class History* (New York: Verso, 1994), esp. pp. 181–98.

8 This is reported in the course of an informative overview of controversies over the ethnic and racial categories employed by the federal government: Lawrence Wright, "One Drop of Blood," *New Yorker*, July 25, 1994, p. 47.

 9   For an accessible review of scientific opinion, see James C. King, *The Biology of Race* (Berkeley: University of California Press, 1981).

10   Anthony Appiah, *In My Father's House: Africa in the Philosophy of Culture* (New York: Oxford University Press, 1992), p. 38.

11   The decision: use it in quotation marks in the title of the book, and let it go without quotation marks in the text itself. See Henry Louis Gates, Jr., *"Race," Writing, and Difference* (Chicago: University of Chicago Press, 1986). See especially Gates's concluding remarks, " 'Talkin' That Talk," pp. 402–9.

12   For an informed and accessible discussion of the issue of the racial or ethnic status of Mexican Americans, see Peter Skerry, *The Mexican-Americans: The Ambivalent Minority* (New York: Free Press, 1993), pp. 15–18.

13   I believe this solution meets the objections raised against the dropping of the category race by Michael Omni and Howard Winant, *Racial Formation in the United States from the 1960s to the 1990s*, 2nd edn. (New York: Routledge, 1994), esp. pp. 54–5, 158–9, 181, and is consistent with their understanding of how "races" are socially constructed.

14   Mary C. Waters, *Ethnic Options: Choosing Identities in America* (Berkeley: University of California Press, 1990), p. 147. See also Richard D. Alba, *Ethnic Identity: The Transformation of White America* (New Haven: Yale University Press, 1990).

15   Herbert Gans, "Symbolic Ethnicity in America," *Ethnic and Racial Studies* 2 (1979), pp. 1–20, esp. p. 9.

16   Waters, *Ethnic Options*, pp. 157–8, 164.

17   Ibid., p. 167.

18   Bureau of the Census, *Statistical Abstract of the United States*, 110th edn (Washington, D.C.: U.S. Government Printing Office, 1991), table 53; Wright, "One Drop," p. 49.

19   Carlos A. Fernandez, "La Raza and the Melting Pot," in *Racially Mixed People in America*, ed. Maria P. P. Root (Newbury Park, Calif.: Sage Publications, 1992), p. 139.

20   See, e.g., "U.S. Racial Categories Criticized by Minorities," *San Francisco Chronicle*, July 15, 1994. For a helpful history of the one-drop rule and for a discussion of the basis for its continued support within the ranks of African Americans today, see F. James Davis, *Who Is Black?* (University Park, Pa.: Pennsylvania State University Press, 1991), esp. pp. 180–1.

21   Wright, "One Drop," pp. 54–5.

22   See Paul Spickard, *Mixed Blood: Intermarriage and Ethnic Identity in Twentieth-Century America* (Madison, Wis.: University of Wisconsin Press, 1989), and Paul Spickard, "The Illogic of American Racial Categories," in Root, *Racially Mixed People*, pp. 12–23.

23   Terry Wilson, "Blood Quantum: Native American Mixed Bloods," in Root, *Racially Mixed People*, p. 121.

24   Wright, "One Drop," p. 53.

25   *Malone v. Haley*, Massachusetts Supreme Judicial Court, July 5, 1989.

26   Christopher A. Ford, "The Administration of Identity in Race-Conscious Law," *California Law Review* (October 1994), p. 1282.

27   Ibid., p. 1285.

28   "How Many Racial Categories Should the U.S. Census Have?" *San Francisco Chronicle*, August 22, 1994, p. B3.

29   David Harvey, "Class Relations, Social Justice, and the Politics of Difference," in *Place and the Politics of Identity*, ed. Michael Keith and Steve Pile (New York: Routledge, 1993), p. 64.

10

The Melting Pot: Myth or Reality?

Assimilation's Quiet Tide

Richard D. Alba

Assimilation has become America's dirty little secret. Although once the subject of avid discussion and debate, the idea has fallen into disrepute, replaced by the slogans of multiculturalism. At best, assimilation is considered of dubious relevance for contemporary minorities, who are believed to want to remain outside the fabled "melting pot" and to be, in any event, not wholly acceptable to white America.

However, assimilation was, and is, a reality for the majority of the descendants of earlier waves of immigration from Europe. Of course, it does have its varieties and degrees. Among Americans descended from the immigrants of the nineteenth and early twentieth centuries, assimilation is better viewed as a direction, rather than an accomplished end state.

Assimilation need not imply the obliteration of all traces of ethnic origins, nor require that every member of a group be assimilated to the same degree. That ethnic communities continue to exist in many cities and that many individuals identify with their ethnic ancestry do not indicate that assimilation is a myth. What, then, does assimilation mean when applied to American ethnic groups derived from European immigration?

It refers, above all, to long-term processes that have whittled away at the social foundations for ethnic distinctions. These processes have brought about a rough parity of opportunities to attain such socioeconomic goods as educational credentials and prestigious jobs, loosened the ties between ethnicity and specific economic niches, diminished cultural differences that serve to signal ethnic membership to others and to sustain ethnic solidarity, shifted residence away from central-city ethnic neighborhoods to ethnically intermixed suburbs, and, finally, fostered relatively easy social intermixing across ethnic lines, resulting ultimately in high rates of ethnic intermarriage and ethnically mixed ancestry.

Reprinted with permission of the author from *The Public Interest*, no. 119 (Spring 1995), pp. 3–18. © 1995 by National Affairs, Inc.

The assimilation associated with these outcomes should not be viewed as imposed upon resistant individuals seeking to protect their cultural identities – a common image of assimilation in recent, largely negative, discourse – nor as self-consciously embraced by individuals seeking to disappear into the mainstream (though, in both instances, there may be some who fit the description).

Rather, it is, in general, the perhaps unintended, cumulative byproduct of choices made by individuals seeking to take advantage of opportunities to improve their social situations. For many white ethnics, these opportunities opened especially in the period following World War II, due to more favorable attitudes towards groups such as Jews and Italians, the expansion of higher education and middle-class and upper-middle-class employment, and the mushrooming growth of housing in suburban communities.

The decision to make use of these opportunities sometimes has greater impact on the following generations than on the one responsible for them. When socially mobile families forsake the old neighborhood, where the stamp of ethnic ways on everyday life could be taken for granted, for a suburb, it is the children who grow up in a multi-ethnic, or even non-ethnic, environment.

What's In a Name

The rising tide of assimilation is illustrated by data from the most recent U.S. census (1990). A first sign is given by responses to the ancestry question, which appeared for the first time in the 1980 census. From the 1980 to the 1990 census, there were surprising changes in the way ancestries were reported. In contrast to the racial- and Hispanic-origin data collected by the census, the distributions of responses across European-ancestry categories underwent sharp alterations, which appear to correlate strongly with the specific ancestry examples offered on the census questionnaire. These ancestry examples were listed immediately below the question, and their influence on the resulting responses implies that many whites are suggestible when it comes to the way they describe their ancestry.

For instance, in 1980, "English" was among the first examples given, and 49.6 million Americans claimed English ancestry; in 1990, it was omitted from the list of examples, and the number who identified themselves as of English ancestry fell to 32.7 million, a decline of one-third. Similarly, in 1990, German and Italian were the first two ancestry examples given; though both were also listed in 1980, their positions were not as prominent. Both ancestry groups increased in number by about 20 percent between the two censuses, an increase substantially larger than that for European-ancestry categories in general. Such shifts suggest that ethnic ancestry is not a firmly anchored self-concept for many Americans, and alert us to the need to take ancestry data with a dose of caution, for the "Germans" and "Italians" of 1990 have changed in unknown ways from the "Germans" and "Italians" of 1980.

Increasing Socioeconomic Parity

Historically, one of the most important moorings of ethnicity has been the concentration of different ethnic groups in specific socioeconomic strata. This brings the members of an ethnic group together by circumstances other than ethnicity and gives them common material and other interests arising from their shared situations. As Nathan Glazer and Daniel Patrick Moynihan explained in their seminal book, *Beyond the Melting Pot*, "to name an occupational group or a class is very much the same thing as naming an ethnic group."

However, in recent years, there has been a growing and impressive convergence in the average socioeconomic opportunities for members of white ethnic groups. Convergence here means that the disadvantages that were once quite evident for some groups of mainly peasant origins in Europe, such as the Italians, have largely faded, and their socioeconomic attainments increasingly resemble, if not even surpass, those of the average white American.

This phenomenon is quite demonstrable for education (a convenient indicator because its level is, for the great majority, fixed by the age of 25), but it is hardly limited to this sphere. Table 1 presents the educational attainments of

Table 1a   Educational attainment by ethnic ancestry – men

	Cohort born 1956–65		Cohort born 1916–25	
	% attended college	% completed bachelor's degree	% attended college	% completed bachelor's degree
All non-Hisp. white	55.9	25.5	34.6	16.2
Solely British	66.3	31.8	46.6	23.5
German	57.6	25.9	35.2	16.0
Irish	59.4	26.5	33.8	15.4
French	52.6	21.9	32.4	14.4
Italian	61.9	30.2	25.8	12.1
Polish	61.4	32.9	29.2	14.2
All southern and eastern European	64.4	33.8	32.2	16.0

Source: 1-in-1000 Public Use Microdata Sample of the 1990 Census

Table 1b   Educational attainment by ethnic ancestry – women

	Cohort born 1956–65		Cohort born 1916–25	
	% attended college	% completed bachelor's degree	% attended college	% completed bachelor's degree
All non-Hisp. white	57.7	24.6	25.1	8.7
Solely British	66.3	31.5	38.1	15.7
German	60.7	24.8	25.8	9.2
Irish	60.4	25.0	24.0	7.7
French	56.2	20.3	26.5	9.9
Italian	61.2	27.8	16.5	4.9
Polish	62.2	29.4	14.4	3.8
All southern and eastern European	64.1	31.8	19.3	6.1

Source: 1-in-1000 Public Use Microdata Sample of the 1990 Census

younger and older cohorts for the major European-ancestry categories. The data compiled in the table are limited to "non-Hispanic whites" (a population overwhelmingly of European ancestry) and to individuals born in the United States, thus avoiding any confounding with the characteristics of immigrants themselves. Though the data cannot tell us about the quality of education received, the evidence of convergence is strong.

To evaluate changes, two comparison groups are presented: one contains all non-Hispanic whites and the other individuals whose ancestry is solely from the British Isles (exclusive of the Republic of Ireland). The latter is commonly viewed as one of America's privileged ethnic groups. The other groups presented are the largest non-British groups, divided between the early-arriving groups from northern and western Europe (Germans, Irish, French, in order of size), and the later-arriving groups from southern and eastern Europe Italians, Poles and a separate category containing all individuals with ancestry from southern and/or eastern Europe).

In the case of each ancestry category, individuals are included in the tabulations regardless of whether their ancestry is solely or partly from the category. Limiting tabulations to individuals with ancestry exclusively from one category would in effect, eliminate one of the important mechanisms of assimilation – growing up in an ethnically mixed family.

The groups from southern and eastern Europe are often regarded as the acid test of assimilation because of the relative recency of their arrival and the prominence of their ethnicity in American cities. For the men of these groups who were born between 1916 and 1925, moderate disadvantages are evident when they are compared to the average non-Hispanic white or to men of German, Irish, and French ancestries; the disadvantage appears more substantial when compared to men of exclusively British ancestry. For instance, only a quarter to a third of Italian and Polish men attended college, compared to almost half of the British men. About one in eight Italians and Poles completed bachelor's degrees, compared to nearly one in four British men.

In the cohort born between 1956 and 1965 (whose education was largely complete by the time of the 1990 census), the southern and eastern Europeans have just about pulled even with the British men and are ahead of the average white and the men of other northern- and western-European origins. The figures for southern and eastern Europeans in general and for Poles may be affected by the extraordinary accomplishments of Jewish men (who are nevertheless minorities of these categories), but the same argument cannot be made in the case of the Italians.

The process of convergence is also quite striking among women. For predominantly rural immigrant groups, like the Italians and Poles, the education of daughters was of secondary importance compared to the education of sons. In the older cohort, British women had rates of college attendance and graduation more than twice those of their Italian and Polish contemporaries. This disparity has been largely eradicated in the younger cohort: Italian and Polish women are slightly behind British women in college attendance and graduation but tied with, if not slightly ahead of, the average non-Hispanic white woman as well as those of German, Irish, and French ancestries. The younger women in the general southern- and eastern-European category have above-average educational attainments that are similar to those of British women; this parity represents a marked improvement over their situation in the older cohort.

Decline of European Mother Tongues

Declines in overt cultural differences are a second component of assimilatory change. In census data, these are measurable in terms of the languages spoken in the home. Communication in a mother tongue marks a social boundary, which includes those who share the same ethnic origin and can speak its language and excludes all others. In addition, many aspects of ethnic culture that are embedded in a mother tongue are diminished or lost as exposure and fluency wane.

All available evidence reveals a powerful pattern of conversion to English monolingualism within three generations, from which only a small minority of any group escapes (a pattern first established by the sociologist Calvin Veltman). Consequently, the use in the home of European mother tongues (other than Spanish), and even exposure to them, have dropped off quite precipitously among those with southern- and eastern-European ancestries. Many older members of these groups spoke these languages in the immigrant homes and communities where they grew up. Data collected by the Census Bureau's Current Population Survey in the late 1970s shows that three-quarters of southern- and eastern-European ethnics born in the United States before 1930 grew up in homes where a language other than English was spoken.

The situation for younger members of these and other groups, as depicted in the 1990 census, is presented in table 2 (which omits the English-speaking ethnic categories). The younger cohort contains individuals who were between the ages of five and fourteen in 1990 (the census does not record the language of children under the age of five). In general, 95 percent or more of the children in each ethnic category speak only English at home. There are scarcely differences to be noted among the categories, except perhaps for the slightly higher percentage of German children who speak English only.

Table 2   Language at home by ethnic ancestry

	Cohort born 1976–85 % speak other than English	Cohort born 1916–25 % speak other than English
All non-Hisp. white	3.5	6.1
German	2.2	2.9
French	3.3	13.4
Italian	4.0	19.4
Polish	3.5	24.2
All southern and eastern European	5.1	19.8

Source: 1-in-1000 Public Use Microdata Sample of the 1990 Census

Speaking a mother tongue at home is more common among the older members of these groups. Germans are still an exception, testifying to the deep impact of wartime hostility on the survival of German culture in the United States. For the Italians, Poles, and other southern and eastern Europeans, about 20 percent of their older members continue to speak a mother tongue, presumably on a daily basis. The figure is nearly as high for the French. Of course, still higher percentages spoke mother tongues during their childhoods. A major transition in language is evidently underway.

Qualifiers, however, should not be overlooked here. Perhaps fluency in a language is not required for it to serve an ethnic purpose; the use of words and phrases from a mother tongue, interspersed in English conversation, can signal an ethnic loyalty to others. This sort of knowledge cannot be measured from census data, but it does seem plausible that, where languages cease to be everyday means of communication, knowledge of words and phrases will drop off, too. Also, it is impossible to measure from census data the number of individuals who acquire a mother tongue through schooling or other formal instruction. Yet, given the generally sorry record of Americans' mastery of foreign languages, one would not want to depend too much on this source for cultural support.

The Declining Ethnic Neighborhood

Educational and occupational mobility and language acculturation, combined with the potent catalyst of competition with racial and new immigrant minorities over urban turf, have spurred residential changes. These have brought many white ethnics out of inner-city ethnic neighborhoods and into suburban settings, where ethnic residential concentrations tend to be diluted, if they exist at all. As a result of the continued visibility of surviving ethnic neighborhoods, some of which have become meccas for those seeking an "authentic" ethnic experience, the magnitude and implications of residential shifts are less appreciated than they should be.

In depicting residential shifts, I will switch from the trends in aggregate national census samples to the changes in a single but special geographic context, the Greater New York metropolitan region. This broad swath of cities and suburbs, covering 23 densely settled counties stretching from the Hudson Valley and Long Island in New York to the New Jersey shore, was home to 17 million people in 1990. Examining residential patterns in a single region avoids the risk of decontextualizing residential situations and losing sight of their location in relation to ethnic communities. No doubt due to the New York region's historic role as a gateway for immigrants, white ethnic communities continue to play a visible role in its ethnic geography. If such communities are important anywhere, they are sure to be so here.

Three large groups – Germans, Irish, and Italians – are used to trace residential patterns. Each has between two and three million members in the region, according to both 1980 and 1990 census data, and has figured in significant ways in the region's ethnic neighborhoods in the past. However, based on their histories and the results of past investigations (such as *Beyond the Melting Pot*), the Germans could be expected to be the least residentially distinctive (i.e., with the fewest ethnic areas), while the Italians should be the most.

In fact, all of these groups are now found mainly in the suburban parts of the region, where ethnic residential concentrations are demonstrably thinner (though not nonexistent). By 1980, the Germans and Irish were already disproportionately located in suburbs: roughly three-quarters of both were outside central cities, compared to two-thirds of all non-Hispanic whites (but just one-quarter of Hispanics and nonwhites). Moreover, in suburbia, the residential distributions of the Germans and Irish are barely distinguishable from that of other non-Hispanic whites. In other words, these groups are residentially intermixed.

The Italians present a different, but more dynamic, picture. In 1980, they were slightly less likely to be found in suburbs than the average white (64 percent versus 66 percent), but during the 1980s their numbers in large cities fell while rising in the suburbs. By 1990, 70 percent resided in suburbs. While they were still not as suburbanized as the Germans and Irish, they were more so than the average non-Hispanic white. For the Italians, too, suburban residence means a greater probability of living in an ethnically diverse community.

Ethnic Exodus

This picture gains further credibility when it is taken to the level of specific ethnic neighborhoods. To accomplish this, John Logan, Kyle Crowder, and I have identified the region's ethnic neighborhoods in 1980 and 1990 census data as clusters of census tracts where any of the three groups has an above-average concentration (operationally defined as 35 percent or more of the population).

For the Germans and Irish, these neighborhoods are, generally speaking, few and small; only tiny fractions of each group could be considered to reside in them (just 4 percent of the Irish in 1990, for instance). For the Italians, however, there are a number of these neighborhoods, some of which are quite large and most of which take on familiar outlines, identifiable with well-known Italian areas (such as Brooklyn's Bensonhurst). Nevertheless, it is still the case that just a minority of the group – a quarter in both 1980 and 1990 – resides in Italian neighborhoods.

The Italian neighborhoods, moreover, underwent substantial changes during the 1980s. The outflow of Italians from the region's large cities especially drained inner-city ethnic neighborhoods. Bensonhurst was the largest contiguous Italian area in 1980, home to nearly 150,000 persons of Italian ancestry. By 1990, it had shrunk in its Italian population to less than 100,000, while also diminishing in spatial extent. Most other inner-city Italian neighborhoods also lost population, though not on such a dramatic scale. In effect, this outflow removed Italians from their most ethnic neighborhoods.

The suburban areas with growing numbers of Italians are very different in character. In the first place, the great majority of suburban Italians reside outside of anything resembling an ethnic neighborhood. Moreover, population growth bypassed inner-suburban ethnic neighborhoods, such as the Italian areas of Yonkers, and insofar as growth was funneled into outer-suburban areas of Italian concentration, these are not very ethnic, as measured for example by the number of residents who are intermarried.

In sum, even in the New York region, the ethnic mosaic *par excellence*, trends favor the further residential assimilation of white ethnic groups. The Irish, long a prominent ethnic group in the region, are already residentially intermixed. The Italians, some of whose ethnic communities are still conspicuous, reside mostly in non-ethnic areas, and their continuing suburbanization is eroding the most ethnic Italian neighborhoods.

The Intermarriage Melting Pot

Intermarriage is usually regarded, with justification, as the litmus test of assimilation. This remains true even if marriage can no longer be taken for granted as a lifetime commitment. A high rate of intermarriage signals that individuals of putatively different ethnic backgrounds no longer perceive social and cultural differences significant enough to create a barrier to a long-term union. In this sense, intermarriage could be said to test the salience, and even the existence, of a social boundary between ethnic categories. Moreover, intermarriage carries obvious and profound implications for the familial and, more broadly, the social contexts in which the next generation will be raised. Its significance in this respect is not much diminished by a high rate of divorce because the children of divorces usually carry on close relationships with both sides of their families.

Among whites, intermarriage has advanced to the point where a substantial majority of marriages involve some degree of ethnic intermixing. In 1990 census data, more than half (56 percent) of whites have spouses whose ethnic backgrounds do not overlap with their own at all (included in this count are spouses whose ethnic ancestries are described as just "American" or in some other non-ethnic way). Only one-fifth have spouses with identical ethnic backgrounds. The remainder, not quite one-quarter, have spouses whose ancestries overlap their own in some respect but differ in some other. Of necessity, one or both partners in these marriages have mixed ancestry (as when, for instance, a German-Irish groom takes an Irish-Italian bride).

Intermarriage has had an especially deep impact on the groups from southern and eastern Europe. This is partly because their smaller size (in comparison, say, with the German ancestry group) makes them more vulnerable to what is called "out-marriage." It may also be due to their concentration in regions of the nation where ethnic diversity is greater among whites (the Northeast compared to the South, for instance), increasing the likelihood that they will have close relationships with individuals of diverse backgrounds.

Intermarriage patterns are displayed in table 3 for the seven largest ancestry categories of whites. It shows that, among those aged 25 to 34 in 1990, a majority of each category had married unambiguously outside of it, with out-marriage being more common among the smaller ethnic groups.

Table 3   Marriage patterns of major ancestry groups

Ancestry groups (in order of size)	Cohort born 1956–65 Spouse's ancestry			Cohort born 1916–25 Spouse's ancestry		
	% entirely from group	% partly from group	% not from group	% entirely from group	% partly from group	% not from group
German	22.6	25.6	51.8	26.3	21.3	52.4
Irish	12.7	22.4	64.9	20.1	21.0	58.9
English	17.7	20.4	61.9	24.0	24.7	51.2
Italian	15.0	11.7	73.3	49.2	2.4	48.3
French	12.1	10.0	77.9	13.2	13.0	73.9
Scots/Scots-Irish	7.0	10.8	82.1	11.9	12.8	75.4
Polish	7.6	8.3	84.1	36.0	3.9	60.1

Source: 1-in-1000 Public Use Microdata Sample of the 1990 Census

For the large, long-established categories (English, Germans, and Irish), marriages to individuals whose ancestry is partly from the group figure prominently in the pattern and help explain why the incidence of unambiguous out-marriage is not greater. Perhaps some of these marriages, where there is an ethnic ingredient in common, deserve to be viewed as in-group marriages. However, in the majority of cases, both spouses have ethnically mixed ancestry and share only one ethnic element in common. Thus, they should probably be viewed as akin to intermarriages, even if not so in the strictest sense.

Intermarriage has attained, by any standard, very high levels among the Italians and Poles, the two groups in the table from southern and eastern Europe. Close to three-quarters of the younger Italians have spouses without Italian ancestry; for Poles, the equivalent figure is higher still. However, marriages involving spouses who both have some ancestry from these groups is higher than it would be if marriage were "random" with respect to ancestry, and there is some sign that the increase in intermarriage may be leveling off. A likely forecast is that intermarriage will continue at high levels but that a significant minority of each of these groups will continue to look within for marriage partners.

The rising tide of intermarriage is sweeping over religious barriers as well. This is demonstrated most tellingly by the surge of intermarriage among Jews since the 1960s. Data from the 1990 National Jewish Population Survey reveal that 57 percent of Jews marrying since 1985 have married partners raised in other religions. Just two decades earlier, the figure had been only 11 percent. The consequences of Jewish-Gentile intermarriage are still debatable, at least in principle, because of the possibilities of the non-Jewish spouse converting or of the children being raised as Jewish. However, the data suggest that neither possibility characterizes a majority of intermarried couples. Besides, even if these possibilities were the rule, they do not diminish the import of the fact that religious origins are playing a lesser role in the choice of a spouse than they once did.

An obvious consequence of intermarriage is ethnically mixed ancestry, which holds potentially profound implications for ethnic groups. Though the mere fact of mixed ancestry is certainly no bar to ethnic feelings and loyalties, it is likely to reduce their intensity, especially because most individuals with mixed ancestry are raised with limited exposure to ethnic cultures in their most robust form.

Marriage Across Racial Lines

What is unfolding among whites through intermarriage resembles, then, the proverbial melting pot, but with mainly European ingredients to this point. It is still the case that just a small proportion of marriages by whites (2 percent) are contracted with Hispanics or with nonwhites. The vast majority of their intermarriages, in other words, involve individuals of European ancestries only (the most notable exception being the nontrivial fraction of whites who claim some American-Indian ancestry, typically mixed with European).

Lower rates of racial intermarriage are partly a result of residential segregation, which particularly affects blacks and new immigrant groups, and partly a consequence of the reluctance of many whites, the largest pool of potential marriage partners, to accept a nonwhite or Hispanic spouse. No doubt, there is also a greater desire on the part of many minority-group members to find husbands and wives from their own groups. For the new immigrant groups, from the Caribbean, Latin America, and Asia, the overall intermarriage rate is also driven down by their concentrations in the first and second generations, where intermarriage tends to be lower in general.

The extreme case is that of African Americans ("non-Hispanic blacks" in census terminology). According to 1990 census data, just 4 percent of African Americans have married outside their group. However, this figure hides an important and long-standing gender discrepancy: intermarriage is considerably more prevalent among black men than among black women (6 percent versus 2 percent). For both sexes, most intermarriage takes place with non-Hispanic white partners.

Hispanics on the whole exhibit considerably higher, but still modest, levels of intermarriage, even in the second generation. Seventy percent of U.S.-born Hispanics are married to other Hispanics, mostly to individuals of the same national origin. In the Hispanic case, there is no gender gap in intermarriage. Its frequency does, however, vary considerably by specific group, and the total for Hispanics overall is influenced especially by the high rate of endogamy on the part of the largest Hispanic group, Mexican Americans.

Intermarriage is only a bit more common among U.S.-born Asians overall, two-thirds of whom marry other Asians. As with Hispanics, this total disguises substantial variation by specific national origin and is heavily affected by a high level of endogamy in one group, Japanese Americans, who form the largest contingent among U.S.-born Asian adults.

American Indians bracket the intermarriage spectrum at the high end. More than half have married outside the American-Indian population; the great majority of their intermarriages are to non-Hispanic whites. However, since American Indians represent less than 1 percent of the national population, their intermarriage tendency does not have a great influence on the total pattern.

The predominantly European cast to the contemporary melting of ethnic lines through intermarriage may be changing, at least to some degree. One indication is the higher-than-average frequency of marriage to Hispanics or nonwhites on the part of younger non-Hispanic whites. Among those in the 25 to 34 age group, close to 4 percent have married minority-group members; though still low in absolute terms, this figure represents a measurable increase over past levels.

Rising intermarriage with racial minorities is having its most dramatic effects among African Americans, as the demographer Matthijs Kalmijn first documented (in the September 1993 issue of the journal *Social Forces*) with an analysis of marriages for the two-decade period following the Supreme Court's 1967 invalidation of the last anti-miscegenation law. In 1990 census data, 10 percent of 25- to 34-year-old black men have intermarried, most with white women. This figure, while obviously not high, nevertheless represents a stunning upward shift from the historical level. The change has not been as striking for black women, but the level of intermarriage has risen among younger black women to nearly 4 percent.

Intermarriage involving members of groups from new immigration is virtually certain to increase in the near future, as the ranks of their second- and third-generation adults swell. Yet, whether marriage across social boundaries defined by non-European ancestries will attain the acceptability – indeed the unremarkableness – that intermarriage appears to have attained in the case of European ancestries remains to be seen.

Assimilation's Continuing Relevance

The assimilation trends tracked by the census can, to be sure, appear somewhat crude, lacking the nuanced *chiaroscuro* of personal experience where ethnicity may still he present. Nevertheless, taken together, these trends convincingly show that the social bases for ethnic distinctiveness are eroding among Americans of European ancestry. Indeed, the erosion would continue even if the trends were to come to a halt. As older, currently more ethnic generations are replaced by their children and grandchildren, who are less ethnic on average, the groups as a whole become less ethnic.

Decline, however, does not mean disappearance, certainly not in the foreseeable future. The overall picture is mixed, with the proportions of the different elements – i.e., "assimilated" versus "ethnic," to portray them in their extremes – shifting in the assimilated direction.

A larger question, and an unanswerable one for the moment, concerns the relevance of the European-American experience of assimilation for non-European minorities. Even if one narrows the question by accepting that assimilation is probably most relevant for immigrant groups, as opposed to those whose entry to American society was coerced by enslavement or conquest, the conditions of contemporary immigration are sufficiently different from those prevalent in the past that generalizations based on earlier experience are open to doubt.

Currently, we lack good theories and hard-and-fast empirical knowledge about the genesis of European-American assimilation. To what extent does it reflect persisting forces in American society – the lure of opportunities in the mainstream economy, for instance, or the permeability of ethnic boundaries in a society populated largely by immigration? To what extent is it the product of historically unique events and conditions, such as the period of economic expansion following World War II or the virtual shutdown of immigration after 1930, which prevented the renewal of ethnic communities through continuing immigration? To what extent is it restricted to those with European ancestry and white skin? Without answers to these questions, we will have to wait to observe the trajectories of new immigrant groups to assess the ultimate relevance of assimilation for them. Yet, one has to suspect that assimilation is far from a spent force.

◆

Are the Children of Today's Immigrants Making It?

Joel Perlmann and Roger Waldinger

Thirty years after the Hart-Celler Act brought a wave of new immigrants to the United States, their children are reaching adulthood. These children of immigrants have only recently become a sizable presence in American schools and are just now moving from the schools into the labor market. But recent studies by Herbert Gans, Alejandro Portes, Ruben Rumbaut, and Min Zhou – all leading students of American ethnic life – outline, with clarity and acuity, reasons for concern: having originated from everywhere but Europe, today's newcomers are visibly identifiable in a mainly white society still not cured of its racism. Moreover, changes in the structure of the U.S. economy aggravate discrimination's ill effects. While the poorly educated immigrant parents seem to have had no trouble finding jobs at the bottom of the economic ladder, the shift toward knowledge-intensive jobs means that the next generation will have to do well in school if they wish to surpass the achievements of their parents. But, with big-city schools in more trouble than ever before, the outlook for successful passage through the educational system seems dim. As second generation expectations are unlikely to remain unchanged, we can count on a mismatch between the aspirations of immigrant children and requirements of the jobs that they seek.

The other major factor influencing scholarly views of today's immigrant children has to do with the past. The descendants of the last great migration started out at the very bottom, but they have now either caught up with, or surpassed, their WASP betters of yore. While one might find cause for comfort in their success story, future developments are likely to follow a different, less hopeful path. To begin with, the people of the last great immigration, from the 1890s to the 1920s, shared a common European heritage with the then-dominant WASPs, blunting discrimination's edge. The old factory-based economy also allowed for a multi-generational move up the totem pole. Immigrant children could do better if they just hung on through the high-school years, after which time well-paying manufacturing jobs would await them. The third or fourth generation would continue on through college and beyond, completing the climb from proletarian to plumber to professional. By contrast, the recent restructuring of the U.S. economy gives the children of today's immigrants no time to play catch-up, requiring strong and early performance as the condition for advancement.

Excerpted and reprinted with permission of the authors from *The Public Interest*, no. 132 (Summer 1998), pp. 73–96. ©1998 by National Affairs, Inc.

Is the pessimism of Gans, Portes, Zhou, and others justified? When we consider second-generation upward mobility in the past, and compare it to the prospects of second-generation mobility today, we think not.

Second-Generation Lessons

The 1890–1920 wave, heavily dominated by immigrants from southern and eastern Europe and the last mass immigration to occur before legislation choked off the European flow, provides the crucial reference point. Compared to their predecessors, the immigrants of the turn of the century were far more likely to converge on the nation's cities, and far less likely to move into agriculture – in striking parallel to the situation today. These immigrants of the turn of the century encountered an economy very different from the postindustrial capitalism of late-twentieth-century America. However, their situation was far closer to the present than to the American economy of 1850 or before.

The 1890–1920 wave included relatively few immigrants from Mexico, Asia, and the Caribbean, of course, which some will argue makes comparisons impossible. We disagree. The issue is whether today's immigrant children are likely to adapt in ways that parallel or diverge from the trajectory followed by their second-generation predecessors who were overwhelmingly of southern and eastern European origins. The real question about race is whether being an Asian, black, or Mexican immigrant is a big handicap for today's immigrants, a handicap that distinguishes them from southern and eastern Europeans of the last wave. Asian, black, and Mexican immigrants faced especially destructive discrimination in 1900; the situation is radically different today.

The great majority of the 1890–1920 immigrants entered the American economy and class structure near the bottom, dramatically below the average native-born family's position. True, there were entrepreneurs among the immigrants – mainly persons with a background in trade or crafts (as among Jews) or unskilled laborers who somehow managed to move into entrepreneurial endeavors. Nonetheless, in 1910, immigrants from all major groups, save the British, were far more likely to work at the least skilled jobs than were native whites of native parentage, and all were less likely to work in white-collar jobs of any sort. Low levels of literacy also distinguished these groups from natives and from late-nineteenth-century immigrants from northwestern Europe. Just over half of the "other eastern and southern Europeans" reported that they could read, and just over half of the Italians could not speak English, for example. Though Jews entered America at occupational and literacy levels above their counterparts from southern and eastern Europe, they still began with quite a disadvantage compared to the native born. The children of immigrants were less likely than the children of natives to remain in school, and those who remained in school were more likely to have fallen behind in grade attainment.

*   *   *

The Mexican Factor

Given the distinctive economic characteristics of the post-1965 immigrants, one might not have expected the discussions of their children's prospects to have turned so pessimistic so quickly. In contrast to the immigrants of 1890–1920, concentrated at the bottom of the occupational distribution, socio-economic diversity is a salient feature of the new immigrants.

High-skilled immigrants have played a modest, but significant, role in immigration to the United States ever since the enactment of the Hart-Celler Act in 1965. Notwithstanding charges that America's immigrants are of "declining quality," the 1990 Census found that a college degree was as common among all immigrants as among natives (one out of five). Moreover, the high skilled are often present at levels well above the U.S. average, with the college-graduate share ranging from 27 percent among Russians to 65 percent among Indians. Consequently, a good proportion of the recent arrivals begin not at the bottom but in the middle class or above. In contemporary Los Angeles, for example, coveted professional occupations have become immigrant concentrations. More than 35 percent of the pharmacists in the Los Angeles region are foreign born, as are more than 25 percent of the dentists, and more than 20 percent of the engineers, computer specialists, and physicians.

At the same time, many of today's immigrants do start at the bottom. Thus, in 1990, 5 percent of all U.S.-born adults, but 18 percent of foreign-born adults, had not received any secondary schooling. We can refine this contemporary native–immigrant comparison in a crucial way: a great share of the immigrants coming in at the bottom are from Mexico. Indeed, in 1990, 22 percent of the foreign-born population in the United States was born in Mexico; the next most prominent source country, the Philippines, accounted for less than 5 percent. If we look at the immigrants from the many other sending countries – eight-tenths of the whole – we find that the educational achievements of native- and foreign-born adults no longer appear very different. The foreign born are actually more likely to have reached college than the native born. In other words, were it not for the immigration of Mexicans, immigration would be 80 percent as large as the current one, and its members, on average, would begin their progress through the American economy no worse off, on average, than other Americans who are not immigrants. The usual generalizations about contemporary immigration provide no hint of this reality.

*   *   *

Regardless of comparisons to immigrants past, today's debate asks about the effect of the "new economy." While the new economy may render the children of non-Mexican immigrants vulnerable, it must be having about the same influence on the children of the native born. The new economy may indeed confront children with "missing rungs" on the ladder – but no more so, on average, than it does for children of native-born families. The Mexican immigrant population, therefore, stands most at risk; and its magnitude makes immigrants as a whole appear distinctively exposed to the winds of economic change. By contrast, at the turn of the century, no single group could have altered the generalization that most immigrants were much more likely than natives to start out near the bottom. That generalization applied to every one of the major southern and eastern European groups – the relatively better-skilled Jews included.

Not Black and White

But what about race? The European immigrants of 1890–1920, write Portes and Zhou, were "uniformly white"; consequently, "skin color reduced a major barrier to entry into the American mainstream." Gans concurs: "While dark-skinned immigrants from overseas cultures will also acculturate, racial discrimination will not encourage their assimilation, at least not into white society."

"Race," as historian Barbara Fields has argued, explains nothing but is something that has to be explained. So contentions such as these beg the question at hand: Under what conditions do such distinctions among groups gain significance? A look at other societies demonstrates that neither skin color nor any other physical attribute is a necessary condition for the erection of racial divisions. The central complaint of modern European anti-Semites was precisely that the Jews had become indistinguishable from everyone else. And current French attitudes are far less antagonistic to black Africans or Antilleans than to North Africans. Yet the latter are frequently blond and of fair complexion.

We may see nineteenth-century European immigrants as uniformly "white" today. But that is not the way they were seen then. John Higham's classic, *Strangers in the Land*, showed the influence of racial thinking – with its distinctions among "Nordic," "Alpine," and "Mediterranean" races – common among intellectual and political elites who framed the immigration-restriction legislation of the 1920s. As applied to the European immigrants, those racial classifications often employed visible physical features, including skin color. In the nineteenth century, the Irish were considered a "race" and regularly characterized as "savage," "simian," "low-browed," and "bestial." Black Americans were referred to as "smoked Irishmen," suggesting that these two groups were then looked at through a remarkably similar racial lens. Later observers stressed the "Saracen blood" of the southern Italians, whose "dark complexion... sometimes resembles African more than Caucasian hues." Similar doubts about the "whiteness" of immigrants were extended to Slavs and Jews.

Moreover, these racial divisions faded at a very gradual pace. Social scientists today will make sport of turn-of-the-century sociologist E. A. Ross, whose book *The Old World and the New* contains such gems as this quote from a physician who claimed that "the Slavs are immune to certain kinds of dirt. They can stand what would kill a white man." As late as 1945, a University of Chicago sociologist, W. L. Warner, and his co-author, Leo Srole, could distinguish between "light" and "dark" "Caucasoids"; the latter, "a mixture of Caucasoid and Mongoloid" blood, were expected to undergo a glacially paced assimilation – anywhere from six generations to "a very long time in the future which is not yet discernible."

It could not have been more than a few years after 1945 that Warner and Srole's "dark Caucasoids" became "white ethnics." Racial perceptions changed as the Irish, Poles, Italians, and Jews moved ahead; in this sense, for the descendants of the European immigrants, race was an achieved, not an ascribed, status. Yet today we are told that the earlier immigrants were able to move ahead because they were white, and that the immigrants of today will have trouble doing so because they are not white. At best, this view drastically needs to be fleshed out with historical detail and more nuance; at worst, it mistakes cause and effect.

The New Immigrants and Blacks

The recent historical treatment of "whiteness" attends to the processes by which European immigrants distanced themselves from natives of African descent. In the words of social historian Robert Orsi, "Proximity – real and imagined – to the dark-skinned other was pivotal to the emergence" of the hyphenated identities that the European ethnics established in their own quest for acceptance in America. The struggle for place in a contested, ethnic order provided ample motivations for the newcomers to resolve any ambiguity over how their racial identity was to be defined. As Orsi writes, the "effort to establish the border against the dark-skinned other required an intimate struggle, a contest against the initial uncertainty over which side of the racial dichotomy the swarthy immigrants were on and against the facts of history and geography that inscribed this ambiguity on the urban landscape." Labor competition furnished additional incentives, though, as the Italians often found themselves pitted against the Irish, and the Irish against the Germans, the conflict over jobs does not suffice to explain why they all became white. But they did; and, in becoming white, the immigrants and their descendants also became party to strategies of social closure that maintained black exclusion and ensured more stable employment and better wages for others of their own kind.

Can today's immigrants draw on a similar ethnic card? The answer is not yet in, but there is no question that they certainly can try, especially when it comes to differentiating themselves from poorer, less educated African Americans who fall at the bottom of the racial order. We all know about the tensions that suffuse the relations between African Americans and the new middleman minorities that run businesses in the Harlems and Watts of today's United States. These conflicts enable entrepreneurial, but visibly identifiable, immigrants to move to the advantaged, "white" side of America's racial division.

It is not that difficult to imagine that professional or entrepreneurial immigrants find rewards for falling on the "right side" of the color divide. We suggest that the same can even be said for the labor migrants, whose presence so many Americans now seem to dislike. That distaste notwithstanding, urban employers in New York, Los Angeles, or Chicago have come to prefer them to native-born American blacks.

As in the past, such racial conflict coexists with tensions among workers of diverging national or regional attachments. In Roger Waldinger's interviews with employers in the Los Angeles region, he repeatedly heard reports of bad blood between Mexicans and various Central American groups, as well as of intra-ethnic conflict within Central American populations. Nevertheless, far more Latino hostility seems to be directed towards blacks. "And I have to tell you that there is natural resentment between the two races," reported one manager referring to blacks and Latinos. "They do not get along well together in manufacturing." The owner of a large furniture company, with almost 40 years in the business, reported that

> the shop has always been 98 percent Latino. I have hired some blacks. But you put two men on a machine, Mexicans won't work with a black. [They will] aggravate him till he quits. They can't make it inter-racially. I'm not going to be a sociologist and tell them "you're in the same boat, you ought to work together." The only place where we have blacks is in the trucks, because they work by themselves.

Today, as at the turn of the century, the second generation will benefit from their parents' efforts to distance themselves from native blacks. But there is a rejoinder to the argument just advanced, namely the contention that the geographic and ethnic origins of the new immigrants leave them in no position to play the "race card." From this perspective, the influence of the past is important in that it defines today's newcomers as "people of color." Consequently, immigrants from Latin American, the Caribbean, or Asia will not be able to avoid being treated like a caste, unlike earlier immigrants.

One need only look at the present dynamics of white–Asian relations today to realize that the argument for this sort of historical continuity falls short. It is not just that legislated racial divisions now seem curiously barbarous; in crucial respects, the eradication of the legal barriers is paralleled by changes in social conditions. Asians at the bottom of the class structure there may be; but Asians throughout the class structure there are as well, in impressive numbers. And the educational achievement of large numbers of Asians ensures that, for significant numbers of second-generation Asians, the disappearance of low-skilled factory jobs will not be relevant to their economic advancement. Moreover, trends in intermarriage between the offspring of new Asian immigrants are far closer to historic trends in immigrant-native intermarriage than to historic trends in black-white intermarriage.

In contrast to the pattern that prevailed during the great immigrations of 1830–1920, a plurality of "races" is now evident in large numbers, nationwide. At the same time, white, Asian, Hispanic, and Native-American groups are intermingling in large numbers. The conjunction of these two facts alone may help diminish the significance of the black-white divide in American life. Another relevant factor is that a large portion of the numerous Latin American arrivals come with an interracial legacy, having "Indian" and/or black ancestors as well as white ancestors, adding a new layer of complexity to the race equation in America. The arrival of these new immigrants may end up helping to erode the centrality of the black-white divide.

The End of Classifications?

Ackowledging these tendencies, we think, yields a pessimistic and an optimistic scenario. The pessimistic scenario suggests that the crucial line will remain between blacks and all others. Some "segmented assimilation" will occur, leading a fraction of the second generation to integrate into the black population and the rest into some, as yet, undefined category that may not be "white" in any meaningful sense. All we lack to make this scenario more plausible is a term in the popular culture to replace white – a term that can include Asians and Hispanics easily enough and that essentially means "native-born and not black." If that term does emerge, it would be a worrisome development.

The more optimistic forecast rests on the evolution of black-white relations themselves. It may seem worse than polyannaish in a period of black-white tension to insist on the prospect for qualitative change in relations across that divide. Nevertheless, during the last presidential race, Republican leaders donned sackcloth and ashes because Colin Powell would not run as their candidate for the presidency. By contrast, during the previous great wave of immigration, a president who ate lunch at the White House with a black was obliged to claim that the luncheon was necessitated by busy schedules and was not a social function.

One needn't argue that black-white dynamics are at a happy pass to understand that they have shifted enormously for the better in the past six decades. It is significant that black-white intermarriage remains low; but, with 10 percent of young black men now marrying whites, intermarriage is no longer negligible and continues to increase. If the social class and educational situation of inner-city blacks is a national disaster, there is, nevertheless, also a serious growth in the black middle class and in black collegiate enrollment. The point is simply that the black-white divide, while remaining salient, is different from what it once was.

One measure of change, even in the most recent years, is the fate of the phrase, "the Browning of America." It no longer seems likely that the crucial divide of the future will be between non-Hispanic whites and all others who would be loosely united as "browns." Indeed, the term "the Browning of America" is as common today as was the term "the Greening of America" a generation ago – and about as reliable in predictive value. Another measure, along a different dimension, is the problem that federal agencies have in their attempts to fit the children of racial intermarriages into their racial classification systems. In our reading, these problems should be viewed as symptoms of transition to a time when those classifications seem quaintly passé.

Quotas, Jews, and Asians

There is little question that many, possibly even most, of today's second-generation children are heading upward, as exemplified by the large number of Asian students enrolled in the nation's leading universities, some the children of workers, others the descendants of immigrants who moved right into the middle class. The rapid Asian ascent evokes parallels with the past, most clearly the first- and second-generation Russian Jews who began appearing at the City College of New York, and then Harvard, Columbia, and other prestigious schools shortly after 1900. If there is similarity between past and present experiences of second-generation movement into the middle class, we are more struck by the distinctive institutional reactions to the Jewish, and later the Asian, inflows into higher education.

The history of the quotas against Jewish students is well known. By the second decade of the twentieth century, the number of Jews seeking admission to elite academic institutions was still a relatively small minority of the Jewish age cohort, but the numbers were nonetheless large enough to create a notable presence and to discomfit the then-dominant WASPs. By the end of the 1920s, Harvard, Yale, Princeton, and a host of other institutions, including public state universities, had all adopted measures that restricted Jewish enrollment. Professional schools followed suit. Decisive in changing these restrictive policies was the new legal and social environment that emerged during World War II and thereafter. By the 1960s, public opinion had changed, along with the law, ending the era of anti-Jewish discrimination in higher education.

An echo of this earlier controversy arose in the 1980s, amidst charges that prestigious colleges, private and public, had established quotas against Asians, just as they had against Jews several decades before. Asian students with records comparable to those of their white counterparts were not doing as well when it came to admission to the most selective, private institutions. And Asian enrollments, which had been rising quite sharply in the late 1970s and early 1980s, suddenly flattened out at schools like Princeton, Brown, Harvard, and Stanford.

If the pattern was reminiscent of the earlier Jewish experience and the underlying cause familiar – competition with white elites over scarce and valued resources – the controversy worked itself out very differently. In contrast to the earlier experience, Asian administrators, faculty, and students were numerous and influential, sufficiently so that their voices could not be ignored. Several of the universities accused of discrimination – Princeton, Harvard, Stanford, and Brown, to name just a few – took a critical look at their own admissions practices and then took steps that led to significant increases in Asian-American admissions.

Unlike the Jews, who in the 1920s and 1930s were isolated politically and intimidated by a rising tide of anti-Semitism, Asian-American organizations were able and willing to use political influence; which, in turn, galvanized the scrutiny of outside monitors. In California, admissions policies at UC Berkeley became highly suspect; then, as political scientist Don Nakanishi has described, the state's leading Democratic politicians "held numerous fact-finding hearings, intervened by bringing together university officials and Asian-American community leaders, passed special resolutions on admissions, and had the state Auditor General undertake an unprecedented audit of admissions policies." In Washington, both liberals and conservatives kept the spotlight on allegations of discrimination in admissions. The Office of Civil Rights undertook a major investigation of Harvard, eventually clearing it of charges of discrimination (though it did find that Asians suffered from preferences granted to alumni children and athletes).

There are a number of lessons to be drawn from the story of Asian and Jewish efforts to scale the ivy walls. In the strongly nativist, anti-Semitic environment of the 1920s and 1930s, organized efforts to overturn discriminatory practices were of little avail. Hence, the second generation was forced to fall back on the institutions of the ethnic community, which by the 1930s included civil-service employment as well as a large business sector. Changed power relations after World War II upended the exclusionary practices put into place during the inter-war years. Once quotas were removed, the Jewish presence on campuses swelled.

The Asian controversy arose in a completely different historical moment: earlier struggles against discrimination – the struggles over the Jewish quotas themselves, the post-World War II political climate, and, not least, the civil-rights movement – had changed the rules of the game. It had become far more difficult for dominant groups to engage in strategies of social closure than it had been earlier in the century. The advantages derived from the more open society of the late twentieth century should temper generalizations about the determining position of skin pigmentation in the fate of the new second generation of immigrants.

The Hourglass Economy

But there is still the change in the economy to be considered. Portes and Zhou, as well as Gans, argue that the mismatch between aspiration and opportunity is greater today than before. In their view, the conundrum of the contemporary second generation lies in the continuing transformation of the U.S. economy. The manufacturing economy of old allowed immigrants and their descendants to advance economically and socially in the course of three of four generations. By contrast, occupational segmentation today has (in the words of Portes and Zhou) "reduced the opportunities for incremental upward mobility through well-paid, blue-collar positions." The declining viability of small business is thought to reduce the possibilities for advancement among immigrants' descendants. And the general stalling of mobility reduces the chances for ethnic succession: Jews and Italians followed the Irish into the public sector, as the latter moved on to more lucrative pursuits. Today's civil servants are unlikely to enjoy the same options, closing off this path of mobility for today's second-generation immigrants. Thus emerges the "hourglass economy" – many good jobs at top, many bad jobs at bottom, few decent jobs in the middle. How then will the second generation move up? This economic problem, coupled with the racial origins of the second generation, drives scholars like Portes and Zhou and Gans to their pessimism.

An exception to the hourglass effect is the offspring of the large fraction of immigrants who arrive with useful skills and educational attainments – let us say, educational attainments comparable to the median among American white workers. These immigrants can and do support an extended education for their second-generation children. The children of immigrants comprise 41 percent of the first-year students enrolled in the City University of New York – a rate that leaves immigrant children over-represented in the third largest public system of higher education in the United States by a factor of almost 50 percent. The New York experience is not unique: nationwide, 74 percent of all college-age immigrants are enrolled in some form of post-secondary schooling, as opposed to 65 percent among the native born; likewise, in-school rates for 18- to 21-year-old immigrants are above native-born levels.

But what of the rest? First, recall that it is not only the supposed decline in demand for low-skilled work in the "new economy" that matters; there is also the matter of the supply of low-skilled workers, given several decades of high-volume immigration. The ratio of the two is what determines the fortunes of low-skilled workers, whether native or foreign born.

But this consideration aside, it does seem likely that the less educationally successful of today's second generation, especially those from the immigrant families entering near the bottom, will run into trouble. But do they differ, in this respect, from their counterparts of the past? Questions about the future of yesterday's second generation were a commonplace earlier in the century. At the time, contemporaries did not fret over the possibility that large numbers of jobs would remain at the bottom of an hourglass economy. Nevertheless, they observed that increasing proportions of decent jobs required extended levels of schooling. They also pointed out that the children of workers, generally, and the children of immigrant workers, in particular, would not obtain those jobs, unless they remained in school longer than it seemed their wont to do. The situation is remarkably similar today.

Finally, it should be emphasized that most employed persons without college degrees are neither immigrants, nor their children, nor native-born racial minorities. Thus, if the new hourglass economy obstructs the upward mobility of the children of immigrants or blacks, it thereby confronts American society, and all of its working-class families, with a very serious problem. For once it would seem true that we really can ignore ethnicity and focus on class.

*   *   *

Future Prospects

The descendants of the last great immigration to the United States have now moved far up the totem pole; from the perspective of the 1990s, it is hard to imagine that their adaptation to America could have turned out differently. But this view of an inexorable climb up the social ladder is certainly not how the children and grandchildren of the European immigrants experienced the process themselves. Their beginnings, as we have noted, were not particularly promising; nor were the established groups of the time ready to accept the newcomers and their descendants. Even the most skilled of the lot, the Jews, found that rapid acculturation and the acquisition of schooling were not sufficient to open doors. The acquisition of full membership was an uncertain, protracted process to which the immigrants and their descendants contributed – both through attempts to undo obstacles to progress and to place themselves on the white side of America's racial divide.

At a minimum, this portrait of the past suggests that, overall, the children of the post-1965 immigration begin with disadvantages no greater than those encountered by immigrant children before. On the one hand, the class composition of today's immigrants is more heavily weighted toward the middle class than was true earlier in the century. And on the other hand, American society is more receptive to immigrants – in large measure because of efforts by earlier groups of outsiders (including native-born blacks) to widen access to opportunity.

We would conclude with two points – the relevance of class and agency. *Class*: While America's new immigrant population is extraordinarily diverse, its overwhelmingly largest component – the Mexicans – falls at the very bottom of the skill ladder; the Mexicans are even more heavily represented among the immigrants' children. Absent the Mexicans, today's second generation looks little different from the rest of the American population in socio-economic characteristics. Those characteristics: are not sufficient to guarantee satisfactory adjustment to the economy of the next generation; but the same can be said for young, third-generation-plus Americans of any ethnic stripe. The immigrant children most notably at risk are the Mexicans (most notable, surely, in numbers and as notable as any other immigrant group in the low level of economic well-being). It is the presence of a single large group, so far below the others in skills, that distinguishes today's from yesterday's second generation. However, we note that the advent of the new economy means trouble for the children of the native-born members of America's working class, who also find themselves in conflict with the middle-class values and expectations of schools. These are the main reasons why we should worry about the future for the offspring of Mexican immigrants and of other less-skilled newcomers.

Agency: As did their predecessors, the children of today's new immigrants will transform America. The relatively high class background of so many immigrant children makes it more likely that they will do so quickly and on their own terms – witness the contrast between the Jewish and Asian fate in higher education. That higher class standing is also likely to change the import of race, historically fluid except at the black-white divide, and currently under rapid transition even there. One can certainly imagine that some section of African Americans, Latin Americans, and Asian Americans will find themselves pigeonholed in some new, but stigmatized and subordinated "other" category. But there are other possibilities; and the ever growing ethnic diversity of American life – thanks, in large measure to immigration itself – suggests that these other possibilities are more likely. We expect that today's second generation will make itself busy reshaping the meaning of race – an endeavor to be pursued with at least some success.

11

The Immigration Debate

The Immigrant Contribution to the Revitalization of Cities

Thomas Muller

> The richest regions are those with the highest proportion of immigrants.... Their industry, their skills and their enterprises were major factors in the economic development that made these regions prosperous.
>
> President's Commission on Immigration and Naturalization, 1953

Immigration has had its deepest and most sustained impact on what can be called "gateway cities." The most important examples of these are Los Angeles County, Miami/Dade County, New York City, and the city of San Francisco; Washington, D.C., and possibly Chicago qualify as second-tier gateways. These cities share several important demographic characteristics. Their population growth since the 1970s is attributable exclusively to immigration. The majority of the population in each city is some combination of Asian, black, and Hispanic, with only two of every five residents a non-Hispanic white. Immigrants have flocked to the cities for generations, and these urban centers have become dependent on their labor.

* * *

Gateway cities also share several economic characteristics linked to immigration and international activity. Two-thirds of all foreign bank branches in the United States are located in gateway cities, and gateway ports account for nearly two-fifths of all U.S. exports. In the central business districts (CBDs) of the four gateway cities, foreign investors in 1987 held office buildings valued at more than $12 billion, or 60 percent of total overseas investment in office real estate within the United States. Almost one-half of the office space in downtown Los Angeles, for example, is owned by foreign, mostly Japanese,

Excerpted from Thomas Muller, *Immigrants and the American City* (New York: New York University Press, 1993), chapter 4.

groups. Conversely, international investors are practically absent from Baltimore, Cincinnati, Phoenix, and other large urban centers with few immigrants. The prevalence of foreign bank branches, foreign investment, and immigrant-based commercial activity, together with the presence of many large domestic financial institutions, has helped integrate these gateways into a worldwide commercial network.

* * *

The concept of gateway cities is related to the notion of "primary core world cities" used by urban planners and social scientists, but it differs in several critical respects. John Friedmann's list of "world cities" – Chicago, Houston, Los Angeles, Miami, New York, San Francisco, and a dozen others located outside the United States – overlaps with the roster of gateway cities presented above. However, Friedmann makes mostly negative assertions about those cities. He argues that world cities, by attracting so many internal migrants as well as immigrants, are growing at such a rapid rate that their social costs are outstripping their financial resources.[1] He also maintains that growth in corporate headquarters, international finance, and related commercial activities leads to the creation of low-wage service jobs at the expense of high-wage employment. Friedmann strongly suggests that these world cities will eventually collapse under the weight of the poor masses flowing into them. A similar view is held by Saskia Sassen-Koob, who believes that world cities require for their well-being the presence of a growing underclass.[2] The positive assessment registered in this [essay] – that immigration to American gateway cities has contributed to their economic and social vitality – is partially attributable to the economic success of many recent arrivals, mainly non-European immigrants, as a consequence of the 1965 Immigration Act.

The Immigrant City Anew

In the decades following the passage of the national origins legislation in 1924, the immigrant role in cities diminished as the aging foreign-born population and their children joined the exodus to suburbs. But after the 1965 Immigration Act became effective, the inflow of non-European legal aliens and illegal workers accelerated, with the result that numerous places – once the homes of the newest European aliens – again became immigrant cities. These places include not only the six gateway areas specified, but also other large and small urban centers that have been affected by the growing immigrant presence.

The net population increase in the United States due to immigration between 1970 and 1990 is estimated at well over 10 million and accounts for about a fourth of the overall population gain the nation has experienced over twenty years. This estimate does not fully incorporate the probable magnitude of illegal immigration that has taken place during the past two decades, which would increase the total by perhaps another two million. Over four-fifths of the newcomers to our shores settle in metropolitan areas – most of them in central cities. Of all immigrants arriving in New York State during the 1980s, almost 90 percent gave New York City as their destination; three of every five arrivals in Illinois listed Chicago. Overall, the majority of aliens choose to live in a handful of areas, with New York and Los Angeles in the lead, followed by Chicago, San Francisco, Washington, D.C., and Miami. The number initially settling in places like Buffalo, Indianapolis, Memphis, and Pittsburgh is negligible, although even these areas are being "penetrated" by Asian entrepreneurs and professionals.

The ethnic distribution of aliens in our major cities reflects historical patterns and geography. There are reliable figures only for legal entrants; of these, New York attracts about two-thirds of all Dominicans, one-half of all Russians, one-fourth of all Chinese, and one-third of all Colombians. But fewer than one in one hundred Mexicans settles in New York. They prefer Los Angeles County, where nearly four in ten residents enumerated in 1990 were Hispanic; the same is true of Koreans, Salvadorans, and Vietnamese. Chicago attracts more than one-fourth of all Poles, while Miami is a magnet for Cubans, Haitians, and Central Americans. San Francisco boasts the largest Chinese community in the nation; about three in ten residents of that city are Asian. As for illegals, Mexicans, Koreans, and Central Americans gravitate to Los Angeles, Chinese to San Francisco, and Caribbean nationals to New York. The latest among illegal entrants are the Irish, who, driven by a stagnating economy in Ireland that has failed to provide enough jobs for those leaving school, can be seen much as they were a century earlier, working on construction crews on the streets of New York.

The ethnic composition of immigrants has shifted from Europe to Asia and the Western Hemisphere since the 1950s, but the occupational patterns of aliens who enter legally (with the exception of Mexicans) has remained essentially stable. Professional and blue-collar positions continue to attract immigrants in greater proportions than among the native-born work force. The groups with the highest proportion of professionals are Indians, Filipinos, and Britons, with percentages well exceeding the average for urban natives; by contrast, Mexicans, Vietnamese, and Haitians tend to be blue-collar workers.

The growing presence of non-European immigrants, together with the high birthrates of new entrants and native minorities, is also affecting the size and ethnic distribution of the nation's labor force. To the envy of other Western nations, the United States gained twenty-three million jobs between 1977 and 1987. Hispanics, blacks, and Asians account for somewhat more than two of every ten residents but supplied four of every ten workers added during the decade. In central cities, both large and small, these three groups accounted for almost one-half of the growth in the labor force, mostly through immigration. The number of Hispanics in the work force more than doubled, while the number of Asians increased 134 percent during the ten-year span, to 1.9 million. Job gains for blacks have been somewhat higher than the national average. However, a substantial number of blacks gaining employment in New York and particularly Miami were recent immigrants. All in all, immigration is helping to bring about a change in the racial composition of the labor force unseen since the late seventeenth century, when black slaves became a critical component in the Southern colonies.

Immigrants coming to live in the inner cities are now filling the void left by those moving to the suburbs. This process is by no means recent. In earlier periods it was rural migrants, blacks, and immigrants who flowed into the urban core. Today, those first two categories have run dry. America's rural agricultural population has been so diminished that only minimal outmigration can be expected in the future. And blacks are now more likely to be leaving rather than entering large cities. Moreover, in a period of low birthrates, natural increase cannot be expected to maintain a growing labor force. That leaves immigrants. A large enough number of recent immigrants have settled in inner cities to have a measurable effect on their population size, age distribution, and work force characteristics.

The effects of a shrinking population base on urban life have been amply chronicled. Schools grow empty, housing is abandoned, infrastructure crumbles. As more buildings are taken off the tax rolls, a city's ability to maintain services is further diminished. Abandoned buildings breed crime, which leads to a further deterioration in neighborhood life. Commuters come to work in downtown office towers but spend their earnings in the suburbs. So do many of the remaining inner-city residents, causing a drop in sales tax receipts.

Such was the experience of the gateway cities – and most others – during the 1970s. But the situation would have been far worse in the absence of immigration. For instance, New York, a city of more than 7 million residents, lost 700,000 persons during the decade; without immigrants, the decline would have exceeded 1.5 million. During the 1980s, the city officially gained 251,000 residents; were it not for the 854,000 legal immigrants who settled there, New York's downward spiral would have continued, although more slowly. Had legal and undocumented immigration ceased in the mid-1960s, the city would probably now have considerably fewer than six million inhabitants.

In some circumstances, inner cities could benefit from reduced population. No doubt many New Yorkers, faced with crowded subway cars, clogged streets, and rising rents, would prefer a city of six million. If New York had been able to adjust to a lower population while also retaining a strong middle-class presence, its quality of life may well have improved. But in reality, population losses are selective. Outmigrants from cities tend to be better educated and more affluent than those remaining: New York had a net loss of 40,000 college graduates between 1975 and 1980.[3] In the absence of immigration, the city's share of middle-class families and active workers would have fallen further. Between 1975 and 1980 the vast majority of those leaving the city had household incomes between $25,000 and $50,000. The city's poor population, meanwhile, increased by 36,000.

Most residents of Los Angeles County, frustrated by traffic congestion and air pollution, would also favor fewer people. Similar to New York, the Los Angeles County population, which remained stable in the 1970s, would have declined by up to one million had no immigrants settled there. The county's population gain of 1,386,000 during the 1980s is primarily attributable to the immigrant inflow. The county has experienced no net migration from other parts of the nation since the early 1970s despite considerable economic growth. Without the alien contribution, the population in the two other gateway cities,

San Francisco and Miami, would unquestionably have fallen.[4] The upturn in the number of immigrants during the 1980s reversed the population decline in Boston and San Francisco, although the economic health of these cities during the 1980s certainly aided their stability.

These population effects of immigration assume that the alien influx is unrelated to the departure of the middle-class from cities. It may be that, in the absence of renewed immigration, more natives would have remained. During the 1980s the number of non-Hispanic whites declined by over one million in the four gateway urban centers combined, with the steepest fall (over 22 percent) in Miami/Dade county. Part of the outflow from Miami is attributable to immigration, but to what extent the losses in Los Angeles and New York are linked to the growing alien presence is difficult to assess. However, among the nation's twenty largest cities, Baltimore, Cleveland, Detroit, Milwaukee, and Philadelphia have attracted few immigrants and, not coincidentally, lost 5 percent or more of their population in the 1980s. This supports the thesis that the absence of immigration does not constrain the flight of middle-class residents to the suburbs. The inability of these industrial cities to attract immigrants has further weakened their economic base.

Achieving a stable population by itself adds little to a local economy. In fact, a population with a high proportion of children and the aged can actually weaken economic activity. However, fewer than 4 percent of recent immigrants are over the age of sixty-five (compared to 11.5 percent of the total U.S. population), and the percentage under the age of eighteen is similar to the native-born population. Therefore, a high proportion of new immigrants are in the working-age category. In addition, immigrants also have higher labor force participation rates than the population at large. Since their rate of unemployment is only somewhat higher than average, immigrants are overall more apt to be in the work force than native residents.

Dishwashers and Engineers

New immigrants are most likely to be seen working at sewing machines in apparel factories, as engineers in high-technology industries, washing dishes in restaurants, and as shop owners in central-city ghettos. Such diversity should not be surprising since, conservatively, one of every five workers entering the nation's labor force in the 1970s and 1980s was a recent immigrant, and in central cities the proportion was much higher. If these workers – six million or more in all – had not come to our shores, would these jobs have been taken by others, remained unfilled, or created at all in the first place? This is a critical question because immigrants have been portrayed alternately as unwanted aliens taking jobs from Americans, as competitors causing wages to decline, or, more benignly, as laborers who accept jobs that natives shun. All these images have some validity. There is no doubt that some immigrants take jobs that would otherwise go to natives. And the wages paid to unskilled workers can be depressed by an immigrant-fed labor surplus. Many aliens, meanwhile, take on such unwanted jobs as dishwasher and hotel maid.

But immigration has also helped create new jobs – in some cases for members of the same ethnic group, in other cases for native workers. The chief effect of immigration on the urban occupational structure, from the perspective of native white workers, has been to supplant low-wage blue-collar and service jobs with white-collar and public-sector positions. Many new immigrants, particularly undocumented workers and Hispanics, accept work in hotels, restaurants, and low-wage manufacturing establishments that are unattractive to most natives. Their earnings stimulate employment in higher-paying jobs, including finance, utilities, and local government.

*   *   *

Almost one-third of all new immigrants in 1980 worked in manufacturing a much higher rate than for nonimmigrants. Among undocumented workers, more than one-half are employed in the production of apparel and other manufactured goods.[5] Given that the number of manufacturing jobs (unlike jobs in other sectors) has remained stable since the late 1960s, immigrants are taking the place of domestic workers, especially those engaged in low-wage production jobs in cities.

The role of manufacturing in urban economic life began to recede after World War II. By the 1960s, with factories relocating first to other parts of the country and then overseas, most cities experienced a sharp decline in their manufacturing fortunes. Hardest hit were apparel, textiles, shoes, furniture, and electronics. Where immigrants were present, however, the trend was slowed. This was nowhere more apparent than in Los Angeles. Between 1972 and 1986, as manufacturing employment nationwide dropped slightly, it grew in Los Angeles County by almost 20 percent. This was due primarily to the presence of Hispanics willing to work for low wages. With the exception of high-wage sectors like aerospace, Hispanics had by the late 1980s become the backbone of the county's industrial work force.

*   *   *

In New York, as in Los Angeles, immigrants have played an important role in the manufacturing sector, which has suffered for numerous reasons – foreign and domestic competition, a weak regional economy, the high cost of doing business in Manhattan, and obsolete facilities. The availability of immigrant labor in New York, although not enough in itself to reverse the loss of manufacturing jobs, has apparently slowed the rate of decline.

The importance of undocumented aliens in several manufacturing sectors is readily illustrated in statistics. In 1980, according to one estimate, 39 percent of all jobs in apparel, 37 percent in leather and footwear, and 36 percent in canned foods and vegetables across the nation were held by illegal workers.[6]

Apparel production in gateway cities is the sector most dependent on immigrant labor, and as such it demonstrates the impact of recent entrants on low-wage manufacturing. The high concentration of immigrants in the field is not a new phenomenon. At the turn of the century, workers from Eastern Europe and Italy in the Northeast and Chinese workers in San Francisco provided the low-wage labor force in this highly competitive industry.

Although apparel employment in the nation declined substantially between 1972 and 1987, there was a considerable increase in Los Angeles. A survey found that almost all of the 80,000 apparel workers in the region were female illegal aliens.[7] In 1979 undocumented workers in the local apparel industry earned only $2.75 per hour – considerably below the $3.68 earned by U.S. citizens. Wages in Los Angeles for all apparel workers fell from 102 percent to 94 percent of the U.S. average between 1972 and 1987.

Immigrant labor likewise enabled New York City to maintain its historically important role in the apparel sector, particularly women's clothing (although at somewhat reduced levels). During the 1970s and early 1980s, the rate of job loss in this industry in New York was only slightly more rapid than it was nationally. Employment in apparel and textiles in the borough of Queens rose modestly in the mid-1980s, suggesting that the industry has remained competitive. The growing use of low-wage immigrant labor did not appear to diminish the historically high productivity of the New York labor force in this sector; rather, productivity in New York remained above the national average, allowing the industry to maintain a presence in the area.

*   *   *

Many employers could not have obtained, at prevailing wages, sufficient native workers in apparel and other low-wage industries to maintain profitable operations. Without such labor these jobs presumably would have been moved to other countries with lower labor costs. This would have resulted in higher imports and larger balance-of-payment deficits. Manufacturing jobs were also retained in industries supplying materials to apparel, furniture, and metal-products firms and other sectors dependent on alien workers.

Immigrants, undocumented workers in particular, are also represented disproportionately in service industries, especially in restaurants, hotels, hospitals, and as private household help. These are typically low-paying jobs that require only limited English-language or other skills. Undocumented workers comprise 80 percent of all Hispanics exployed in Los Angeles restaurants. Hispanics, in turn, form the majority of all such workers in the city. Virtually every restaurant in Miami, New York, and San Francisco depends on immigrant dishwashers and bus-boys. Hotels in gateway cities are also dependent on immigrants to work in their kitchens, clean rooms, and maintain the grounds. Employment in restaurants and hotels doubled between 1970 and the late 1980s; such growth could not have been sustained without the alien presence. About 7 percent of all hotel and restaurant jobs in 1980 were held by illegal workers,[8] and that figure has increased during the 1980s to perhaps 10 percent or more of the total.

Although immigrants are popularly seen as holding the types of jobs discussed so far, others are skilled craftsmen and professional workers. Thus, it is not only through their willingness to perform undesirable tasks that immigrants contribute to urban economies; they also bring – or develop in the United States – badly needed skills. In the New York area, more than eleven thousand of those who arrived during the 1970s were employed as craft workers in manufacturing. A good example is the production of precious jewels.

New York accounts for more than one-third of total national output, centered in the "Diamond District." The aging local labor force in cutting and setting jewels – many in the industry were refugees who arrived in the late 1930s – has been rejuvenated through the arrival of new immigrant craftsmen, mostly of European origin. The presence of foreign-born workers is similarly important in furs (Soviet Jews), wigs (Koreans), and other highly specialized fields.

The importance of skilled immigrant labor is not limited to the manufacturing sector. Since the late 1960s (repeating the pattern of the late 1930s), this nation has attracted many well-educated professionals from overseas. Most of them have settled in the large coastal cities of California and the New York megalopolis. In New York City, the percentage of recent arrivals who are professionals is considerably higher than that for the European immigrants who came prior to 1970. Among the city's recent Asian immigrants, the proportion of professionals is almost as high as that among the native white population.

For the most part, these professionals are concentrated in two fields – health care and engineering sciences. In many public hospitals in gateway cities, the majority of interns and other staff workers are foreign nationals. During the late 1970s, more than one-half of all interns in New York City municipal hospitals were Asians; in Brooklyn Hospital, a private, nonprofit institution, the percentage was even higher. Unfamiliarity with English often creates difficulties in communicating with patients, but without these immigrants, our nation's public hospitals – inside and outside big cities – would probably suffer a shortage of doctors.

*   *   *

Foreign-born engineers and scientists, meanwhile, have made an important contribution to the nation's technological standing. The 1980 census identified more than seventy thousand Asian-born engineers and natural scientists, 97 percent of them employed in metropolitan areas. Immigration statistics indicate that nearly one-third of the college-educated immigrants who arrived in the early 1970s held scientific or technical jobs. According to a National Science Foundation study, foreign-born individuals account for almost 20 percent of the scientific staff in the nation's largest firms. Electronics firms are likely to hire aliens because Americans with similar qualifications are not readily available. Usually located in urban areas, electronics companies have a large pool of immigrant professionals at their disposal. In 1982, noncitizens and naturalized citizens accounted for 26 percent of all engineers with master's degrees and 36 percent of those with Ph.D.'s.[9]

*   *   *

The economic value of attracting trained professionals from other nations can be calculated not only by their contributions to their occupations but by the cost of their education, paid in their country of origin. One estimate is that $500 million was saved by the prior education and training of physicians, engineers, and others who emigrated to the United States in 1971. This "brain drain" has had an adverse effect on countries of emigration by depleting their human resources.

For this reason, some countries have adopted strategies to limit enrollment of their nationals in the U.S. universities. The Chinese, for example, curtailed the flow of their Ph.D. students in some scientific fields to the United States – even prior to the May 1989 bloody upheaval in Beijing – because a large number never returned. These students are now being sent to Western Europe (the former Soviet Union in no longer favored), where they are less likely to find employment, permanent jobs, or social acceptance than in this country.

Immigrants who have come to the United States legally since the late 1960s have higher educational achievement levels than earlier entrants or native-born Americans. In 1982, 11.6 percent of recent immigrants had four years of college and 11.8 percent had graduate-level training.[10] Among natives, 10.6 percent had sixteen years and 7.9 percent had seventeen or more years of schooling. Recent entrants are overrepresented at both ends of the educational spectrum – with Hispanic immigrants below the American average, Asians above the average.

The Middle-Class Entrepreneurs

For centuries commercial activity has been a dominant feature in the growth and economic vitality of central cities. In fact, a city's economic health can be roughly gauged by changes in the number of its retail and service establishments. In the 1972–82 period, the number of retail stores in most industrial cities fell. Across the country the total count remained essentially unchanged, although retail employment rose. The national trend was shifting from small, family-operated businesses to larger operations, but the pattern in three of the four gateway cities countered the trend, thanks to the growth in Asian- and Hispanic-owned stores. Had that number of Asian businesses remained constant, both Los Angeles and San Francisco would have experienced declines in retail stores. Similarly, the absence of new Cuban enterprises in Miami would have reversed the growth pattern.

Between 1972 and 1982, the number of retail businesses in New York City actually declined, as did the number of jobs in stores. The sharpest decline came in establishments without payrolls, that is, mom-and-pop stores that employ only family members. This falloff reflected two developments – the loss of clients due to outmigration and the consolidation of stores into larger, more efficient units. In the following five years, however, New York retail trade recovered in response to modest population growth and a rise in income at a rate exceeding the national average. Paralleling this economic expansion, the number of Asian and Hispanic retail establishments grew, and retail employment increased by 14 percent (though a weak regional economy in the early 1990s reversed the employment gains).

In gateway and other cities, immigrants have made an important contribution to retail growth. A disproportionate share of non-Hispanic immigrants work as entrepreneurs, and most favor retail trade or services. More than one-tenth of all recent immigrants are self-employed (a category that includes professionals and business owners); among Asians the rate is even higher. In fact, in 1987 Asians owned 4.1 percent of all retail stores across the nation, a percentage considerably in excess of their share of the population. This high rate of self-employment set Asian immigrants apart from blacks, who in that same year owned only 3.1 percent of business establishments (and comprised 12 percent of the population), as well as Hispanics, with one notable exception – about 20 percent of all Cubans are self-employed; another 30 percent worked for other Cubans. In the four gateway cities, two out of every nine Asian households owned a business enterprise in 1987.

Immigrant entrepreneurs are helping to revive the small neighborhood stores that were common in the nation's cities prior to World War II. Arabs in Detroit and Chicago, and Cubans and Nicaraguans in Miami, have helped confound the predictions of some economists that large corporations would take over the retail trade, forcing many independent merchants out of business.

Nowhere is the proliferation of immigrant businesses more evident than in New York. Many Greeks own coffee shops; Koreans, fruit and vegetable markets; Dominicans, construction firms; Asian Indians, travel agencies; and Chinese, restaurants. In Los Angeles, Koreans are concentrated in the proprietorship of liquor stores, gasoline stations, and hamburger stands, while Indian immigrants own motels and dry cleaning establishments.

Much smaller in number but equally enterprising in their own way – and certainly more exotic – are recent African immigrants. The several hundred Senegalese peddlers who crowd the sidewalks of New York in their native garb are no doubt the city's most colorful self-employed group. Although many of these activities are not legal (because the peddlers lack licenses), their uncanny ability to materialize with umbrellas in the midst of unexpected downpours has elicited the appreciation of many a Manhattanite. These small-time black entrepreneurs purchase their goods from Chinese and Korean wholesalers in the city, thus further promoting ethnic business activity.[11]

No group better exemplifies the entrepreneurial spirit than Asians. Remarkably driven, they have grabbed an increasingly large, but by no means dominant, share of retail establishments in Los Angeles, New York, Houston, and other metropolises. Perhaps it should not be surprising that Houston, the embodiment of the freewheeling Texans, would be attractive to equally freewheeling entrepreneurs from the Far East. The Asian population in this city has risen from 2,500 in 1965 to 67,000 in 1990. In Houston's downtown, with its own, more genuine Chinatown, 39 percent of all commercial buildings are owned by foreign, mostly Asian, investors – the highest percentage of such ownership in the country, with the exception of Los Angeles. Asians are estimated to own (in the early 1990s) two out of five retail stores in Los Angeles County, and one-third in the San Francisco metropolitan area, although high-volume chain stores remain predominantly in white hands. There are a dozen or more Asian Indian, Chinese, and Korean businesses in every state, including the Dakotas, Maine, and Vermont.

Of all Asian groups, the Koreans have progressed most rapidly in the shortest period of time. The total number admitted to this country during the 1950s was only 6,000 – mostly wives of American soldiers – rising to 35,000 in the 1960s, 268,000 in the following decade, and 334,000 in the 1980s. Remarkably, for every thousand Korean residents, there were more than one hundred Korean-owned enterprises in 1987. This means that every third Korean household owned a business – a rate much higher than that for other ethnic groups.

*   *   *

Cities in a Competitive Market

Perhaps the most important effect of recent immigration has been the restoration of urban competitors in particular sectors. This has been achieved by immigrants in their roles as low-wage workers, professionals, and entrepreneurs who encourage and contribute investment. To evaluate immigrant workers' importance in the urban economy, their roles must be considered in the context of the larger labor market.

Economists frequently view the labor market as composed of two sectors. The first is the primary market where workers are subject to standard labor laws. A set of formal rules and regulations governs the relationship between employers and workers. Enterprises include the government, large corporations, and institutions that are frequently unionized, with wages negotiated through collective bargaining. This sector has been diluted by falling union membership in manufacturing, once the mainstay of organized labor, and by significant job cuts in large, service-oriented enterprises, particularly those in communications and finance in the early 1990s. Native workers are more likely than immigrants to be employed in the primary sector.

Characteristics distinguishing the secondary sector include a labor market that is not unionized, with few regulations and wages set by supply and demand. The majority of new immigrants, particularly undocumented workers employed within ethnic enclaves or toiling in restaurants and personal service businesses, are likely to be in the secondary labor market.

The presence of secondary-market workers has enabled cities to compete at two levels: with the suburban areas that have become the new centers of metropolitan commercial activity and with other nations that export their products to the United States. Revitalized inner-city commercial areas, including ethnic enclave businesses, reduce the outflow of city shoppers to suburban malls and smaller shopping centers.

As noted earlier, immigrants are overrepresented in low-wage industries such as apparel, shoes, and furniture, which have traditionally depended on alien labor. Immigrant workers in California and Texas cities have made these areas rich in such industries. Do cities actually benefit from the presence of these low-wage sectors? Would it not be better to locate such factories in a less-developed country with abundant cheap labor and retain for ourselves the higher-wage industrial jobs? The labor movement struggled for decades to rid the United States of sweatshops, and yet we now appear to applaud the proliferation of such enterprises in American cities.

In reality, older American cities in particular would have difficulty with the concentrated production of capital-intensive goods, which require high technology. Most of these cities are not considered by investors as potential sites for new industry. Shortages of undeveloped land, obsolete physical plants, excessive tax rates, and high transportation costs are among the drawbacks cited to explain the lack of private investment. Privately, foreign enterprises are fearful that a central-city facility would be exposed to the urban ills and dangers portrayed almost daily in the American and international media. For a stagnating urban economy, any productive economic activity is a plus. A Newark, New Jersey, is not likely to attract large research laboratories and certainly not a Japanese automaker. But with both commercial space and immigrant labor available at low cost, older cities can attract labor-intensive manufacturing and service industries. If the United States aimed to produce only high-tech goods, not only would its trade balance be distorted by the move, but the effort would exacerbate its difficulties in the competitive world market as a result of overspecialization.

*　　*　　*

The benefits of relatively low-wage industries extend well beyond the employment they provide. First of all, these plants pay local taxes. They also generate business for local suppliers. The workers at manufacturing plants spend most of their paychecks locally, helping to stimulate retail sales. All in all, older cities that have difficulty attracting high-tech business enterprises can benefit mightily from industries that at first glance might seem less than glamorous.

Highly skilled immigrants also make a valuable contribution to urban economies. These craftsmen – stonemasons, jewelers, and others – help fill the gap left by the reluctance of our talented high school graduates to learn skilled trades, despite the relatively high wages they offer. Many immigrant workers are trained by their parents and grandparents; others receive more formal instruction in technical schools in their native lands prior to settling in this country. The city provides them the opportunity to earn a higher wage than they would in their country of origin.

Native workers with specialized skills may have once worked in the urban core, but they have increasingly been lured to more attractive positions in the suburbs. Immigrants help fill the gap. The availability of a skilled labor force can offset some of the disadvantages common to central-city locations, such as congestion and high taxes, that discourage industries from expanding their operations within the inner city. Generally speaking, the absence of a ready pool of both unskilled and skilled workers has contributed to the decision of companies to move from central cities.

Even more valuable than skilled immigrants are those who come to our shores with professional training, particularly in science and engineering. The ability of cities to attract these immigrants has allowed some small firms to maintain their operations within the urban core. The 1980 census enumerated 23,300 Asian-born engineers and natural scientists living in central cities. Upward of 95 percent of all such foreign-born professionals reside in urban areas. In the economically stagnating city of Detroit, 44 percent of all Asians are professionals. Many trained immigrants find jobs with ethnic entrepreneurs who, having some scientific training themselves, have established small companies. Asians have been particularly successful in combining technological and managerial skills to create companies that produce technologically advanced products.

Immigration, Jobs, and Wages

Cities as a whole clearly derive many advantages from the presence of immigrants. But cities are made up of many groups – employers and workers, sellers and consumers, rich and poor, white and black, young and old, owners and renters – each with distinct interests. Which groups and classes benefit from immigration?

The effects on workers are considered first because the fear of job competition and lower wages has fueled the most bitter anti-immigrant sentiment. In the earlier discussion of how immigration laws evolved, "taking jobs from American workers" was found to be the most consistent theme voiced by opponents of liberal entry policies, whatever their actual motivation may have been. Although the claim that native workers as a group were harmed was never substantiated, the relationship between job opportunities for these workers and immigration is complex and not fully understood by economists.

The analysis presented in this chapter and observation of the labor market in gateway cities during the 1970s and 1980s suggest that the addition of immigrant workers to a local economy enhances the competitiveness of its industries. Concurrently, the demand for locally produced goods and services rises. This is especially apparent in New York and Los Angeles, where a large population base and a diversified economy mean that many of the goods consumed in the area are also produced there. Expanded payrolls thus have a large "employment multiplier effect" on the entire region.

Some of the jobs that immigrants help to create – notably in retail trade and personal services– are taken by other immigrants. But in many other areas – utilities, banking, finance, real estate, and communications – new jobs tend to be filled by natives. Similarly, added economic activity creates new demand for nontechnical professionals – lawyers, accountants, and bankers – primarily natives because language and licensing requirements make it difficult for immigrants to enter these fields. For example, the 1980 census found that only 320 recent male immigrants in New York were working as professionals in the legal field – a mere 0.5 percent of all male attorneys in the city.

Generally speaking, immigrants create substantially more jobs than they take in such fields as communications and utilities. By contrast, they take more jobs than they create in manufacturing, retail trade, and restaurants. Thus, in Los Angeles, New York, San Francisco, and other cities, the net effect of immigration has been to *redistribute* the jobs available for native workers away from manufacturing and lower-skill services toward the white-collar sector, particularly in management and the professions. This redistribution, which began in the 1970s, accelerated during the 1980s, with more and more native men and women shifting to white-collar jobs, while immigrants, particularly Hispanics, expanded their hold on manufacturing. By 1991, 23 percent of all blacks, but only 10 percent of all Hispanics, working in Los Angeles held professional or managerial positions. In the same year, nondurable goods manufacturing attracted fewer than 13,000 blacks compared to 194,000 Hispanics.[12]

The vast majority of jobs taken by immigrants are in the private sector. The proportion of recent immigrants holding nonprofessional public-sector jobs is extremely small. But the presence of immigrants expands the demand for public services and increases local tax revenue, leading to an expansion of public, particularly municipal, employment. The number of teachers, for example, rises in almost direct proportion to increased enrollment. The demand for other municipal services – police, utilities, social services – is also linked to population growth. About one in seven persons employed in the New York metropolitan area, and one in nine in Los Angeles County, works for the local, state, or federal government. Of course, population is not the only factor determining public employment levels. During the 1970s, New York City's fiscal crisis was primarily responsible for severe reductions in municipal employment. During the 1980s, however, as economic conditions improved and population grew modestly (owing exclusively to immigration), municipal employment expanded significantly again. The 1990–91 fiscal crisis forced New York City once more to curtail municipal jobs, but the employment level remained well above the low point that followed the earlier cutbacks.

Public-sector jobs are more important for blacks than for whites, Asians, or Hispanics. In New York City[13] almost one-fourth of all black men and one-third of all black women in 1980 worked for local, state, or federal government. All net gains in jobs experienced by native blacks during the 1970s were generated by the public sector. This pattern continued into the next decade. Between 1983 and 1989, blacks gained fifty-nine thousand jobs in government at all three levels, which accounted for about seven out of ten new jobs for blacks in the city. Among the 508,000 government jobs in 1991, almost two out of five were held by blacks, although blacks constitute only about one-fourth of the employed labor force. The gains accrue primarily to native blacks; aside from the health-care field, relatively few black immigrants obtain public-sector jobs. On a per capita basis, black women in New York are seven times more likely to hold jobs in the public sector than women who are recent immigrants.

Moreover, for blacks the public sector means not only more stable jobs than typically found in the private sector but also relatively high pay. The earnings of blacks in government exceed earnings in the private sector. Blacks employed by the police and fire departments in California earn one-third more than blacks in the private sector. Because wage gains in government have outpaced private industry and a disproportionately high number of blacks work in the public sector, this has contributed toward reducing wage disparities, particularly between black women and other women.

On the whole, native workers are benefiting (as have previous generations) from their transition to white-collar jobs, a process accelerated by the presence of immigrant workers. As older, urban-dwelling native workers in manufacturing retire or decide to take jobs in other sectors, immigrants emerge as the newest generation of industrial workers. In several large urban areas, the percentage of industrial workers that were immigrants in the early 1990s approached (and in Los Angeles and Miami exceeded) the historic peak of immigrants' share in the manufacturing work force nationwide attained during the early decades of the twentieth century. There were, nonetheless, notable differences from the earlier period. High-wage, unionized Pennsylvania steel mills and Michigan assembly plants, industries dominated by immigrants in 1910, saw few foreign-born workers eight decades later.

Job expansion nationally and in gateway cities that can be linked to immigrant consumers and entrepreneurs has probably equaled, and in some areas exceeded, jobs taken by immigrant workers. The most visible impact of their entry into the labor force is the overall growth in employment levels and the change in sectoral distribution of jobs among native workers. In this respect, the impact of immigration parallels the experience during earlier periods when foreign-born workers filled the nation's factories and small immigrant shops lined the ethnic neighborhoods of American cities.

The relationship between immigrant workers and wages has been a matter of controversy for a century or more. An increase in the number of workers, regardless of their origin, competing for the same job can be expected to result in wage depression. Fortunately, because not all immigrants are concentrated in one occupation or industry, substantial wage effects are rarely observed.

Since the late nineteenth century there have been numerous attempts to correlate wages with immigration, none of which demonstrated conclusively long-term effects. Following the economic downturn in 1894, Congress debated the cause of the general wage decline and appointed a commission to determine the linkage between immigration, wages, and the economic climate. The report, quoted in the House of Representatives, found no such relationship.[14] Recent research finds the effects of immigrants on native worker earnings to be temporary and minor. This conclusion is shared by Robert Topel, an economist at the University of Chicago, who found the impact of foreign-born workers on native wages in 1987 to be, in most instances, negligible.[15] Similarly, a study determined that wage effects associated with undocumented Mexican workers also appear to be small.[16]

Immigration had a more significant impact on low-skilled workers in Los Angeles, where wages in the metropolitan area during the 1970s declined in comparison to the nation as a whole. This trend was due in part to the presence of immigrants, particularly illegal entrants, during a period of slow growth.[17] Immigrants themselves, and to a lesser extent native Hispanics, absorbed a considerable share of the fall in wages in Los Angeles as natives left low-paying jobs for more lucrative positions. By the mid-1980s immigrants dominated the work force in several Los Angeles industries. Their presence encouraged the inflow of more undocumented workers as jobs expanded. Laborers to fill these low-paying jobs could be most readily obtained only a few hours away across the international border. Wages dropped as a result in the apparel industry, but because virtually all production workers were Hispanic immigrants, the native population was little affected. Among the beneficiaries of lower wages were those holding white-collar jobs in apparel factories and those supplying goods and services to the apparel industry.

*   *   *

The Middle Class as Beneficiaries

Several groups benefit from the immigrant presence. These include consumers, property owners, businesses dependent on low-wage labor, and families seeking domestic help.

Ethnic enclaves are popular destinations for shoppers, who frequently find goods that are either unavailable or for sale at substantially higher prices elsewhere. The popularity of restaurants that have proliferated in ethnic neighborhoods is a measure of both their affordability and of the variety sought by consumer palates. When immigrants own stores outside their ethnic enclaves, they are often in poorer neighborhoods, and these businesses are typically open fourteen or more hours a day, providing customers with virtually around-the-clock convenience. These enterprises are usually small and rely on free family labor, so overhead expenses tend to be modest, enabling neighborhood grocery stores, for example, to charge prices no higher than supermarkets. Customers are usually known by name, and some are given credit, a practice supermarkets would not tolerate. Convenience, service, and price are ingredients for successful immigrant stores outside enclaves.

The ability of small Asian enterprises to remain in business is well illustrated by examining the operation of a local Chinese restaurant in a neighborhood shopping center in northern Virginia. The enterprise is typical of others sprouting in shopping centers across the land. The average hourly wage for its employees – all but one a member of an extended family, including two teenage boys – is well below the minimum wage. American teenagers would probably not tolerate going to school, working six to eight hours a day, and studying, with little sleep. But because immigrants will, consumers find meals prepared to order on the premises at a cost comparable to the fast-food outlets with which the ethnic restaurants compete.

Consumers of ethnic products are not limited to a particular segment of society in American cities. Nonetheless, it would be difficult to argue against the proposition that more affluent groups gain the most from the immigrant presence. This pattern is consistent with the distribution of benefits associated with earlier waves of aliens who came to American cities. As shoppers, middle-class families obtain some goods and numerous services at lower prices than would be the case in the absence of immigrants. Restaurant prices, housekeeping, and gardening services, in particular, are moderated by the availability of immigrant labor. Because families that dine in restaurants and hire help have above-average earnings, they stimulate much of the demand for undocumented workers in cities. Similarly, business clients and the more affluent families stay in hotels and utilize tourist services, which creates employment for immigrants.

Immigrant production workers, on the other hand, benefit people at all income levels because apparel, furniture, food products, shoes, and textiles are purchased – in differing quantities and qualities – by all income groups. Factory owners also gain from the use of immigrant labor. Interestingly, when California residents were asked whether consumers or owners benefited from the presence of illegal workers, more than four out of five believed all the benefits accrued to employers.[18] In their view (but contrary to economic theory for competitive sectors), savings from lower wages were not passed on to the consumer.

As property owners, natives profit from the increase in property values that immigrants induce. Within or on the periphery of immigrant enclaves – be it the Lower East Side of Manhattan; Flushing, New York; the Ironbound section of Newark, New Jersey; the mid-Olympic area of Los Angeles; or Westchester County, New York – property prices have uniformly soared. Native property owners have sold their real estate at prices far in excess of what they would have received if immigrants had not increased the demand for it. In some cases the original properties – boarded-up buildings – were almost valueless, with unpaid taxes exceeding the market price.

*   *   *

On the level of the individual family, immigrant housekeepers play a key (but not widely recognized) role in enabling both husband and wife to work. Without Mexicans and Central Americans (mostly illegal in this case) willing to work for low wages (the number of illegal housekeepers is unknown – the census enumerated only a small fraction of the total), thousands of Californian two-income families would simply not be able to afford a clean house and care for the children. Families in very affluent as well as middle-class neighborhoods in large cities have discreetly managed to obtain alien domestic help. The phenomenon of housekeepers is most visible in Los Angeles, the Washington, D.C., suburbs, and other urban centers with a large Hispanic presence. To a lesser extent, Caribbean housekeepers have taken the place of native blacks in the New York region; within one generation, the native black housekeeper all but disappeared from the domestic scene, too expensive a proposition for most families.

*   *   *

The economic vitality of gateway cities has been strengthened by immigrants – Hispanic, Asian, and European. Population stability is the most obvious impact, but it is not the most important. Immigrants, ranging from young, unskilled entrants to highly trained scientists, make a major contribution to the nation's labor force. By spurring neighborhood revitalization, immigration has enhanced the ability of cities to retain middle-class residents.

Ethnic entrepreneurs are thriving in America's cities not only because of their own ambition but also because of the vitality and openness of our economic system. There are perhaps fewer impediments to starting a business in the United States than anywhere else in the world. We have no constraints on the amount of capital that can be brought into the country, no citizenship requirements, and no special rules and regulations that would prevent aliens from owning businesses. Most receptive of all are large cities, which lack the self-protective businesses elite common in smaller, tightly knit communities.

Despite all the structural changes that have occurred in our economy, cities continue to offer business opportunities to all those willing to work hard and take risks. Immigrants who are supported by an ethnic cohort network are particularly well situated to take advantage of these opportunities. In the process of bettering their own position, these entrepreneurs are also helping to revive commercial and residential activity in formerly deteriorating neighborhoods.

Not that immigrants are immune from the economic downturns that periodically trouble the nation. But the ethnic enclave is more resilient and can better endure economic hardships than the more open economy.

Focusing unduly on aggregate measures of the economic benefits of immigration, however, can be misleading. First, impressive totals, such as changes in per capita income, can mask less benign redistributional effects upon the working class and native minorities in particular. Second, while immigration generally has a positive impact on private enterprise, its effects on the public sector may be less in evidence. Finally, an analysis concentrating on economic issues can easily overlook pressing social problems.

Earlier, the economic benefits of immigration were shown to date back many years, to a period before the Republic itself was founded. Congress mandated immigration constraints in the 1920s less out of economic than social concerns. Americans feared that a continuing influx of immigrants would dilute traditional values, undermine the nation's social stability, and alter its political balance. These potentially negative consequences of immigration, both economic and social, perceived and real, remain fixed in the minds of many people as we move into a decade in which the number of immigrants will probably exceed the record attained in the first decade of the twentieth century.

Notes

1 John Friedmann, "The World City Hypothesis," *Development and Change* 17, no. 1 (January 1986), pp. 69–83.
2 Sassen-Koob also identifies "global cities" and considers New York and Los Angeles to be the foremost of these cities. Her position is that such cities, in particular, require large numbers of low-wage jobs and contribute to the expansion of an underclass. Sassen-Koob argues further that the "expulsion of middle-income jobs" is especially pronounced in global cities. See Saskia Sassen-Koob, "The New Labor Demand in Global Cities," in *Cities in Transformation: Class, Capital and the State*, ed. Michael P. Smith (Beverly Hills, Calif.: Sage Publications, 1984), pp. 139–69.
3 Richard D. Alba and Michael J. Batusis, *The Impact of Migration on New York State*, a report for the Public Policy Institute and the Job Training Partnership Council by the Center for Social and Demographic Analysis, State University of New York, Albany, 1984.
4 Net outmigration from San Francisco accelerated from 19,100 in 1960–5 to 43,082 in 1970–5, slowing to 22,610 in the 1975–80 period. The slowdown and consequent change in direction in the 1980s can be attributed primarily to the Asian influx and the entry of nearly 30,000 Southeast Asian refugees. For discussion, see *Migration Patterns in the San Francisco Bay Area*, Association of Bay Area Governments, Oakland, November 1987.
5 John K. Hill and James E. Pearce, "Enforcing Sanctions against Employers of Illegal Aliens," *Economic Review*, Dallas Federal Reserve Bank, May 1987, pp. 1–15.
6 Ibid.
7 Benjamin Mark Cole, "Abundance of Space, Cheap Labor Pool Boost Local Manufacturing Employment," *Los Angeles Business Journal*, December 1, 1986, p. 8.

8   Hill and Pearce, "Enforcing Sanctions against Employers of Illegal Aliens."
9   National Research Council, *Foreign and Foreign-Born Engineers in the United States* (Washington, D.C.: National Academy Press, 1988), p. 2.
10 Ellen Sehgal, "Foreign-Born Workers in the U.S. Labor Market: The Results of a Special Survey," *Monthly Labor Review* 108, no. 7 (July 1985), pp. 18–24.
11 "Street Peddlers from Senegal Flock to New York," *New York Times*, November 10, 1985, p. 52.
12 U.S. Department of Labor, Bureau of Labor Statistics, *Geographic Profile of Employment and Unemployment 1991*, BLS Bulletin 2410, August 1992. In 1989, blacks held about 20 percent of all professional jobs and Hispanics (who make up 62 percent of school enrollment) only 12 percent of these jobs in Los Angeles schools. See Los Angeles Unified School District, *Ethnic Survey Report: Fall 1989*, publication no. 111, Los Angeles, January 1990.
13 The importance of government employment for blacks extends well beyond New York. Almost three out of ten blacks employed in Los Angeles County and Miami/Dade County in 1991 worked for the government. In Chicago, Detroit, Houston, and nearly all other large cities, blacks' share of public-sector jobs is disproportionately high. About as many Hispanics as blacks work for the government in Los Angeles, although Hispanics outnumber blacks in the labor force by a ratio of more than three to one. Hispanics generally hold many fewer government jobs, except in San Antonio, which has a majority Hispanic population. In most other cities an expansion in the public sector means more jobs for blacks rather than Hispanics.
14 *Congressional Record*, May 19, 1896, p. H5423.
15 Robert H. Topel, "The Impact of Immigration on the Labor Market" (mimeo), University of Chicago and National Bureau of Economic Research, Cambridge, Mass., January 1988.
16 Testimony of Frank D. Bean, in U.S. Congress, Joint Economic Committee, Subcommittee on Economic Resources, Competitiveness, and Security Economics, "Impact of Undocumented Mexican Immigration on the Earnings of Other Groups in Metropolitan Labor Markets in the United States," 99th Cong., 2nd sess., May 29, 1986.
17 Thomas Muller and Thomas J. Espenshade, *The Fourth Wave: California's Newest Immigrants* (Washington, D.C.: Urban Institute Press, 1985).
18 "A Telephone Survey of Public Attitudes toward Immigration and Related Issues among California Adults" (mimeo), survey prepared for the Urban Institute by Field Research Corporation, San Francisco, June 1983.

◆

Immigration Policy and the U.S. Economy: An Institutional Perspective

Vernon M. Briggs, Jr.

By virtue of events that have already transpired and public policies already in place, the 1990s will witness the largest inflow of immigrants into the population and labor force of the United States of any decade in the nation's history. The revival of the phenomenon of mass immigration from out of the nation's past began in 1965. Policymakers did not intend for it to happen, and its consequences were unanticipated by the nation's citizenry. But it has. Indeed, a comprehensive study by an international panel of social science scholars concluded its assessment of U.S. society with the observation that "America's biggest import is people" and determined that "at a time when attention is directed to the general decline in American exceptionalism, American immigration continues to flow at a rate unknown elsewhere in the world" (Oxford Analytica 1986, p. 20). Moreover, unlike earlier mass immigration periods to the United States, the post-1965 wave of immigrants shows "no sign of imminent decline" (Bouvier 1991, p. 18).

For a variety of reasons, immigration is a subject that is especially amenable to study and interpretation by institutional economists. In today's world setting, international migration is a discretionary action that is regulated by the specific actions of the governments of individual nation-states. To the degree mass immigration takes place, it is a policy-driven phenomenon.

There is no international obligation for any nation to allow others to enter or to work or to permanently settle within its geographical borders. In fact, most nations do not admit immigrants for permanent settlement. The Universal Declaration of Human Rights states that no nation-state should force people to stay within its borders; but there is no parallel obligation on any nation to accept outsiders into its sovereign territory (United Nations 1948). It is, therefore, one area of economic policymaking where market forces are not permitted to function.

*   *   *

The Evolution of U.S. Immigration Policy

Immigration played a major role in the first half of the nineteenth century when the United States began to industrialize. Following the end of its colonial era in 1776, the new nation expanded geographically to embrace a vast land

Excerpted from *Journal of Economic Issues* 30 (June 1996), pp. 371–89.

area that had an abundance of natural resources and a temperate climate but relatively few people. Throughout its first century, the country had neither ceilings nor screening restrictions on the number and types of people permitted to enter for permanent settlement. The economy was dominated by agricultural production and farm employment. Most jobs required little in the way of training or educational preparation. An unregulated immigration policy was consistent with the nation's basic labor market needs during this crucial period of nation building.

When the industrialization process began in earnest during the latter decades of the nineteenth century, immigration again became of critical importance to the assembly of an urban labor force. The newly introduced technology of mechanization required mainly unskilled workers to fill manufacturing jobs in the nation's rapidly expanding urban labor markets as well as in the related-employment growth sectors of mining, construction, and transportation. As Stanley Lebergott (1964, p. 28) observed in his epic study of the development of the U.S. labor force, "somewhat surprisingly, the greatest beneficiaries of the flow of immigrant labor [in the nineteenth century] was never agriculture though farming was our primary industry." Rather, it was the urban economy and its vast need for unskilled workers whose ranks were expanded by the arrival of immigrants.

There were surplus pools of native-born workers who were poorly skilled and barely educated who remained marginalized throughout the 1880–1914 era when the industrialization process took hold in earnest. They could have filled many of these new jobs. They were mostly native-born workers who were underemployed in the rural sectors of the economy. The most numerous were native-born whites, but the most obvious were the freed blacks of the former slave economy of the rural South. The noted black educator Booker T. Washington, in his famous Atlanta Exposition speech in 1895, pleaded with the white industrialists of that era to draw upon the available black labor force instead of seeking immigrants to fill the new jobs that industrialization was creating (Washington 1965, p. 147). If blacks were incorporated at this critical juncture of American economic development when entirely new industries were coming into being and an entirely new occupational structure was being created, Washington (1965, p. 148) said we could make "the interests of both races one." His advice was ignored. Mass immigration from Asia and Europe became the alternative of choice. Before long, immigration from China and Japan was banned in response to nativist reactions, so various ethnic groups from Eastern and Southern Europe became the primary sources of unskilled workers of that era.

Putting aside the equity opportunity that was lost and turning to the issue of efficiency, the mass immigration of the late nineteenth and early twentieth centuries was consistent with the prevailing labor market needs of the nation. The jobs created during this expansive era typically required little in the way of skill, education, literacy, numeracy, or fluency in English from the work force. The enormous supply of immigrants generally lacked these human capital attributes. As Peter Roberts, an immigration scholar at that time, wrote: "We may yearn for a more intelligent and better trained worker from the countries of Europe, but it is questionable whether or not that type of man would have been so well fitted for the work America had to offer" (Roberts 1913, p. 61). In the same vein, Handlin (1915, p. 5) wrote: "It was the unique quality of the 19th Century immigration that the people who moved, entered the life of the United States at a status equal to that of the older residents. The newcomers were one with those long settled in the New World." In terms of their political entitlements, their paucity of human capital endowments, and their low income status, there was little difference between the immigrants and the native-born workers of that era.

When America's frontiers were overcome in the 1890s, it was not long before immigration was sharply restricted – beginning in 1914 with the events associated with World War I and followed by newly adopted immigration laws in the early 1920s. In part, the imposition of legal restrictions reflected legitimate economic concerns that the mass immigration of the preceding three decades had depressed wages, hampered unionization, and caused unemployment. In part, they also reflected nativist social reactions to the ethnic, racial, and religious diversity that the mass immigration of that era also brought (Briggs 1984, pp. 31–54). The Immigration Act of 1924 (also known as the National Origins Act) not only imposed the first permanent legislative ceiling on immigration (at a low annual level of about 154,000 immigrants), but it also included an ethnic screening system that was highly discriminatory as to who could enter and who could not (favoring immigrants from Northern and Western European countries and disfavoring or prohibiting immigration from all other Eastern Hemisphere nations). Its restrictions, however, did not apply to countries of the entire Western Hemisphere.

For the next 50 years, the quantitative significance of immigration rapidly receded, and the expansion of the economy became dependent on the utilization of domestic labor reserves. Originally, it was those people in the nation's vast rural areas, where workers were being displaced by the rapid mechanization of agriculture, who were finally given the opportunity to compete for jobs in urban America. Among the major beneficiaries of the cessation of mass immigration was the nation's black population. It was not until mass immigration ended in 1914 that "the Great Migration" of blacks to the North and the West could commence. And it did. Later, during the war years of the 1940s, women, youth, disabled, and older workers, as well as minorities, were recruited and employed in the nation's economic mainstream for the first time.

Indicative of the declining significance of immigration on American life over this time span is the fact that the percentage of the U.S. population that was foreign-born consistently fell from 14.6 percent in 1910 to 4.7 percent in 1970 (the lowest percentage since before the Civil War). During this long interval of the receding influence of immigration, the U.S. economy sustained the greatest increases in real wages, employment levels, and production output in its economic history. It was also the time when the nation adopted an extensive array of progressive social policies pertaining to labor standards, collective bargaining, and civil rights. It was also a period when income inequality within the population was significantly reduced for the first time since the nation was founded.

The Revival of Mass Immigration

In the mid-1960s, the phenomenon of mass immigration was accidently revived as a result of domestic political pressures. The primary concern of immigration reformers at the time was to end the discriminatory "national origins" admission system. Having just enacted the Civil Rights Act of 1964 that was designed to end overt racial and ethnic discrimination in the nation's internal relationships, the logical next step was to end overt discrimination in the nation's external relationships with the international community. The immigration reformers, however, "were so incensed with the ethnocentrism of the laws of the past that they spent virtually all of their energies seeking to eliminate the country of origin provisions" and, as a consequence, "they gave very little attention to the substance or long range implications of the policy that would replace them" (North and Houstoun 1976, p. 5). In a nutshell, that is what has subsequently occurred. It is a story of unintended consequences (Briggs 1992, ch. 6).

There was no intention to raise the level of immigration by any appreciable amount or to open the admission door to large numbers of unskilled and poorly educated persons. There was no shortage of labor in 1965 that required an increase in immigration. Indeed, 1965 was exactly the year that the postwar "baby boom" hit the labor market. One million more people turned 18 years old (the primary labor force entry age for full-time job seeking) that year, and the high level of entry persisted for the next 16 years. Already worried about the adverse effects of foreign workers on citizen workers, the Johnson administration had terminated the Mexican Labor Program (i.e., the infamous "bracero program") only 10 months before the Immigration Act of 1965 was signed. Moreover, in the presidential campaign of 1964, the Republican party had raised the specter of massive job displacement if the proposed immigration legislation (initially proposed in 1963 by the Kennedy administration) were to be enacted by the Johnson administration after the election ("Should the Gates..." 1964, p. 114). Congress was sensitive to the charge of possible adverse labor market impacts of immigrants and, for that reason, it significantly tightened the labor certification requirements that applied to non-family and non-refugee admissions that were contained in the Immigration Act of 1965.

The key features of the Immigration Act of 1965 that have instrumentally affected subsequent events transcend the vision of ending overt ethnocentrism. Prior to its passage, the preference system that had been in place since 1952 and that was superimposed on the basic national origins selection system was one that set human resource concerns as the major objective of the nation's immigration policy. Half of all available visas were set aside for this group. The Immigration Act of 1965, however, introduced the notion of "family reunification" as the highest priority – setting aside 74 percent of the visas for such persons (later increased to 80 percent in 1980). The concept embraces not only nuclear family members, but also extended family members. In the process, it downgraded labor needs of the nation to both smaller numbers and lower preference levels. Thus, the focus of the nation's immigration policy shifted. Had the scale of immigration remained at its low pre-1965 levels, this shift in focus may not have proved significant. But, immigration has increased dramatically, and the human capital attributes of ensuing inflow has been entirely counter to the post-1965 trends of the labor market.

Furthermore, the Immigration Act of 1965 also introduced a preference category for the admission of refugees. This is the first time in the history of the U.S. immigration law that refugees were given statutory recognition as being a permanent feature of the U.S. immigration policy. Refugees, mostly from the Third World, have proven to be a major source of post-1965 immigrants and, subsequently, of additional family-related immigrants.

The Act of 1965 is also significant for what it did not do. Namely, it failed to address the ongoing problem of illegal immigration. It did not contain any forms of deterrence. By its silence, the legal loophole in earlier legislation that exempted employers from being prosecuted for hiring illegal immigrants was perpetrated. Following its passage, illegal immigration simply exploded in scale.

It is obvious, in retrospect, that the nation-changing ramifications of the Immigration Act of 1965 were not foreseen by its proponents at the time of its passage. In testimony prior to its passage, Secretary of State Dean Rusk stated that "the significance of immigration for the United States now depends less on numbers than on the quality of the immigrants" ("'Statement' of Secretary..." 1965, p. 276). Congressman Emanuel Celler, the sponsor of the bill in the House of Representatives, stated during the final floor debate that "there will not be comparatively, many Asians or Africans entering the country... since few could immigrate from those countries because they have not family ties to the United States" (U.S. Congress 1965b, p. 21, 758). Senator Edward Kennedy, the floor manager of the bill in the Senate, stated "this bill is not concerned with increasing immigration to this country, nor will it lower any of the high standards we apply in the selection of immigrants" (U.S. Congress 1965c, p. 24, 225). Kennedy also said "our cities will not be flooded with a million immigrants annually"; that "the ethnic mix of this country will not be upset"; and "it (the pending bill) would not cause American workers to lose their jobs" (U.S. Congress 1965a, pp. 1–3). As subsequent research has shown, none of these assurances proved to be true.

Subsequent legislation and related developments have also greatly expanded the number of foreign nationals who are legally permitted to work temporarily in the United States in occupations that compete with U.S. citizens. These foreign workers (who are called "non-immigrant workers" in immigration law) cover the gamut of occupations (e.g., apple pickers, fast food servers, nurses, engineers, computer programmers, and professors) (Briggs 1984, pp. 172–7; 1983, pp. 609–30). They may work in the United States for periods that range from a few months to up to six years. More than one-half million such workers are legally admitted to work each year. Also, in 1980, U.S. immigration policy was expanded by the addition of a political asylum policy (Briggs 1984, pp. 128–50). It was intended to address the issue of persons who arrive in the United States (as opposed to refugees who are screened for admission abroad) and who claim they will be persecuted if they are forced to return to their homelands. The full implications of this policy were not thought through at the time. Consequently, it has become a major source of controversy over the succeeding years as it has become involved in U.S. foreign policy issues (e.g., persons fleeing from Cuba versus those from Haiti) and contemporary political disputes (e.g., people fleeing from China's "one child per couple" population policy). As a consequence, there were 425,000 back-logged asylum cases pending as of the beginning of 1995. Immigration policy, therefore, has multiple dimensions.

The Economic Consequences of Post-1965 Immigration

The Immigration Act of 1965 was a turning point in the history of U.S. immi-gration policy. The most obvious effect of the changes caused by that legisla-tion (which have been followed by the Refugee Act of 1980, the Immigration Reform and Control Act of 1986, and the Immigration Act of 1990) has been a significant increase in the size of the foreign-born population. The foreign-born population has grown from 4.7 percent of the total population in 1970 to 8.7 percent of the population in 1994 (or about one of every eleven people in the population). In absolute terms, the foreign-born population has increased from 9.6 million persons in 1970 to 22.8 million persons in 1994 (an increase of 137 percent). Of these, 4.5 million persons arrived since 1990. Making an allowance of the undercount of illegal immigrants, the actual inflow has certainly exceeded a million a year in most of the 1980s and all of the 1990s to date. The inflow, however, has been exceedingly uneven in terms of where the immigrants have come from. Twenty-eight percent of the entire foreign-born population in 1994 have come from only one country – Mexico.

But the immigrant population is younger than the native-born population and contains more men than women; hence, the impact of immigration on the labor force is significantly greater than is revealed by population statistics. Indeed, in 1994 the foreign-born accounted for 10.8 percent of the labor force (or one of every nine members of the U.S. labor force) (U.S. Department of Labor 1995). These figures must also be viewed as minimal rates as there is a sizable undercount of the number of illegal immigrants present in the country.

If the revival of mass immigration since 1965 had been evenly distributed across the country, the incongruity of the subsequent immigrant inflow would have been less dramatic than it has been. A key feature of the post-1965 mass immigration, however, has been its geographic concentration. Five states (California, New York, Florida, Texas, and Illinois) account for 65 percent of the entire foreign-born population and 68 percent of the entire foreign-born labor force. It is also the case that the foreign-born are overwhelmingly con-centrated in only a handful of urban areas. But these particular labor markets are among the nation's largest in size, which greatly increases the significance of their concentration. These five metropolitan areas in 1994 were Los Angeles, New York, Miami, Chicago, and Washington, D.C. Collectively, they accounted for 51 percent of all foreign-born workers in 1994. The con-centration in the central cities of the nation is even more extreme. The 1990

Census, for instance, revealed that the percentage of the population that is foreign-born of Miami was 60 percent; in New York City, 28 percent; for Los Angeles, 38 percent; for San Francisco, 34 percent; and for Chicago, 17 percent. The percentage of the labor force that was foreign-born, of course, is higher in each of these cities than these population percentages show.

The flow of immigrants into the United States has tended to be bimodal in terms of their human capital attributes (as measured by educational attainment), but the highest concentration by far is in the lowest end of the nation's human capital distribution. The 1990 Census revealed that the percentage of foreign-born adults (25 years and over) who had *less than* a ninth grade education was 25 percent (compared to only 10 percent for native-born adults) and whereas 23 percent of native-born adults did not have a high school diploma, 42 percent of foreign-born adults did not. Immigration, therefore, is a major contributor to the nation's adult illiteracy problem. On the other hand, both foreign-born adults and native-born adults had the same percentage of persons who had a bachelor's degree or higher (20.3 percent and 20.4 percent, respectively), but with regard to those who had graduate degrees, foreign-born adults had a considerably higher percentage than did the native-born, 3.8 percent versus 2.4 percent. Thus, it is at both ends of the U.S. labor force that immigration has its greatest impacts – at the bottom and at the top of the economic ladder.

In the low-skilled labor market, immigration has increased the competition for whatever jobs are available. In recent years, unskilled jobs have not been increasing as fast as have the number of unskilled workers. As for skilled jobs, immigration can be useful in the short run as a means of providing qualified workers where shortages of qualified domestic workers exist. But, the long-term objective should be that these jobs should go to citizens and resident aliens. As the Commission on Workforce Quality and Labor Market Efficiency warned the U.S. Secretary of Labor in 1989, "by using immigration to relieve shortages, we may miss the opportunity to draw additional U.S. workers into the economic mainstream" (CWQLME 1989, p. 32). It concluded by stating that public policy should "always try to train citizens to fill labor shortages" (CWQLME 1989, p. 32). No industry should have unlimited access to the possibility of recruiting immigrant and non-immigrant foreign workers. Shortages should be signals to the nation's education and training system to provide such workers and for private employers to initiate actions to overcome these shortages. They should not be excuses to increase skilled immigration per se.

The effects of the human capital variation between the foreign-born and native-born, not surprisingly, are reflected in a comparison of their 1994 occupational distributions. Twenty-six percent of the foreign-born labor force were employed in the low-skilled and semi-skilled occupations as operatives, laborers, or farm workers (compared to 17 percent of native-born workers).

The disproportionate concentration of the foreign-born who lack even a high school diploma is also reflected in their unemployment experiences. The overall unemployment rate of foreign-born workers in 1994 was 9.2 percent, while the comparable national unemployment rate at the time was 6.5 percent. Consequently, immigration is pulling up the national unemployment rate.

The unemployment rate for foreign-born workers with less than a ninth grade education in 1994 was 13 percent; for those with some high school but no diploma, it was 15.2 percent. The comparable rates for native-born workers were 13.5 percent and 29.9 percent. Consequently, the greatest labor market impact of immigration is in the sector of the labor market that is already having the greatest difficulty finding employment. It is, therefore, the least skilled segment of the labor force (using educational attainment as the usual proxy for skill) who are bearing the brunt of the direct job competition with immigrant workers. There certainly is no shortage of unskilled native-born workers as indicated by their high unemployment rates and by the number of adult illiterates (estimated to be more than 27 million persons).

As for the racial and ethnic composition of the immigration phenomenon, immigrants from Asia and Latin America overwhelmingly dominate the current inflow. Immigrants from Asia and Latin America account for more than 80 percent of the post-1965 immigrants. Indeed, Asia emerged in the 1990s as the primary immigrant source region. As of 1994, 62 percent of the Asian population of the United States were foreign-born with 92 percent of such persons entering the United States since 1970. As for the Hispanic population, 39 percent were foreign-born in 1994 with more than one-half of the Hispanic labor force being foreign-born (51.2 percent). In contrast, only 3 percent of the non-Hispanic white labor force were foreign-born and only 4 percent of the black non-Hispanic labor force in 1994 were foreign-born. Thus, the most distinguishing feature of the Asian and Hispanic labor forces is the inordinately high proportion who are foreign-born. Immigration, accordingly, is significantly altering the racial and ethnic composition of both the nation's population and labor force.

The 1990 Census also disclosed that 79.1 percent of the foreign-born population (five years old and over) speak a language other than English (compared to 7.8 percent of the native-born) and that 47.0 percent of the foreign-born (five years and over) reported that they do not speak English "very well." The ability to speak English in an increasingly service-oriented economy has been definitively linked to the ability to advance in the U.S. labor market of the post-1965 era (Chiswick 1992, p. 15).

For these reasons and others, it should come as no great revelation that the incidence of poverty among families of the foreign-born population in 1990 was 50 percent higher than that of native-born families or that 25 percent of the families with a foreign-born householder who entered the country since 1980 were living in poverty in 1990. Nor is it surprising to find that immigrant families make greater use of welfare than do native-born families (Borjas and Trejo 1991, pp. 195–211).

The human capital deficiencies of adult immigrants has dire intergenerational consequences on the preparation of their children to become future workers. It is estimated that two million immigrant youth enrolled in U.S. public schools in the 1980s. Studies of these immigrant children indicate that they are "twice as likely to be poor as compared to all students, thereby straining local school resources" (U.S. General Accounting Office 1994, p. 2). Moreover, "many immigrants, including those of high school age, have had little or no schooling and are illiterate even in their native languages" (U.S. General Accounting Office 1994, p. 2). New demands for the creation of bilingual programs and special education classes have significantly added to the costs of urban education and have frequently led to the diversion of funds from other important programs for other needy children (Rivera-Batiz 1995, pp. 84–9). Overcrowding of urban school systems, already confronting enormous educational burdens, has frequently occurred with devastating impacts on the educational process (e.g., Firestone 1994, p. A1). Other educational costs to social policy are more subtle but equally as significant as the financial concerns. Namely, the societal goal of desegregated urban schools has been greatly retarded by the arrival of immigrant children because it has increased the racial isolation of inner-city black children (Fiske 1988, p. A16).

There is also the issue of job competition, which is the hardest to prove. Logic would indicate that, if immigrants are disproportionately concentrated in the nation's largest urban labor markets and if foreign-born workers are disproportionately lacking in human capital attributes, and if they are overwhelmingly minority group members themselves, it would be similarly situated native-born workers (actual and potential) who experience the greatest competition with immigrants for jobs. But developing a methodology to measure displacement has proven to be an insurmountable feat. Not only is it impossible to prove that if one person is hired, someone else has been displaced, but even if such a straightforward approach were feasible, it would not settle the issue. There is no way to ascertain who else would have moved to the high-immigrant impact cities if the immigrants were not pouring into those same labor markets. Moreover, there is no way to measure the number of people who have left these same local labor markets in despair who might otherwise have retained their jobs or had higher wages if not for the presence of newly arrived immigrants. Research on these mobility issues has found that the internal immigration patterns of the native-born labor force to the urban areas where immigrants are concentrated has been reduced (Walker et al. 1992, pp. 234–48). Still other research has found that immigrants themselves are less likely to move out of states where they are concentrated than are the native-born (Kritz and Nogle 1994, pp. 1–16). Both features can cause an accentuation of the impact on those labor markets where immigrants are concentrated. Furthermore, research shows those urban cities in California that have experienced quantum increases in immigration have seen the "flight" of low-income, poorly educated citizen workers out of their former communities to outer fringes of their metropolitan areas or to other states (Frey 1995, pp. 353–75). This means that they have lost the competitive struggle for jobs with low-skilled, poorly educated immigrants and that these other labor markets are now not confronted with trying to accommodate the outflows of unskilled citizen and resident alien job seekers. The same can be said of wage rates. If the immigrants had not entered these local labor markets in substantial numbers, wages should have risen, which would have attracted citizens to move in or to stay in these cities.

While the direct displacement issue cannot be definitively resolved, the substitution of immigrant workers for native-born workers can be described.

Unfortunately, this type of work requires case studies of occupational patterns in high immigrant impact cities. Few have been conducted. One excellent study in southern California clearly documented the situation whereby black janitorial workers, who had successfully built a strong union in the 1970s that provided high wages and good working conditions, were almost totally displaced and the union broken by Hispanic immigrants in the 1980s who were willing to work for far lower pay and with few benefits (Mines and Avina 1992, pp. 429–48). More such case research is desperately needed.

Finally, but without question, the most serious finding concerning post-1965 immigration is the adverse effect it has had on income distribution. The *Economic Report of the President: 1994* stated that "immigration has increased the relative supply to less educated labor and appears to have contributed to the increasing inequality of income" in the United States (*Economic Report* 1994, p. 170). Given the aforementioned indicators, this conclusion is not a surprise, but it is the most significant indictment of prevailing policy.

The Post-1965 Transformation of U.S. Employment Patterns

Although the signs were already present in the mid-1960s that the demand for labor in the United States was being transformed, it was still a subject of debate – not yet a confirmed reality. Labor economists were arguing that the structure of labor demand was being reconstituted. But the warnings were ignored at the time by those who said that the unemployment of that era was essentially a cyclical issue. By the 1990s, virtually everyone acknowledges that unemployment is a structural issue and that the imbalance between the demand and the supply of labor is growing worse. Employment growth in the major goods-producing sectors that had spawned economic growth in the first half of the twentieth century is no longer occurring. A significant shift to the service sector is in progress. It has accounted for literally all of the job growth that has occurred since the mid-1960s. By 1994, almost 80 percent of all jobs were in the service sector, and it is projected that 95 percent of the job growth in the remainder of 1990s will occur in the service sector. The greatest growth in service employment has occurred in the occupations that have the highest requirements for educational achievement (i.e., jobs in the professional, managerial, executive, administrative, and technical occupations). The shift to services has placed an emphasis on cognitive abilities, not manual effort. Technological development, spawned by the computer revolution, has led to increases in output but with declining needs for labor inputs (Franklin 1993, pp. 41–57). In every occupational category, the percentage of workers in non-production (i.e., white-collar workers) has increased sharply, while the proportion in production jobs (i.e., blue-collar jobs) has fallen precipitously. It has been jobs at the lower skill levels that have been most impacted by these contractive trends. But in the 1990s, even jobs for many skilled workers have come under attack. The unexpected end of the Cold War has led to extensive reductions in the ranks of the armed forces and the work forces of the private sector defense contractors (Saunders 1993, pp. 3–10). Likewise, the corporate fad in the 1990s to downsize their employment rolls and the surge in mega-mergers to reduce the number of competitors have both added to the employment instability of workers at all skill levels (Cappelli 1994, pp. 5–11; Katz 1994, pp. 15–19).

All of this uncertainty has been compounded by the decision of the United States in the early 1960s to embrace international competition. The U.S. economy was not built on the principle of free trade. Indeed, it was built behind high protective tariff walls that existed until the 1960s (and in practice until the 1980s). The implementation of free trade policies has been a voyage into unchartered waters. The advent of U.S. participation in the North American Free Trade Agreement and adherences to the provisions of the General Agreement on Tariffs and Trade have all led to a greater vulnerability of U.S. workers to international job competition and of the U.S. economy to job losses.

Theoretically, the benefits of free trade are based on the premise that it will cause income distribution changes to occur within each trading nation. But, as Lester Thurow (1992, p. 82) has poignantly written: "…average incomes will go up with free trade, but there will be millions of losers in each country…. The theory simply maintains that the losses of the losers will simply be smaller than the winnings of winners." The job losers, in the contemporary case of the United States, are those unskilled and poorly educated workers who, under protectionism, were previously able to secure jobs – often with high wages. Disproportionately, they are workers from minority groups. Those in the manufacturing sector have been especially vulnerable. The winners are high-skilled and better-educated workers who often are employed in service industries. Thurow (1992, p. 82) also notes that "…the theory assumes that the winners will compensate the losers so that everyone in each country has an incentive to move to free trade but, in fact, such compensation is almost never paid." With the exception of a few provisions for retraining some displaced workers, there are no compensation provisions in any of the new trade policies adopted by the United States. Even those few retraining programs, however, are currently under attack by budget cutters in Congress.

Political Rhetoric and Non-Repetitive Circumstances

When the "nation of immigrants" rhetoric is put aside, it is clear that immigration is not a universal principle whose efficacy is immune from the changes in economic circumstances. In the nineteenth and early twentieth centuries, mass immigration was consistent with the economic needs of the nation. Agriculture was still the major employment sector, but the non-agricultural sector was in the process of being industrialized. The introduction of mechanization created millions of jobs for unskilled, poorly educated, non-English speaking workers in urban centers. It was a time when high tariffs were in place that protected the business sector from foreign competitors. It was when the work standards (i.e., laws covering minimum wages, child labor, hours worked, health and safety requirements, and collective bargaining protection) were virtually nonexistent. There were no income maintenance programs in place to provide a safety net for the uncertainties of life (e.g., unemployment compensation, food stamps, supplemental security income, aid for dependent children, Social Security, or Medicare and Medicaid). Likewise, it was a period when there was no concern about equal employment opportunity needs for native-born citizens.

As discussed, the phenomenon of mass immigration then went into remission for 50 years in 1914 before being accidentally revised in 1965. Unfortunately, while the post-1965 immigrants resemble in many ways the immigrants of the earlier era in terms of their economic characteristics and their settlement patterns, the U.S. economy in no way is similar to that of the earlier era. As a consequence, the immigrants are quite different from the general citizen population in terms of their human capital attributes and employment patterns. The immigrants are disproportionately poor, uneducated, unskilled, non-English speaking, and are overwhelmingly members of racial and ethnic groups themselves. Like in the past, the immigrants tend to settle in the central cities of the nation's largest labor markets.

But the jobs that are now being created are knowledge-based. They require workers who are empowered with skills and education to fill them. It is a service oriented economy and not a goods-producing economy. Cognitive abilities – reading, writing, and speaking of English – are employment imperatives. The ability to work with other employees, to follow employers' instructions, and to relate directly to customers are all essential communication skills. The employment growth centers are more dispersed because, unlike the employment patterns of the earlier goods-producing enterprises, which were geographically concentrated, service jobs are less geographically concentrated because they have to be provided where people actually are. Job growth is not in the central cities but, rather, in surrounding metropolitan areas. Furthermore, the nation has developed a costly social system that is designed to protect those in our society who experience unemployment and social hardship but which has its political limits in terms of the adequacies of its coverages and benefit levels it is willing to and can provide. It is also a time when the labor market is under unprecedented challenges to purge itself of past discriminatory behavior and to incorporate previously excluded groups, and when the labor force has been experiencing unprecedented growth that is generated by internal forces. These growth forces are associated with the demographic positioning of the "baby boom" generation into its primary working age as well as the unprecedented increases in the labor force participation of women. Likewise, the economy has been opened to foreign competition for the first time. In such a situation, productivity is the only way for the country to remain competitive, for real wages to increase, and for jobs to remain available within its borders. A highly skilled, motivated, and educated labor force is imperative.

The consequences of the pursuit of the political objective of mass immigration at this juncture in the nation's evolutionary development is in direct conflict with the attainment of the nation's economic objectives. A course correction is long overdue. History, as Hicks said, is not repetitive regardless of opportunistic platitudes by politicians or George Santayana's famous *dictum* to the contrary. The appropriate immigration policy for the nation depends entirely on its congruence with the circumstances of the present, not of the past. As Thorstein Veblen said:

> ... the habits of thought under the guidance of which men live are received from an earlier time.... [As a consequence, they] are adapted to past circumstances, and are, therefore never in full accord with the requirements of the present. (Veblen 1959, p. 133)

The resurrection of mass immigration from out of the nation's distant past was a political accident; its perpetuation in the 1990s is contrary to national interest. Immigration reform, therefore, needs to be the forefront of the nation's economic policy agenda.

References

Borjas, George J., and Stephen J. Trejo. 1991. "Immigrant Participation in the Welfare System." *Industrial and Labor Relations Review* 44, no. 2 (January), pp. 195–211.

Bouvier, Leon. 1991. *Peaceful Invasions: Immigration and Changing America.* Washington, D.C.: Center for Immigration Studies.

Briggs, Vernon M., Jr. 1983. "Non-Immigrant Labor Policy in the United States." *Journal of Economic Issues* 17, no. 3 (September), pp. 609–30.

———. 1984. *Immigration Policy and the American Force.* Baltimore: The Johns Hopkins University Press.

———. 1992. *Mass Immigration and the National Interest.* Armonk, N.Y.: M.E. Sharpe, Inc.

Cappelli, Peter. 1994. "Forces Driving the Restructuring of Employment." *Looking Ahead* 16, nos. 2–3, pp. 5–11.

Chiswick, Barry R., ed. 1992. *Immigration, Language, and Ethnicity: Canada and the United States.* Washington, D.C.: The American Enterprise Institute.

CWQLME. 1989. "Investing in People: A Strategy to Address America's Workforce Quality and Labor Market Efficiency." U.S. Department of Labor. Washington, D.C.: U.S. Government Printing Office.

Economic Report of the President: 1994. Washington, D.C.: U.S. Government Printing Office.

Firestone, David. 1994. "Crowded Schools in Queens Find Class Spaces in Unusual Places." *New York Times*, June 8, p. A1.

Fiske, E. 1988. "Racial Shifts Challenge U.S. Schools." *New York Times*, June 23, p. A16.

Franklin, James C. 1993. "Industry Output and Employment." *Monthly Labor Review* 116, no. 11 (November), pp. 41–57.

Frey, William. 1995. "Immigration and Internal Migration." *Population and Environment* 16, no. 4 (March), pp. 353–75.

Handlin, Oscar. 1951. *The Uprooted.* New York: Grosset and Dunlap Publishers.

Katz, Harry C. 1994. "Downsizing and Employment Security." *Looking Ahead* 16, nos. 2–3, pp. 15–19.

Kritz, Mary, and June Marie Nogle. 1994. "Nativity Concentration and Internal Migration Among the Foreign-Born." *Demography* 31, no. 3 (August), pp. 1–16.

Lebergott, Stanley. 1964. *Manpower in Economic Growth.* New York: McGraw Hill Book Company.

Mines, Richard, and Jeffrey Avina. 1992. "Immigrants and Labor Standards: The Case of California." In *U.S. Mexico Relations: Labor Market Interdependence*, ed. Jorge Bustamonte et al. Stanford: Stanford University Press, pp. 429–48.

North, David, and Marion Houstoun. 1976. *The Characteristics and Role of Illegal Aliens in the U.S. Labor Market: An Exploratory Study*. Washington D.C.: Linton and Company, Inc.

Oxford Analytica. 1986. *America In Perspective*. Boston: Houghton-Mifflin.

Rivera-Batiz, F. 1995. "Immigrants and Schools: The Case of the Big Apple." *Forum for Applied Research and Public Policy* 10, no. 3 (Fall), pp. 84–9.

Roberts, Peter. 1913. *The New Immigration*. New York: The Macmillan Company.

Saunders, Norman. 1993. "Employment Effects of the Rise and Fall in Defense Spending." *Monthly Labor Review* 116, no. 11 (November), pp. 3–10.

"Should the Gates be Opened Wider?" 1964. *Business Week* (October 17), p. 114.

"Statement" of Secretary of State Dean Rusk before the Subcommittee on Immigration, U.S. Senate, Committee on the Judiciary as reprinted in "Department Urges Congress to Revise Immigration Laws." 1965. *The Department of State Bulletin*. Washington, D.C.: U.S. Department of State, August 24, p. 276.

Thurow, Lester. 1992. *Head to Head: The Coming Economic Battle Among Japan, Europe, and America*. New York: William Morrow and Co., Inc.

United Nations. 1948. Declaration of Human Rights, Articles 13 and 14. Adopted by the General Assembly of the United Nations on December 10, 1948.

United States Congress. 1965a. Senate, Subcommittee on Immigration and Naturalization of the Committee on the Judiciary. *Hearings*, February 10, 1965. Washington, D.C.: U.S. Government Printing Office, pp. 1–3.

———. 1965b. House of Representatives, *Congressional Record*. 89th Congress, 1st Session, August 25, 1965. Washington, D.C.: U.S. Government Printing Office, p. 21,758.

———. 1965c. Senate, *Congressional Record*. 89th Congress, 1st Session. September 17, 1965. Washington, D.C.: U.S. Government Printing Office, p. 24,225.

U.S. Department of Labor. 1995. "Labor Force, Income, and Poverty Statistics for the Foreign-Born Using the March 1994 Current Population Survey," *Special Report*. Washington, D.C.: Bureau of International Labor Affairs.

U.S. General Accounting Office. 1994. "Statement of Linda Morra, Director of Education and Employment Issues, Health Education, and Human Services Division to U.S. Senate Committee on Labor and Human Resources." *Immigrant Education*. GAD/T-HEHS-94-1946 (April 14, 1994).

Veblen, Thorstein. 1959. *The Theory of the Leisure Class*. New York: The New American Library.

Walker, Robert, Mark Ellis, and Richard Barff. 1992. "Linked Migration Systems: Immigration and Internal Labor Flows in the United States." *Economic Geography* 68, no. 3 (July), pp. 234–48.

Washington, Booker T. 1965. "The Atlanta Exposition Address." *Up from Slavery* as reprinted in *Three Negro Classics*. New York: Avon Books, pp. 145–57.

12

Multicultural Education

Multiculturalism: E Pluribus Plures

Diane Ravitch

Questions of race, ethnicity, and religion have been a perennial source of conflict in American education. The schools have often attracted the zealous
attention of those who wish to influence the future, as well as those who wish
to change the way we view the past. In our history, the schools have been not
only an institution in which to teach young people skills and knowledge, but
an arena where interest groups fight to preserve their values, or to revise the
judgments of history, or to bring about fundamental social change. In the
nineteenth century, Protestants and Catholics battled over which version of
the Bible should be used in school, or whether the Bible should be used at all.
In recent decades, bitter racial disputes – provoked by policies of racial segregation and discrimination – have generated turmoil in the streets and in the
schools. The secularization of the schools during the past century has
prompted attacks on the curricula and textbooks and library books by fundamentalist Christians, who object to whatever challenges their faith-based
views of history, literature, and science.

   Given the diversity of American society, it has been impossible to insulate
the schools from pressures that result from differences and tensions among
groups. When people differ about basic values, sooner or later those disagree-
ments turn up in battles about how schools are organized or what the schools
should teach. Sometimes these battles remove a terrible injustice, like racial
segregation. Sometimes, however, interest groups politicize the curriculum and
attempt to impose their views on teachers, school officials, and textbook publishers. Across the country, even now, interest groups are pressuring local
school boards to remove myths and fables and other imaginative literature
from children's readers and to inject the teaching of creationism in biology.
When groups cross the line into extremism, advancing their own agenda without regard to reason or to others, they threaten public education itself, making

Excerpted from *The American Scholar* 59, no. 3 (Summer 1990), pp. 337–54. Copyright ©
1990 by the author.

it difficult to teach any issues honestly and making the entire curriculum vulnerable to political campaigns.

For many years, the public schools attempted to neutralize controversies over race, religion, and ethnicity by ignoring them. Educators believed, or hoped, that the schools could remain outside politics; this was, of course, a vain hope since the schools were pursuing policies based on race, religion, and ethnicity. Nonetheless, such divisive questions were usually excluded from the curriculum. The textbooks minimized problems among groups and taught a sanitized version of history. Race, religion, and ethnicity were presented as minor elements in the American saga; slavery was treated as an episode, immigration as a sidebar, and women were largely absent. The textbooks concentrated on presidents, wars, national politics, and issues of state. An occasional "great black" or "great woman" received mention, but the main narrative paid little attention to minority groups and women.

With the ethnic revival of the 1960s, this approach to the teaching of history came under fire, because the history of national leaders – virtually all of whom were white, Anglo-Saxon, and male – ignored the place in American history of those who were none of the above. The traditional history of elites had been complemented by an assimilationist view of American society, which presumed that everyone in the American melting pot would eventually lose or abandon those ethnic characteristics that distinguished them from mainstream Americans. The ethnic revival demonstrated that many groups did not want to be assimilated or melted. Ethnic studies programs popped up on campuses to teach not only that "black is beautiful," but also that every other variety of ethnicity is "beautiful" as well; everyone who had "roots" began to look for them so that they too could recover that ancestral part of themselves that had not been homogenized.

As ethnicity became an accepted subject for study in the late 1960s, textbooks were assailed for their failure to portray blacks accurately; within a few years, the textbooks in wide use were carefully screened to eliminate bias against minority groups and women. At the same time, new scholarship about the history of women, blacks, and various ethnic minorities found its way into the textbooks. At first, the multicultural content was awkwardly incorporated as little boxes on the side of the main narrative. Then some of the new social historians (like Stephan Thernstrom, Mary Beth Norton, Gary Nash, Winthrop Jordan, and Leon Litwack) themselves wrote textbooks, and the main narrative itself began to reflect a broadened historical understanding of race, ethnicity, and class in the American past. Consequently, today's history textbooks routinely incorporate the experiences of women, blacks, American Indians, and various immigrant groups.

Although most high-school textbooks are deeply unsatisfactory (they still largely neglect religion, they are too long, too encyclopedic, too superficial, and lacking in narrative flow), they are far more sensitive to pluralism than their predecessors. For example, the latest edition of Todd and Curti's *Triumph of the American Nation*, the most popular high-school history text, has significantly increased its coverage of blacks in America, including profiles of Phillis Wheatley, the poet; James Armistead, a revolutionary war spy for

Lafayette; Benjamin Banneker, a self-taught scientist and mathematician; Hiram Revels, the first black to serve in the Congress; and Ida B. Wells-Barnett, a tireless crusader against lynching and racism. Even better as a textbook treatment is Jordan and Litwack's *The United States*, which skillfully synthesizes the historical experiences of blacks, Indians, immigrants, women, and other groups into the mainstream of American social and political history. The latest generation of textbooks bluntly acknowledges the racism of the past, describing the struggle for equality by racial minorities while identifying individuals who achieved success as political leaders, doctors, lawyers, scholars, entrepreneurs, teachers, and scientists.

As a result of the political and social changes of recent decades, cultural pluralism is now generally recognized as an organizing principle of this society. In contrast to the idea of the melting pot, which promised to erase ethnic and group differences, children now learn that variety is the spice of life. They learn that America has provided a haven for many different groups and has allowed them to maintain their cultural heritage or to assimilate, or – as is often the case – to do both; the choice is theirs, not the state's. They learn that cultural pluralism is one of the norms of a free society; that differences among groups are a national resource rather than a problem to be solved. Indeed, the unique feature of the United States is that its common culture has been formed by the interaction of its subsidiary cultures. It is a culture that has been influenced over time by immigrants, American Indians, Africans (slave and free) and by their descendants. American music, art, literature, language, food, clothing, sports, holidays, and customs all show the effects of the commingling of diverse cultures in one nation. Paradoxical though it may seem, the United States has a common culture that is multicultural.

Our schools and our institutions of higher learning have in recent years begun to embrace what Catherine R. Stimpson of Rutgers University has called "cultural democracy," a recognition that we must listen to a "diversity of voices" in order to understand our culture, past and present. This understanding of the pluralistic nature of American culture has taken a long time to forge. It is based on sound scholarship and has led to major revisions in what children are taught and what they read in school. The new history is – indeed, must be – a warts-and-all history; it demands an unflinching examination of racism and discrimination in our history. Making these changes is difficult, raises tempers, and ignites controversies, but gives a more interesting and accurate account of American history. Accomplishing these changes is valuable, because there is also a useful lesson for the rest of the world in America's relatively successful experience as a pluralistic society. Throughout human history, the clash of different cultures, races, ethnic groups, and religions has often been the cause of bitter hatred, civil conflict, and international war. The ethnic tensions that now are tearing apart Lebanon, Sri Lanka, Kashmir, and various republics of the Soviet Union remind us of the costs of unfettered group rivalry. Thus, it is a matter of more than domestic importance that we closely examine and try to understand that part of our national history in which different groups competed, fought, suffered, but ultimately learned to live together in relative peace and even achieved a sense of common nationhood.

Alas, these painstaking efforts to expand the understanding of American culture into a richer and more varied tapestry have taken a new turn, and not for the better. Almost any idea, carried to its extreme, can be made pernicious, and this is what is happening now to multiculturalism. Today, pluralistic multiculturalism must contend with a new, particularistic multiculturalism. The pluralists seek a richer common culture; the particularists insist that no common culture is possible or desirable. The new particularism is entering the curriculum in a number of school systems across the country. Advocates of particularism propose an ethnocentric curriculum to raise the self-esteem and academic achievement of children from racial and ethnic minority backgrounds. Without any evidence, they claim that children from minority backgrounds will do well in school *only* if they are immersed in a positive, prideful version of their ancestral culture. If children are of, for example, Fredonian ancestry, they must hear that Fredonians were important in mathematics, science, history, and literature. If they learn about great Fredonians and if their studies use Fredonian examples and Fredonian concepts, they will do well in school. If they do not, they will have low self-esteem and will do badly.

At first glance, this appears akin to the celebratory activities associated with Black History Month or Women's History Month, when schoolchildren learn about the achievements of blacks and women. But the point of those celebrations is to demonstrate that neither race nor gender is an obstacle to high achievement. They teach all children that everyone, regardless of their race, religion, gender, ethnicity, or family origin, can achieve self-fulfillment, honor, and dignity in society if they aim high and work hard.

By contrast, the particularistic version of multiculturalism is unabashedly filiopietistic and deterministic. It teaches children that their identity is determined by their "cultural genes." That something in their blood or their race memory or their cultural DNA defines who they are and what they may achieve. That the culture in which they live is not their own culture, even though they were born here. That American culture is "Eurocentric," and therefore hostile to anyone whose ancestors are not European. Perhaps the most invidious implication of particularism is that racial and ethnic minorities are not and should not try to be part of American culture; it implies that American culture belongs only to those who are white and European; it implies that those who are neither white nor European are alienated from American culture by virtue of their race or ethnicity; it implies that the only culture they do belong to or can ever belong to is the culture of their ancestors, even if their families have lived in this country for generations.

The war on so-called Eurocentrism is intended to foster self-esteem among those who are not of European descent. But how, in fact, is self-esteem developed? How is the sense of one's own possibilities, one's potential choices, developed? Certainly, the school curriculum plays a relatively small role as compared to the influence of family, community, mass media, and society. But to the extent that curriculum influences what children think of themselves, it should encourage children of all racial and ethnic groups to believe that they are part of this society and that they should develop their talents and minds to the fullest. It is enormously inspiring, for example, to learn about men and women from diverse backgrounds who overcame poverty, discrimination, physical handicaps, and other obstacles to achieve success in a variety of fields. Behind every such biography of accomplishment is a story of heroism, perseverance, and self-discipline. Learning these stories will encourage a healthy spirit of pluralism, of mutual respect, and of self-respect among children of different backgrounds. The children of American society today will live their lives in a racially and culturally diverse nation, and their education should prepare them to do so.

The pluralist approach to multiculturalism promotes a broader interpretation of the common American culture and seeks due recognition for the ways that the nation's many racial, ethnic, and cultural groups have transformed the national culture. The pluralists say, in effect, "American culture belongs to us, all of us; the U.S. is us, and we remake it in every generation." But particularists have no interest in extending or revising American culture; indeed, they deny that a common culture exists. Particularists reject any accommodation among groups, any interactions that blur the distinct lines between them. The brand of history that they espouse is one in which everyone is either a descendant of victims or oppressors. By doing so, ancient hatreds are fanned and recreated in each new generation. Particularism has its intellectual roots in the ideology of ethnic separatism and in the black nationalist movement. In the particularist analysis, the nation has five cultures: African American, Asian American, European American, Latino/Hispanic, and Native American. The huge cultural, historical, religious, and linguistic differences within these categories are ignored, as is the considerable intermarriage among these groups, as are the linkages (like gender, class, sexual orientation, and religion) that cut across these five groups. No serious scholar would claim that all Europeans and white Americans are part of the same culture, or that all Asians are part of the same culture, or that all people of Latin-American descent are of the same culture, or that all people of African descent are of the same culture. Any categorization this broad is essentially meaningless and useless.

Several districts – including Detroit, Atlanta, and Washington, D.C. – are developing an Afrocentric curriculum. *Afrocentricity* has been described in a book of the same name by Molefi Kete Asante of Temple University. The Afrocentric curriculum puts Africa at the center of the student's universe. African Americans must "move away from an [*sic*] Eurocentric framework" because "it is difficult to create freely when you use someone else's motifs, styles, images, and perspectives." Because they are not Africans, "white teachers cannot inspire in our children the visions necessary for them to overcome limitations." Asante recommends that African Americans choose an African name (as he did), reject European dress, embrace African religion (not Islam or Christianity) and love "their own" culture. He scorns the idea of universality as a form of Eurocentric arrogance. The Eurocentrist, he says, thinks of Beethoven or Bach as classical, but the Afrocentrist thinks of Ellington or Coltrane as classical; the Eurocentrist lauds Shakespeare or Twain, while the Afrocentrist prefers Baraka, Shange, or Abiola. Asante is critical of black artists like Arthur Mitchell and Alvin Ailey who ignore Afrocentricity. Likewise, he speaks contemptuously of a group of black university students who spurned the Afrocentrism of the local Black Student Union and formed an organization called Inter-race: "Such madness is the direct consequence of self-hatred, obligatory attitudes, false assumptions about society, and stupidity."

The conflict between pluralism and particularism turns on the issue of universalism. Professor Asante warns his readers against the lure of universalism: "Do not be captured by a sense of universality given to you by the Eurocentric viewpoint; such a viewpoint is contradictory to your own ultimate reality." He insists that there is no alternative to Eurocentrism, Afrocentrism, and other ethnocentrisms. In contrast, the pluralist says, with the Roman playwright Terence, "I am a man: nothing human is alien to me." A contemporary Terence would say "I am a person" or might be a woman, but the point remains the same: you don't have to be black to love Zora Neale Hurston's fiction or Langston Hughes's poetry or Duke Ellington's music. In a pluralist curriculum, we expect children to learn a broad and humane culture, to learn about the ideas and art and animating spirit of many cultures. We expect that children, whatever their color, will be inspired by the courage of people like Helen Keller, Vaclav Havel, Harriet Tubman, and Feng Lizhe. We expect that their response to literature will be determined by the ideas and images it evokes, not by the skin color of the writer. But particularists insist that children can learn only from the experiences of people from the same race.

Particularism is a bad idea whose time has come. It is also a fashion spreading like wildfire through the education system, actively promoted by organizations and individuals with a political and professional interest in strengthening ethnic power bases in the university, in the education profession, and in society itself. One can scarcely pick up an educational journal without learning about a school district that is converting to an ethnocentric curriculum in an attempt to give "self-esteem" to children from racial minorities. A state-funded project in a Sacramento high school is teaching young black males to think like Africans and to develop the "African Mind Model Technique," in order to free themselves of the racism of American culture. A popular black rap singer, KRS-One, complained in an op-ed article in the *New York Times* that the schools should be teaching blacks about their cultural heritage, instead of trying to make everyone Americans. "It's like trying to teach a dog to be a cat," he wrote. KRS-One railed about having to learn about Thomas Jefferson and the Civil War, which had nothing to do (he said) with black history.

*   *   *

The efficacy of particularist proposals seems to be less important to their sponsors than their value as ideological weapons with which to criticize existing disciplines for their alleged Eurocentric bias. In a recent article titled "The Ethnocentric Basis of Social Science Knowledge Production" in the *Review of Research in Education*, John Stanfield of Yale University argues that neither social science nor science are objective studies, that both instead are "Euro-American" knowledge systems which reproduce "hegemonic racial domination."

The claim that science and reason are somehow superior to magic and witch-craft, he writes, is the product of Euro-American ethnocentrism. According to Stanfield, current fears about the misuse of science (for instance, "the nuclear arms race, global pollution") and "the power-plays of Third World nations (the Arab oil boycott and the American–Iranian hostage crisis) have made Western people more aware of nonscientific cognitive styles. These last events are beginning to demonstrate politically that which has begun to be under-stood in intellectual circles: namely, that modes of social knowledge such as theology, science, and magic are different, not inferior or superior. They repre-sent different ways of perceiving, defining, and organizing knowledge of life experiences." One wonders: If Professor Stanfield broke his leg, would he go to a theologian, a doctor, or a magician?

*   *   *

It is hardly surprising that America's schools would recognize strong cul-tural ties with Europe since our nation's political, religious, educational, and economic institutions were created chiefly by people of European descent, our government was shaped by European ideas, and nearly 80 percent of the people who live here are of European descent. The particularists treat all of this history as a racist bias toward Europe, rather than as the matter-of-fact consequences of European immigration. Even so, American education is not centered on Europe. American education, if it is centered on anything, is cen-tered on itself. It is "Americentric." Most American students today have never studied any world history; they know very little about Europe, and even less about the rest of the world. Their minds are rooted solidly in the here and now. When the Berlin Wall was opened in the fall of 1989, journalists discov-ered that most American teenagers had no idea what it was, nor why its open-ing was such a big deal. Nonetheless, Eurocentrism provides a better target than Americentrism.

In school districts where most children are black and Hispanic, there has been a growing tendency to embrace particularism rather than pluralism. Many of the children in these districts perform poorly in academic classes and leave school without graduating. They would fare better in school if they had well-educated and well-paid teachers, small classes, good materials, encourage-ment at home and school, summer academic programs, protection from the drugs and crime that ravage their neighborhoods, and higher expectations of satisfying careers upon graduation. These are expensive and time-consuming remedies that must also engage the larger society beyond the school. The lure of particularism is that it offers a less complicated anodyne, one in which the children's academic deficiencies may be addressed – or set aside – by inflating their racial pride. The danger of this remedy is that it will detract attention from the real needs of schools and the real interests of children, while simulta-neously arousing distorted race pride in children of all races, increasing racial antagonism and producing fresh recruits for white and black racist groups.

*   *   *

The rising tide of particularism encourages the politicization of all curricula in the schools. If education bureaucrats bend to the political and ideological winds, as is their wont, we can anticipate a generation of struggle over the content of the curriculum in mathematics, science, literature, and history. Demands for "culturally relevant" studies, for ethnostudies of all kinds, will open the classroom to unending battles over whose version is taught, who gets credit for what, and which ethno-interpretation is appropriate. Only recently have districts begun to resist the demands of fundamentalist groups to censor textbooks and library books (and some have not yet begun to do so).

The spread of particularism throws into question the very idea of American public education. Public schools exist to teach children the general skills and knowledge that they need to succeed in American society, and the specific skills and knowledge that they need in order to function as American citizens. They receive public support because they have a public function. Historically, the public schools were known as "common schools" because they were schools for all, even if the children of all the people did not attend them. Over the years, the courts have found that it was unconstitutional to teach religion in the common schools, or to separate children on the basis of their race in the common schools. In their curriculum, their hiring practices, and their general philosophy, the public schools must not discriminate against or give prefer-ence to any racial or ethnic group. Yet they are permitted to accommodate cultural diversity by, for example, serving food that is culturally appropriate or providing library collections that emphasize the interests of the local com-munity. However, they should not be expected to teach children to view the world through an ethnocentric perspective that rejects or ignores the common culture. For generations, those groups that wanted to inculcate their religion or their ethnic heritage have instituted private schools – after school, on week-ends, or on a full-time basis. There, children learn with others of the same group – Greeks, Poles, Germans, Japanese, Chinese, Jews, Lutherans, Catholics, and so on – and are taught by people from the same group. Valuable as this exclusive experience has been for those who choose it, this has not been the role of public education. One of the primary purposes of public education has been to create a national community, a definition of citizenship and culture that is both expansive and *inclusive*.

The curriculum in public schools must be based on whatever knowledge and practices have been determined to be best by professionals – experienced teachers and scholars – who are competent to make these judgments. Pro-fessional societies must be prepared to defend the integrity of their disciplines. When called upon, they should establish review committees to examine dis-putes over curriculum and to render judgment, in order to help school officials fend off improper political pressure. Where genuine controversies exist, they should be taught and debated in the classroom. Was Egypt a black civilization? Why not raise the question, read the arguments of the different sides in the debate, show slides of Egyptian pharoahs and queens, read books about life in ancient Egypt, invite guest scholars from the local university, and visit muse-ums with Egyptian collections? If scholars disagree, students should know it. One great advantage of this approach is that students will see that history is a lively study, that textbooks are fallible, that historians disagree, that the writing of history is influenced by the historian's politics and ideology, that history is written by people who make choices among alternative facts and interpretations, and that history changes as new facts are uncovered and new interpretations win adherents. They will also learn that cultures and civilizations constantly interact, exchange ideas, and influence one another, and that the idea of racial or ethnic purity is a myth. Another advantage is that students might once again study ancient history, which has all but disappeared from the curricula of American schools. (California recently introduced a required sixth grade course in ancient civilizations, but ancient history is otherwise *terra incognita* in American education.)

The multicultural controversy may do wonders for the study of history, which has been neglected for years in American schools. At this time, only half of our high school graduates ever study any world history. Any serious attempt to broaden students' knowledge of Africa, Europe, Asia, and Latin America will require at least two, and possibly three years of world history (a requirement thus far only in California). American history, too, will need more time than the one-year high-school survey course. Those of us who have insisted for years on the importance of history in the curriculum may not be ready to assent to its redemptive power, but hope that our new allies will ultimately join a constructive dialogue that strengthens the place of history in the schools.

As cultural controversies arise, educators must adhere to the principle of "E Pluribus Unum." That is, they must maintain a balance between the demands of the one – the nation of which we are common citizens – and the many – the varied histories of the American people. It is not necessary to denigrate either the one or the many. Pluralism is a positive value, but it is also important that we preserve a sense of an American community – a society and a culture to which we all belong. If there is no overall community with an agreed-upon vision of liberty and justice, if all we have is a collection of racial and ethnic cultures, lacking any common bonds, then we have no means to mobilize public opinion on behalf of people who are not members of our particular group. We have, for example, no reason to support public education. If there is no larger community, then each group will want to teach its own children in its own way, and public education ceases to exist.

History should not be confused with filiopietism. History gives no grounds for race pride. No race has a monopoly on virtue. If anything, a study of history should inspire humility, rather than pride. People of every racial group have committed terrible crimes, often against others of the same group. Whether one looks at the history of Europe or Africa or Latin America or Asia, every continent offers examples of inhumanity. Slavery has existed in civilizations around the world for centuries. Examples of genocide can be found around the world, throughout history, from ancient times right through to our own day. Governments and cultures, sometimes by edict, sometimes simply following tradition, have practiced not only slavery, but human sacrifice, infanticide, cliterodectomy, and mass murder. If we teach children this, they might recognize how absurd both racial hatred and racial chauvinism are.

What must be preserved in the study of history is the spirit of inquiry, the readiness to open new questions and to pursue new understandings. History, at its best, is a search for truth. The best way to portray this search is through debate and controversy, rather than through imposition of fixed beliefs and immutable facts. Perhaps the most dangerous aspect of school history is its tendency to become Official History, a sanctified version of the Truth taught by the state to captive audiences and embedded in beautiful mass-market text-books as holy writ. When Official History is written by committees respond-ing to political pressures, rather than by scholars synthesizing the best available research, then the errors of the past are replaced by the politically fashionable errors of the present. It may be difficult to teach children that history is both important and uncertain, and that even the best historians never have all the pieces of the jigsaw puzzle, but it is necessary to do so. If state education departments permit the revision of their history courses and textbooks to become an exercise in power politics, then the entire process of state-level curriculum-making becomes suspect, as does public education itself.

The question of self-esteem is extraordinarily complex, and it goes well beyond the content of the curriculum. Most of what we call self-esteem is formed in the home and in a variety of life experiences, not only in school. Nonetheless, it has been important for blacks – and for other racial groups – to learn about the history of slavery and of the civil rights movement; it has been important for blacks to know that their ancestors actively resisted enslavement and actively pursued equality; and it has been important for blacks and others to learn about black men land women who fought coura-geously against racism and who provide models of courage, persistence, and intellect. These are instances where the content of the curriculum reflects sound scholarship, and at the same time probably lessens racial prejudice and provides inspiration for those who are descendants of slaves. But knowing about the travails and triumphs of one's forebears does not necessarily translate into either self-esteem or personal accomplishment. For most chil-dren, self-esteem – the self-confidence that grows out of having reached a goal – comes not from hearing about the monuments of their ancestors but as a consequence of what they are able to do and accomplish through their own efforts.

As I reflected on these issues, I recalled reading an interview a few years ago with a talented black runner. She said that her model is Mikhail Baryshnikov. She admires him because he is a magnificent athlete. He is not black; he is not female; he is not American-born; he is not even a runner. But he inspires her because of the way he trained and used his body. When I read this, I thought how narrow-minded it is to believe that people can be inspired *only* by those who are exactly like them in race and ethnicity.

♦

The Great Multicultural Debate

Gary B. Nash

"The civil rights battles of the '50s and '60s were fought in the courtroom," says David Nicholson of the *Washington Post*, "but in the '90s the struggle for cultural parity will take place in the classroom as blacks and other minorities seek to change what their children are taught."[1] Now, only two years into the decade, the swirling multicultural debate around the country is proving Nicholson correct. But the debate has gone far beyond the subject of what is taught and has led to some remarkable – and troubling – notions of what we are as a people and a society.

Often lost in the present furor is even an elementary sense of how far the writing and teaching of history have moved away from the male-oriented, Eurocentric, and elitist approaches that had dominated for so long at all levels of the American educational system. It is important to understand this because new calls for change often ignore what has already occurred in the rethinking and rewriting of history and, in so doing, sometimes prescribe new formulae that contain hidden dangers.

Reimagining the Past

Among academic historians, agreement is widespread today that history has been presented in a narrow and deeply distorted way, not just in the United States but in every country. In the 1930s, when he was writing *Black Reconstruction*, W. E. B. Du Bois wrote: "I stand at the end of this writing, literally aghast at what American historians have done to this field ... [It is] one of the most stupendous efforts the world ever saw to discredit human beings, an effort involving universities, history, science, social life, and religion."[2] Few white historians would have agreed with Du Bois at the time, for in fact he was attacking their work. But a half-century later, the white president of the Organization of American Historians, Leon Litwack, agreed with this assessment. In his presidential address in 1987, Litwack charged that "no group of scholars was more deeply implicated in the miseducation of American youth and did more to shape the thinking of generations of Americans about race and blacks than historians."[3]

The narrow and distorted lenses through which historians looked for years – which in the main reflected the dominant biases of white, Protestant America – extended far beyond the history of black Americans. Du Bois would surely have been equally dismayed if he had read one of the most widely used books in Western Civilization courses in the 1960s, where the much honored

Excerpted from *Contention*, 1992, pp. 1–28.

British historian, Hugh Trevor-Roper, magisterially proclaimed that it was useless to study African history because this would only be to inquire into "the unrewarding gyrations of barbarous tribes...whose chief function in history...is to show to the present an image of the past from which, by history, it has escaped."[4]

Similar mental constructions prevailed in regard to Native American history. In introducing Douglas Leach's history of King Philip's War in 1676, the bloodiest Indian war of the seventeenth century in North America, Samuel Eliot Morison, writing in 1958, instructed readers how to view both colonial–Indian relations and the decolonization movements in the Third World after World War II: "In view of our recent experiences of warfare, and of the many instances today of backward peoples getting enlarged notions of nationalism and turning ferociously on Europeans who have attempted to civilize them, this early conflict of the same nature cannot help but be of interest."[5]

The paradigmatic shift in the writing of history is far from complete, but some of those who currently protest about Eurocentric or racist history take little account of how resolutely the present generation of historians – scholars and teachers alike – have come to grips with older conceptualizations of history. Academic historians, most of them detached from what is going on in the primary and secondary schools of the country unless they have school age children enrolled in public schools, are often puzzled by the furor over the question of "whose history shall we teach" because they have watched – and participated in – wholesale changes in their own discipline in the last thirty years or so. African American history, women's history, and labor history are taught in most colleges and universities; Asian American, Hispanic American, and Native American history are taught in many. These courses are built on an outpouring of scholarship in this generation.

African American history can be taken as an instructive example. Even fifteen years ago, John Hope Franklin, author of the leading textbook in African American history, wrote of "a most profound and salutary change in the approach to the history of human relations in the United States," and he noted that in the process of this change "the new Negro history has come into its own."[6] Since 1977, this blossoming of black history has continued unabated. In compiling a bibliography of African American history for just the period from 1765 to 1830 for the forthcoming *Harvard Guide to Afro-American History*, I tracked down over 200 books and more than 400 articles published since 1965. The proliferation of scholarship for the period after 1830 is even greater. When the *Harvard Guide* is completed, it will detail thousands of books, articles, and doctoral dissertations – an enormous flowering of scholarship.

In women's history, the amount and range of scholarship – and sophisticated courses built upon it – is equally impressive. So too, younger scholars are building on the work of a few old hands to create the knowledge for a thorough understanding of the history, literature, art, music and values of Native Americans, Asian Americans, and other groups. In fact, among professional historians, the big debate is not about the need to recapture the lost past of so many groups and so many struggles over power and wealth in

American society and so many neglected parts of world history but about whether this quest, in going so far, has shattered the coherence and usability of history.

In the current atmosphere of heated debate, it is worth some reflection on why and how change has occurred in the writing of history. Four developments have intersected to cause a major transformation. First – and largely forgotten in the current debates – is the wholesale change in the recruitment of professional historians, the people who do historical scholarship, teach at the collegiate level, and, ultimately, are responsible for the textbooks used in the schools. Before World War II, professional historians were drawn almost exclusively from the ranks of white, male, Protestant, and upper-class society. From their perspective, it was entirely fitting that they should be the keepers of the past because they believed that only those of the highest intellect, the most polished manners, and the most developed aesthetic taste could stand above the ruck and look dispassionately at the annals of human behavior. Such a view conformed precisely to the centuries-old view of the elite that ordinary people were ruled by emotion and only the wealthy and educated could transcend this state and achieve disinterested rationality. Pitted against this thoroughly dominant group since the early nineteenth century was a small number of women, African Americans, and white radicals who worked without much recognition as they tried to create alternative histories.

Small cracks in the fortress of the historical profession began to appear in the 1930s as Jews struggled for a place in the profession. Peter Novick's book on the historical profession, *That Noble Dream: The "Objectivity Question" and the American Historical Profession*, gives a vivid picture of the way the profession grudgingly yielded to Jewish aspirations. When applying for his first teaching job, Richard Leopold – who would emerge as a major historian of diplomacy – was described by a graduate mentor at Harvard as "of course a Jew, but since he is a Princeton graduate, you may be reasonably certain he is not of the offensive type." Bert Lowenberg was described in a letter of recommendation as "by temperament and spirit … [he] measures up to the whitest Gentiles I know."[7]

Not until after World War II would more than a handful of Jews gain admission to the historical profession. By that time, the GI bill was opening the doors of higher education to broad masses of Americans. This rapidly enlarged and diversified the historians' guild. Religious barriers continued to fall and class barriers began to fall as well, though not without creating consternation in many quarters. At Yale, George Pierson, the chairman of the history department, wrote the university's president in 1957 – in a period when the growth of American universities demanded thousands of newly trained professors – that while the doctoral program in English "still draws to a degree from the cultivated, professional, and well-to-do classes … by contrast, the subject of history seems to appeal on the whole to a lower social stratum." Pierson complained that "far too few of our history candidates are sons of professional men; far too many list their parent's occupation as janitor, watchman, salesman, grocer, pocketbook cutter, bookkeeper, railroad clerk, pharmacist, clothing cutter, cable tester, mechanic, general clerk, butter-and-egg jobber, and the like." Five years later, Carl Bridenbaugh, the president of the American Historical Association, lamented what he called "The Great Mutation" that he believed was undermining the profession. "Many of the younger practitioners of our craft, and those who are still apprentices, are products of lower middle-class or foreign origins, and their emotions not infrequently get in the way of historical reconstructions."[8]

The notion that lower-class and foreign-born backgrounds disabled apprentice historians by conditioning them to substitute emotion for reason was revived when racial and gender barriers began to fall in the 1960s. The historical profession had for many decades included a small number of notable women and African Americans, and an occasional Native American, Hispanic American, and Asian American. But women began to enter the profession in substantial numbers only in the 1960s, while members of racial minority groups have increased since that time only slowly. Charges that emotions outran analytic insight were again heard from members of the old guard, none of its members more vocal than Oscar Handlin, whose Jewish background had nearly stopped him from entry into the profession a generation before.[9] But by this time, the old guard had been swamped, and social history had surged forward to displace the traditional emphasis on male- and elite-centered political and institutional history and on intellectual history that rarely focused on the thought and consciousness of people who were not of European descent.

Given these changes in the composition of the profession, it is not surprising that new questions have been posed about the past – questions that never occurred to a narrowly constituted group of historians. The emphasis on conflict rather than consensus, on racism and exploitation, on history from the bottom up rather than the top down, on women as well as men, is entirely understandable as people whose history had never been written began recovering it for themselves. Step by step, new historians (including many white males) have constructed previously untold chapters of history and have helped to overcome the deep historical biases that afflicted the profession for many generations.

Sustaining and strengthening the transformation that was beginning to occur because of the different background of historians was the dramatic period of protest and reform that occurred in American society in the 1960s and 1970s. The struggles of women, people of color, and religious minorities to gain equal rights spurred many historians (many of whom were involved in these movements) to ask new questions about the role of race and gender relations in the nation's history and to examine racial minorities, women, and working people as integrally involved in the making of American society. They were not breaking new ground altogether; for many decades, reaching back to the early nineteenth century, individual scholars had tilled the fields of women's and minority history, and the events of the 1930s spurred interest in labor history. But their colleagues in the profession had offered little appreciation of their work, and certainly their efforts to recover the history of women and people of color rarely found its way into textbooks used at the primary, secondary, or even collegiate level.

A third development fueling the change in the writing and teaching of history has been the growing interdependence of the nations of the world. Especially in the public schools this has increased the awareness of the importance of studying the histories of many cultures and of teaching world history rather than simply the history of western civilization. The internationalization of economic, political, and cultural affairs has driven home the point to historians and teachers that a Eurocentric history that measures all progress and renders all historical judgments on the basis of the experience of one part of the world will not equip students for satisfactory adult lives in the twenty-first century.

Lastly, and crucially, teachers have seen the composition of their own classrooms change dramatically in the last two decades. The public schools especially have been repopulated with people of different skin shades, different native languages, different accents, and different cultures of origin. More than two thirds of the children in public schools in New York City, Houston, Dallas, Baltimore, San Francisco, Cleveland, and Memphis are not white. In Los Angeles, Chicago, Philadelphia, Detroit, San Antonio, Washington, D.C., El Paso, and New Orleans children of color occupy more than three quarters of all classroom seats in the public schools and in a few of these cities comprise more than 90 percent of all public schoolchildren.

Such a demographic revolution – accounted for by the century-long migration of rural southern African Americans to the cities and by the Immigration acts of 1965 and 1990 which have opened the doors especially to people from Asia and Latin America – reminds us that this nation has always been a rich mosaic of peoples and cultures. It reminds us also that we cannot begin to understand our history without recognizing the crucial role of racial and religious prejudice and exploitation in our past as well as the vital roles of people from many different ethnic, racial, and religious backgrounds in building American society and making American history. The more usable past that a new generation of historians had been creating since World War II became all the more imperative in the schools as new immigrants and people of color became numerically dominant in most of the large urban public school systems.

To what extent, then, has the presentation of history changed in the public schools? In 1979, reviewing American history textbooks as they had been written for schoolchildren from the early twentieth century forward, Frances FitzGerald concluded that "The texts of the sixties contain the most dramatic rewriting of history ever to take place in American schoolbooks."[10] In FitzGerald's view, one of the largest changes was in the textbooks' new presentation of the United States as a multiracial society – a signal revision brought about, in her view, more because of the pressure of school boards in cities with a high percentage of black and Hispanic students – Newark, New Jersey, and Detroit particularly – than because of the influence of new historical scholarship on writers of textbooks for the schools. Yet FitzGerald admitted that by the late 1970s, textbooks were far from cleansed of Eurocentric bias and represented a "compromise ... among the conflicting demands of a variety of pressure groups, inside and outside the school systems" – a compromise "full of inconsistencies." (Among which, she noted, was an almost absolute ban on any discussion of economic life, social and economic inequality, and violence and conflict in American life.)

Why was it that the flowering of social history in the universities that made such important gains in breaking through Eurocentric conceptualizations of American history and world history made only limited gains for the teaching of a less nationalistic, white-centered, hero-driven, and male-dominated history in the schools? In theory, the schools might have been expected to reflect the remarkable changes in historical scholarship. This proved not to be the case for several reasons. First, most teachers who ended up teaching social studies had only a smattering of history in their Bachelor of Arts education – a few courses or a minor for the large majority of them. Second, most teachers were trained at schools where the new scholarship was only palely represented because the 1970s were years in which new faculty appointments were few, especially in the state universities where most teachers are trained. Third, the books used in the schools, though often produced by professional historians, only cautiously incorporated the new social history of women, laboring people, and minorities because publishers who catered to a national market were far more timid than university presses about publishing history that radically revised our understanding of the past, especially the American past. Thus, by the early 1980s, the textbooks in United States history for the secondary schools reflected far less of the new scholarship than textbooks written for college survey classes.

If the 1960s and 1970s brought only a partial transformation of the curriculum, the 1980s have been a period in which the reconceptualization of history, as presented in the schools, has made impressive gains, even though it has had to struggle against a resurgent conservatism, inside and outside the historical profession, that opposes even the partial reforms of the last generation. The barrage of responses to the rewriting of history in the last generation confirms J. H. Plumb's remark that the "personal ownership of the past has always been a vital strand in the ideology of all ruling classes."[11]

The conservative opposition, growing out of the white backlash to the liberal programs of the Kennedy-Johnson era, was led from the top but it reverberated deep into the ranks of white blue-collar America. In the early 1970s, Jules Feiffer captured the disgruntlement of the man in the streets in a cartoon about the white hard-hat worker who complained: "When I went to school I learned that George Washington never told a lie, slaves were happy on the plantation, the men who opened the West were giants, and we won every war because God was on our side. But where my kid goes to school he learns that Washington was a slaveowner, slaves hated slavery, the men who opened the West committed genocide, and the wars we won were victories for U.S. imperialism. No wonder my kid's not an American. They're teaching him some other country's history." Feiffer's cartoon captured the essence of Plumb's observation that history is a powerful weapon traditionally in the arsenal of the upper class: even an elitist, male-dominated, Eurocentric history appealed to the white working class because, while they were largely excluded from it, they were also the beneficiaries of it relative to women and people of color.

In the last decade, some members of the historical profession have taken stands much like Feiffer's blue-collar white parent. Articles began to appear about 1980 complaining about the "crisis in history" – a crisis, it was argued, caused by the rise of the new social history that traced the historical struggles and contributions of the many groups that had attracted little notice from most historians. C. Vann Woodward called for a return to narrative history because, he maintained, historians had lost their way in the welter of narrow quantitative and technical monographs that could not be synthesized into a broad interpretation of American history suitable for schoolchildren. Henry Steele Commager, Page Smith, and Bernard Bailyn similarly advised their colleagues to get back to what historians were once noted for – absorbing narrative history. "The sheer disarray and confusion in the proliferation of analytical historiography" and the consequent loss of coherence in the master lessons of history was ruining the profession, Bailyn claimed in his American Historical Association address in 1981.[12] Most of these attacks, while genuinely concerned with how the enormous output of specialized scholarship could be digested and synthesized, were also seen by some as veiled attacks on the writing of the history of race, class, and gender relations in the history of the United States, Europe, and other parts of the world.

Thus, unlike in the period from the 1930s through the 1950s, when opposition to a reconceptualized history was expressed in terms of the unsuitability of the "outsiders" entering the profession, the current debates within the historical profession focus on the kind of history that is being written. The former outsiders are now within the academic gates, and it will not do any longer to attack them as sociologically and temperamentally unsuited for the work they do; rather, it is the history they write that has come under fire.

Opponents see the new history of women, laboring people, religious and racial minorities – sometimes lumped together under the rubric "social history" – as creating a hopelessly chaotic version of the past in which no grand synthesis or overarching themes are possible to discern and all coherence is lost. Of course, the old coherence and the old overarching themes were those derived from studying mostly the experiences of only one group of people in American society or in grounding all the megahistorical constructs in the Western experience. The contribution of the social historians is precisely to show that the overarching themes and the grand syntheses promulgated by past historians will not hold up when we broaden our perspectives and start thinking about the history of all the people who constituted American society, French society, or any other society. If the rise of women's history, African American history, labor history, and other group histories has created a crisis, we must ask "whose crisis?" For example, it is not a crisis for those interested in women's history because students of women's history know they have been vastly enriched by the last generation's scholarship. Moreover, they know that they have not only gained an understanding of the history of women and the family but in the process have obliged all historians to rethink the allegedly coherent paradigms for explaining the past that were derived from studying primarily the male experience. Nor is the current state of scholarship a crisis for those interested in African American history. With our knowledge so vastly enlarged in this area, we can see how correct Du Bois was in his assessment of a viciously distorted history presented to his generation, and we can go on with the work of reconstructing our history. The crisis, in fact, is the crisis of those whose monopolistic hold on the property of history has been shattered. The democratization of the study of history has undermined the master narratives of those who focused on the history of elites and particularly on grandiose syntheses of "the rise of American democracy" or the majestic "rise of Western civilization" – syntheses that, in spite of claims of objectivity, have been highly subjective and selective in the organizing questions asked, the evidence consulted, and the conclusions drawn.[13]

Joan Wallach Scott has argued that what is most disturbing to those who oppose the transformation of the historical profession in the last generation is that the new social history "has exposed the politics by which one particular viewpoint established its predominance."[14] Perhaps even more threatening, however, is the fact that the new history that pays close attention to gender, race, and class – and in so doing demonstrates that historical experiences varied with the position and power of the participants – promises to end forever any single interpretation or completely unified picture of American history (or the history of any society). By showing that different groups experienced a particular era or movement in starkly different ways, such terms as "The Jacksonian Age of the Common Man," the "Westward Movement," the "Progressive Era," or the post-1945 "Affluent Society" become only the telltale labels of a narrowly conceived history. What is not new is historians arguing over a particular movement or era. They have always argued – for example, about how radical or conservative the American Revolution was, about the profitability of slavery, or about the character of Progressivism. But these arguments took place within certain conceptually defined spaces where race and gender – and often class – were hardly regarded as usable categories.

Many traditional historians have found it painful to watch time-worn labels and characterizations of staple chapters of history vaporize under the impact of the new social history. To a historical profession dominated by white males, it was fun to argue, for example, about the origins of capitalism or about Turner's frontier thesis – whether the frontier truly was a crucible of democratic ideas and institution-creating behavior, a place where democratic values were continuously replenished. But to these historians, it is painfully unsettling – little fun at all – to consider the westward movement from the perspectives of Native Americans watching the wagon trains appearing from the east, Mexican ranchers and miners of the Southwest who found themselves demographically overwhelmed by the arriving Euroamericans, and Chinese contract laborers brought to the Pacific slope in the 1870s. For each of these groups the "frontier movement" was anything but heroic, anything but the westward "march of democracy." The deepest threat of a new history built upon a consideration of alternative experiences and perspectives is that it goes beyond incorporating notable figures who were women or people of color into the traditional storyline and searches for an altogether new storyline based on the historical experiences of the entire society under investigation.

Notwithstanding the sharp attacks on social history in recent years, multiculturalism – defined as the integration of the histories of both genders and people of all classes and racial or ethnic groups – has proceeded rapidly in the last few years. Multicultural curricula, "stressing a diversity of cultures, races, languages, and religions," and eliminating "ethnocentric and biased concepts and materials from textbook and classroom" have been adopted by school systems throughout the United States.[15] California has implemented an explicitly multicultural history-social science curriculum and many other states and individual school districts are following the same path, though with many variations.

Afrocentrism and Multiculturalism

How do these debates among professional historians connect with and affect the current debates over multiculturalism in the schools? And how do they allow us to appraise the rise of the Afrocentric perspective – a powerful movement within the public schools of the nation's largest cities? Perhaps it is not surprising, given how long it has taken for textbooks and school curricula to change that, while some members of the historical profession were resisting the movement toward a history that pays attention to gender, race, and class, some school reformers, especially those who were not part of the while majority, would find the reforms of the last two decades too slow and too fragmentary. For some educators, particularly a group of African Americans, the reforms were altogether wrongheaded, so that greater speed and thoroughness toward a multicultural approach was not at all desirable.

*   *   *

Designed primarily to nurture self-esteem in black children by teaching them of the greatness of ancestral Africa and the contributions that Africans of the diaspora have made in many parts of the world, the Afrocentric approach is mostly the work of non-historians. Its most widely visible and vocal leaders are Molefi Kete Asante, whose degree is in rhetoric and communications; Asa Hilliard, whose degree is in education; and Leonard Jeffries, City College in the City University of New York, whose degree is in political science. Such educators surely cannot be faulted for regarding the dropout rates, low achievement scores, and lives blighted by drugs, violence, and early pregnancies of young African Americans as a national tragedy – and one that white America is largely uninterested in addressing. For these educators an Afrocentric curriculum that sees all knowledge and values from an African perspective is a cure. "The only issue for us," says Jeffrey Fletcher, who is part of the Black United Front for Education Reform in Oakland, California, "is how we can get out of this plight. It's like if you have someone around your throat choking you. It's nice to know about the baseball scores and other cultures, but the only thing you need to know is how to get those fingers off your neck."[16]

Afrocentrism is both an intellectual construction and a social-psychological remedy, and the two parts of it deserve separate discussion. As an intellectual construction, Molefi Kete Asante explains, Afrocentricity means "literally placing African ideals at the center of any analysis that involves African culture and behavior."[17] If this means homogenizing all of the many distinct African cultures and blending the entire gamut of religious, moral, and political ideals from Muslim Africa to Christian Africa to the animist rain forest dwellers and blurring the many distinct historical experiences over many centuries of culturally distinct peoples, then most scholars would have much to discuss with Asante. But if Afrocentrism means simply that any consideration of African history or the history of Africans of the diaspora must take account of the culture of the homeland and the way it was transmitted and maintained, at least partially, outside of Africa, then a great many scholars of the black experience – historians, ethnomusicologists, cultural anthropologists, art historians, linguistic scholars, and so forth – have been Afrocentrist for a long time. Certainly I was an Afrocentrist in this sense twenty years ago when I wrote *Red, White, and Black: The Peoples of Early America* because the main thrust of that book was to demonstrate that eastern North America in the seventeenth and eighteenth century was a merging ground for distinct cultures – European, African, and Indian (each distinctly divided within itself) – and that each culture had to be understood on its own terms if the interaction among them was to be fully comprehended.

Hence, Afrocentrists, in insisting on appreciating the integrity of African cultures and the persistence of many of their elements during and beyond the diaspora are building on a decades-old movement to overturn the European colonizers' mindset – a movement to which people of many ethnic and racial identities of the last generation have contributed in sometimes separate and sometimes intersecting ways. In this sense, the claim of Asante that "Few whites have ever examined their culture critically" and his claim that those who have, such as the British historian of Africa, Basil Davidson, have "been severely criticized by their peers," is discouragingly uninformed.[18] Asante's account of what he believes is stubbornly Eurocentric scholarship on African and African American history ignores the work of two generations of African and African American historians, including those who are English, French, Caribbean, and American and who are of various racial inheritances.

In building on a tradition of ridding ourselves of a Eurocentric approach, Afrocentrism as practiced by some of its proponents, virtually none of whom are historians, has produced some notable contradictions and ironies and a great many oversimplifications. For example, though striving to undermine the significance of Western culture, its most trumpeted message is that Egypt was black and African (a distortion and oversimplification in itself) and that black Egyptians taught the ancient Greeks most of what they knew, which is to presume that what the Greeks knew was significant. An irony in Afrocentrism is that its proponents take great pains to find great figures of Western culture, such as Alexander Dumas and Aleksandr Pushkin, who had an African ancestor, and claim them as evidence of the superiority of African culture. Since white America, for more than two centuries, defined anyone with any small portion of African ancestry as black, the Afrocentrists can chortle as they discover that Beethoven's great-grandfather may have been a Moorish soldier in the Spanish army (an assertion, first made by J. A. Rogers, a black journalist a generation ago but still far from proved).[19] But if Beethoven had a black ancestor, the Afrocentrists still have to live with the contradiction of celebrating someone who has been thoroughly a part of western culture while downgrading that culture in the interest of claiming the superiority of African culture as the place where modern science, mathematics, and other disciplines had their origin.

In its treatment of Egypt, Afrocentrists such as Asante and Hilliard are out of touch with most reputable scholarship on the ancient world and give precedence to a part of Africa with which most African Americans had little cultural connection. For Asante, the "Afrocentrist analysis reestablishes the centrality of the ancient Kemetic (Egyptian) civilization and the Nile Valley cultural complex as points of reference for an African perspective."[20] It is certainly true that most 19th- and 20th-century scholars in the West have taken Africans out of Egypt and taken Egypt out of Africa, relocating it in the Middle East. But in correcting this, following the work of the Senegalese Africanist Chiekh Anta Diop and more recently by using very selectively Martin Bernal's *Black Athena: The Afroasiatic Roots of Classical Civilization*, Afrocentrists have tried to turn all of the mixed-race Egyptians into African blacks and to make most of European civilization derivative from black Africa. Moreover, in arguing that the cultures of ancient Egypt and the Nile Valley are the main reference points for an African perspective, such Afrocentrists defy most of the scholarship of the last generation on most of the Africans of the diaspora, whose cultures in West Africa were hardly the same as the culture of the Nile. The *Portland African-American Baseline Essays*, the most comprehensive attempt to set forth an Afrocentric curriculum, clearly follow this misleading path, urging teachers to "identify Egypt and its civilization as a distinct African creation" (that is without Asian or European influences). The Social Studies essay devotes more than three times as much space to the history and culture of ancient Egypt as to the history and culture of West Africa in the period before the beginning of the Atlantic slave trade.[21]

*   *   *

The non-scholarly form of Afrocentrism, drawing on a long-established movement to stop measuring all things by the European cultural yardstick, has moved perilously close to holding up a new yardstick which measures all things by how nearly they approach an African ideal. When we get beyond labels and cultural yardstick waving, what will be enduringly important for those who wish to study the interaction of African peoples and Europeans, in whatever part of the world, is an ability to look through several sets of lenses. Most of us learned a long time ago that this was what good history and good anthropology are all about. It is hardly arguable that to understand African literature or African American history or Afro-Brazilian music one must have an understanding of African culture as well as the cultures with which

Africans were interacting. Nor is it deniable that the stigmatizing of African culture and its derivative cultures of the diaspora has been an essential part of white supremacist thought and that it has been institutionalized in our culture and in the cultures of all societies where Europeans were the cultural arbiters. But Afrocentrism becomes a new and dangerous ethnocentrism of its own when it adopts the colonizers' old trick of arranging cultures on a continuum ranging from inferior to superior. It is this aspect of Afrocentrism that disturbs black scholars such as Henry Louis Gates, Jr., who decries such "ethnic fundamentalism" and attempts "to reduce the astonishing diversity of African cultures to a few simple-minded shibboleths."[22] As long ago as 1945, Emery Reves wrote in *The Anatomy of Peace*: "Nothing can distort the true picture of conditions and events in this world more than to regard one's own country [or culture] as the center of the universe and to view all things solely in their relationship to this fixed point."[23] We seem destined to relearn this lesson.

When Afrocentrism makes the leap from theory and scholarly perspective to a curricular prescription for the schools, its problems and dangers multiply. Asante believes that "most African-American children sit in classrooms yet are outside the information being discussed." If he means this statement to apply to modern mathematics, science, and computer skills, or even to reading and writing skills, and if the remedy is to learn about ancient Egyptian concepts of science and magic, then black children taught in an Afrocentric curriculum will not acquire the skills and knowledge without which they can move forward in modern society. In social studies classrooms, knowledge of African history and of the many rich and complex traditions in the period before contact with Europeans, can certainly awaken the interest of African American children (and other children too, one assumes) and can stimulate their sense of how African peoples, interacting with other societies, have been an essential part of the history of humankind. But getting beyond romantic notions of African history will require that they learn that ethnic and national identities have been stronger than pan-Africanism on the African continent, both before and after the long era of the slave trade and European colonization. Equally important, African American children, as much as any other children, need to learn about the history of many cultures and historical experiences. The ultimate goal of a multicultural education is to create mutual respect among students of different religions, races, and ethnic backgrounds by teaching them that rich cultural traditions have existed for centuries in every part of the world. "The natural inclination in people to fear and distrust what they find alien and strange," writes Robert K. Fullinwider, "is tempered by an education that makes students' religions, languages, customs, and values familiar to each other, thereby encouraging in students a sympathetic imagination, a generosity of spirit, and an openness to dialogue."[24]

Perhaps too much emphasis has been placed, in the Afrocentrist educators' program, on the power of pride in African ancestry. In itself, of course, ancestral pride and group pride, when kept in bounds, are conducive to a healthy sense of one's potential. For example, there is little doubt, as Roger Wilkins has written, that it was of great importance to the Civil Rights activists to assert "a human validity that did not derive from whites" and to understand that "the black experience on this continent and in Africa was profound, honorable, and a source of pride."[25] But ancestral and group pride cannot solve the deep social and economic problems that confront so many youth who live in black communities today. If the most radical black educators devote their energies to refashioning children's self-image through an oversimplified and often invented history, what energy will go toward fighting for structural reforms that provide jobs, equal opportunities, decent housing, and a more stable family life for millions of people trapped in poverty and despair? The black historian John Bracey describes the "glories of Ancient Africa" as a understandable but sadly insufficient response "to the harsh realities of the West Side of Chicago, or BedStuy, or the gang mayhem of Los Angeles."[26]

*   *   *

Still other explosives infest the minefield of extreme Afrocentrism. If the Afrocentrists are correct that their curriculum will raise self-esteem, and therefore performance levels – a disputed point with little solid evidence – then it is logical to suppose that what is sauce for the goose is sauce for the gander. The logical extension of their reasoning is that a Hispanocentrist approach ought to be instituted for children of Hispanic backgrounds; children of Chinese ancestry in this country ought to receive a Sinocentrist education; a Khmercentrist approach is the best road ahead for the thousands of immigrant children from Cambodia; and so forth. Indeed, logic would require the reinstitution of a Eurocentric approach for low-achieving white children, or a series of nation-specific or European ethnic group-specific approaches to help underachieving children of these backgrounds overcome their disadvantages. But what approach would be employed in thousands of classrooms in large cities across the country where children of a great variety of ethnic, racial, and religious backgrounds mingle? Which ethnically specific curriculum should be taught to the growing number of mixed-race children in a society where miscegenation laws, after a long struggle, no longer exist and the rate of interracial marriage is at an all-time high and is increasing yearly?

Separate Ground and Common Ground

Except among the David Dukes and Pat Buchanans, who so far have had little influence on curricular change, there is little argument about the desirability of including people of all classes, colors, and conditions in our accounts of how history unfolds – indeed, this is simply sound historical analysis. Nor is there much doubt that children will find history more compelling and relevant when they recognize that people of their religion, color, region, ethnic background, or class played active roles in the making of American society. But students also need to discover through history the common humanity of all individuals while discovering the historical relevance of gender, race, religion, and other categories that help shape their identity. And whatever our origins and characteristics, we should hope that all students will find inspiring figures of different colors, genders, and social positions. Harriet Tubman and Ida B. Wells should inspire all students, not simply African American females. Likewise, all students can gain wisdom from studying the trial of Anne Hutchinson or the Lincoln-Douglass debates and draw inspiration from the courage and accomplishments of Black Hawk, John Brown, Elizabeth Blackwell, A. Philip Randolph, Louis Brandeis, Dolores Huerta, and a thousand more. W. E. B. Du Bois knew that the history he was taught was wildly distorted and used as an instrument of white supremacy. But he also understood that he benefitted greatly from reading the great writers of many cultures. "I sit with Shakespeare and he winces not. Across the color line I move arm in arm with Balzac and Dumas, where smiling men and welcoming women glide in gilded halls ... I summon Aristotle and Aurelius and what soul I will, and they come all graciously with no scorn nor condescension. So, wed with Truth, I live above the veil."[27]

The veil of which Du Bois wrote was the color line, of course, and he is only one of a long line of brilliant black scholars who drew sustenance from all parts of humanity. Ralph Ellison, growing up in Macon County, Alabama, remembered that he "read Marx, Freud, T. S. Eliot, Pound, Gertrude Stein, and Hemingway. Books which seldom, if ever, mentioned Negroes were to release me from whatever 'segregated' idea I might have had of my human possibilities."[28] C. L. R. James, the Trinidadian historian and author of *Black Jacobins*, still after forty years the most important book on the Haitian Revolution, writes movingly of his education in the classics of English literature in the schools of Trinidad. As an adult, James came to understand "the limitation of spirit, vision, and self-respect which was imposed on us by the fact that our masters, our curriculum, our Code of morals, *everything* began from the basis that Britain was the source of all light and leading, and our business was to admire, wonder, imitate, learn." But he went on to read and learn from French and Russian literary greats and to find an authentic voice of his own, much enriched by his cosmopolitan education.[29] His accomplishments are a reminder that a curriculum organized around only one vantage point for learning, whether English, European, or African, will limit the vision of students and therefore keep them from being all that they can be.

Thirteen years ago, looking at the way multiculturalism was proceeding in its earlier stage, Frances FitzGerald worried that the rise of the new social history that concerned the forgotten elements of the population would lead to a history that was a bundle of fragmented group histories. This, she said, would teach that "Americans have no common history, no common culture and no common values, and that membership in a racial cultural group constitutes the most fundamental experience of each individual. The message would be that the center cannot, and should not, hold."[30]

Today, FitzGerald's question about what holds us together, whether we have a common culture, is all the more relevant. If multiculturalism is to get beyond a promiscuous pluralism that gives every thing equal weight and adopts complete moral relativism, it must reach some agreement on what is at the core of American culture. The practical goal of multiculturalism is to foster mutual respect among students by teaching them about the distinct cultures from which those who have come to the United States derive and the distinctive historical experiences of different racial, ethnic, religious, and gender groups in American history. Multicultural education, writes Robert Fullinwider, is "the conscious effort to be sensitive, both in teacher preparation and in curriculum construction, to the cultural, religious, ethnic, and racial variety in our national life in order to (1) produce an educational environment responsive to the needs of students from different backgrounds and (2) instill in students mutual understanding and respect."[31] But nurturing this mutual respect and an appreciation of cultural diversity can only be maintained if parents, teachers, and children reach some basic agreement on some core set of values, ways of airing disputes, conducting dialogue – in short, some agreement on how to operate as members of a civic community, a democratic polity. For a democratic polity to endure, the people of a society made up of many cultures must both "be willing to forbear from forcing onto fellow citizens one proper and approved way of life,... must possess a certain amount of respect for one another and a certain amount of understanding of one another's beliefs,... and [must] want to participate in a common 'civic culture'."[32]

If the mutual respect that is at the heart of genuine multiculturalism cannot live "in isolation of specific cultural forms and supports," what are these forms and supports?[33] They are, in essence, the central, defining values of the democratic polity. The pluribus in e pluribus unum can be upheld in all manner of cultural, religious, and aesthetic forms – from the clothes an individual or group chooses to wear, to their cuisine, their artistic preferences and styles, the dialect and linguistic constructions of their internal social life, their religious beliefs and practices, and so forth. But pluribus can flourish in these ways only if unum is preserved at the heart of the polity – in a common commitment to core political and moral values. Chief among these values is the notion that under our founding political principles government is derived from the people, that we live under a government of laws, that certain basic rights as spelled out in the first ten amendments to the Constitution are a precious heritage, and that all citizens – apart from whatever group attachments they claim – have a common entitlement as individuals to liberty, equal opportunity, and impartial treatment under the law. This, of course, is a system of political ideals, not a description of political or social reality. But the ideals are clearly stated in the founding documents and have been reference points for virtually every social and political struggle carried out by women, religious minorities, labor, and people of color. Our entire history can be read as a long, painful, and often bloody struggle to bring social practice into correspondence with these lofty goals. But it is the political ideals that still provide the path to unum. In his classic study of race relations, Gunnar Myrdal focused on the central contradiction of a democracy that would not extend equal rights to Jews, black Americans, and other "outsiders" and thereby engaged in a massive hypocrisy. But at the same time, Myrdal recognized that such disadvantaged groups "could not possibly have invented a system of political ideals which better corresponded to their interests."[34] That a struggle has occurred – and is still occurring – is no argument against the ideal of a common core culture.

It is only a reminder of an agenda still waiting to be completed, of what the African American historian Vincent Harding has poignantly called "wrestling toward the dawn."[35]

Notes

1   David Nicholson, "Afrocentrism and the Tribalization of America," *Washington Post*, September 23, 1991, p. B1.
2   W. E. B. Du Bois, *Black Reconstruction: An Essay toward a History of the Part Which Black Folk Played in the Attempt to Reconstruct Democracy in America, 1860–1880* (New York: Harcourt, Brace, and Co., 1935), pp. 725, 727.
3   Leon Litwack, "Trouble in Mind: The Bicentennial and the Afro-American Experience," *Journal of American History* 74 (1987), p. 326.
4   Hugh Trevor-Roper, *The Rise of Christian Europe* (New York: Harcourt, Brace & World, 1965), p. 9.
5   Douglas Edward Leach, *Flintlock and Tomahawk: New England in King Philip's War* (New York: Macmillan, 1958), p. ix.
6   John Hope Franklin, "The New Negro History," in John Hope Franklin, *Race and History: Selected Essays, 1938–1988* (Baton Rouge: Louisiana State University Press, 1989), p. 46.
7   Peter Novick, *That Noble Dream: The "Objectivity Question" and the American Historical Profession* (Cambridge: Cambridge University Press, 1988), p. 173.
8   Ibid., pp. 366, 339.
9   Oscar Handlin, *Truth in History* (Cambridge, Mass.: Harvard University Press, 1979), passim.
10 Frances FitzGerald, *America Revised: History Schoolbooks in the Twentieth Century* (Boston: Little, Brown & Co., 1979), p. 58.
11 Quoted in Gary B. Nash, *Race, Class, and Politics: Essays on American Colonial and Revolutionary Society* (Urbana and Chicago: University of Illinois Press, 1986), p. xviii.
12 Bernard Bailyn, "The Challenge of Modern Historiography," *American Historical Review* 87 (1982), p. 3.
13 On these points, see also Joan W. Scott, "Liberal Historians: a Unitary Vision," *Chronicle of Higher Education*, September 11, 1991, pp. B1–2.
14 Joan W. Scott, "History in Crisis? The Others' Side of the Story," *American Historical Review* 94 (1989), p. 690; equally pertinent is Lawrence W. Levine, "The Unpredictable Past: Reflections on Recent American Historiography," *American Historical Review* 94 (1989), pp. 671–9.
15 Robert K. Fullinwider, "The Cosmopolitan Community," unpublished mss, pp. 2–3.
16 Quoted in David L. Kirp, "The Battle of the Books," *San Francisco Chronicle*, "Image" section, February 24, 1991.
17 Molefi Kete Asante, *The Afrocentric Idea* (Philadelphia: Temple University Press, 1987), p. 6.
18 Molefi Kete Asante, "Multiculturalism: An Exchange," *American Scholar*, Spring 1991, p. 268.
19 J. A. Rogers, *100 Amazing Facts About the Negro: With Complete Proof: A Short Cut to the World History of the Negro* (New York: F. Hubner, n.d.), pp. 5, 21–2.

20 Asante, *The Afrocentric Idea*, p. 9.

21 John Henrik Clarke, "Social Studies African-American Baseline Essay" (Portland: Portland Public Schools, 1989), pp. SS-12–13 and passim.

22 Henry Louis Gates, Jr., "Beware of the New Pharoahs," *Newsweek*, September 23, 1991, p. 47.

23 Emery Reves, *The Anatomy of Peace* (New York: Harper & Brothers, 1945), p. 1.

24 Robert K. Fullinwider, "Multicultural Education," *The University of Chicago Legal Forum*, 1991, p. 80.

25 Roger Wilkins, *A Man's Life: An Autobiography* (New York: Simon and Schuster, 1982), p. 184.

26 John Bracey, in *African Commentary*, November 1989, p. 12.

27 W. E. B. Du Bois, *Souls of Black Folk: Essays and Sketches* (Chicago: A. C. McClurg & Co., 1903), p. 82.

28 Ralph Elison quoted in Jim Sleeper, *The Closest of Strangers: Liberalism and the Politics of Race in New York* (New York: W. W. Norton, 1990), p. 234.

29 C. L. R. James, *Beyond a Boundary* (London: Hutchinson & Co., 1963), pp. 38–9, 70, and passim.

30 FitzGerald, *America Revised*, p. 104.

31 Fullinwider, "Multicultural Education," p. 77.

32 Ibid., p. 81.

33 Fullinwider, "Cosmopolitan Community," p. 21.

34 Gunnar Myrdal, *An American Dilemma: The Negro Problem and Modern Democracy* (New York: Harper & Brothers, 1944), p. 13.

35 Vincent Gordon Harding, "Wrestling toward the Dawn: The Afro-American Freedom Movement and the Changing Constitution," *Journal of American History* 74 (1987), p. 31.

13

Language Politics

♦

Lingo Jingo: English-Only and the New Nativism

Geoffrey Nunberg

For most of our history, language has not been a major theme in American political life. The chief reason for that, to be sure, is that God in his wisdom has given us a single dominant language, with few real dialects or patois of the sort that European nations have had to deal with in the course of their nation building. (One notable exception is the post-Creole variety spoken by many African Americans.) It's true that America has always had substantial communities of speakers of non-English languages: indigenous peoples; groups absorbed in the course of colonial expansion, like the Francophones of Louisiana and the Hispanics of the Southwest; and the great flows of immigrants from 1880 to 1920 and during the past 30 years. And since the eighteenth century there have been recurrent efforts to discourage or suppress the use of other languages by various minorities, particularly at the time of the nativist movement of the turn of the century. But the focus on language has always been opportunistic, a convenient way of underscoring the difference between us and them; the issue has always subsided as minorities have become anglicized, leaving little symbolic residue in its wake. Unlike the Slovakians, the Italians, the Germans, or those paragons of official orality, the French, we have not until now made how we speak an essential element of what we are.

Given the minor role that language has played in our historical self-conception, it isn't surprising that the current English-only movement began in the political margins, the brainchild of slightly flaky figures like Senator S. I. Hayakawa and John Tanton, a Michigan ophthalmologist who co-founded the U.S. English organization as an outgrowth of his involvement in zero population growth and immigration restriction. (The term "English-only"

was originally introduced by supporters of a 1984 California initiative opposing bilingual ballots, a stalking horse for other official-language measures.
Leaders of the movement have since rejected the label, pointing out that they
have no objection to the use of foreign languages in the home. But the phrase
is a fair characterization of the goals of the movement so far as public life is
concerned.)

Until recently, English-only was not a high priority for the establishment
right. President Bush was opposed to the movement, and Barbara Bush once
went so far as to describe it as "racist." And while a number of figures in the
Republican leadership have been among the sponsors of official-language bills,
most did not become vocal enthusiasts of the policy until the successes of
English-only measures and of anti-immigrant initiatives like California's
Proposition 187 persuaded them that anti-immigrant politics might have
broad voter appeal. Senator Dole endorsed English-only in the 1996 presidential campaign, and Newt Gingrich recently described bilingualism as a menace
to American civilization.

The successes of English-only are undeniably impressive. Polls show
between 65 percent and 86 percent of Americans favoring making English the
official language, and the U.S. English organization currently claims more
than 650,000 members. Largely owing to its efforts, 18 states have adopted
official-language measures via either referenda or legislative action, with legislation pending in 13 more (four other states have official-language statutes
that date from earlier periods). The majority of these laws are largely symbolic, like the 1987 Arkansas law – which President Clinton now says it was
"a mistake" to sign – that states merely, "The English language shall be the
official language of the state of Arkansas." But a few are more restrictive,
notably the measure adopted by Arizona voters in 1988, which bars the state
or its employees from conducting business in any language other than English,
apart from some narrow exceptions for purposes like health and public safety.
In 1996 the House passed H.R. 123, which is similar in most respects to the
Arizona law. (Its title is the "English Language Empowerment Act," which as
the writer James Crawford has observed is a small assault on the language in
its own right.) The Senate did not act on the bill, but it has been reintroduced
in the current session; given the present makeup of the Congress, there is a fair
chance that some legislation will be enacted in this session – though perhaps in
the watered-down version preferred by some Senate Republicans who are
apprehensive about offending Hispanic constituents. In that form, as little
more than a symbolic affirmation of the official status of English, the bill
would likely win the support of some Democrats, and might prove difficult for
President Clinton to veto.

In any case, to the extent that the bill is symbolic, its adoption is more or
less facultative; the movement achieves most of its goals simply by raising the
issue. At the local level, the public discussion of English-only has encouraged
numerous private acts of discrimination. In recent years, for example, dozens
of firms and institutions have adopted English-only workplace rules that bar
employees from using foreign languages even when speaking among themselves or when on breaks. More generally, the mere fact that politicians and

the press are willing to take the proposals of English-only seriously tends to establish the basic premise of the movement: that there is a question about the continued status of English as the common language of American public discourse. In the end, the success of the movement should be measured not by the number of official-language statutes passed, but by its success in persuading people – including many who are unsympathetic to the English-only approach – to accept large parts of the English-only account of the situation of language in America.

Is English Really Endangered?

In rough outline, the English-only story goes like this: the result of recent immigration has been a huge influx of non-English speakers, who now constitute a substantial proportion of the population. Advocates of English-only often claim that there are 32 million Americans who are not proficient in English, a figure that will rise to 40 million by the year 2000. Moreover, these recent arrivals, particularly the Hispanics, are not learning English as earlier generations of immigrants did. According to Senator Hayakawa, "large populations of Mexican Americans, Cubans, and Puerto Ricans do not speak English and have no intention of learning."

The alleged failure to learn English is laid to several causes. There are the ethnic leaders accused of advocating a multiculturalist doctrine that asserts, as Peter Salins describes it, that "ethnic Americans [have] the right to function in their 'native' language – not just at home but in the public realm." Government is charged with impeding linguistic assimilation by providing a full range of services in other languages, even as bilingual education enables immigrant children to complete their schooling without ever making the transition to English. Moreover, it is claimed, the peculiar geographic situation of Hispanics creates communities in which linguistic or cultural assimilation is unnecessary. For example, Paul Kennedy (himself no supporter of English-only) writes of an impending "Hispanicization of the American Southwest," where

> Mexican-Americans will have sufficient coherence and critical mass in a defined region so that, if they choose, they can preserve their distinctive culture indefinitely. They could also undertake to do what no previous immigrant group could ever have dreamed of doing: challenge the existing cultural, political, legal, commercial, and educational systems to change fundamentally not only the language but also the very institutions in which they do business.

Once you accept all this, it is not hard to conclude, as Congressman Norman Shumway puts it, that "the primacy of English is being threatened, and we are moving to a bilingual society," with all the prospects of disorder and disunity that bilingualism seems to imply. As Senator Hayakawa wrote:

> For the first time in our history, out nation is faced with the possibility of the kind of linguistic division that has torn apart Canada in recent years; that has been a major feature of the unhappy history of Belgium, split into speakers of

French and Flemish; that is at this very moment a bloody division between the Sinhalese and Tamil populations of Sri Lanka.

A U.S. English ad makes the point more graphically: a knife bearing the legend "official bilingualism" slashes through a map of the United States.

But the English-only story is nonsense from beginning to end. Take, for starters, the claim that there are 32 million Americans who are not proficient in English. To see how wild that figure is, consider that the total number of foreign-born residents over five years old is only 18 million, some of them immigrants from other English-speaking countries and most of the rest speaking English well. The actual Census figure for residents over five who speak no English is only 1.9 million – proportionately only a quarter as high as it was in 1890, at the peak of the last great wave of immigration. And even if we include people who report speaking English "not well," the number of residents with limited English proficiency stands at around six million people in all. This is not a huge figure when you consider the extent of recent immigration and the difficulty that adults have in acquiring a new language, particularly when they are working in menial jobs that involve little regular contact with English speakers. (Or to put it another way: more than 97 percent of Americans speak English well, a level of linguistic homogeneity unsurpassed by any other large nation in history.)

What is more, recent immigrants are in fact learning English at a faster rate than any earlier generations of immigrants did – and by all the evidence, with at least as much enthusiasm. Whatever "multiculturalism" may mean to its proponents, it most assuredly does not involve a rejection of English as the national lingua franca. No ethnic leaders have been crazy enough to suggest that immigrants can get along without learning English, nor would any immigrants pay the slightest attention to such a suggestion if it were made. According to a recent Florida poll, 98 percent of Hispanics want their children to speak English well. And the wish is father to the deed: immigrants of all nationalities are moving to English at a faster rate than even before in our history. The demographer Calvin Veltman has observed that the traditional three-generation period for a complete shift to English is being shortened to two generations. A recent RAND Corporation study showed that more than 90 percent of first-generation Hispanics born in California have native fluency in English, and that only about 50 percent of the second generation still speak Spanish.

That latter figure suggests that for recent Hispanic arrivals, as for many groups of immigrants that preceded them, becoming American entails not just mastering English but also rejecting the language and culture of one's parents. It is a regrettable attitude (and the very one that English-only has battened on), but the process seems inevitable: relatively few Hispanics display the fierce religious or patriotic loyalty to their mother tongue that the Germans did a hundred years ago. The only exception is the Cubans, who have a special political motivation for wanting to hang on to Spanish, but even here the preference for English is increasingly marked – a survey of first- and second-generation Cuban college students in Miami found that 86 percent preferred

to use English in speaking among themselves. It is only the assimilated third-
and fourth-generation descendants of immigrants who feel the loss of languages keenly, and by then it is almost always too late. (For a linguist, there is
no more poignant experience than to watch a class of American college fresh-
men struggling to master the basic grammer of the language that their grandparents spoke with indifferent fluency.)

A number of factors contribute to the accelerated pace of language shift
among immigrants: the increased mobility, both social and geographical, of
modern life; the ubiquity of English-language media; universal schooling; and
the demands of the urban workplace. In the nineteenth century, by contrast,
many immigrants could hold on to their native language for several generations at no great cost: some because they lived in isolated farming communities and required very little contact with English speakers, others because they
lived in one of the many states or cities that provided public schooling in their
native tongues. At the turn of the century, in fact, more than 6 percent of
American schoolchildren were receiving most or all of their primary education
in the German language alone – programs that were eliminated only around
the time of the First World War.

All of this underscores the irony of the frequent claims that unlike earlier
generations, modern immigrants are refusing to learn English – or that modern bilingual education is an "unprecedented" concession to immigrants who
insist on maintaining their own language. In point of fact, there's a good
chance that great-grandpa didn't work very hard to learn English, and a fair
probability that his kids didn't either. Today, by contrast, all publicly supported bilingual education programs are aimed at facilitating the transition to
English. The programs are unevenly implemented, it's true, owing to limited
funding, to the resistance of school administrators, and to the shortage of
trained teachers. (An early study found that 50 percent of teachers hired in
"bilingual" programs lacked proficiency in their students' native languages.)
And in any case such programs are available right now for only about 25
percent of limited-English students. Still, the method clearly works better than
any of the alternatives. An extensive 1992 study sponsored by the National
Academy of Sciences found that, compared with various types of "immersion"
programs, bilingual education reduces the time to reach full English fluency by
between two and three years.

What of the other government programs that critics describe as opening the
door to "official bilingualism"? Measured against the numerous social and
economic motivations that limited-English immigrants have for learning
English, the availability of official information in their own language is a negligible disincentive, and there are strong arguments for providing these services. To take an example that the English-only people are fond of raising,
why in the world would we want to keep immigrants with limited English
from taking their driver's license tests in their native languages? Do we want
to keep them from driving to work until they have learned the English word
pedestrian? Or to be more realistic about it – since many of them will have no
choice but to drive anyway – do we want to drive to work on roads full of
drivers who are ignorant of the traffic laws?

In any event, these programs are extremely, even excessively, limited. Federal law mandates provision of foreign-language services only in a handful of special cases – interpreters must be provided for migrant worker health care centers and for certain Immigration and Naturalization Service procedures, for example – and a recent General Accounting Office survey found that the total number of federal documents printed in languages other than English over the past five years amounted to less than one-tenth of 1 percent of the total number of titles, hardly a sign of any massive shift to multilingualism in the public realm.

Language as Symbolism

Considered strictly in the light of the actualities, then, English-only is an irrelevant provocation. It is a bad cure for an imaginary disease, and moreover, one that encourages an unseemly hypochondria about the health of the dominant language and culture. But it is probably a mistake to try to engage the issue primarily at this level, as opponents of these measures have tried to do with little success. Despite the insistence of English-only advocates that they have launched their campaign "for the immigrants' own good," it's hard to avoid the conclusion that the needs of non-English speakers are a pretext, not a rationale, for the movement. At every stage, the success of the movement has depended on its capacity to provoke widespread indignation over allegations that government bilingual programs are promoting a dangerous drift toward a multilingual society. The movement's supporters seem to have little interest in modifying that story to take the actual situation of immigrants into account. To take just one example, there are currently long waiting lists in most cities for English-language adult classes – around 50,000 people in Los Angeles County alone – but none of the English-only bills that have been introduced in the Congress make any direct provision for funding of such programs. Who, after all, would care about that?

One indication of just how broadly the movement transcends any immediate, practical concerns about immigrants is the success it has had in regions where issues like immigration and multiculturalism ought by rights to be fairly remote concerns. Of the states that have passed official-English laws in recent years, only four (California, Florida, Arizona, and Colorado) have large immigrant populations. The remainder consist of western states like Montana, North and South Dakota, and Wyoming; Indiana and new Hampshire; and all of the southern and border states except Louisiana (apart from Florida, the only state in the region with substantial numbers of non-English speakers). The breadth of support for these measures seems to increase as its local relevance diminishes, as witness the 89 percent majority that the measure won in an Alabama referendum and the unanimous or near-unanimous legislative votes for English-only measures in states like Arkansas, Georgia, Tennessee, Kentucky, and Virginia. These are not the sorts of places where voters could feel any imminent threat to English from the babel of alien tongues, or indeed, where we would expect to see voters or legislators giving much attention to immigration at all.

At the national level, then, English-only is not strictly comparable to explicit anti-immigrant measures like Proposition 187, which raise genuine substantive issues. The English-only movement has been successful because it provides a symbolic means of registering dissatisfaction with a range of disquieting social phenomena – immigration, yes, but also multiculturalism, affirmative action, and even public assistance. (Not missing a trick, U.S. English advocates like to describe bilingual programs as "linguistic welfare.") By way of response, the movement offers an apparently minimal conception of American identity: We are at the very least a people who speak English.

It seems an unexceptionable stipulation. Even Horace Kallen, who introduced the notion of "cultural pluralism" 70 years ago as a counter to the ideology of the melting pot, readily acknowledged that all Americans must accept English as "the common language of [our] great tradition." But the decision to invest a language with official status is almost never based on merely practical considerations. Language always trails symbolic baggage in its wake and frames the notion of national identity in a particular way. That is why the designation of a national language is controversial wherever the matter arises.

However, the actual significance varies enormously from one nation to the next. Sometimes language is made the embodiment of a liturgical tradition, as in various Balkan countries, and sometimes of a narrowly ethnic conception of nationality, as in Slovakia or the Baltic states. In the recent French debates over the status of the language and the use of English words, the language is standing in more than anything else for the cultural authority of traditional republican institutions – a recent constitutional amendment declared French not the national language, but *la langue de la République.*

Even in the American context, the case for English has been made in very different ways over the course of the century. For the nativists of Kallen's time, language was charged with a specifically ideological burden. The imposition of English was the cornerstone of an aggressive program of Americanization, aimed at sanitizing immigrant groups of the undemocratic doctrines they were thought to harbor. The laws passed in this period undid almost all the extensive public bilingualism of the late nineteenth century, particularly in the civic and political domains. The ability to speak English was made a condition for citizenship in 1906, and in 1915 an English-literacy requirement was added, over President Wilson's veto. A 1919 Nebraska statute stipulated that all public meetings be conducted in English; Oregon required that foreign-language periodicals provide an English translation of their entire contents. More than 30 states passed laws prohibiting or restricting foreign-language instruction in primary schools.

The justification provided for these measures was a peculiar doctrine about the connection between language and political thought, which held that speaking a foreign language was inimical to grasping the fundamental concepts of democratic society. The Nebraska supreme court, for example, warned against the "baneful effects" of educating children in foreign languages, which must "naturally inculcate in them the ideas and sentiments foreign to the best interests of their country." English was viewed as a kind of "chosen language," the consecrated bearer of "Anglo-Saxon" political ideals and institutions. A New York official told immigrants in 1916: "You have got to learn our language because that is the vehicle of the thought that has been handed down from the men in whose breasts first burned the fire of freedom." (Like many other defenders of this doctrine, he dated the tradition from the Magna Carta, a text written, as it happens, in Latin.)

Taken literally, the chosen-language doctrine does not stand up under scrutiny, either linguistically or philosophically. Nothing could be more alien to the Enlightenment universalism of the Founders than the notion that the truths they held to be "self-evident" were ineffable in other languages. But it is almost always a mistake to take talk of language literally. It was not our democratic ideals that seemed to require expression in English, but the patriotic rituals that were charged with mediating the sense of national identity in the period, such as the obligatory school-room declamations of the sacred texts of American democracy; and more broadly, the Anglo culture in which those rituals were embedded. Theodore Roosevelt made the connection clear when he said: "We must ... have but one language. That must be the language of the Declaration of Independence, of Washington's Farewell Address, of Lincoln's Gettysburg speech and second inaugural." The list is significant in its omissions. English might also be the language of Shakespeare, Emerson, and Melville, but its claim to merit official recognition had to be made on political grounds, as the only cloth from which our defining ideals could be woven.

In this regard, the "new nativism" is greatly different from the old. The modern English-only movement makes the case for a national language in what seem to be apolitical (or at least, nonideological) terms. English is important solely as lingua franca, the "social glue" or "common bond" that unites all Americans. Indeed, advocates are careful to avoid suggesting that English has any unique virtues that make it appropriate in this role. A U.S. English publication explains: "We hold no special brief for English. If Dutch (or French, or Spanish, or German) had become our national language, we would now be enthusiastically defending Dutch." (It is hard to imagine Theodore Roosevelt passing over the special genius of English so lightly.)

On the face of things, the contemporary English-only movement seems a less coercive point of view. Indeed, the movement often seems eager to discharge English of any cultural or ideological responsibility whatsoever. Its advocates cast their arguments with due homage to the sanctity of pluralism. As former Kentucky Senator Walter Huddleston puts it, Americans are "a generous people, appreciative of cultural diversity," and the existence of a common language has enabled us "to develop a stable and cohesive society that is the envy of many fractured ones, without imposing any strict standards of homogeneity." At the limit, advocates seem to suggest that Americans need have nothing at all in common, so long as we have the resources for talking about it.

That is misleading, though. Language is as much a proxy for culture now as it was at the turn of the century, except that now neither English nor Anglo culture needs any doctrinal justification. This explains why English-only advocates are so drawn to comparisons with polities like Canada,

Belgium, and Sri Lanka. Turn-of-the century nativists rarely invoked the cases of Austria-Hungary or the Turkish empire in making the case against multilingualism, not because such scenarios were implausible – after all, the nativists had no qualms about invoking equally implausible scenarios of immigrant hordes inciting revolution – but because they were irrelevant: What could Americans learn about their national identity from comparisons with places like those? And the fact that Americans are now disposed to find these specters plausible is an indication of how far the sense of national identity has moved from its doctrinal base. The ethnic divisions in Canada and Belgium are generally and rightly perceived as having no ideological significance, and the moral seems to be that cultural differences alone are sufficient to fragment a state, even this one.

There are a number of reasons for the shift in emphasis. One, certainly, is a generally diminished role for our particular political ideology in an age in which it seems to lack serious doctrinal rivals. Over the long term, though, the new sense of the role of a common language also reflects the emergence of new mechanisms for mediating the sense of national community – radio, film, television – which require no direct institutional intervention. And the effects of the new media are complemented by the techniques of mass merchandising, which ensure that apart from "colorful" local differences, the material setting of American life will look the same from one place to another. ("To be American is to learn to shop," Newt Gingrich observed not long ago, without apparent irony.)

As Raymond Williams noted, the broadcast media aren't direct replacements for traditional institutions: they do not inculcate an ideology so much as presuppose one. In this sense they are capable of imposing a high degree of cultural and ideological uniformity without explicit indoctrination, or indeed, without seeming to "impose" at all. This may help to explain why the English-only movement appears indifferent to the schools or the courses in citizenship that played such an important part in the program of the turn-of-the-century Americanization movement, as well as to the theories about the special mission of English that were so prominent then. It's hard to imagine anyone making the case for English as the language of Washington's farewell speech or Lincoln's second inaugural, when students are no longer required to memorize or even read those texts anymore. Of all our sacred texts, only the Pledge of Allegiance and the national anthem are still capable of rousing strong feelings. But these are, notably, the most linguistically empty of all the American liturgy (schoolchildren say the first as if it were four long words, and I have never encountered anybody who is capable of parsing the second), which derive their significance chiefly from their association with the non-linguistic symbol of the flag.

Cherished Conformity

It is inevitable, then, that modern formulations of the basis of national identity should come to focus increasingly on the importance of common experience and common knowledge, in place of (or at least, on an equal footing with) common political ideals. Michael Lind, for example, has argued that American identity ought to be officially vested in a national culture, which has native competence in American English as its primary index but is also based on American "folkways" that include

> particular ways of acting and dressing; conventions of masculinity and femininity; ways of celebrating major events like births, marriages, and funerals; particular kinds of sports and recreations; and conceptions of the proper boundaries between the secular and religious spheres. And there is also a body of material – ranging from historical events that everyone is expected to know about to widely shared but ephemeral knowledge of sports and cinema and music – that might be called common knowledge.

Once we begin to insist on these cultural commonalities as necessary ingredients of national identity, it is inevitable that the insistence on English will become more categorical and sweeping. Where turn-of-the-century Americanizationists emphasized the explicitly civic uses of language, English-only casts its net a lot wider. It's true that the movement has tended to focus its criticism on the government bilingual programs, but only because these are the most accessible to direct political action; and within this domain, it has paid as much attention to wholly apolitical texts like driver's license tests and tax forms as to bilingual ballots. Where convenient, moreover, English-only advocates have also opposed the wholly apolitical private-sector uses of foreign languages. They have urged the California Public Utilities Commission to prohibit Pac Tel from publishing the Hispanic Yellow Pages; they have opposed the FCC licensing of foreign-language television and radio stations; they have proposed boycotts of Philip Morris for advertising in Spanish and of Burger King for furnishing bilingual menus in some localities. For all their talk of "cherished diversity," English-only advocates are in their way more intolerant of difference than their nativist predecessors. "This is America; speak English," English-only supporters like to say, and they mean 24 hours a day.

The irony of all this is that there was never a culture or a language so little in need of official support. Indeed, for someone whose first allegiance is to the English language and its culture, what is most distressing about the movement is not so much the insult it offers to immigrants as its evident lack of faith in the ability of English-language culture to make its way in the open market – and this at the very moment of the triumph of English as a world language of unprecedented currency. (A Frenchman I know described the English-only measures as akin to declaring crabgrass an endangered species.) The entire movement comes to seem tainted with the defensive character we associate with linguistic nationalism in other nations. I don't mean to say that English will ever acquire the particular significance that national languages have in places like Slovakia or France. But it's getting harder to tell the difference. .

English Only: The Tongue-Tying of America

Donaldo Macedo

During the past decade conservative educators such as ex-secretary of education William Bennett and Diane Ravitch have mounted an unrelenting attack on bilingual and multicultural education. These conservative educators tend to recycle old assumptions about the "melting pot theory" and our "common culture," assumptions designed primarily to maintain the status quo. Maintained is a status quo that functions as a cultural reproduction mechanism which systematically does not allow other cultural subjects, who are considered outside of the mainstream, to be present in history. These cultural subjects who are profiled as the "other" are but palely represented in history within our purportedly democratic society in the form of Black History Month, Puerto Rican Day, and so forth. This historical constriction was elegantly captured by an 11th-grade Vietnamese student in California:

> I was so excited when my history teacher talked about the Vietnam War. Now at last, I thought, now we will study about my country. We didn't really study it. Just for one day, though, my country was real again. (Olsen 1988, p. 68)

The incessant attack on bilingual education which claims that it serves to tongue-tie students in their native language not only negates the multilingual and multicultural nature of U.S. society, but blindly ignores the empirical evidence that has been amply documented in support of bilingual education. An example of a truly tongue-tied America materialized when the ex-foreign minister of the Soviet Union, Mr. Eduard Shevardnadze, began to deliver a speech in Russian during a recent commencement ceremony at Boston University. The silence that ensued was so overwhelming that one could hear a pin drop. Over 99% of the audience was saved from their monolingualism thanks to the intervention of an interpreter. In fact, the present overdose of monolingualism and Anglocentrism that dominates the current educational debate not only contributes to a type of mind-tied America, but also is incapable of producing educators and leaders who can rethink what it means to prepare students to enter the ever-changing, multilingual, and multicultural world of the 21st century.

It is both academically dishonest and misleading to simply point to some failures of bilingual education without examining the lack of success of linguistic minority students within a larger context of a general failure of public education in major urban centers. Furthermore, the English Only position points to a pedagogy of exclusion that views the learning of English as education

Excerpted and reprinted from *Journal of Education*, Boston University School of Education, 173, no. 2 (1991), pp. 9–20, with permission from the Trustees of Boston University (copyright holder) and the author.

itself. English Only advocates fail to question under what conditions English will be taught and by whom. For example, immersing non-English-speaking students in English as a Second Language programs taught by untrained music, art, and social science teachers (as is the case in Massachusetts with the grandfather clause in ESL Certification) will hardly accomplish the avowed goals of the English Only Movement. The proponents of English Only also fail to raise two other fundamental questions. First, if English is the most effective educational language, how can we explain that over 60 million Americans are illiterate or functionally illiterate (Kozol 1985, p. 4)? Second, if education solely in English can guarantee linguistic minorities a better future, as educators like William Bennett promise, why do the majority of Black Americans, whose ancestors have been speaking English for over 200 years, find themselves still relegated to ghettos?

I want to argue in this paper that the answer lies not in technical questions of whether English is a more viable language of instruction or the repetitive promise that it offers non-English-speaking students "full participation first in their school and later in American society" (Silber 1991, p. 7). This position assumes that English is in fact a superior language and that we live in a classless, race-blind society. I want to propose that decisions about how to educate non-English-speaking students cannot be reduced to issues of language, but rest in a full understanding of the ideological elements that generate and sustain linguistic, racial, and sex discrimination. That is, educators need to develop, as Henry Giroux has suggested, "a politics and pedagogy around a new language capable of acknowledging the multiple, contradictory and complex subject positions people occupy within different social, cultural, and economic locations" (1991, p. 27). By shifting the linguistic issue to an ideological terrain we will challenge conservative educators to confront the Berlin Wall of racism, classism, and economic deprivation which characterizes the lived experiences of minorities in U.S. public schools. For example, J. Anthony Lukas succinctly captures the ideological elements that promote racism and segregation in schools in his analysis of desegregation in the Boston Public Schools. Lukas cites a trip to Charlestown High School, where a group of Black parents experienced firsthand the stark reality their children were destined to endure. Although the headmaster assured them that "violence, intimidation, or racial slurs would not be tolerated," they could not avoid the racial epithets on the walls: "Welcome Niggers," "Niggers Suck," "White Power," "KKK," "Bus is for Zulu," and "Be illiterate, fight busing." As those parents were boarding the bus, "they were met with jeers and catcalls 'go home niggers. Keep going all the way to Africa!'" This racial intolerance led one parent to reflect, "My god, what kind of hell am I sending my children into?" (Lukas 1985, p. 282). What could her children learn at a school like that except to hate? ...

Against this landscape of violent racism perpetrated against racial minorities, and also against linguistic minorities, one can understand the reasons for the high dropout rate in the Boston public schools (approximately 50%). Perhaps racism and other ideological elements are part of a school reality which forces a high percentage of students to leave school, only later to be profiled by the very system as dropouts or "poor and unmotivated students." ...

It is very curious that this new-found concern of English Only advocates for limited English proficiency students does not interrogate those very ideological elements that psychologically and emotionally harm these students far more than the mere fact that English may present itself as a temporary barrier to an effective education. It would be more socially constructive and beneficial if the zeal that propels the English Only movement were diverted toward social struggles designed to end violent racism and structures of poverty, homelessness, and family breakdown, among other social ills that characterize the lived experiences of minorities in the United States. If these social issues are not dealt with appropriately, it is naive to think that the acquisition of the English language alone will, somehow, magically eclipse the raw and cruel injustices and oppression perpetrated against the dispossessed class of minorities in the United States. According to Peter McLaren, these dispossessed minority students who

> populate urban settings in places such as Howard Beach, Ozone Park, El Barrio, are more likely to be forced to learn about Eastern Europe in ways set forth by neo-conservative multiculturists than they are to learn about the Harlem Renaissance, Mexico, Africa, the Caribbean, or Aztec or Zulu culture. (McLaren 1991, p. 7)

While arguing for the use of the students' native language in their educational development, I would like to make it very clear that the bilingual education goal should never be to restrict students to their own vernacular. This linguistic constriction inevitably leads to a linguistic ghetto. Educators must understand fully the broader meaning of the use of students' language as a requisite for their empowerment. That is, empowerment should never be limited to what Stanley Aronowitz describes as "the process of appreciating and loving oneself" (1985). In addition to this process, empowerment should also be a means that enables students "to interrogate and selectively appropriate those aspects of the dominant culture that will provide them with the basis for defining and transforming, rather than merely serving, the wider social order" (Giroux and McLaren 1986, p. 217). This means that educators should understand the value of mastering the standard English language of the wider society. It is through the full appropriation of the standard English language that linguistic minority students find themselves linguistically empowered to engage in dialogue with various sectors of the wider society. What I must reiterate is that educators should never allow the limited proficient students' native language to be silenced by a distorted legitimation of the standard English language. Linguistic minority students' language should never be sacrificed, since it is the only means through which they make sense of their own experience in the world.

Given the importance of the standard English language in the education of linguistic minority students, I must agree with the members of the Institute for Research in English Acquisition and Development when they quote Antonio Gramsci in their brochure [1990]:

> Without the mastery of the common standard version of the national language, one is inevitably destined to function only at the periphery of national life and, especially, outside the national and political mainstream.

But these English Only advocates fail to tell the other side of Antonio Gramsci's argument, which warns us:

> Each time that in one way or another, the question of language comes to the fore, that signifies that a series of other problems is about to emerge, the formation and enlarging of the ruling class, the necessity to establish more "intimate" and sure relations between the ruling groups and the popular masses, that is, the reorganization of cultural hegemony. (Gramsci 1971, p. 16)

This selective selection of Gramsci's position on language points to the hidden curriculum with which the English Only movement seeks to promote a monolithic ideology. It is also part and parcel of an ongoing attempt at "reorganization of cultural hegemony" as evidenced by the unrelenting attack by conservative educators on multicultural education and curriculum diversity. The ideological force behind the call for a common culture can be measured by the words of syndicated columnist Pat Buchanan, who urged his fellow conservatives "to wage a cultural revolution in the 90's as sweeping as the political revolution of the 80's" (Giroux 1991, p. 15). In other words, as Henry Giroux has shown, the conservative cultural revolution's

> more specific expressions have been manifest on a number of cultural fronts including schools, the art world, and the more blatant attacks aimed at rolling back the benefits constructed of civil rights and social welfare reforms constructed over the last three decades. What is being valorized in the dominant language of the culture industry is an undemocratic approach to social authority and a politically regressive move to reconstruct American life within the script of Eurocentrism, racism, and patriarchy. (Giroux 1991, p. 15)

Derrick Z. Jackson, in his brilliant article "The End of the Second Reconstruction," lays bare the dominant conservative ideology that informs the present cultural hegemony when he argues that "From 1884 to 1914, more than 3,600 African-Americans were lynched. Lynching is passé today. AIDS, infant mortality, violence out of despair, and gutted public education do the same trick in inner cities neatly redlined by banks" (1991, p. 27). In contrast to the zeal for a common culture and English only, these conservative educators have remained ominously silent about forms of racism, inequality, subjugation, and exploitation that daily serve to wage symbolic and real violence against those children who by virtue of their language, race, ethnicity, class, or gender are not treated in schools with the dignity and respect all children warrant in a democracy. Instead of reconstituting education around an urban and cultural studies approach which takes the social, cultural, political, and economic divisions of education and everyday life as the primary categories for understanding contemporary schooling, conservative educators have recoiled in an attempt to salvage the status quo. That is, they try to keep the present unchanged even though, as Renato Constantino points out:

> Within the living present there are imperceptible changes which make the status quo a moving reality. . . . Thus a new policy based on the present as past and not

on the present as future is backward for it is premised not on evolving conditions
but on conditions that are already dying away. (1978, p. 201)

One such not so imperceptible change is the rapid growth of minority representation in the labor force. As such, the conservative leaders and educators
are digging this country's economic grave by their continued failure to educate
minorities. As Lew Ferlerger and Jay Mandle convincingly argue, "Unless the
educational attainment of minority populations in the United States improves,
the country's hopes for resuming high rates of growth and an increasing standard of living look increasingly dubious" (1991, p. 12).

In addition to the real threat to the economic fabric of the United States, the
persistent call for English language only in education smacks of backwardness
in the present conjuncture of our ever-changing multicultural and multilingual
society. Furthermore, these conservative educators base their language policy
argument on the premise that English education in this country is highly effective. On the contrary. As Patrick Courts clearly argues in his book *Literacy for
Empowerment* (1991), English education is failing even middle-class and upper-
class students. He argues that English reading and writing classes are mostly
based on workbooks and grammar lessons, lessons which force students
to "bark at print" or fill in the blanks. Students engage in grudgingly banal
exercises such as practicing correct punctuation and writing sample business letters. Books used in their classes are, Courts points out, too often in the service
of commercially prepared ditto sheets and workbooks. Courts's account suggests that most school programs do not take advantage of the language experiences that the majority of students have had before they reach school. These
teachers become the victims of their own professional ideology when they
delegitimize the language experiences that students bring with them into the
classroom.

Courts's study is basically concerned with middle-class and upper-middle-
class students unburdened by racial discrimination and poverty, students who
have done well in elementary and high school settings and are now populating
the university lecture halls and seminar rooms. If schools are failing these
students, the situation does not bode well for those students less economically,
socially, and politically advantaged. It is toward the linguistic minority
students that I would like to turn my discussion now.

The Role of Language in the Education of
Linguistic Minority Students

Within the last two decades, the issue of bilingual education has taken on a
heated importance among educators. Unfortunately, the debate that has emerged
tends to recycle old assumptions and values regarding the meaning and useful-
ness of the students' native language in education. The notion that education
of linguistic minority students is a matter of learning the standard English language still informs the vast majority of bilingual programs and manifests its
logic in the renewed emphasis on technical reading and writing skills.

I want to reiterate in this paper that the education of linguistic minority students cannot be viewed as simply the development of skills aimed at acquiring the standard English language. English Only proponents seldom discuss the pedagogical structures that will enable these students to access other bodies of knowledge. Nor do they interrogate the quality of ESL instruction provided to the linguistic minority students and the adverse material conditions under which these students learn English. The view that teaching English constitutes education sustains a notion of ideology that systematically negates rather than makes meaningful the cultural experiences of the subordinate linguistic groups who are, by and large, the objects of its policies. For the education of linguistic minority students to become meaningful it has to be situated within a theory of cultural production and viewed as an integral part of the way in which people produce, transform, and reproduce meaning. Bilingual education, in this sense, must be seen as a medium that constitutes and affirms the historical and existential moments of lived culture. Hence, it is an eminently political phenomenon, and it must be analyzed within the context of a theory of power relations and an understanding of social and cultural reproduction and production. By "cultural reproduction" I refer to collective experiences that function in the interest of the dominant groups rather than in the interest of the oppressed groups that are objects of its policies. Bilingual education programs in the United States have been developed and implemented under the cultural reproduction model leading to a de facto neocolonial educational model. I use "cultural production" to refer to specific groups of people producing, mediating, and confirming the mutual ideological elements that merge from and reaffirm their daily lived experiences. In this case, such experiences are rooted in the interest of individual and collective self-determination. It is only through a cultural production model that we can achieve a truly democratic and liberatory educational experience. I will return to this issue later.

While the various debates in the past two decades may differ in their basic assumptions about the education of linguistic minority students, they all share one common feature: they all ignore the role of language as a major force in the construction of human subjectivities. That is, they ignore the way language may either confirm or deny the life histories and experiences of the people who use it.

The pedagogical and political implications in education programs for linguistic minority students are far-reaching and yet largely ignored. These programs, for example, often contradict a fundamental principle of reading, namely that students learn to read faster and with better comprehension when taught in their native tongue. The immediate recognition of familiar words and experiences enhances the development of a positive self-concept in children who are somewhat insecure about the status of their language and culture. For this reason, and to be consistent with the plan to construct a democratic society free from vestiges of oppression, a minority literacy program must be rooted in the cultural capital of subordinate groups and have as its point of departure their own language.

Educators must develop radical pedagogical structures which provide students with the opportunity to use their own reality as a basis of literacy. This includes, obviously, the language they bring to the classroom. To do otherwise is to deny minority students the rights that lie at the core of a democratic education. The failure to base a literacy program on the minority students' language means that oppositional forces can neutralize the efforts of educators and political leaders to achieve decolonization of schooling. It is of tantamount importance that the incorporation of the minority language as the primary language of instruction in education of linguistic minority students be given top priority. It is through their own language that linguistic minority students will be able to reconstruct their history and their culture.

I want to argue that the minority language has to be understood within the theoretical framework that generates it. Put another way, the ultimate meaning and value of the minority language is not to be found by determining how systematic and rule-governed it is. We know that already. Its real meaning has to be understood through the assumptions that govern it, and it has to be understood via the social, political, and ideological relations to which it points. Generally speaking, this issue of effectiveness and validity often hides the true role of language in the maintenance of the values and interests of the dominant class. In other words, the issue of effectiveness and validity becomes a mask that obfuscates questions about the social, political, and ideological order within which the minority language exists.

If an emancipatory and critical education program is to be developed in the United States for linguistic minority students in which they become "subjects" rather than "objects," educators must understand the productive quality of language. James Donald puts it this way:

> I take language to be productive rather than reflective of social reality. This means calling into question the assumption that we, as speaking subjects, simply use language to organize and express our ideas and experiences. On the contrary, language is one of the most important social practices through which we come to experience ourselves as subjects. ... My point here is that once we get beyond the idea of language as no more than a medium of communication, as a tool equally and neutrally available to all parties in cultural exchanges, then we can begin to examine language both as a practice of signification and also as a site for culture struggle and as a mechanism which produces antagonistic relations between different social groups. (Donald 1982, p. 44)

It is to the antagonistic relationship between the minority and dominant speakers that I want to turn now. The antagonistic nature of the minority language has never been fully explored. In order to more clearly discuss this issue of antagonism, I will use Donald's distinction between oppressed language and repressed language. Using Donald's categories, the "negative" way of posing the minority language question is to view it in terms of oppression – that is, seeing the minority language as "lacking" the dominant standard features which usually serve as a point of reference for the minority language. By far the most common questions concerning the minority language in the United States are posed from the oppression perspective. The alternative view of the minority language is that it is repressed in the standard dominant language. In this view, minority language as a repressed language could, if spoken, challenge the privileged standard linguistic dominance. Educators have failed to recognize the "positive" promise and antagonistic nature of the minority language. It is precisely on these dimensions that educators must demystify the standard dominant language and the old assumptions about its inherent superiority. Educators must develop liberatory and critical bilingual programs informed by a radical pedagogy so that the minority language will cease to provide its speakers the experience of subordination and, moreover, may be brandished as a weapon of resistance to the dominance of the dominant standard language of the curriculum.

In this sense, the students' language is the only means by which they can develop their own voice, a prerequisite to the development of a positive sense of self-worth. As Giroux elegantly states, the students' voice "is the discursive means to make themselves 'heard' and to define themselves as active authors of their worlds" (Giroux and McLaren 1986, p. 235). The authorship of one's own world also implies the use of one's own language, and relates to what Mikhail Bakhtin describes as "retelling a story in one's own words" (Giroux and McLaren 1986, p. 235).

A Democratic and Liberatory Education for Linguistic Minority Students

In maintaining a certain coherence with the educational plan to reconstruct new and more democratic educational programs for linguistic minority students, educators and political leaders need to create a new school grounded in a new educational praxis, expressing different concepts of education consonant with the principles of a democratic, multicultural, and multilingual society. In order for this to happen, the first step is to identify the objectives of the inherent colonial education that informs the majority of bilingual programs in the United States. Next, it is necessary to analyze how colonialist methods used by the dominant schools function, legitimize the Anglocentric values and meaning, and at the same time negate the history, culture, and language practices of the majority of linguistic minority students. The new school, so it is argued, must also be informed by a radical bilingual pedagogy, which would make concrete such values as solidarity, social responsibility, and creativity. In the democratic development of bilingual programs rooted in a liberatory ideology, linguistic minority students become "subjects" rather than mere "objects" to be assimilated blindly into an often hostile dominant "common" culture. A democratic and liberatory education needs to move away from traditional approaches, which emphasize the acquisition of mechanical basic skills while divorcing education from its ideological and historical contexts. In attempting to meet this goal, it purposely must reject the conservative principles embedded in the English Only movement I have discussed earlier. Unfortunately, many bilingual programs sometimes unknowingly reproduce one common feature of the traditional approaches to education by ignoring the important relationship between language and the cultural capital of the students at whom bilingual education is aimed. The result is the development

of bilingual programs whose basic assumptions are at odds with the democratic spirit that launched them.

Bilingual program development must be largely based on the notion of a
democratic and liberatory education, in which education is viewed "as one
of the major vehicles by which 'oppressed' people are able to participate in
the sociohistorical transformation of their society" (Walmsley 1981, p. 74).
Bilingual education, in this sense, is grounded in a critical reflection of the cultural capital of the oppressed. It becomes a vehicle by which linguistic minority students are equipped with the necessary tools to reappropriate their
history, culture, and language practices. It is, thus, a way to enable the linguistic minority students to reclaim "those historical and existential experiences
that are devalued in everyday life by the dominant culture in order to be both
validated and critically understood" (Giroux 1983, p. 226). To do otherwise
is to deny these students their very democratic rights. In fact, the criticism that
bilingual and multicultural education unwisely question the traditions and values of our so-called "common culture" as suggested by Kenneth T. Jackson
(1991) is both antidemocratic and academically dishonest. Multicultural education and curriculum diversity did not create the S & L scandal, the Iran-
Contra debacle, or the extortion of minority properties by banks, the stewards
of the "common culture," who charged minorities exorbitant loan-sharking
interest rates ... .

The learning of English language skills alone will not enable linguistic
minority students to acquire the critical tools "to awaken and liberate them
from their mystified and distorted views of themselves and their world"
(Giroux 1983, p. 226). For example, speaking English has not enabled
African-Americans to change this society's practice of jailing more Blacks than
even South Africa, and this society spending over 7 billion dollars to keep
African-American men in jail while spending only 1 billion dollars educating
Black males (Black 1991).

Educators must understand the all-encompassing role the dominant ideology has played in this mystification and distortion of our so-called "common
culture" and our "common language." They must also recognize the antagonistic relationship between the "common culture" and those who, by virtue of
their race, language, ethnicity, and gender, have been relegated to the margins.
Finally, educators must develop bilingual programs based on the theory of
cultural production. In other words, linguistic minority students must be
provided the opportunity to become actors in the reconstruction of a more
democratic and just society. In short, education conducted in English only
is alienating to linguistic minority students, since it denies them the fundamental tools for reflection, critical thinking, and social interaction. Without the
cultivation of their native language, and robbed of the opportunity for reflection and critical thinking, linguistic minority students find themselves unable
to recreate their culture and history. Without the reappropriation of their culture, the valorization of their lived experiences, English Only supporters'
vacuous promise that the English language will guarantee students "full participation first in their school and later in American society" (Silber 1991,
p. 7) can hardly be a reality.

References

Aronowitz, S. 1985. "Why should Johnny read." *Village Voice Literary Supplement*, May, p. 13.

Black, C. 1991. "Paying the High Price for Being the World's no. 1 Jailor." *Boston Sunday Globe*, January 13, p. 67.

Constantino, R. 1978. *Neocolonial Identity and Counter Consciousness*. London: Merlin Press.

Courts, P. 1991. *Literacy for Empowerment*. South Hadley, Mass.: Bergin & Garvey.

Donald, J. 1982. "Language, Literacy, and Schooling." In *The State and Popular Culture*. Milton Keynes, UK: Open University Culture Unit.

Ferlerger, L. and J. Mandle. 1991. *African-Americans and the Future of the U.S. Economy*. Unpublished manuscript.

Giroux, H. A. 1983. *Theory and Resistance: A Pedagogy for the Opposition*. South Hadley, Mass.: Bergin & Garvey.

Giroux, H. 1991. *Border Crossings: Cultural Workers and the Politics of Education*. New York: Routledge.

Giroux, H. A. and P. McLaren. 1986. "Teacher Education and the Politics of Engagement: The Case for Democratic Schooling." *Harvard Educational Review*, 56 (3), pp. 213–38.

Gramsci, A. 1971. *Selections from Prison Notebooks*, ed. and trans. Quintin Hoare and Geoffrey Nowell. New York: International Publishers.

Jackson, D. 1991. "The End of the Second Reconstruction." *Boston Globe*, December 8, p. 27.

Jackson, K. T. 1991. Cited in a *Boston Sunday Globe* editorial, July 7.

Kozol, J. 1985. *Illiterate America*. New York: Doubleday Anchor.

Lukas, J. A. 1985. *Common Ground*. New York: Alfred A. Knopf.

McLaren, P. 1991. "Critical Pedagogy: Constructing an Arch of Social Dreaming and a Doorway to Hope." *Journal of Education*, 173 (1), pp. 9–34.

Olsen, L. 1988. *Crossing the Schoolhouse Border: Immigrant Students and the California Public Schools*. San Francisco: California Tomorrow.

Silber, J. 1991. *Boston University Commencement Catalogue*, May.

Walmsley, S. 1981. "On the Purpose and Content of Secondary Reading Programs: Educational and Ideological Perspectives." *Curriculum Inquiry*, 11, pp. 73–9.

14

Self-Segregation on College Campuses

Degree of Separation at Yale

Peter Beinart

For decades at Cornell University, minority students have opted out of regular dorms and into ethnic theme houses. Last year, Cornell's president proposed changing that slightly: students should wait to enter the Ujamaa house or the Latino Living Center until after their freshman year. The response? Fifteen undergrads went on a hunger strike, hundreds laid down in the street, and Reverend Al Sharpton dropped in to accuse the administration of trying to make black and Latino students "merge in with everyone else so we don't know they're here."

This is the kind of thing that gives conservative critics of political correctness a reason to get up in the morning. And it occasioned the usual shoutfest about diversity, forced integration, and self-segregation – followed by a weak-kneed administration compromise.

So far, so predictable. But right-wing outrage over separatism at Cornell raises an interesting question: Why on Earth are conservatives supporting the five Orthodox Jewish students who won't live in the regular dormitories at Yale? The answer is one of the ironies of the culture war: when it comes to religion, the real multiculturalists are all on the Right.

The Yale case and the Cornell case are essentially the same. It's true that the Yalies are asking to move off campus, but that's only because Yale doesn't have specialty houses. If it had a single sex dorm, or a "no-premarital sex" dorm, the Orthodox five would live there. And it's true that the Cornell radicals say they're fleeing racism while the Yale faithful say they're fleeing condoms. But it amounts to the same thing. Yale freshman Elisha Dov Hack's older brother told him that dorm life has made previous Orthodox students less observant. Hunger-striking black senior Dana Miller told *The New York*

Times last year that Cornell's proposed change was "an attempt to socialize students into a homogeneous group." Hack and Miller are both really fleeing assimilation.

That's why it's so remarkable that champions of the melting pot like Charles Krauthammer, William Buckley, Kate O'Beirne, and the editors of *The Weekly Standard* have risen to the Yale Five's defense. This, after all, is the same Charles Krauthammer who recently decried "the tragic turn towards black separatism," and the same *Standard* which in September coined the phrase, "diversity gulag."

Conservative views about separatism, it turns out, depend on who's doing the separating. Consider these words, written in September by frequent *National Review* contributor Jacob Neusner: "cripples have their ramps, homosexuals their K-Y dispensers and double beds, blacks their ghettos, Hispanics their barrios, voyeurs their unisex toilets, all courtesy of university housing directors. But rather than extend the same 'sensitivity' to scarcely a minyan – a quorum – of Orthodox Jews, Yale would rather humiliate itself." This tasteful nugget gets to the heart of the issue. All this time everyone thought conservatives opposed "ghettos" and "barrios" on principle. But now it turns out they're just mad that P.C. radicals get them and prudish believers do not.

A good example of this multicultural me-tooism is the Right's support for charter schools. On August 16, 1996, *The Washington Times* called the accreditation of charter schools in the District of Columbia a "ray of hope." Three and a half months later, the principal of the Afrocentric Marcus Garvey Public Charter School assaulted a *Washington Times* reporter. A *Times* commentator, Ernest Lefever, called the attack "the latest in a long string of outrages committed in the name of multiculturalism."

He's right, but the *Times* was asking for it. Multiculturalism isn't just the ideology of the Marcus Garvey charter school, it's the ideology of charter schools, period. Charter schools are based on the idea that communities should be able to fashion their own institutions with minimal interference from outsiders. They represent a rejection of the principle that public schools educate all students in a common curriculum or a common culture. That is why Michael Kelly wrote in this space last December that charter schools "take from the pluribus to destroy the unum." In their mania for local autonomy, conservative educational reformers have recreated the publicly funded black nationalist schools that arose in late 1960s New York under radical chic Mayor John Lindsey – most notoriously in Ocean Hill-Brownsville, Brooklyn.

Their motivation, of course, is different. For liberals, multiculturalism offered emancipation from racial oppression; for conservatives, it's about religion. Charter schools, combined with vouchers for private and parochial schools, and subsidies for home schooling, constitute the multiculturalist Right's assault on a common school system. Many Christian conservatives believe that regular public schools promote an immoral, godless ideology. Like the Orthodox Jews at Yale, they want to separate – and take their money with them. And just as liberals are instinctively (sometimes mindlessly) sympathetic to demands made in the name of anti-racism, secular conservatives jump to defend the beleaguered faithful. In so doing, they end up supporting a multi-culturalism of their own. Once upon a time, liberals and conservatives believed in Norman Podhoretz's "brutal bargain." Assimilation was hard and even demeaning, but it bought you entrance into a common American culture. That didn't mean the culture was static; over time it might absorb a bit of your particular ethos. But you pushed from the inside, conscious that you could not both reject assimilation and expect its fruits.

In the 1960s, the Left decided this model wouldn't work for blacks. It believed, naively, that African Americans could remain separate from whites while making ever greater moral claims on them. The result, of course, was a tremendous backlash, as working-class whites learned how to stake the claims of identity themselves.

As conservatives line up behind their own brand of separatism, they should take care not to be similarly naive. The options are these: you either commit to common institutions, and accept the old, painful disjuncture between home and school, or you accept marginality. It is a far different thing to call for prayer in public schools than it is to demand that the citizenry fund religious schools. And it is a far different thing to participate fully in a university while maintaining your identity than it is to expect a university to accept you fully while refusing to give yourself fully to it. If conservatives really cared about the Yale Five, they would tell them what they told the hunger-strikers at Cornell: assimilation is the American way.

♦

Understanding Self-Segregation on the Campus

Troy Duster

In the last decade, the increasing social and ethnic heterogeneity of the nation's college campuses has captured the attention of media pundits, higher-education administrators, and many faculty members. Unfortunately, the troublesome aspects of this development have dominated most of the public debate.

One major issue that has absorbed the media is that many students' social lives are segmented in ways that reaffirm their ethnic, racial, and cultural identities. This segmentation, now routinely referred to as "Balkanization," causes surprise, chagrin, and even some derision. It is characterized as an unseemly reversion to "tribalism" that gets in the way of the search for common ground.

There is something both old and new here. Although typically treated as a new and alarming development, such segmentation is quite an old phenomenon and has been replayed throughout the history of higher education in America. Social historians who study U.S. colleges and universities know that the Hillel and Newman foundations played similar important roles for Jewish and Catholic students, respectively, for much of this century. With the assistance of such organizations, parties, dances, recreation, study groups, and sometimes residences were routinely "self-segregated," often in response to active discrimination against Jews and Catholics elsewhere on campus.

Today's critics are suffering from a selective cultural amnesia when they portray African-American theme houses and Chinese student associations as newly created enclaves that destroy the search for common ground. Even into the last decade, the most prestigious fraternities at Yale, Michigan, Harvard, and Berkeley had never admitted a Jew, much less an African American or an Asian. The all-Jewish fraternity was common as late as the 1960s, and when a Chinese American, Sherman Wu, pledged a fraternity at Northwestern in 1956, it was such a sensation that it made national news and generated a folk song. Over the years, some mild hand wringing occurred about such discrimination, but no national campaign was launched against the "self-segregation" of the all-white, all-Anglo fraternities.

Yet despite this long tradition, I believe something new *is* occurring on campuses that may help explain the hysterical response that we have been hearing. The new development is a demographic shift that the long-dominant white majority sees as threatening its cultural hegemony.

At the Berkeley campus of the University of California, the undergraduate student body has been rapidly and dramatically transformed. In 1960, more than 90 per cent of the students were white. In 1980, the figure was about

Reprinted from *Chronicle of Higher Education*, September 25, 1991, pp. 81–2.

66 per cent. Today, it is about 45 per cent. The freshman class this fall signals an even more striking change for those who still think of Berkeley in 1960s terms. For the first time in history, whites do not make up the largest proportion of the incoming class; instead, it is Asian Americans, who account for about 35 per cent. Only 30 per cent of the class are Americans of European ancestry. In addition, nearly 20 per cent of the class are Chicanos/Latinos, and nearly 8 per cent African Americans. If this pattern holds, well over 60 per cent of Berkeley students will be "of color" within the next five years.

Although it will not be quite as dramatic in some other regions of the country, this coloring of the campus landscape reflects a vital and constantly unfolding development in American social life. Although symbolized by dramatic figures such as those at Berkeley, the ramifications go far beyond the percentages of different ethnic and racial groups admitted to college campuses. The ramifications of demographic change certainly tug at the curriculum and challenge the borders of faculty turf and expertise. But the fundamental issues tapped by this change go to the heart of American identity and culture.

Bubbling just beneath the surface of all the national attention devoted to "political correctness" and "quotas" is a complicated question that, stated most simply, is: "What does it mean to be an American?" And the related question is, "How does one become an American?"

The controversy over diversity at Berkeley, much like the battle over the social-studies curriculum in New York State, is a struggle over who gets to define the idea of America. Are we essentially a nation with a common – or at least dominant – culture to which immigrants and "minorities" must adapt? Or is this a land in which ethnicity and difference are an accepted part of the whole; a land in which we affirm the richness of our differences and simultaneously try to forge agreement about basic values to guide public and social policy?

Critics of the current, visible wave of segmentation argue that "Balkanization" threatens the ties that bind civil society. But civil society in a nation of immigrants is forever in flux, and the basic issue always has been which group has the power to define what the values and structures of that common society will be. We should learn something from our history.

Being an American is different from being French or Japanese or almost any other nationality because, except for Native Americans, there actually is no such thing as an American without a hyphen. We are a nation of immigrants. Generations of immigrants have struggled to balance both sides of the hyphen, to carry on some aspects of the culture of the old country while adopting the norms and customs of the new. Today, many of their descendants continue to find comfort in an identification with the old country, however tenuous it may be. In a diverse nation, such identification can provide a sense of belonging to a recognizable collectivity. It helps give a sense of belonging – of being one with others like oneself – that helps to overcome the isolation of modern life, while paradoxically also allowing a sense of uniqueness.

This is the same phenomenon we see being reenacted on campuses all over the country today, the difference being that the actors are no longer all white.

At a place like Berkeley, there is no longer a single racial or ethnic group with an overwhelming numerical and political majority. Pluralism is the reality, with no one group a dominant force. This is completely new; we are grappling with a phenomenon that is both puzzling and alarming, fraught with tensions and hostilities, and yet simultaneously brimming with potential and crackling with new energy. Consequently, we swing between hope and concern, optimism and pessimism about the prospects for social life among peoples from differing racial and cultural groups. Are members of particular groups isolated or interacting, segregating or integrating, fighting or harmonizing? Who is getting ahead or falling behind?

It may well be that we have too narrowly conceived the options as *either/or*. It may be that as a nation we have cast the problem incompletely and thus incorrectly by posing the matter as either one of assimilation to a single, dominant culture where differences merge and melt away – or one of hardened, isolated, and self-segregated groups retreating into ethnic and racial enclaves, defeating the very purpose of trying to achieve diversity.

The findings from a two-year study of student life on the Berkeley campus in which I participated strongly suggest that these are not the only two alternatives before us. Other avenues are possible. In that research, we discovered an emerging vision of one of these options, a "third experience" of diversity. In this "third experience," the whole is greater than the sum of the various parts. In it, for example, collective problem solving by individuals from different backgrounds produces superior results precisely because of the synergy that develops from different approaches being brought to bear on the same problem.

At the public level, we see the possibility of people with strong ethnic and racial identities (including ethnically homogeneous affiliations and friendships) also being able to participate effectively in heterogeneous educational or work settings. These public spheres are enriched precisely because people bring to them the strengths of different cultural and ethnic identities forged out of their unique experiences and "separateness."

In the private arena, individuals with strong ethnic and racial identities also can form friendships that cross racial lines, for example, as students meet each other as equals in the dorms, classrooms, and quads. Although only a small proportion of students currently achieve this, students from different backgrounds can come to see one another as resources by recognizing different, yet complementary, competencies.

One of my favorite examples at Berkeley is an advanced student in computer sciences, an African American, who is acting as a mentor to two first-generation, Asian émigrés. He is teaching them computer technology and such nuances of American culture as the unique role of charitable organizations. The Asian students, in turn, are teaching him about subjects ranging from traditional Chinese medicine to the symbolic importance of gift giving among Koreans. While this kind of learning has always occurred when there is contact between people from different cultures, the potential scale of this contact among "equals" at places like Berkeley is quite new – and holds out the promise of significant changes in social interaction over the long term.

Some of our students, no less than some of our leading pundits, such as George Will and Arthur Schlesinger, Jr., see "self-segregation" as an assault upon their idea of a common community. But other students understand that people living among their ethnic or racial peers are trying to forge an identity and support group to help them in a difficult and often alien world.

The all-black dining table in the dormitory or the all-Asian dance is visually striking, it is true, and stands in sharp relief against student life in earlier periods, when the social segregation among white ethnic students was much less obvious. We should not forget the invidious distinctions made in earlier periods, however. When I was an undergraduate at Northwestern University, I learned about the virulence of anti-Semitism from Christians and about vicious anti-Irish and anti-Italian sentiment from the Anglo upper crust in Evanston. But those distinctions did not reach *Time* and *Newsweek* or the national television networks, and columnists did not talk about the "Balkanization" of our college campuses. Race somehow matters more.

Wholesale condemnation of self-segregation is too simple and simpleminded. Just as Jewish students have found Hillel and a common ethnic/cultural identity the basis for self-affirmation, so too do today's ethnic and racial "minorities" often need to draw upon the social, cultural, and moral resources of their respective communities.

We must also remember that the European ancestry of the Jewish and Catholic students segregated into enclaves in the earlier part of the century was rather better reflected in the existing curriculum than are the ancestries of today's Asian, Latino, or African-American students. While the earlier "out" groups were generally content to receive the established curriculum, today's students are likely to challenge both the curriculum and the pedagogy used to deliver it.

What ultimately bothers today's critics most is not the racial or ethnic segregation of students' social lives, but the challenges that the growing numbers of Asian, Latino, and African-American students pose to the faculty once they find their ancestors' histories and contributions largely ignored in the classroom. That is what really rankles the critics and explains the depth of their anxiety; they recognize that the challenges to the curriculum represent a real and powerful confrontation over who answers, "What does it mean to be an American?"

The Debate Over "Identity Politics"

The Rise of "Identity Politics"

Todd Gitlin

The rise of "identity politics" forms a convergence of a cultural style, a mode of logic, a badge of belonging, and a claim to insurgency. What began as an assertion of dignity, a recovery from exclusion and denigration, and a demand for representation, has also developed a hardening of its boundaries. The long overdue opening of political initiative to minorities, women, gays, and others of the traditionally voiceless has developed its own methods of silencing.

At the extreme, in the academy but also outside, "genealogy" has become something of a universal solvent for universal ideas. Standards and traditions now are taken to be nothing more than the camouflage of interests. All claims to knowledge are presumed to be addressed from and to "subject positions," which, like the claims themselves, have been "constructed" or "invented" collectively by self-designated groups. Sooner or later, all disputes issue in propositions of the following sort: the central subject for understanding is the difference between X (for example, women, people of color) and Y (for example, white males). P is the case because my people, X, see it that way; if you don't agree with P, it is (or more mildly, is probably) because you are a member of Y. And further: since X has been oppressed, or silenced, by Y – typically, white heterosexual males – justice requires that members of X, preferably (though not necessarily) adherents of P, be hired and promoted; and in the student body, in the curriculum, on the reading list, and at the conference, distinctly represented.

This is more than a way of thought. Identity politics is a form of self-understanding, an orientation toward the world, and a structure of feeling that is frequent in developed industrial societies. Identity politics presents itself as – and many young people experience it as – the most compelling remedy for anonymity in an impersonal world. This cluster of feelings seems to answer the questions, Who am I? Who is like me? Whom can I trust? Where do I belong?

Reprinted from *Dissent* 40 (Spring 1993), pp. 172–7.

But identity politics is more than a sensibility felt and lived by individuals. It is a search for comfort, an approach to community. The sense of membership is both a defense and an offense. It seems to overcome exclusion and silencing. Moreover, in a world where other people seem to have chosen up sides and worse, where they approach you – even menace you – because you belong to a particular group, it seems a necessity to find or invent one's strength among one's people. From popular culture to government policy, the world has evidently assigned you a membership. Identity politics turns necessity to virtue.

But there is a hook: for all the talk about "the social construction of knowledge," identity politics in practice slides toward the premise that social groups have essential identities. At the outer limit, those who set out to explode a shrunken definition of humanity end by shrinking their definitions of blacks or women. In separatist theory, they must be, and have always been, all the same. After a genuflection to historical specificity, anatomy once again becomes destiny. This identity politics is already a tradition in its second generation, transmitted and retransmitted, institutionalized in jargons, mentors, gurus, conferences, associations, journals, departments, publishing subfields, bookstore sections, jokes, and, not incidentally, in affirmative action and the growing numbers of faculty and students identified and identifying themselves as "of color."

In this setting, identity politics promises a certain comfort. But what was, at first, an enclave where the silenced could find their voices tends now to harden into a self-enclosed world. In the academy, the pioneering work in the early 1970s toward making women's studies legitimate, bolstering labor studies, rethinking the damage done by slavery and the slaughter of the Indians, opening up the canon to hitherto silenced traditions – all this work was done by scholars who had one foot in the civil rights and antiwar movements and who came to their specialties already bearing something of a universalist or cosmopolitan bent. But much of the succeeding work tended to harden and narrow. Identity politics in the strict sense became an organizing principle among the academic cohorts who had no political experience before the late sixties – those now in their twenties and early thirties. After the late 1960s, as race and gender (and sometimes class) became the organizing categories by which critical temperaments addressed the world in the humanities and social sciences, faculty people working this territory came to display the confidence of an ascending class speaking predictably of "disruption," "subversion," "rupture," "contestation," "struggle for meaning." The more their political life is confined to the library, the more aggressive their language.

But identity politics is not simply a product of the academic hothouse. It also thrives in the society at large – in the media of the mass and margins alike, in schools and in street lore. Some students carry the rhetoric of their particular group to campus with them. Alert to slights, they cultivate a cultural marginality both defensive and aggressive. Fights over appropriate language, over symbolic representation (whether in the form of syllabus or curriculum or faculty or even cuisine), over affirmative action and musical styles and shares of the public space *are, to them, the core of "politics." Just as these cohorts have their clothes and their music, they have "their politics" – the principal, even the only form of "politics" they know.*

The specialists in difference may do their best to deny the fact that for a quarter of a century, they have been fighting over the English department while the right held the White House as its private fiefdom. But academic currents are not so insulated from the larger social world as parochial theory may presume. The legitimacy of racial animus on a national scale, the boldness of right-wing politicians, the profusion of straightforward race prejudice among students have all made the academic left edgier and more offensive. Affirmative action has been successful enough to create a critical mass of African Americans who feel simultaneously heartened, challenged, and marooned. The symbolic burden they bear is enormous. In the absence of plausible prospects for fighting the impoverishment of the cities, unemployment, police brutality, crime, or any of the economic aspects of the current immiseration, it is more convenient – certainly less risky – to accuse a liberal professor of racism. Identity politics is intensified when antagonistic identities are fighting for their places amid shrinking resources. The proliferation of identity politics leads to a turning inward, a grim and hermetic bravado celebrating victimization and stylized marginality.

The thickening of identity politics is relative. We have to ask, Thickening compared to what? Compared to "universalism," "common culture," "the human condition," "liberality," "the Enlightenment project" – the contrary position wears different labels. I shall group them all (at Robert Jay Lifton's suggestion) under the heading of commonality politics – a frame of understanding and action that understands "difference" against the background of what is *not* different, what is shared among groups. This distinction is one of shadings, not absolutes, for differences are always thought and felt against a background of that which does not differ, and commonalities are always thought and felt in relation to differences. Still, the shadings are deeply felt. whence the intellectual polarization that shows up in debates about the complex of problems including the curriculum, diversity, and so on.

The point I wish to assert is that the thickening of identity politics is inseparable from a fragmentation of commonality politics. In large measure, things fell apart *because* the center could not hold. For chronologically, the breakup of commonality politics predates the thickening of identity politics. The centrifugal surge, on campus and off, is the product of two intersecting histories. There is, obviously, the last quarter century of America's social and demographic upheavals. But these, in turn, have taken place within the longer history that snakes forward throughout the West since the revolutions of 1776, 1789, and 1848. Throughout this period and beyond, believers in a common humanity clustered around the two great progressive ideals: the liberal ideal enshrined in the Declaration of Independence and, later, in the Declaration of the Rights of Man and Citizen; and the radical ideal that crystallized as Marxism.

Such legitimacy as the left enjoyed in the West rested on its claim to a place in the story of universal human emancipation. Two hundred years of revolutionary tradition, whether liberal or radical, were predicated on the ideal of a universal humanity. The left addressed itself not to particular men and women but to all, in the name of their common standing. If the population at large was incapable, by itself, of seeing the world whole and acting in the general interest, some enlightened group took it upon itself to be the collective conscience, the Founding Fathers, the vanguard party. Even Marx, lyricist of the proletariat, ingeniously claimed that his favored class was destined to stand for, or become, all humanity. Nationalist revolutions – from 1848 to the present – were to be understood as tributaries to a common torrent, the grand surge of self-determination justified by the equivalent worth of all national expressions. Whether liberals or socialists, reformers or revolutionaries, the men and women of the left aimed to persuade their listeners to see their common interest as citizens of the largest world imaginable. *All* men were supposed to have been created equal, workingmen of *all* countries were supposed to unite. Historians of women are right to point out that the various founding fathers were not thinking of half the species; yet potentially inclusive language was in place. The power of the discourse of political rights was such that it could be generalized by extrapolation. Thus, within fifty years, women – grossly subordinated in the antislavery movement – were working up a politics based on their constituting half of a human race that had been decreed to share equal rights.

Marxism, in all its colorations, became the core of what may be called the idea of the left – the struggle to usher in and to represent common humanity. There exists, Marx asserts in his early writings, a universal identity: the human being as maker, realizing his "species being" in the course of transforming nature. With the audacity of a German idealist primed to think in first principles, Marx adapts from Hegel the idea that a "universal class" will give meaning to history – though not without help. To accomplish its mission, this class to end all classes requires a universal midwife: the revolutionary. To every particular circumstance and cause, the universal priesthood of communists is charged with bringing the glad tidings that History is the unfolding of Reason. The communist party, like God, has its center everywhere and nowhere. The proletariat is his nation. Like the emigré Marx, he is at home nowhere and everywhere, free to teach people of all nations that not a historical event or a struggle against oppression rises or falls which does not have its part to play in the great international transfiguration.

Such is the lyric of Marxism, the rhetoric that appealed to revolutionaries for a century after the death of the founding father. And therefore Marxism-Leninism, the universalist technology of revolution and rule later codified by Stalinists, is, if not the unshakable shadow of Enlightenment Marxism, at least its scion. Lenin's Bolshevik party thrives on and requires this lineage, even if Lenin and Marx are not identical. Under Lenin, the party, this directive force that sees all and knows all and acts in the ostensibly general interest, becomes the incarnation of the Enlightenment's faith in the knowability of the human situation. Farther down a road already surveyed by Marx, Lenin makes intellectuals essential to the revolution, thereby securing the dominion of universal ideals.

From 1935 to 1939 and again during World War II, the Popular Front could even conjure a new commonality – a cobbled-together anti-Fascist fusion. In the end, Marxists could always ask rhetorically, what was the alternative that promised universal justice, a single humanity? And so, partly by default, from one revision to the next, Marxism remained the pedigreed theoretical ensemble hovering over all left-wing thought. And yet, once the anti-Fascist alliance was broken, the universalist promise of Marxism proceeded to unravel.

From this point of view, the intellectual radicalism of the early sixties can be seen as a search for a substitute universalism. Having dismissed Marxism for what C. Wright Mills called its "labor metaphysic," the New Left tried to compose a surrogate universal. "The issues are interrelated" was the New Left's approach to a federation of single-issue groups – so that, for example, the peace, civil rights, and civil liberties movements needed to recognize that they had a common enemy, the "Dixiecrats" who choked off any liberal extension of the New Deal. More grandly, in a revival of Enlightenment universalism, Students for a Democratic Society's Port Huron Statement spoke self-consciously in the name of all humanity. The universal solvent for particular differences would be the principle that "decision-making of basic social consequence be carried on by public groupings": that is, participatory democracy. In theory, participatory democracy was available to all. In practice, it was tailored to students, young people collected at "knowledge factories" as the industrial proletariat has been collected at mills and mines; young people who were skilled in conversation, had time on their hands, and, uprooted from the diversities of their respective upbringings, were being encouraged to think of themselves as practitioners of reason. When the early New Left set out to find common ground with a like-minded constituency, it reached out to the impoverished – the Student Non-violent Coordinating Committee to sharecroppers and SDS to the urban poor, who, by virtue of their marginality, might be imagined as forerunners of a universal democracy. If students and the poor were not saddled with "radical chains" in the system of production, at least they could be imagined with radical *needs* for political participation.

But the student movement's attempts at universalism broke down – both practically and intellectually. In fact, the ideal of participatory democracy was only secondary for the New Left. The passion that drove students – including Berkeley's Free Speech Movement – was the desire to support civil rights as part of a movement with a universalist design. The New Left was a movement-for-others searching for an ideology to transform it into a movement-for-itself, but participatory democracy was too ethereal an objective with which to bind an entire movement, let alone an entire society. Freedom as an endless meeting was only alluring to those who had the time and taste to go to meetings endlessly. The universalist impulse regressed. Enter, then, the varieties of Marxism by which universalist students could imagine either that they were entitled to lead a hypothetical proletariat (Progressive Labor's Stalinism) or that they themselves already prefigured a "new working class."

But these attempts at recomposing a sense of a unified revolutionary bloc were weak in comparison with centrifugal pressures. Such unity as had been felt by the civil rights movement began to dissolve as soon as legal segregation was defeated. Blacks began to insist on black leadership, even exclusively black membership. Feminist stirrings were greeted with scorn by unreconstructed men. If white supremacy was unacceptable, neither could male supremacy be abided. One group after another demanded the recognition of difference and the protection of separate spheres for distinct groupings. This was more than an *idea* because it was more than strictly intellectual; it was more a whole way of experiencing the world. Difference was now lived and felt more acutely than unity.

The crack-up of the universalist New Left was muted for a while by the exigencies of the Vietnam War and the commonalities of youth culture. If there seemed in the late 1960s to be one big movement, it was largely because there was one big war. But the divisions of race and then gender and sexual orientation proved far too deep to be overcome by any rhetoric of unification. The initiative and energy went into proliferation – feminist, gay, ethnic, environmentalist. The very language of collectivity came to be perceived by the new movements as a colonialist smothering – an ideology to rationalize white male domination. Thus, by the early 1970s, the goals of the student movement and the various left-wing insurgencies were increasingly subsumed under the categories of identity politics. Separatism became automatic. Now one did not imagine oneself belonging to a common enterprise; one belonged to a caucus.

But note: the late New Left politics of dispersion and separateness, not the early New Left politics of universalist aspiration, were the seed-ground of the young faculty who were to carry radical politics into the academy in the 1970s and 1980s. The founders of women's and black studies had a universalist base in either the Old or the New Left. But their recruits, born in the early or later 1950s, did not. By the time they arrived on campuses in the early seventies, identity politics was the norm. They had no direct memory of either a unified left or a successful left-of-center Democratic party. In general, their experience of active politics was segmented. The defeat of the left was so obvious it was taken for granted. For these post-1960s activists, universalist traditions seemed empty.

The profusion of social agents took place throughout the society, but nowhere more vigorously than in the academy. Here, in black and ethnic studies, women's studies, gay and lesbian groupings, and so on, each movement could feel the exhilaration of group-based identity. Each felt it had a distinct world to win – first, by establishing that its group had been suppressed and silenced; then by exhuming buried work and exploring forms of resistance; and, finally, by trying to rethink society, literature, and history from the respective vantages of the silenced, asking what the group and, indeed, the entire world would look like if those hitherto excluded were now included. And since the demands of identity politics were far more winnable in the university than elsewhere, the struggles of minorities multiplied. When academic conservatives resisted, they only confirmed the convictions of the marginal – that their embattled or not-yet-developing perspectives needed to be separately institutionalized. In the developing logic of identity-based movements, the world was all periphery and no center, or, if there was a center, it was their own. The mission of insurgents was to promote their own interests; for if they would not, who would?

From these endeavors flowed genuine achievements in the study of history and literature. Whole new areas of inquiry were opened up. Histories of the world and of America, of science and literature, are still reverberating from what can legitimately be called a revolution in knowledge. But as the hitherto excluded territories were institutionalized, the lingering aspiration for the universal subject was ceded. A good deal of the Cultural Left felt its way, even if half-jokingly, toward a weak unity based not so much on a universalist premise or ideal but rather on a common enemy – that notorious White Male. Beneath this, they had become, willy-nilly, pluralists, a fact frequently disguised by the rhetoric of revolution hanging over from the late sixties.

Soon, difference was being practiced, not just thought, at a deeper level than commonality. It was more salient, more vital, more present – all the more so in the 1980s, as practical struggles for university facilities, requirements, and so forth culminated in fights over increasingly scarce resources. For the participants in these late-sixties and post-sixties movements, the benefits of this pursuit were manifold – an experience of solidarity, a ready-made reservoir of recruits. Seen from outside as fragments in search of a whole, the zones of identity politics came to be experienced from within as worlds unto themselves. The political-intellectual experience of younger academics could be mapped onto other centrifugal dispositions in post-Vietnam America. Group self-definitions embedded in political experience merged with other historicist and centrifugal currents to form the core and the legitimacy of the multicultural surge, the fragments of the Cultural Left. The idea of a common America and the idea of a unitary Left, these two great legacies of the Enlightenment, hollowed out together.

Thus a curious reversal of left and right. In the nineteenth century, the right was the property of aristocracies who stood unabashedly for the privileges of the few. Today, the aspiring aristocrats of the academic right tend to speak the language of universals – canon, merit, reason, individual rights, transpolitical virtue. For its part, seized by the logic of identity politics, committed to pleasing its disparate constituencies, the academic left has lost interest in the commonalities that undergird its obsession with difference.

♦

Identity Politics and Class Struggle

Robin D. G. Kelley

I find it ironic that at the very moment when radical renewal might actually be on the horizon, a handful of self-proclaimed spokespersons on the Left have practically written the "Left's" epitaph. The most vocal and visible of the bunch are Todd Gitlin (*Twilight of Our Common Dreams: Why America is Wracked by Culture Wars* [New York: Metropolitan Books, 1995]) and Michael Tomasky (*Left for Dead: The Life, Death and Possible Resurrection of Progressive Politics in America* [New York: Free Press, 1996]), but some of their ideas have been echoed by the likes of Richard Rorty, Sean Wilentz, Robert McChesney, and Jim Sleeper, to name a few. (I suppose Robert Hughes' *Culture of Complaint* might qualify since he writes about the absence of class analysis, but it is so polemical and so anti-Marxist that his passing suggestions for a renewed "Left" seem gratuitous.) Tomasky and Gitlin, in particular, set out to explain why the Left failed to mobilize a mass-based response to the rise of the Right, why it remains small, divided, and parochial, entrenched for better or worse in the groves of academe. Their explanation: "The Left" has lost touch with its Enlightenment roots, the source of its universalism and radical humanism, and instead has been hijacked by a "multicultural left" wedded to "identity politics" which has led us all into a cul-de-sac of ethnic particularism, race consciousness, sexual politics, and radical feminism.

Much of the blame is assigned to women, gays and lesbians, and colored people for fracturing the American Left, abandoning honest class struggle, and alienating white men who could be allies but aren't because of the terrible treatment meted out to them by the Loud Minority. Universal categories such as class have fallen before the narrow, particularistic mantras of radical chic: race, gender, sexuality, and disability. Indeed, in their view class is not just another identity, it transcends identity. If the "Left" wants to save itself, we must abandon our ever shrinking identity niches for the realm of majoritarian thinking. After all, we're told, the majority of Americans are white and heterosexual and have little interest in radical feminism, minority discourse, and struggles centered on sexual identity.

In some ways, I can sympathize with these people about the limitations of "identity politics." While the growing interest in the politics of identity has extended our analytical scope to overlooked or trivialized cultural spheres and expanded our understanding of intellectual history, in some circles it has also tended to limit discussions of power to cultural politics. And while so-called "identity politics" has always profoundly shaped labor movements and – even more than vague, abstract notions of class unity – has been the glue for class solidarity, by the same token it has also become a noose around the necks of

Excerpted from *New Politics*, Winter 1997, pp. 84–96.

oppressed people, as in the case of white racism or certain variants of black nationalism.

On the other hand, whatever cul-de-sacs we might have entered, the "Enlightenment train" will not lead us out. These people assume that the universal humanism they find so endearing and radical can be easily separated from the historical context of its making; indeed, that it is precisely what can undo the racism and modern imperialism it helped to justify. The racialism of the West, slavery, imperialism, the destruction of indigenous cultures in the name of "progress," are treated as aberrations, coincidences, or not treated as all. They insist that these historical developments do not render the Enlightenment's radical universalism any less "radical," and those who take up this critique are simply rejecting Enlightenment philosophers because they're "dead white males." Their uncritical defense of the Enlightenment (which includes a strange tendency to collapse Marx, Locke, and Jefferson into the same category), betrays an unwillingness to take ideas, let alone history, seriously. Gitlin certainly acknowledges these contradictions inherent in Enlightenment philosophy, as well as the historical context of slavery, racism, and colonialism. But in an intellectual sleight of hand he brackets these contradictions, reduces a huge body of complex, historically specific ideas to transhistorical abstractions (which he uses selectively to make his case against "identity politics"), and then presumes that Enlightenment thought constitutes the central reservoir of ideas for the very identity movements he criticizes. Says Gitlin:

> The Enlightenment is not to be discarded because Voltaire was anti-Semitic or Hume, Kant, Hegel, and Jefferson racist, but rather further enlightened – for it equips us with the tools with which to refute the anti-Semitism of a Voltaire and the racism of the others....In none of these cases was bigotry at the core of the man's intellectual system; it reflected the routine white prejudice of the time. The Enlightenment is self-correcting. The corrective to darkness is more light. (p. 215)

Good liberalism, to be sure, but its analytical insight leaves much to be desired. To pose the question as pro or con, keep the Enlightenment or discard it, sidesteps fundamental questions such as the legacy of 18th century social thought for modern conceptions of race or the philosophical underpinnings of racial slavery in an age when free labor and free market ideology triumphed. For example, while racialist ideas can be traced to ancient thought and forms of domination internal to Europe, the Enlightenment also ushered in a transformation in Western thinking about race. How could it not? After all, as many commentators since the French Revolution have observed, the expansion of slavery and genocidal wars against non-European peoples took place alongside, and by some accounts made possible bourgeois democratic revolutions that gave birth (in the West) to the concept that liberty and freedom are inalienable rights. This contradiction is fundamental to Enlightenment philosophy, notions of progress, and developments in scientific thinking.

*   *   *

Besides assuming that the "universal" is truly "self-evident," the neo-Enlightenment Left cannot conceive of movements led by African Americans, women, Latinos, gays and lesbians, speaking for the whole or even embracing radical humanism. The implications are frightening: the only people who can speak the language of universalism are white men (since they have no investment in identity politics beyond renewed ethnic movements arising here and there) and women and colored people who have transcended or rejected the politics of identity. Moreover, they either don't understand or refuse to acknowledge that class is lived through race and gender. There is no universal class identity, just as there is no universal racial or gender or sexual identity. The idea that race, gender, and sexuality are particular whereas class is universal not only presumes that class struggle is some sort of race and gender-neutral terrain but takes for granted that movements focused on race, gender, or sexuality necessarily undermine class unity and, by definition, cannot be emancipatory for the whole.

Don't get me wrong. I'm not giving priority to "identity politics" over the struggle to dismantle capitalism and to build a world we've never seen before – a world free of market forces and all the terrible things that go with it. Rather, I have trouble with their characterization of race, gender, and sexuality as narrow identity politics while "class" is regarded as some transcendent, universal category that rises above these other identities. Indeed, Gitlin calls the first three, "birthrights," and despite an obligatory nod to Anthony Appiah, he fails to treat these categories as social constructs that have enormous consequences for how class is lived. Along with these so-called "identities" come regimes of oppression. Are churches being burned because black people are alienating white folks? Is that why the Justice Department focuses much of its investigation on black congregations rather than white supremacist groups? Is pro-Prop 187 sentiment and callousness toward immigrants the result of Mexican and Central American immigrants' refusal to be "inclusive?"

I find the neo-Enlightenment position incredibly problematic given what we know of the history of class struggle in the U.S. It rests, not on a serious analysis of the social movements lumped together under the heading "identity politics," but on caricature, stereotypes, omissions, innuendo, and historical analysis that borders on the comical at times. Indeed, these movements are rarely ever named and their positions never spelled out in any detail. Yet, despite the lack of depth and scholarly rigor, as well as an over-reliance on personal impressions, these arguments seem to be winning over a broad section of high profile liberals/leftists who believe the time has come for us to "transcend" all this race and gender stuff and get to the matter at hand: class warfare against the bosses. During the recent labor teach-in at Columbia University, for example, both Betty Friedan and Richard Rorty, taking a page from Gitlin's book, told the audience that the time had come to graduate from narrow identity movements to the bigger picture. It was as if antiracist and antisexist struggles were not fundamental to the struggles of working people across race and gender lines, or worse, that they had been essentially resolved and were no longer pressing problems.

Although their books have been widely reviewed, we have yet to subject the neo-Enlightenment position to a serious political critique. I don't know how many times I've been told, "Don't attack them, they're on our side!" Besides the obvious analogy to the issue of the Left's stance toward Clinton, I'm always inclined to repeat Tonto's response to the Lone Ranger: "What do you mean 'we'?" Of course, to say "we" invites accusations of "identity politics," of identifying with colored people at the expense of the poor Lone Ranger, who is merely low-level manager of capital rather than an owner. But this is precisely the problem: the "we" I'm speaking of includes all oppressed people, including Mr. Ranger if he chooses to join. The Gitlin/Tomasky group makes the grave error of rendering movements struggling around issues of race, gender, and sexuality as inherently narrow and particularistic. The failure to conceive of these social movements as essential to the emancipation of the whole remains the fundamental stumbling block to building a deep and lasting class-based politics.

Part of their problem has to do with their failure to take seriously the ideas coming out of these "identity movements." Their arguments rest less on what these movements espouse than on their racial, ethnic or gender make-up or their sexual orientation. "Choose a nonwhite ethnicity," Tomasky sneers, "combine it with a sexual practice or a physical condition, and there probably exists a movement to match" (p. 89). Let us take one of their favorite whipping girls: the "black feminist," particularly of the lesbian variety. In a bizarre tautology, black feminists are narrowly concerned with their race and sex because they are black feminists. In fact, aside from Alice Walker and the statement issued by the Combahee River Collective (a radical black feminist group founded in the mid-1970s), black feminists in their texts have no names or organizations – they function as little more than signifiers (or, to put them in a more traditional context, as scapegoats). Tomasky was kind enough to quote one line from the Combahee River Collective's 1977 statement, though the line he quotes is intended to demonstrate how narrow identity politics can get. For him, the principles of black feminism are succinctly expressed in the following sentence: "We believe that the most profound and potentially most radical politics come directly out of our own identity." What he neglected to mention, however, is that the same statement proposed a clear socialist agenda, arguing that emancipation for everyone could not take place until racism, homophobia, sexism, and capitalism are annihilated, and criticized mainstream feminist organizations for not being inclusive enough – for not dealing adequately with the needs of the poor or with racist oppression of men and women. Nor did Tomasky acknowledge the important line in the statement that "as Black women we find any type of biological determinism a particularly dangerous and reactionary basis upon which to build a politic."

In other words, had Tomasky and Gitlin taken the time to read the material written by black feminists instead of simply reducing them to caricatures of their own imagination, they might have discovered some of the most sophisticated statements of the kind of radical humanism they claim to embrace. Anna Julia Cooper, whose writings continue to have a profound impact on black feminism, wrote in 1893:

> We take our stand on the solidarity of humanity, the oneness of life, and the unnaturalness and injustice of all special favoritisms, whether of sex, race,

country or condition. ... The colored woman feels that woman's cause in one and universal; and that ... not till race, color, sex, and condition are seen as accidents, and not the substance of life; not till the universal title or humanity to life, liberty, and the pursuit of happiness is conceded to be inalienable to all; not till then is woman's lesson taught and woman's cause won – not the white woman's nor the black woman's, not the red woman's but the cause of every man and every woman who has writhed silently under a mighty wrong.

This radical humanism, as theorist Patricia Hill Collins points out, has been a consistent principle of black feminist thought. Alice Walker insists that a "womanist" is "committed to the survival and wholeness of entire people, male and female," and is "not a separatist" but "traditionally a universalist." Pauli Murray is even more explicit:

> The lesson of history that all human rights are indivisible and that the failure to adhere to this principle jeopardizes the rights of all is particularly applicable here. A built-in hazard of an aggressive ethnocentric movement which disregards the interests of other disadvantaged groups is that it will become parochial and ultimately self-defeating in the face of hostile reactions, dwindling allies, and mounting frustrations.

One could see this vision in the writings of many black feminists, including June Jordan, Barbara Christian, Angela Davis, Elsa Barkley Brown, Pearl Cleage, Audre Lorde, Pat Parker, Barbara Smith, Cheryl Clarke, Julianne Malveaux, bell hooks, Margaret Simms, and Filomina Steady, to name a few.

Of course, had Tomasky and Gitlin actually read this stuff, they might jump up in agreement and dismiss these statements as exceptions to the rule. (Whatever the rule is, however, always goes unnamed.) But a close reading reveals that they are not saying the same thing. "If all human rights are indivisible," then why privilege majoritarian concerns over all others and ridicule movements organized around sex, race, and gender? Why presume that such movements are necessarily narrow simply because black women and their concerns are central to them? Nothing could be further from the truth. One vital outgrowth of radical black feminism has been the black women's healthcare movement, its most notable manifestation being the National Black Women's Health Project. Among other things, they have sought to create a healthier environment for poor and working-class women and reduce women's dependence on a health care system structured by capitalism and run primarily by men. If they succeed, imagine how such a transformation might benefit all of us, irrespective of race or gender?

Unfortunately, these neo-Enlightenment Leftists are blind to the radical humanist traditions that have undergirded black feminist movements, and this blindness has kept them from seeing how black feminism could contribute to their own emancipation. Similarly, they don't see how gay and lesbian movements might also contribute to our collective emancipation – a criticism made eloquently by Martin Duberman in his review of Tomasky's book in *The Nation*. Some things are obvious: the continuing struggle of gays and lesbians against discrimination in public and private life have important implications for national civil rights law; the work of ACT UP and other movements have made AIDS visible – a disease that's killing many heterosexual people, especially poor black women. Less obvious is the role of scholarship coming out of Gay and Lesbian Studies programs as well as Women's Studies programs – grist for the anti-identity politics mill. Queer theory, for example, begins with the premise that sexuality is a vital part of human existence, and that the way sexual identities are defined (and policed) has to do with social relations of power, the role of the state, public institutions, and social movements. The best work understands that sexual identities and practices are lived through race and class and can only be understood historically. What does this scholarship have to do with the rest of us? What are the implications for the "universal"? For one, we know now that there is no universal masculinity or femininity. The idea of "normal" behavior is a social construction, which means that there is nothing natural or inevitable about male dominance, the overrepresentation of men in positions of power, or the tendency of men to use violence to resolve conflict. These are all obvious points, to be sure. But how many heterosexual men and women stop to think about the emancipatory potential of a more flexible sexual and gender identity for all of us? Besides reducing homophobic anxieties, freeing up self-expression, and enabling us to reconstruct our relationships to one another (isn't that what revolution is all about?), I believe a less rigid definition of masculinity may actually reduce violence – from police brutality to domestic abuse.

While Gitlin tends to be slightly more sympathetic to feminism and gay and lesbian movements than Tomasky, they both view them as prime examples of dead-end identity politics. On the other hand, when they proclaim a movement or issue "universal," they don't stop to analyze how race and gender shape various responses to issues. For example, Tomasky believes he hit on a common value/agenda when he writes: "Working people in this country need a movement that will put their interests and livelihoods first." Fair enough. But without an analysis that takes racism, sexism, and homophobia seriously, or considers deep historical differences, we won't know what "interests" mean. Let's take crime and the issue of neighborhood safety, an issue on which many people across race, gender, and even class lines can find common ground. Yet, racism – not narrow identity politics – persuaded many African Americans to oppose Clinton's $22 billion Crime Bill, and the majority of white voters to support it. For many black people, the issue of neighborhood safety is not just about more police but the kind of police – where they live, how they relate to the community. Indeed, no matter what we might think of the Nation of Islam (NOI), many non-Muslims see its fight against drug dealers in black communities as more effective than the police.

It is precisely this kind of economism that enables these people to claim, without evidence, that declining wages is universally more important to most black people than police brutality or having to wait an hour for a seat at Denny's. One is hard economics that unites people; the other is just narrow identity politics. Thus, when black gays and lesbians take to the streets to protest violence against them, that's "identity politics." When angry white males claim that affirmative action is taking jobs from them, that's class politics muffled beneath a racial blanket they themselves don't understand. When white people vote for David Duke and Pat Buchanan, that's class politics, not identity politics. Something's wrong with this picture.

* * *

Rather than worry about offending "majoritarian sensibilities," the labor movement must make antiracism, antisexism, and homophobia foundational. The absurd argument that minority aggressiveness is responsible for white male backlash at the tail end of the 1960s masks the fact that it has been white racism that has tragically inhibited the growth of most progressive movements in the U.S. As W. E. B. Du Bois, Dave Roediger, Alexander Saxton, Ted Allen, Noel Ignatiev, Michael Goldfield, Eric Lott, David Wellman and others have demonstrated, racism has been a noose around white workers' necks since the American Revolution. In the South during Reconstruction, a misguided white majority sided with the wrong class and rejected the black workers and sharecroppers who proposed a Democratic South with massive land redistribution. Despite the fact that the black freedom struggle, in alliance with the radical wing of the Republican Party, enfranchised poor whites who didn't have the right to vote before the 15th Amendment, the vast majority of exploited white labor still chose color over class. And in California, it was precisely anti-Chinese sentiment that galvanized the multi-ethnic "white" working class and forged a dynamic union movement on the West Coast during the late 19th century. Of course, white workers were never uniformly racist and there are enough stories of interracial working-class solidarity to fill volumes. But we also must recognize the price these men and women had to pay: white workers willing to commit "race suicide" often faced the worst of state repression, ostracism, and sometimes hostility within their own ranks. It's not an accident, for example, that the most militantly antiracist unions emerging out of the CIO campaigns of the 1930s and 40s were the main targets of McCarthyite witch hunts.

I can't stress enough the importance of the fight against racism right now, especially with a growing backlash against affirmative action under the guise of supporting a "color blind" society. Anyone seriously concerned about the labor movement and building multiracial unity must recognize the fundamental role racism has played in destroying internationalism. Anti-immigrant sentiment, for instance, is not just about class anger, because there really is no mobilization against Canadians or European immigrants taking what are essentially skilled jobs. It's about dark people, whether some invisible Pacific Rim empire run by "sneaky Orientals" or "wetbacks." The history of conquest and, later, repatriation in the Southwest is fundamental to understanding anti-immigrant sentiment, the English-only movement, and pro-Prop 187. Blanket support for "majoritarian" positions simply plays into American nationalism and chauvinism.

So, how might people build class solidarity without suppressing or ignoring differences? How can we build on differences – by which I mean different kinds of oppression as well as different identities – rather than in spite of them?

One way to conceive of alliances across race and gender is as a set of "affiliations," of building unity by supporting and perhaps even participating in other people's struggles for social justice. Basically, that old fashioned IWW slogan, "An injury to one is an injury to all!" After all, contrary to the neo-Enlightenment narratives, African-American social movements have been practicing the principle of "an injury to one is an injury to all" for a very long time: black male abolitionists supported women's suffrage when few white men would; black radicals throughout the early part of the century supported the Irish struggle for self-determination; black soldiers and journalists shed tears at the sight of Nazi death camps; and since Roosevelt, we have been mainstays in the Democratic Party even to our own detriment. Black trade unions were never exclusionary; black labor leaders did not implement Jim Crow locals. And when the Chinese Exclusion Act seemed to have universal support among non-Asian workers, it was a black man, James Ferrell of the Knights of Labor, who told his comrades that they ought to organize the Chinese rather than attack them.

The good news is that most elements of the labor movement understand this, unlike many academics who apparently find the idea of multiple identities too complicated to deal with. Despite their uncritical support of the Democratic Party, the current leadership of the AFL-CIO seems to understand that the labor movement is not about transcending these other social movements derisively labelled "identity politics" but about building alliances and affiliations and learning from them.

*   *   *

It's ludicrous to blame so-called identity politics of the 1960s for the collapse of the left, the derailment of progressive social movements, or our inability to roll back poverty and unbridled corporate wealth. We have others to thank for that: Richard Nixon, Ronald Reagan, George Bush, Bill Clinton, Cointelpro, white flight, red squads, red-lining, Contra-backed crack dealers, economic restructuring, the NRA, right-wing think tanks, complacent labor leaders ... and the list goes on. Of course, the Left – whatever that means now – is not blameless. The scars of sectarianism run deep and trace their roots to the glorious days when the Old Marxists were supposedly more "universal." Street fights erupted between socialists and anarchists; battles raged between the Trotskyists and Stalinists and a variety of sects claiming to be the true heirs of Lenin. And then China entered the picture, along with Albania. These battles within the Marxist world contributed more to the internal implosion and proliferation of left-wing parties than feminism and black nationalism.

Index